FLY BOY HEROES

The Stories of the Medal of Honor Recipients
of the Air War against Japan

JAMES H. HALLAS

STACKPOLE
BOOKS

Guilford, Connecticut
Blue Ridge Summit, Pennsylvania

STACKPOLE BOOKS

An imprint of Globe Pequot, the trade division of The Rowman & Littlefield Publishing Group, Inc.
4501 Forbes Blvd., Ste. 200
Lanham, MD 20706
www.rowman.com

Distributed by NATIONAL BOOK NETWORK

British Library Cataloguing in Publication Information available

Library of Congress Cataloging-in-Publication Data
978-0-8117-7131-3 (cloth)
978-0-8117-7132-0 (electronic)

♾™ The paper used in this publication meets the minimum requirements of American National Standard for Information Sciences—Permanence of Paper for Printed Library Materials, ANSI/NISO Z39.48-1992.

CONTENTS

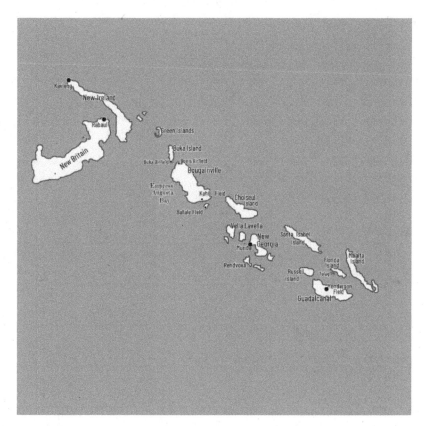

Map of Bougainville-Guadalcanal.

Map of New Guinea.

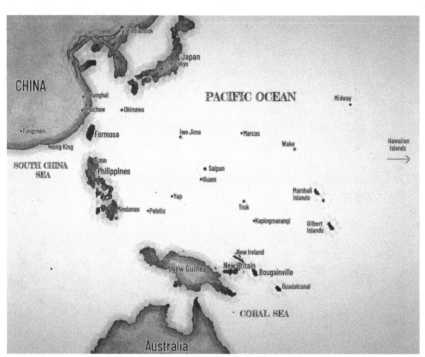

Map of Pacific overview.

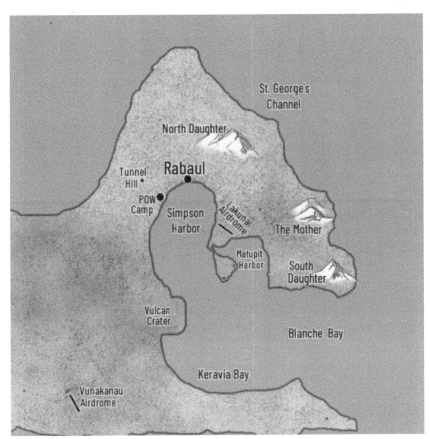

Map of Rabaul.

Introduction

On the morning of December 7, 1941, Chief Aviation Ordinanceman (AOCM) John W. Finn, though suffering multiple wounds, continued to man his machine gun as Japanese planes attacked Kaneohe Naval Air Station on Oahu in the opening hours of the war with Japan. Just over three years later, as that war struggled into its final months, a B-29 radioman named Red Erwin literally embraced death to save his fellow crewmen in the skies off the Japanese home islands.

They were the first and the last of the thirty U.S. Navy, Army, and Marine Corps aviation personnel awarded the Medal of Honor for their actions against the Japanese during World War II: twelve men from the Army, seven from the Navy, and eleven from the Marine Corps. They included pilots and crewmen manning everything from fighters and dive bombers to lumbering flying boats, B-17s, and medium bombers—and one man, Chief Finn, whose job wasn't to fly aircraft but to service them. One was a general. Another was a sergeant. Some were recognized for shooting down large numbers of enemy aircraft in aerial combat. Others were singled out for putting mission over self or for extraordinary leadership and combat initiative that helped shape events. They included at least two men who never fired a gun in anger but risked everything to save others.

The following narrative is not intended as a study of the evolution of U.S. airpower in the Pacific or of strategy or tactics or as a history of the air campaigns beyond what is necessary to provide context for the individual accounts. Nor does it attempt to delve into the technical minutiae of aircraft. Rather, it seeks to relate the stories of the select few who received the Medal of Honor in the air war against Japan—a handful of men out of the many tens of thousands who served in Army air squadrons, on Navy carriers, or with the Marine air arm in the Pacific theater. Today, more than seventy-five years after the end of World War II, few of their names would resonate with the American public. Who were these largely forgotten men? Where did they come from? What inspired them to rise "above and beyond"? What, if anything, made them different?

Virtually all had one thing in common: they'd always wanted to fly. Those who flew against the Japanese—and for that matter, those who flew in Europe—came from a generation steeped in the romanticism of World War I's "Knights of the Air," a generation that venerated that war's aces, including American Ace of Aces Eddie Rickenbacker, who became a national hero with twenty-six victories in aerial combat over the Western Front. The national fascination with aviation reached further heights following Charles ("Lucky") Lindbergh's heroic transatlantic flight in 1927 and continued to be fueled by the excitement generated by the postwar collection of barnstormers, wing-walkers, air shows, races, and highly publicized air-speed and distance records, not to mention the exploits of daring aviators such as Amelia Earhart. Boys built models of planes, pinned newspaper clippings of aircraft on their bedroom walls, pored over pulp magazine accounts of aerial adventures, and dreamed of one day taking to the skies themselves.

Some of the men represented in the following pages scrimped and saved to pay for private flying lessons prior to ending up in the service. Others decided to let Uncle Sam fund their passion and enlisted in the armed forces. An early hurdle was a requirement that officer candidates—and pilots were typically officers—must have at least two years of college. That requirement was eventually dropped in favor of a simple entrance examination, but many a would-be aviator dutifully put in his obligatory two years of college before dropping out to sign up for flight training. As the prospect of war neared, the opportunity to learn to fly grew substantially as the government—intent on establishing a cadre of trained pilots—instituted the Civilian Pilot Training Program on college campuses in late 1938.

In 1939, the Army Air Corps (in 1941 it would be redesignated the U.S. Army Air Forces) had a personnel strength of only 26,000. By the time of the Japanese attack on Pearl Harbor, the Army Air Forces had expanded to roughly 350,000 personnel and had 12,300 aircraft of all types on hand, though large numbers consisted of obsolete bombers and fighters. The Navy had about 5,300 aircraft of all types, many of which were also outdated. The best U.S. fighters were inferior to the German Messerschmitt Bf-109, the British Spitfire, and, as pilots would learn the hard way, the Japanese A6M Zero.[1] Better planes were on the way—the Navy was in the process of transitioning from biplane fighters to the F4F Grumman Wildcat—but during the first few months of the war, many an American would go to his death in inferior aircraft such as the Brewster Buffalo or the Douglas Devastator.

Col. Claire Chennault, commanding the American Volunteer Group—the famed "Flying Tigers"—flying against the Japanese in China before America's entry into the war, recognized the danger early on. He warned Washington about the capabilities of the Japanese Zero, but it does not appear that anyone listened. Nor does anyone seem to have appreciated the high quality of Japanese airmen—Japanese naval pilots in particular. The consensus, steeped in the racism of the day, insisted that Japanese planes were little more than bamboo kites operated by near-sighted monkeys. That ignorance—some might say arrogance—killed many an American pilot before tactics were amended to counter the Zero's superior maneuverability.

The pitfalls of preconceived notions were not limited to the nimble Zero. Early in the war, B-17 bombers were sent out on futile high-altitude attacks on enemy ships; it was wrongly believed that dive bombers could substitute as fighters, and there was a lack of appreciation for the great vulnerability of bombers and torpedo planes attempting missions without adequate fighter protection. All these lessons came at the price of men's lives.

At the same time, aviators in the Pacific theater found a war that was markedly different from that in Europe. Facilities were often primitive. The "Germany first" policy ensured that the war in Europe took precedence when it came to equipment, parts, aircraft, and manpower, often leaving air operations in the Pacific to be conducted on a shoestring. Forced to fly long distances over water and uninhabited jungle, pilots and crews faced fearsome weather fronts as well as the ever-present possibility of losing their way over the trackless ocean and running out of fuel or experiencing mechanical malfunctions that would send them into the water or near-impenetrable jungle.

An aviator downed over Europe was likely to find civilization—roads, towns, people—near at hand. Not so in the Pacific. Many an airman successfully bailed out of his doomed plane and managed to clamber into his life raft in the sea below only to have vanished when—or if—rescuers arrived at the scene hours or days later. Others bailed out over trackless jungle and simply disappeared. The Japanese routinely murdered captured airmen, often by beheading. At least seventy U.S. Army, Navy, and Marine Corps prisoners of war were executed or died of neglect on Rabaul alone between 1942 and 1945. Some of them are commemorated in the following pages.

Victory in the air war against Japan was not easy, and it was not cheap. The U.S. Army Air Forces lost 15,694 dead and missing in the Pacific war. The Navy lists a total of 12,133 deaths among aviation personnel from all causes. The Marine Corps lists 794 aviators killed in action, 560 killed in overseas operational accidents, and 319 missing in action.[2]

Thanks in part to that sacrifice, on Sunday morning, September 2, 1945, under overcast skies, eleven Japanese delegates filed somberly aboard the USS *Missouri* in Tokyo Bay to sign the instrument of surrender ending nearly four years of bitter warfare. Their cities lay in ruins. Their once vaunted navy lay rusting on the seabed from Midway to the Philippines and beyond; their air forces, once the scourge of the Pacific, had been swept from the skies. As the signatures were inscribed and the proceedings came to a close, the roar of engines drowned out conversation as masses of carrier planes and B-29 Superfortresses—some 2,000 in all—passed low overhead to punctuate the despair of a defeated nation.

The demonstration of aerial might was no empty gesture. In the Pacific war, more so than in Europe, victory or defeat hung on domination of the air. It was control of the skies that allowed domination of the seas—a reality sometimes obscured by the iconic images of landing craft churning toward hostile beaches or the famous flag-raising on Iwo Jima's Mount Suribachi. Often overlooked is that the landing craft were heading toward the beaches for one reason: to seize existing airfields or the ground to build new ones. Each island hop allowed the Allies to extend the umbrella of air/sea domination as their amphibious forces moved ever closer to Japan itself.

It was airpower that allowed this inexorable advance. It was airpower that eviscerated the Imperial Navy, annihilated opposition in the skies, rained fire on Japanese cities, and finally brought the war to a close with a pair of radioactive mushroom clouds over Hiroshima and Nagasaki. Battered and bloodied in the opening months of the war, the United States emerged four years later with the most powerful air forces in the world, having progressed in that short span of time from biplanes to jets. The large numbers of obsolete or obsolescent planes in service at the start of the war had been replaced by ever more lethal aircraft—Hellcats, Corsairs, P-38s, B-29s, and Mustangs—first contesting, then crushing Japanese domination of the skies. The Army Air Forces, which began the war with about 350,000 men in uniform and 4,477 combat aircraft, ended it in August 1945 with over 2.2 million men under arms and 41,163 combat aircraft.[3]

It is safe to assume we will never see a conflict like World War II in the Pacific again. Men might not change, but technology moves on. The prospect of swarms of piston-driven aircraft machine-gunning each other at point-blank range or dive-bombing enemy ships in this age of missiles and standoff weaponry is about as likely as the redeployment of muzzle-loading cannons aboard warships. Similarly, U.S. Ace of Aces Dick Bong's record of forty enemy planes downed in air-to-air combat is unlikely to be equaled or surpassed on any future battleground.

Thirty Medals of Honor were awarded to aviation personnel for actions against the Japanese during World War II. The likelihood of receiving the nation's highest military decoration varied depending on the phase of the war and, to some degree, on the branch of service. The Navy, for instance, was much less likely than the Army or Marine Corps to award the Medal of Honor simply for shooting down a large number of enemy planes. Virtually all of the Marine Corps awards were made for actions in the pivotal Solomon Islands campaign. Similarly, most of the Army awards were given for actions—both by fighter pilots and bomber crews—in the prolonged effort to control New Guinea and isolate the Japanese stronghold at Rabaul. In all three services, leadership was often a factor in the award.

As serious students of military history are well aware, the award of decorations can be fickle. Cases abound where an individual receives a medal for an action, while others who do as much or more go unrecognized. Those who receive the Medal of Honor tend to be well aware of that reality: at least two of the men whose actions are recounted in the following pages actually attempted to decline the award. None of this diminishes what they did; it merely serves to remind us that not all heroes wear medals. Perhaps more to the point, while we tend to celebrate the few, wars are won by the many. The air war against Japan was no exception.

1

First to Fight

THE JAPANESE WERE ON THE MOVE.

After many months of frustration, fruitless negotiation, anger, and mistrust, Japan had decided on war with the West. The militarists had prevailed. The goal was simple: destroy Western forces in the Pacific; seize Allied colonies and possessions with their much-needed resources (particularly oil); and then deign to negotiate a peace with a demoralized enemy, emerging with a diplomatic settlement that would leave Japan in command of a Pacific empire.

If the anticipated outcome demonstrated a gross misunderstanding of the West in general and the United States in particular, the plan itself was a masterpiece, the military execution brilliant. The opening move in the early morning hours of December 7, 1941—an aerial attack launched from six carriers to remove the threat posed by the U.S. Pacific Fleet at Pearl Harbor in the Hawaiian Islands—was a stunning success.

AOCM John W. Finn
Kaneohe Naval Air Station
December 7, 1941

War came to thirty-two-year-old John Finn on the morning of Sunday, December 7, 1941, as he lay naked in bed with his wife in their married housing quarters at the naval air station at Kaneohe Bay, Hawaii. Finn, the chief aviation ordnanceman for Patrol Squadron 14 (VP-14), was entertaining lascivious thoughts about how to spend his morning off duty when he heard planes passing low overhead. The planes were not adhering to the normal flight pattern. Stranger still, they sounded like single-engine aircraft, not the big twin-engine PBY amphibious flying boats flown by the three patrol squadrons at the naval air station. Then Finn heard gunfire in the near distance. If anyone was scheduled to test-fire machine guns on the base, as chief aviation ordnanceman, he should have been alerted to the fact.

As his mind slowly shifted gears from romance to business, there came a frantic knocking on the door downstairs. Forgoing his skivvies, Finn hurriedly pulled on his dungaree pants and answered the door to find his neighbor's wife on the step. "They want you down at the hangar right away," she exclaimed. Before Finn could get a word out, she "turned and run like a deer."[1] Without bothering with the skivvies, Finn shrugged into his shirt, pulled on socks and shoes, grabbed his hat, and headed out to his 1938 Chevrolet. Also alerted, his neighbor, CPO Eddie Sullivan, piled into the passenger seat, and they started down the winding road toward the PBY hangar area about a mile away.

Studiously observing the 20 mph base speed limit, Finn paused briefly to pick up a young sailor hiking down the road on foot. He had scarcely resumed his leisurely "Sunday morning drive to church," as he put it later, when a plane came roaring up from behind at low level. Finn glanced out the car window as the aircraft came abreast. "I looked out there and this plane made a wingover and I looked up and saw two great big dirty red balls," he remarked.[2] "It looked almost like the red ball had been mixed with mud. They were not bright red and pretty."[3] Finn had been to China, and he knew which nation painted red discs on their aircraft. He turned to Sullivan and exclaimed, "Sully, this is the real McCoy. It's the Japs."[4] He stomped on the accelerator and raced down the mountain toward the hangar area and, as it turned out, toward history. "I threw it into second and it's a wonder I didn't run over every sailor in the air station," he joked later.[5]

At the time of the Japanese attack on the Pacific Fleet, John William Finn had been in the Navy for fifteen years. Born on July 24, 1909, in Los Angeles, he grew up outside Compton. His father worked as a caretaker for the Los Angeles County Water District. Young Finn had a mechanical bent, but he hated school. After repeating the eighth grade, he told his father he was going to quit. The senior Finn said he'd prefer that John finish his education, but if the boy was set on quitting, he wouldn't stand in the way. "So I quit school," remarked Finn.[6] He was thirteen years old.

He worked for a farmer for a year or so, then joined an older cousin in a Los Angeles factory assembling bristles and hair into different types of brushes. The factory lacked ventilation, and it was dirty, unhealthy work. The cousin started talking about getting out of there and joining the Navy. The cousin never followed through, but Finn knew a good idea when he heard one. Two or three weeks before his seventeenth birthday, he went down to the recruiting station and filled out the paperwork to enlist. He returned with his mother as soon as he turned seventeen; she signed off on all the forms, and Finn found himself in the United States Navy. "I looked like I was about twelve years old," he laughed later. "I didn't shave for two years after I got in the Navy. I never had any whiskers."[7]

Finn quickly decided he liked just about everything about the Navy, starting with his first meal at boot camp: sliced roast beef and gravy. All he could eat. "Man, I just couldn't believe that food. . . . I thought I died and went to heaven," he recalled.[8] After recruit training, Finn was selected for the Aviation General Utility School at Great Lakes, Illinois. "Well, I didn't know what 'general utility' meant," he said. "I thought I went up there to learn how to fly an airplane, but that was the last thing you did. . . . It was a general utility school" designed to train airplane mechanics.[9]

Ironically, completion of aviation school kept him on shore for most of his first enlistment. "I went right in to the A and R Shops where you built airplanes," he recalled. Among his jobs was sewing fabric onto the wings. But Finn really wanted to work with weapons. "All I wanted to do is get over [to] that Ordnance Department where I could have guns, machine guns and all that stuff."[10]

He eventually managed to wrangle an assignment to the Ordnance Department at the naval air station at North Island, California. "I became an aviation ordnanceman—ordnance is anything that belongs with gunnery. . . . [I]t's not only guns and ammunition and torpedoes and rockets, it's all the equipment—complicated equipment that you use—to enable you to use the explosive! The stuff that kills people . . . that goes out there and does the damage."[11]

Toward the end of his first enlistment, Finn finally got to go to sea aboard the USS *Lexington*. Reenlisting, he served aboard a succession of ships, including a tour with the Asiatic Fleet aboard the heavy cruiser USS *Houston*. While stationed in San Diego in 1932, he encountered Nebraska-born Ruby Alice Dilts. A shipmate had met twenty-year-old Alice, as she preferred to be called, at a dance. He introduced her to Finn, who was immediately smitten. The attraction was mutual, and the two were married on June 21, 1933. Finn was promoted to chief petty officer, the highest enlisted rating in the Navy at that time, in 1935 after only nine years of active duty. By then he had decided on a career in the Navy. "Everybody thought I was a boy wonder," he chuckled.[12]

In April 1941, following a tour in Alaska, his PBY flying boat squadron, VP-14, was sent to join two other patrol squadrons—VP-11 and VP-12—at the brand-new naval air station at Kaneohe Bay 15 miles north of Pearl Harbor.[13] Construction on the base began in September 1940 and was still a work in progress when Patrol Squadron 14 (VP-14) arrived. Two large hangars had been built by the shore with another under construction. There was also a smaller maintenance hangar. Expansive ramps or aprons for each squadron's twelve PBY-5s led down to the water. Produced by Consolidated Aircraft, the massive seaplanes had come into service in late 1936. Nearly 64 feet long and powered by two 1200-power Pratt & Whitney "Twin Wasp" 14-cylinder, air-cooled radial piston engines, the aircraft carried a ten-man crew, had a cruise speed of 125 mph and a range of over 2,500 miles, making it an ideal patrol plane.

VP-14 had "ready duty" the morning of December 7. At 6:15 a.m. three planes lumbered into the air to patrol assigned sectors. Shortly before 7 a.m., while Finn was still in bed, one of those aircraft, piloted by twenty-four-year-old Ens. William P. Tanner, spotted an unauthorized submarine on the surface about a mile off the entrance to Pearl Harbor. The PBY attacked in conjunction with the destroyer USS *Ward*. The destroyer took the sub under fire with its deck guns and subsequently with depth charges. Tanner swooped low overhead and dropped another depth charge just ahead of the intruder as the doomed sub disappeared beneath the surface. It was later learned that their victim was a two-man

Japanese midget sub, one of five assigned to penetrate the harbor in conjunction with the early-morning aerial attack.

Forty-five minutes later, Japanese planes heading for the naval air station aroused Finn from what was supposed to be a leisurely Sunday morning. VP-14's war diary reported, "At about 0745 the squadron hangar, planes and area was subjected to a severe strafing attack by about nine (9) Japanese Type 0 fighter planes. Two planes [PBYs] on the water and three on the ramp were set on fire during this attack."[14] In fact, the war diary slightly underestimated the numbers. There were eleven Mitsubishi A6M2 Type 0 fighters (later code-named Zeros by the Allies), five from the carrier *Shōkaku* and six from the *Zuikaku*, each with two forward-firing 7.7mm machine guns and two wing-mounted 20mm cannons.

Arriving in the midst of the attack, Finn sped toward the hangar line in his car. "When I got down to the end of that road, I was going like a scalded tail ape," he remarked.[15] VP-11 was at Hangar 1. Next in line was the maintenance hangar, then VP-14's Hangar 2. Finn yelled over his shoulder to the young sailor in the backseat, asking where he wanted to get out. "Right here!" the youngster shouted as they got to VP-11's hangar. "I skidded to a stop there; he opened the door and got out and I looked in rearview mirror and he was just standing in the middle of the street," remembered Finn. "His hangar had just started to burn."[16] Out in the water, two anchored PBYs were also burning, along with three others on the ramp, pillars of black smoke billowing from their pyres.

Finn sped down to Hangar 2 and out of sheer force of habit parked the car in the official lot before sprinting to the armory area in the cavernous building. Sailors were already shooting back at the enemy planes with guns stripped from PBYs parked on the hangar apron and with rifles and machine guns from the armory. A sailor had shot the padlock off the ready room locker and was handing out arms and ammunition.

Finn heard the clatter of machine-gun fire just outside the door that led from the armory to the apron where the squadron's planes were parked. "I run out there and I peeked out the door," he said. "I didn't want to get shot by our own guns, which could happen very easily." Standing by the side of the hangar, radioman Robert J. Peterson—"a little blonde kid" from Colorado whose eyes were now wide as saucers—was manning a .30-caliber machine gun as planes roared overhead. Almost in Peterson's line of fire, AOM3c James ("Bucky") Walters had set up a .50-caliber machine gun.

"Move your gun out, Pete!" yelled Finn. "You're going to shoot the top of Bucky's head off!"

"We cain't, Chief!" exclaimed Peterson, indicating Japanese planes. "They're shooting at us!"

Finn dashed outside and grabbed Peterson's .30-caliber, which had been set on a tripod mount used for training. "I grabbed that .30-caliber gun, more or less took it away from Pete," he said. He lugged the gun about 20 yards out onto the open apron area, where he could see over the hangar and had a better field of fire. "Right off the bat there was some Jap planes came and I started firing at them with the .30-caliber gun."[17] Fighters would come through strafing, then circle away to line up a return run. "All I did was shoot at every one I could," said Finn. "You don't knock 'em down out of the air. That plane is going close to 200 knots, just a flick, and he's gone. You might not get fifteen or twenty seconds—that's a long blast."[18]

Taking advantage of lulls in the strafing, Finn periodically ran back into the hangar where men were belting ammunition for the machine guns. "I went in and out of my armory all during that battle and repaired machine guns and got other guns going—anything I could do," he said.[19] During one visit, he noticed five or six bomb-handling carts loaded with 500-pound depth charges. Brought in to arm PBYs on antisubmarine duty, the depth charges now posed a major hazard. If they were detonated by a strafing enemy fighter, it was possible the whole hangar would be leveled. Spotting his former car passenger, Eddie Sullivan, Finn exclaimed, "Sullivan, get those damn things out of here!"[20]

Another problem proved harder to resolve: there were scarcely any ground mounts for the machine guns, which were intended for use in the squadron's aircraft. Finn himself was using a training mount designed to stabilize the gun while students learned how to operate the weapon. "It was never ever designed to shoot a machine gun, but I fired thousands of rounds from that thing," he said.[21] Other sailors used whatever they could find—including pipes driven into the ground and even piles of lumber—to support the scavenged machine guns. Despite the growing volume of machine-gun fire directed at the attacking planes, the sailors could see little effect. "I can't tell you how many Japanese planes I shot at," said Finn. "I shot at every one that I could bear on. . . . I did not see a single plane go down. And that began to worry me. Christ, I [couldn't] even seem to get one of them."[22]

At about 9 a.m. the second attack wave of two nine-plane divisions (known as *chutais*), each consisting of Nakajima B5N2 Type 97 attack bombers from the Japanese carrier *Shōkaku*, approached the air station. Given the Allied code name Kate later in the war, the single-engine B5Ns were armed with two 250-kilogram (550-pound) bombs and carried a three-man crew consisting of pilot, navigator/bombardier, and radio operator/gunner. Finn looked up and saw five planes approaching as the first *chutai* swung in for a bomb run. He pulled the charging bolt on his machine gun and waited. "[I] saw those Japs coming and I got right on 'em and I followed them up, fired the whole 100-round belt at them." He watched his tracers float right into a bomber's propeller—"the only plane I know I absolutely hit," he said later. "I grabbed another belt off that pile of ammunition and . . . slapped it in." He looked up at an approaching aircraft and saw "little black . . . little tiny specks coming out of the plane." They were bombs.[23]

Finn paused, thinking the bombs might fall short or go over—then he realized he was standing out in the open without the least bit of protection. He turned and made a dash for the hangar. "I left that gun, dropped that ammunition on the deck and dived into the corner of a stairwell," he said. "And I no sooner hit the deck and the deck rose up, just like a carpet blowing in the wind." Massive explosions blew in all the heavy-glass hangar windows, showering him with shards as he huddled by the concrete stairs. "I jumped up and shook myself and started to run back out. . . . I run out there and one of those bombs had almost made a direct hit on that .30-caliber machine gun. The center of the crater was only about ten feet from the base of that gun."[24] There had been eighteen bombs in all. Eight, including one dud, struck along the paved apron; the rest had fallen just offshore, leaving large muddy rings in the shallow water. "I thought, gee whiz, you're lucky you can run fast," he remarked years later of his narrow escape.[25]

The gun was still operable. Finn shook the bomb debris out of the ammunition belt as the second *chutai* approached. "I saw a flight of planes coming. . . . And they were making a circle going to make a tree top level [run] back on us." As he braced himself, a sailor manning a .50-caliber machine gun started toward him, yelling something unintelligible. "And I had this gun all loaded and was getting ready to fire on this incoming flight of planes. I think it was three or four of them."

"Get the hell back to your gun!" Finn yelled at the man.

The sailor took three or four steps toward him and again yelled something Finn could not make out. Again, Finn told him to get back on his gun. The man kept coming. "My gun is jammed!" he yelled.[26]

Finn dashed over to the .50-caliber, quickly cleared the jam, and trained the gun on the bombers now approaching only about 2,000 feet off the deck. A hail of fire rose toward the *chutai* as Finn and dozens of others opened up with everything from machine guns to rifles and pistols. Apparently confused by the smoke rising from the air station and daunted by the amount of ground fire, the *chutai* broke off and began to circle around to attack from higher altitude. The interlude, noted VP-14's war diary, "was immediately followed by another strafing attack by nine (9) to twelve (12) Type 0 fighters. The two latter attacks succeeded in firing all but one of the remaining planes and in only one case could the fires be extinguished, and that not until the plane had been severely damaged."[27] The strafing was followed by more explosions as the Japanese bombers returned and scored several hits on Hangar 1, killing or wounding a large number of men inside.

Fully exposed on the open tarmac, Finn fired away throughout the attack. "Finally, pretty soon I looked and looked and didn't see any more planes," Finn recalled. He suddenly realized he was bleeding from multiple wounds, most of them fragmentation wounds from exploding 20mm shells fired by the attacking Zeros during their strafing runs. "When those things hit the shrapnel would go all over," he explained.[28] "I got shot in the left arm and shot in the left foot, broke the bone. I had shrapnel blasts in my chest and belly and right thumb."[29] "I went to charge the gun; my arm didn't have any strength at all. I looked down. . . . My left foot had got shot. I was walking around on my heel. I had shrapnel in my chest."[30]

With one arm useless, he reached over with the other to charge the gun, but the Japanese were gone. Scanning the skies, he finally saw one, "a little black speck up to the north." The PBYs on the bay were emitting heavy black smoke as they burned down to the waterline. "That Jap plane disappeared behind that smoke. And I thought, he's coming out and I don't care how far it is, when he comes out to the south end of that smoke, I'm going to let him have it."[31]

The enemy fighter—it was a Zero—burst out of the smoke "right down the barrel of that machine gun. . . . The instant it come out, I started firing," said Finn. "If I didn't hit him, it was just a goddamn miracle."[32] The plane roared overheard. "He was so close to me, over me that the air pressure of that plane just forced me . . . I was standing on one leg hanging onto the gun . . . and forced me right down to the ground on my knees. I came right up, 'cause I had powerful legs, came right up, strong, and tried to get on him as he flew over my head," but the plane had vanished over the hangar.[33]

It was the last Japanese plane Finn saw that day. As he stood down, it seemed as though the whole battle had lasted no more than about fifteen minutes. He was astonished when a sailor told him it was 10:15 a.m.—he had been fighting for over two hours. He was a bloody mess from his multiple wounds, including one to his scalp that was bleeding down onto his face. "Finn, you look like you had your head blown off," observed a sailor.[34] The bones in his left foot were broken, his left arm hung useless, and he had metal fragments sticking out of his chest. He had been hit over twenty times, though "some were just scratches," he insisted later.[35] The Japanese had made an equal mess out of the air station. "All I could see was planes burned up and wreckage everywhere. . . . I started cursing. I was so mad at what they'd done to us."[36]

All planes actually at the air station at the time of the attack had been put out of commission (thirty-three PBYs, one OS2U-1 "Kingfisher" observation floatplane, and a J2F-1 "Duck" single-engine amphibious biplane). The only PBYs still operational were the three sent out on patrol before the attack, though one of those had been shot up by enemy Zeros. VP-14 lost one man killed by a 20mm shell that hit him in the back, probably in the final strafing. Eleven men, including Finn, had been wounded. VP-11 lost seven killed and three seriously wounded, while VP-12 lost nine killed and four wounded. Hangar 1 had been destroyed.[37]

The damage inflicted on the Japanese was difficult to assess. According to the VP-14 war diary, "During the second attack many guns were in action and returning the enemy fire with telling effect. Two planes, one fighter and one bomber, were observed to have been seriously fired and when last seen were headed to seaward and were losing altitude rapidly. Several other planes were observed to have been heavily hit."[38] Japanese records confirm that several planes were heavily damaged. However, there appears to have been only one confirmed loss, this being a Zero piloted by Lt. Fusato Iida, which crashed on the air station grounds. It is likely that Iida's plane was the one fired on by Finn—and dozens of others—at the end of the engagement as it made one last lone strafing run. Japanese sources indicate Iida's Zero had previously been hit in the fuel tank. Without enough gas left to return to his carrier, he signaled to his comrades that he intended to crash his Zero into the enemy base. Considering how many men were firing at the low-flying plane, it is impossible to say just who had hit Iida's Zero in the gas tank or who, if anyone, may have downed him on his final run.

Sent to have his wounds tended to, Finn hobbled into the medical dispensary, where a corpsman began picking metal out of his chest with a pair of tweezers. However, as more seriously wounded men streamed in, Finn pushed his way out and caged a ride back to his quarters, where Alice fixed him up as well as she could. Finn told her to gather the other wives to make bandages out of sheets and pillowcases. "They need 'em at sick bay," he said.[39] He then returned to the hangar line where he stayed through that day and into the next as his ordnance men dug foxholes, welded up makeshift mounts for their machine guns, and braced for possible further attacks. Finally, at 1 p.m. on December 8, he reported back to the medical dispensary. The doctor put a stethoscope on his chest. "Chief, I think the shrapnel has penetrated your chest cavity," he said.

"And I knew damn well it had because I could hear all kinds of blood gurgling around inside of me," recalled Finn. His injuries included twenty-one shrapnel wounds. Fortunately, none of the big pieces had hit him. "It wasn't my day to die," he remarked.[40]

Finn remained in sick bay until the day before Christmas. "When I got out of there I was on crutches with my leg in a cast. Because they—these bones in my foot—were broken."[41] A few months later, after he had recuperated, a Navy yeoman who worked in the office approached him. "Chief," said the yeoman, "you're going to get the Medal of Honor."[42] The award had yet to be announced, but the yeoman had seen the paperwork go by in the office.

On September 15, 1942, Adm. Chester Nimitz presented the Medal of Honor to AOCM John Finn in a ceremony aboard the USS *Enterprise* at Pearl Harbor. Finn was one of fifteen men awarded the medal for actions during the Japanese attack and the only one serving at Kaneohe Naval Air Station. All the rest were given for actions at Pearl Harbor itself, most awarded for efforts to save ships or personnel. Ten were posthumous. "Come to find out, I was the only damn guy there [at the awards ceremony] that actually fired at Japs," remarked Finn.[43]

Because the naval air station was attacked several minutes before Pearl Harbor, Finn is often credited with being the first Medal of Honor recipient of World War II. Years later, reflecting on that Sunday morning, he observed, "I didn't have enough sense to come in out of the rain. But I was mad a lot of the time, pissed off. I can truthfully say I don't remember being scared to death. But I was goddamn mad."[44]

In June 1942, Finn was temporarily commissioned as an ensign, rising in rank to lieutenant two years later. After a series of stateside assignments, he served aboard the carrier USS *Hancock* as the fleet closed on the Japanese home islands during the final months of the war. Following his transfer to the Fleet Reserve in March 1947, he reverted to his enlisted rate of chief petty officer. In 1956 he was placed on the retired list as a lieutenant. In civilian life, Finn and Alice moved to a 93-acre ranch near Pine Valley, California, where Finn had plenty of room to ride his motorcycle, shoot guns, accumulate junk cars and tractors, and adopt an assortment of animals that at one point totaled nineteen dogs. He and Alice had no children of their own but fostered five Native American children, establishing a close bond with the Campo Band of Diegueno Mission Indians. Alice passed away in 1990.

John died at the age of 100 on May 27, 2010, at a veterans' home in Chula Vista, California. He was the last surviving Medal of Honor recipient from the attack on Pearl Harbor and the oldest living recipient at the time of his death. He remains the only aviation ordnanceman ever to receive the medal.

In interviews after the war, Finn was quick to point out that he was not the only sailor to man a machine gun and fire on the Japanese that Sunday morning at Kaneohe Bay. "Personally I did no more than my shipmates," he insisted.[45] "That damned hero stuff is a bunch [of] crap, I guess," he reflected in a 2009 interview. Many people are innately brave, he suggested, but never have an opportunity to demonstrate their courage. "You gotta be in that position. You gotta understand that there's all kinds of heroes, but they never get a chance to be in a hero's position."[46]

Eighteen American warships, including all eight of the Pacific Fleet's battleships, were sunk or heavily damaged in the Pearl Harbor attack; 200 aircraft were destroyed, most on the ground; and over 2,400 U.S. servicemen were killed. By a stroke of good fortune, both U.S. carriers were at sea and escaped destruction in the confines of the harbor, but by any measure the attack was an unmitigated disaster for the U.S. Navy.

With the U.S. naval power shattered, the Japanese prepared to run rampant across the Pacific. The ambitious target list included the Philippines, the Dutch East Indies, Burma, Malaya, Thailand, parts of India, and sundry Central Pacific islands. Among the smaller prizes was a miniscule patch of sand 2,000 nautical miles west of Pearl Harbor. It was called Wake Island.

Capt. Henry T. Elrod
Wake Island
December 8–23, 1941

Afterward they would be called the "Lost Squadron."

They were Marine Fighter Squadron 211 (VMF-211): thirteen pilots and twelve F4F-3 Grumman Wildcats serviced by a forty-nine-man ground crew. The pilots touched down on the newly constructed crushed coral runway at Wake—strategically located between Midway and Guam—on December 4, only three days before the attack on Pearl Harbor. They joined 449 Marines from the 1st Defense Battalion, 68 naval personnel, and 5 luckless U.S. Army soldiers. There were also 1,146 civilian construction workers who had arrived in January to work on the island's defenses as relations with Japan deteriorated.

The dozen Grumman Wildcats from VMF-211 were commanded by Maj. Paul Putnam, described by a fellow officer as "calm, quiet, soft-spoken . . . a determined sort of fellow."[47] Equally determined, but considerably less soft-spoken, was Putnam's boisterous executive officer, thirty-six-year-old Capt. Henry Talmadge Elrod. Captain Elrod, to put it mildly, was a handful.

Born in Rebecca, Georgia, on September 27, 1905, "Talmadge," as he was called by his family, grew up outside Thomasville. His father, a former schoolteacher and Baptist minister turned businessman, was superintendent of the expansive Sinkola Plantation. Family lore paints him as a stern, rigid disciplinarian. Talmadge was cut from different cloth—a "moody, somewhat off-beat boy," a hellion whose reckless antics could drive his father to distraction, observed Talmadge's nephews.[48] Athletics provided one organized outlet for the boy's restless energy. He excelled on the high school football team and was an excellent tennis player. Only those very close to Elrod knew that his bouts of exuberant energy were mirrored by equally extreme emotional lows. It is telling, perhaps, that while he does not seem to have lacked for friends, during his senior year at high school he also won the "meanest kid in the class award"—receiving a powder puff in recognition of that honor.[49]

Following graduation from high school in 1923, Elrod enrolled at the University of Georgia. He lettered on the football team but transferred to Yale before his junior year. He was apparently contemplating a career as an architect or a physician, though his restlessness, physical energy, and lack of discipline would seem to make either a poor choice. Melancholia also continued to dog him. In a letter to a girlfriend, he referred to himself as "worthless" and admitted, "I would give anything to always be a child—to never grow up. . . . I hate responsibility. I don't want to be under obligations to anyone but myself."[50]

Elrod's studies at Yale ended after only a few months, cut short in tragic fashion when his father was found dead of what was deemed to be a self-inflicted gunshot wound. Elrod rushed home and never returned to Yale. In the family turmoil that followed, he had a falling out with his mother, an estrangement that would never be repaired. His sister, Farrar Elrod Ramsey, remarked later that her brother was much enamored with the novel *Beau Geste*, whose protagonist runs off to join the French Foreign Legion.[51] One November day in 1927, Elrod climbed aboard a passing freight train and headed away from home and his mother, brother, and three sisters. None but Farrar would ever see him again. On December 1, he walked into a recruiting station in Denver, Colorado, and enlisted in the Marine Corps. On the application, he gave his religious affiliation as "atheist."[52]

Elrod served a four-year hitch as an enlisted man before receiving a commission as a second lieutenant in 1931. Four years later he earned his wings as a Marine aviator. Family members recalled that he had been fascinated with flying since childhood and in high school had rarely missed the opportunity to go aloft with visiting barnstormers. Ironically, considering later events, his flying career got off to a rocky start. Washing out of flight training in 1933 (an examiner wrote, "[He] has no feel for plane"), he gained reinstatement the following year, and this time managed to pass.[53] He also acquired a wife, Elizabeth Hogun Jackson, the niece of a Navy admiral. The two married on May 10, 1933, in Escambia, Florida, while Elrod was in flight training. In Elizabeth he found a woman resilient enough to handle his impulsiveness—which at one point included going into debt to buy a polo pony. Perhaps not surprisingly, the horse was repossessed when he failed to keep up with the payments.

Elizabeth may have tempered Elrod's behavior to some degree, but she did not change his basic nature. A daredevil in the air, on the ground he was hard-drinking, aggressive, and physical, quick to indulge in rough horseplay. "When it was Elrod's turn to practice aerial gunnery, he was so determined not to miss that he held his fire until he was about to fly right into the tow target," recalled pilot John F. Kinney.[54] His disregard for the rules was legendary. On one occasion he simply appropriated a plane and flew off to attend a christening ceremony for Farrar's youngest son, who was also his namesake.

Despite his rambunctiousness, by late 1941 Elrod was serving as executive officer of Marine Fighter Squadron 211 (VMF-211). In October the squadron's antiquated F3F-2 biplanes were replaced with F4F-3 Grumman Wildcats, a single-place, single-engine, mid-wing monoplane with retractable landing gear, designed to operate from land bases or U.S. Navy aircraft carriers. Armed with four .50-caliber machine guns, the stubby-winged Wildcats were powered by a 1,200-horsepower Pratt & Whitney "Twin Wasp," 14-cylinder radial engine and were capable of a maximum speed of 331 mph.

"The F4F-3s were the best and latest planes the Navy had available at the time," recalled Lt. John Kinney. "But our mechanics had never even seen one of these planes before, and our pilots had only about thirty hours in the Wildcats, which was barely enough to qualify. None of us had fired our machine guns or dropped a bomb from an F4F-3."[55]

They had little time to familiarize themselves with their new mounts as orders came for twelve pilots to bring their Wildcats aboard USS *Enterprise* on November 28 for transport to Wake Island. The planes still wore their factory gray paint; only six of them had their machine guns installed, and even these were lacking sights. The Marines improvised sights, recalled Kinney. "We would simply mount a bolt in the top of the engine cowling as an aiming point. Then we would paint an oval on the sloping windshield to give us some method by which to lead enemy airplanes into our line of fire."[56]

The Wildcat pilots remained unperturbed by these shortcomings as they arrived at Wake on December 4. Should war break out with Japan, they were confident of their superiority. "We were convinced that even if the Japanese planes were mechanically adequate, it would be all the pilots could do to fly them in straight lines," recalled Kinney. "They would be no match for American aerobatic maneuvers."[57]

Elrod arrived at Wake in typical good spirits. He was "a strong, well-built fellow who liked to take his pleasures the hard way," recalled Maj. Walter Baylor, who had been sent to Wake to establish a base radio station for ground-to-air communications. In one boisterous (presumably alcohol-fueled) incident, Elrod and a noncom indulged in a rough-and-tumble wrestling match in Wake's rudimentary officers club. "They went to it, half-naked, on the bare wooden floor, which was plenty rough itself and splintery," observed Baylor. "Both men emerged with scratches and colorful abrasions from stem to stern."[58]

Elrod's best friend in the squadron was Capt. Frank C. Tharin, a thirty-one-year-old Naval Academy graduate from Washington, DC. Tharin addressed Elrod as "Baron," while Elrod referred to Tharin as "Duke." They were inseparable on the ground and in the air. Tharin's affection for the Baron was not universal. Despite Elrod's position as squadron exec, some officers viewed him as undisciplined and too familiar with the enlisted men. "In case of combat, though, I'd rather be with him than against him," remarked one of the VMF-211 pilots.[59] "He was a man of action, a doer," observed Tharin of his unruly friend.[60]

Combat was closer than anyone knew. Wake being twenty-two hours ahead of Oahu, it was December 8 when word first arrived of the Japanese attack on Pearl Harbor. The uncertainty of what lay in store set nerves on edge, but Elrod took the news with uncharacteristic quietude, recalled survivors of the campaign. He said little, smoked a cigarette, had a cup of coffee, and prepared to take to the air.

Any doubts about the future were erased at 11:58 a.m. with the arrival of thirty-four Mitsubishi G3M2 Type 96 land attack planes (later code-named Nells by Allied forces) launched from the Marshall Islands 600 miles away. Introduced in 1935, the Nell boasted a 20mm cannon in a rear dorsal turret and four 7.7mm Type 92 machine guns located in the cockpit, on the left and right sides, and in a forward dorsal turret. Crewed by seven men, it could carry 1,800 pounds of bombs or one aerial torpedo. The attackers this morning were loaded with bombs.

Four of Wake's Wildcats, including one piloted by Elrod, were in the air on patrol, but the raid caught the other eight on the ground. Lt. Robert J. ("Strawberry") Conderman was mortally wounded by machine-gun fire as he raced for his plane. Lt. George A. Graves made it to the cockpit of his Wildcat only to be killed instantly as the plane received a direct hit from a bomb and burst into flames, incinerating him. Still wearing his parachute, Lt. Frank Holden was riddled by machine-gun bullets as he raced for cover, the silk from his chute spilling out in the widening pool of blood around his corpse.

The main fuel dump went up in a tremendous fireball. Seven of the eight Wildcats on the airfield were demolished in the attack: four, including Graves's plane, took direct bomb hits; three others were set on fire and burned so badly they looked like "brown tin cans," recalled a ground crewman.[61] The eighth didn't burn but was pretty well shot up. In two passes, the Japanese had knocked out over half of Wake's little Air Force. The fifty-six VMF-211 personnel on the airfield at the time of the attack suffered thirty-two casualties, including nineteen officers and men killed outright or fatally wounded. The total included more than half of the squadron's pilots. Japanese bombers also swept over nearby Peale and Wilkes islets, inflicting still more casualties and damage, flying so low that ground personnel could see enemy machine gunners laughing as they fired.

The Wildcats on patrol saw the departing enemy bombers, but it was too late to intervene. Their bad luck continued as Elrod landed. Taxiing around the burning debris, he hit an oil drum that had been blown out onto the runway. The collision bent his prop. One of the eight Wildcats caught on the ground during the attack was subsequently repaired, but the others, including Elrod's plane, were a total loss. The battle had scarcely begun, and Wake's air defense had already been reduced to just four Wildcats.

Twenty-four hours later, the Japanese were back. This time they paid a price. Two Wildcats on patrol sent one of the Nells into the sea in flames, and Marine antiaircraft gunners claimed two more. Nevertheless, the Japanese again inflicted substantial damage, working over the barracks, garage, and machine shop, among other critical areas. They also burned Wake's hospital—apparently unimpressed by the large red cross marking it as a medical facility—killing a number of patients, including three enlisted men from Elrod's squadron. Thirty or more civilian contractors were also killed and about the same number wounded. Elrod and Tharin took up residence in a "hole-away-from-home" stocked with a dozen cases of canned goods, five-gallon containers of water, and (unbeknownst to most) a case of whiskey retrieved from the now abandoned Pan-Am hotel.[62]

Two days into the war, Elrod had yet to close with the enemy, and he was showing his frustration, remembered friends. Finally, on the morning of December 10, he got his chance while flying the only plane in the squadron equipped with a supercharger to boost engine performance. Timing the expected Japanese attack, the four surviving Wildcats launched at 10 a.m. and soon spotted approximately two dozen Nells approaching the island. Elrod charged into the formation. Knocking down one Nell, he ignored the antiaircraft fire blossoming around from below, slicing through the formation again and again until he sent another bomber plummeting earthward. Though the Wildcats could not stop the raid, Elrod's grin was back and his mood much improved when he landed. His audacity in the air also earned him a new nickname. From then on, he was "Hammering Hank" to the Wake defenders.[63]

By now it was clear from the bombing patterns—which avoided the power plant and serious damage to the airstrip itself—that the Japanese intended to seize the atoll. Even as Elrod tore into the Nells that morning, the enemy invasion force was on its way, having sailed from Kwajalein in the Marshall Islands on December 8. Consisting of the light cruisers *Yubari*, *Tatsuta*, and *Tenryu*, six destroyers, two troop-laden patrol boats converted from older Momi-class destroyers and equipped to launch landing craft, two armed transports, and a handful of supporting vessels, the Wake Invasion Force arrived offshore the morning of December 11. The flotilla was commanded by fifty-two-year-old Rear Adm. Sadamichi Kajioka, who presumably did not anticipate a major struggle. Once the target area had been softened up by bombardment, Kajioka intended to send in about 450 Japanese special landing troops to overwhelm any survivors.

At 5:22 a.m. Kajioka's flagship *Yubari*, along with the two accompanying cruisers, commenced bombarding the atoll. Manning Wake's six 5-inch shore guns, the Americans impatiently awaited the order to fire as the warships steamed along a mere 4,500 yards offshore. Finally, at 6:15 a.m., the order came to open up, and Admiral Kajioka paid for his complacency. Adjusting their fire, one U.S. battery hit the *Yubari* amidships at least four times and then once again in the forward gun turret as Kajioka's flagship, enveloped in smoke, fled out to sea beyond range. The same shore battery put a shell into one of the troop-carrying patrol boats, killing two men and wounding fourteen.

At 6:50 a.m., another U.S. gun battery nailed the Japanese destroyer *Hayate* amidships with its third salvo at a range of 7,000 yards. One of the shells penetrated just below the waterline and detonated in a magazine. There was a blinding flash as *Hayate* exploded, broke in two, and sank with all 168 hands. U.S. batteries also scored hits on destroyers *Oite*, *Yayoi*, and *Mutsuki*, along with one of two Japanese transports and one of the remaining two Japanese cruisers.

Stunned, Kajioka broke off the attack at 7 a.m. The Wake Invasion Force disappeared back over the southern horizon toward Kwajalein, but Admiral Kajioka's travails were far from over.

As the shore batteries pounded away, Elrod, Putnam, Tharin, and thirty-four-year-old Capt. Herbert C. Freuler had taken to the air, each Wildcat fitted with a pair of 100-pound bombs slung below the wings on homemade lugs. One young pilot scoffed that it would be impossible to sink a warship with a 100-pound bomb, but Elrod was not dissuaded, retorting, "Well, if it's impossible, it will take a little longer, so let's get started."[64] Setting off after the retreating Japanese, the Wildcat pilots braved antiaircraft fire to strafe and bomb the ships, shuttling back and forth to the island airstrip to refuel and rearm with additional bombs. Over the next hour or so, they dropped twenty bombs and used up 20,000 rounds of armor-piercing .50-caliber ammunition in their attacks on the convoy.

The most spectacular result was notched by Elrod, who paired up with Tharin for two bomb runs on the destroyer *Kisaragi*. Putnam saw one of Elrod's bombs smash through the destroyer's deck, starting a fire in the ship's vitals. *Kisaragi* lost way for about half an hour. She finally staggered off to the south, smoking and trailing oil, but the ship was doomed. At about 8:15 a.m., the destroyer suddenly exploded in a ball of flame. The entire 150-man crew perished in the blast, which apparently occurred when the fire started by Elrod's bomb set off *Kisaragi*'s store of depth charges.[65]

Elrod did not have the satisfaction of observing *Kisaragi*'s demise. A burst of machine-gun fire had riddled his oil system, forcing him to head for home before the engine seized. He made it back to Wake but smashed up his Wildcat in a forced landing on the boulder-strewn beach just short of the airstrip. "At the last critical second, he somehow lifted her the extra few feet which enabled him to make a 'deadstick' landing on the beach, just above the creamy surf," recalled Capt. Walter Baylor, who was watching from below.[66]

Elrod climbed out of the wrecked plane, shaken but unhurt aside from a minor cut on his cheek. He was more upset with himself for having wrecked one of the last surviving fighters. "Honest, I'm sorry as hell about the plane," he lamented as a group of onlookers arrived expecting to pull his dead body from the crash. He continued to apologize all the way back to the airstrip.[67]

The defeat of the landing force raised spirits among the Wake garrison. "The attitude of the men after the December 11 attack was that we could handle pretty much anything," observed PFC James O. King. "There was no doubt that help was coming at this stage. We were all optimistic and never dreamed the Japanese would take the island."[68] King was right: help was coming. Four days after the Japanese landing was repulsed, a relief force left Pearl Harbor bound for Wake. Consisting of the fleet carrier *Saratoga*, the oiler *Neches*, a seaplane tender, the heavy cruisers *Astoria*, *Minneapolis*, and *San Francisco*, and ten destroyers, the convoy carried the 4th Marine Defense Battalion, ammunition for the defense, and Marine Fighter Squadron 221.

On December 20, a PBY flying boat from Midway landed in Wake's lagoon amid a rain squall, the first physical contact the defenders had enjoyed with the outside world since the war began. The pilot brought sealed orders indicating that help was on the way and offered to bring out any mail from the defenders when he left the next morning. In a last letter to his wife, "darling Elizabeth," Elrod observed, "We are still clinging grimly to what little that we can call our own. Everything is very secret to everyone except the Japs who seem to know it all before the rest of us." That same evening, in a last-minute addendum, Elrod remained pessimistic. He would like "to see a good old-fashioned typhoon sweep this entire area," he wrote. With a tenderness that probably would have surprised his fellow pilots, he added, "I'll think of a million things that I should have said after I have gone to bed tonight. But now I am going to say that I love you and you alone always and always and repeat it a million times or so. . . . I know that you are praying for me and I have nothing more to ask than that your prayers be answered."[69]

The rest of the Wake garrison might have been surprised by Elrod's pessimism. "Hammering Hank" had become a favorite among the men. Cpl. Guy J. Kelnhofer, who was assigned to one of Wake's antiaircraft guns, remembered how Elrod would buzz low overhead as he went aloft in his Wildcat. "I can remember Elrod taking off over our position and all of us standing up and applauding him as he went off. . . . All of us, you know, just cheering him because he was such a tremendous pilot and was so, so fearless. . . . And he would wave [to] us . . . and we were all shouting, cheering him."[70]

Two hours after the PBY lumbered into the air the next morning bound for Midway, Japanese planes arrived overhead and began to work over the island's defenses. To the garrison's dismay, these were not the usual land-based bombers but single-engine carrier planes—dive bombers and fighters. Somehow they managed to miss the lone Wildcat sitting out on the runway, but their appearance meant the Japanese were returning in force and this time would have carrier support. "Of course we knew that was the beginning of the end," recalled an Army radioman.[71] The following day the last two Marine Wildcats were lost in a dogfight with six A6M2 Zekes over the island. One pilot survived; the other was killed.

Now without planes, the survivors of VMF-211 joined Wake's ground defenses. Elrod, Tharin, and a group of airmen under Major Putnam trudged out to a three-inch gun commanded by Lt. Robert Hanna defending the beach south of the airfield. They joined a mixed force of Marines and civilians-turned-riflemen forming a screen in the dense undergrowth in front of Hanna's gun position.

Elrod had earlier reminded his fellow pilots of Japanese cruelty. "The Japs don't take prisoners," he observed. Now he confided to Tharin that he did not expect to survive. His pessimism surfaced again in a chat with some enlisted men. Elrod advised them to "clean up," adding darkly, "This may be your last night on earth."

Soon afterward, Elrod ran into Cpl. Robert Page, an easygoing twenty-six-year-old from tiny Holt, Missouri.

"Page," Elrod asked, "do you like to fish?"

"Yes, sir," replied Page. "You're talking my language."

"I'll tell you," promised Elrod, "if we get out of this alive, I'll take you on the damnedest fishing trip you was ever on in your life."[72]

Elrod's pessimism was well founded. Information indicating the presence of two Japanese carriers and two fast battleships (actually heavy cruisers) near Wake Island forced Vice Adm. William S. Pye, the acting commander in chief of the U.S. Pacific Fleet, to reconsider the effort to reinforce the beleaguered garrison. The presence of Japanese carriers dramatically changed the picture. The U.S. Navy simply could not risk losing a carrier following the debacle of Pearl Harbor. The Japanese had beaten them to Wake, and the garrison's capitulation was now inevitable. Hours later, to the everlasting fury of the officers and men in the relief expedition, Pye ordered them to turn back. *Saratoga* was only 425 miles from Wake. But by then, the Japanese landing was already well underway.

Unaware of Pye's heartrending deliberations, the Wake Island defenders were waiting nervously in their positions at about 1 a.m. on December 23 when flares soared skyward from offshore. Beams of light flashed. The Americans hoped against hope that perhaps a relief expedition had arrived. But there was to be no relief for Wake. Admiral Kajioka was back, his previously depleted armada reinforced with four heavy cruisers and air support from two aircraft carriers, the *Hiryū* and *Sōryū*.

Since his gun lacked sights, Hanna bore-sighted the piece at one of two indistinct shapes approaching the shore in a misting rain. The shapes turned out to be a pair of landing barges crammed with Japanese infantry. Hanna waited. One of the boats turned on a searchlight. Hanna commenced firing, hitting the vessel multiple times. Turning their attention to the second barge, Hanna's gun crew hit that craft several times as well, but most of the Japanese Special Landing Force troops aboard had already scrambled out and made it to shore. As they started inland, Elrod's screening force took them under fire with small arms and a couple of .30-caliber machine guns.

Elrod fought like a man possessed. Armed with a Thompson submachine gun, he jumped up, shooting and swearing, "Kill the sons of bitches!" He seemed completely heedless of his own safety. "He was just wild with that Tommy gun," recalled an enlisted Marine.[73]

In the close-quarter fighting, Elrod shot down a Japanese carrying a light machine gun. He handed off his Thompson, picked up the dead man's machine gun, and turned it on the landing force troops filtering through the scrub. A Japanese survivor later described an American who was almost certainly Elrod. "One large figure appeared before us to blaze away with a machine gun from his hips as they do in American gangster films," recalled the man.[74] Some of the Japanese fell almost at Elrod's feet.

The assault faltered. Going to ground, the Japanese pounded the defenders with grenade launchers and picked away with rifle fire. Casualties mounted. Just before daylight, Elrod and a few other defenders worked around to the flank, crawling past a scattering of Japanese corpses to position themselves for the next enemy rush. They bumped into a knot of Japanese also on the move. As Elrod rose to lob a hand grenade, a Japanese concealed among the scattering of corpses squeezed off a shot. Elrod collapsed over "Duke" Tharin. The Duke hosed the Japanese rifleman down with his Tommy gun before leaning over to check on Elrod. His free-spirited friend was dead, shot squarely through the forehead.

An hour later, Wake's defenders, overwhelmed at several points, were ordered to surrender. Of the men at Hanna's gun, only ten were still alive. Of those ten, only Tharin had escaped injury. The contorted bodies of over sixty Japanese lay around the position, intermingled with the American dead. As the survivors threw down their guns and emerged into the open, Putnam, bleeding from a wound to his jaw, approached the ranking Marine on Wake, Maj. James Devereaux. "Jimmy, I'm sorry," he said, "poor Hank is dead."[75]

Following the battle, Marine Cpl. Robert M. Brown was among the prisoners assigned to burial duty by their captors. Brown's detail recovered Hank Elrod's remains a few days after the surrender. The Baron was buried on Wake, and the survivors went into captivity. In California, Elizabeth Elrod held out hope that her husband had survived. In May, she wrote to her sister-in-law that some of the men who had served with Elrod had been reported as prisoners, though there was still no word about him. "However, I do not think that the fact that we have not heard necessarily means bad news," she added. "Now if he will only be calm and settle down to wait it out, I see no reason why he won't be coming back to us when the war is over, and won't he have some rare stories to tell?"[76]

Meanwhile, she took pride in reports of his heroism on Wake as passed along by Walter Baylor, who had escaped the island on the last flight out. "I always knew that he was more of a war-time soldier than a peace-time one, but I am glad that now everybody else knows it too and very proud of him," she wrote.[77]

Elrod's gallant performance in the defense of Wake was not forgotten, though his story did not emerge until after the war when the Wake survivors returned to U.S. control and were formally debriefed. It was then that the public learned about "Hammering Hank" Elrod and his heroic actions in the face of overwhelming odds. On November 8, 1946, Gen. A. A. Vandegrift presented the Medal of Honor to Elizabeth Elrod at ceremonies held at Marine Corps Headquarters.[78] Though the recognition came to him late, chronologically Elrod was the first pilot to earn the Medal of Honor in World War II.

In October 1947—not quite six years after his death on Wake—Elrod was interred at Arlington National Cemetery. Elizabeth subsequently donated his Medal of Honor to the Marine Corps Air Museum in Quantico, Virginia. In 1985, the U.S. Navy named a guided missile frigate in Elrod's honor. He is the only Marine hero from Wake who has had a warship named in his honor—a fitting memorial to a sometimes troubled man who found his true place in the chaos of combat with the enemy.

Two months after Hank Elrod's death at Wake, the American position in the Pacific continued to deteriorate in the face of a Japanese juggernaut. U.S. forces in the Philippines were cornered and under siege; Japanese aircraft had sent the British battleship *Prince of Wales* and battlecruiser *Repulse* to the bottom off the coast of Malaya; Malaya itself was quickly overrun, and the British bastion of Singapore was on the brink of surrender; Hong Kong had been seized; the enemy was about to invade the Dutch East Indies with its valuable oil fields. Disaster loomed on all sides.

In February, in an effort to strike at least a symbolic offensive blow in return, a small task force built around one of the U.S. Pacific Fleet's priceless carriers steamed toward Japanese-held Rabaul on the tip of New Britain, nearly 4,000 statute miles from Hawaii. Newly captured by the Japanese, the former Australian base and airfield seemed an opportune target for a surprise raid to demonstrate that the Allies had not been completely declawed. Among the naval aviators preparing to assist in this lesson was a twenty-seven-year-old fighter pilot from New Jersey named Butch O'Hare.

Lt. Edward Henry O'Hare
Off Rabaul
February 20, 1942

Tens of thousands of travelers pass through Chicago's O'Hare International Airport on a regular basis. Few of those travelers probably know that the airport honors a Medal of Honor recipient whose father was a murder victim. His name was Edward Henry O'Hare, but his friends called him Butch.[79]

Butch O'Hare was born on March 13, 1914, in Saint Louis, Missouri, to Selma and Edgar Joseph ("E. J.") O'Hare. The family initially resided above a grocery store owned by Selma's father, but E. J. had higher aspirations. He took nighttime finance courses, became a licensed attorney, and eventually embarked on a lucrative career as a dog track operator after obtaining the patent rights to the ubiquitous mechanical rabbit used in that sport.

Followed by two sisters, Eddie, as his family called him, was a good-natured, likable youth, though somewhat reserved. Later, in the Navy, his superiors would note he was infallibly polite but "a little diffident and quiet on first acquaintance."[80] He was an intelligent boy and an outstanding student. If Eddie had a weakness, it was his inability to stay away from the cookie jar—he had a legendary affection for sweet rolls and pastries in particular. As his son entered his teens, E. J. began to harbor some concerns about Eddie's expanding waistline and a growing inclination toward what the energetic E. J. interpreted as laziness. When Eddie one day asked to use the car to travel the one-block distance to the bakery, E. J. had seen enough. In September 1927 he packed his reluctant son off to Western Military Academy in Alton, Illinois.

Eddie adapted to military school, though he never lost his fondness for snacks. A mediocre football player, he was an excellent marksman and became president of the rifle club. Meanwhile, by 1930, E. J.'s business was booming, and he moved the family to their very own house, complete with swimming pool and a skating rink. Unfortunately, this affluence came at a price: One was the O'Hare marriage, which fell victim to E. J.'s frequent absences on the road. The other was the substantial criminal element associated with E. J.'s dog track operations—an unavoidable reality that had E. J. rubbing shoulders with mobster Al Capone.

Probably in an effort to steer his son toward more respectable pursuits, E. J. encouraged him to apply to the U.S. Naval Academy after his graduation from Western. Hoping to become a naval aviator, Eddie was amenable but failed to pass the entrance exam. After a course of study at Cochran-Bryan Preparatory School in Annapolis—a school that specifically assists students who aspire to enter the Naval Academy—he passed the exam on his second try and was admitted to the Class of 1937.

Though his four years at the academy were unremarkable scholastically—he graduated 255th in a class of 323—young O'Hare was probably the only cadet who had his own car (a 1933 Chevy) as well as a 27-foot motor sailboat. This display of affluence, courtesy of his doting father, does not seem to have affected Eddie's ability to assimilate with his peers. Affable and unassuming, he was well liked by his classmates, who dubbed him "Butch." The nickname stuck, and to everyone but his family, he was Butch O'Hare from then on.

O'Hare spent the first two years after graduation aboard the battleship USS *New Mexico*, but in June 1939 he reported to Pensacola for flight training. He proved to be a natural. "He had a touch that was unbelievable," observed fellow trainee Willard Smith. "I think he probably flew the airplanes almost as well as most of the teachers did. He was just a completely natural pilot, just tremendous."[81] An evaluation dated June 20 observed, "Student handles plane more like an experienced pilot than a student." Butch was rated "above average officer material." Yet another report observed, "He thinks clearly, is thorough in his work and very dependable. He is a little diffident and quiet on first acquaintance but is unfailingly cheerful and courteous and does not lack self-confidence. He appears to be well liked by his classmates."[82]

Sadly, Butch was to suffer personal tragedy before completing the program. On November 8, as his father drove along a Chicago street in his Lincoln Zephyr, another automobile carrying two men pulled up along-side. A point-blank shotgun blast punched a fist-sized hole through the driver's side window and struck E. J. in the left side of the head. A second blast finished the work as E. J.'s Lincoln jumped the curb and crashed into a pole. The other vehicle drove slowly away, obediently stopped at a traffic light, then turned left and disappeared from view. E. J. died at the scene.

While no one was ever arrested in E. J.'s murder, it was almost certainly a hit ordered by Al Capone. It was later revealed that E. J. had been cooperating with the FBI, and his inside information had been instrumental in putting Capone in prison for tax evasion. Capone apparently learned of E. J.'s betrayal and ordered his assassination. Heartbroken, Butch took a fifteen-day emergency leave to attend his father's funeral before returning to Pensacola to complete flight training, which he wrapped up on May 27, 1940.

Assigned to Fighting Squadron 3 (VF-3) aboard the USS *Saratoga*, Ensign O'Hare was vetted by flight officer Flight Officer Lt. Cmdr. John ("Jimmy") Thach, an experienced pilot who would himself become a naval aviation legend. It was Thach's experience that newly minted fighter pilots were cocky and tended to overestimate their abilities. His job was to provide a reality check by humiliating them in a mock dogfight. Newcomer O'Hare proved to be the exception. "I did everything I could to fool him and shake him, and he came right in on me and stuck there and he could have shot me right out of the air," recalled Thach. Having never been defeated by a novice, Thach expressed his surprise to another pilot. Skeptical, the other pilot challenged Butch and was himself defeated.

"Butch O'Hare was a good athlete. He had a sense of timing and relative motion that he may have been born with, but also he had that competitive spirit," remembered Thach. "When he got into any kind of a fight like this, he didn't want to lose. He really was dedicated to winning, and he probably had worked a lot of this out in his own mind, then read as much as he could. When he first got to the squadron he studied all the documents that we had on aerial combat, and he just picked it up much faster than anyone else I've ever seen. He got the most out of his airplane. He didn't try to horse it around."[83]

Butch also scored a big win on the ground during a trip home to Saint Louis in July 1941. Stopping by the hospital to visit a friend's wife and her newborn baby, he was introduced to the new mother's friend, Rita Wooster, a twenty-three-year-old private nurse originally from Musca-tine, Iowa. Noticing Butch's unconcealed interest, the new mother advised him that Rita had recently broken up with another man and probably wasn't ready for a relationship just yet.

Undeterred, Butch offered to drive Rita home. As they arrived at their destination, he apologized for his forwardness and asked her to marry him. Predictably, Rita demurred. Butch apologized once again. He wasn't a lunatic, he explained; it was just that due to his Navy schedule, he didn't have the time or opportunity to court her in the conventional manner. Six weeks later, the two were married in St. Mary's Catholic Church in Phoenix, Arizona.

The outbreak of war three months later found Butch flying F4F-3 Wildcats with VF-3 off the *Saratoga* as part of the doomed rescue mission to Wake Island. Following that disappointment, on January 11, as the *Saratoga* maneuvered off Hawaii, the Japanese submarine *I-6* put a torpedo into her side. With the *Sara* headed for months of repairs, VF-3 was transferred to the *Lexington*.

In the early morning hours of February 20, Task Force 11, consisting of *Lexington*, two heavy cruisers, seven destroyers, and a fleet oiler, was steaming along less than 500 miles northeast of Japanese-held Rabaul, preparing for a surprise raid on the enemy base at the tip of New Britain Island, 3,900 statute miles from Hawaii. So far, they had remained undetected, but that was about to change. At 10:30 a.m., as pilots were gearing up to launch, a Japanese Kawanishi H6K flying boat arrived on the scene. Known to Allied forces as a "Mavis," the massive four-engine aircraft, which carried a crew of ten and had a range of over 4,000 miles, was one of three launched at dawn that morning from Rabaul's Simpson Harbor. The planes had been directed to scout eastward after Japanese listening posts picked up American radio traffic in the area.[84]

Butch and his wingman, twenty-six-year-old Louisiana-born Lt. (j.g.) Marion W. ("Duff") Dufilho, who had graduated from the Naval Academy a year behind Butch, were among six Wildcats launched as *Lexington*'s radar picked up the enemy flying boat only 35 miles from the task force. To their disappointment, they were ordered to hang back and fly cover for the carrier while Fighting Squadron 3 commander Jimmy Thach and his wingman went after the enemy plane. Shortly after 11 a.m. Thach sent the Mavis plummeting into the sea in flames. "I could see the Japs in the forward part of the plane stand up, but they seemed to make no attempt to jump," recalled Thach. "The plane was almost completely engulfed in flames, and it hit the water with a huge explosion."[85]

An hour later, *Lexington* detected a second Mavis, which was also shot down, also without Butch's assistance. Returning to the carrier, Butch was "fit to be tied" at having missed out on VF-3's first air battle, recalled Thach. "He had a combat spirit; he wanted to get in quick."[86] As it turned out, he would not have long to wait for his chance.

Alerted by his doomed flying boat crews, Vice Adm. Eiji Goto, commanding the *24th Air Flotilla* at Rabaul, waited for more details, but the airwaves remained ominously silent. Finally, at 1:10 p.m. he sent eighteen Mitsubishi G4M1 Type 1 medium bombers from the *4th Air Group* after the American task force. Known to the Allies as "Bettys," the two-engine bombers carried a seven-man crew, were capable of 267 mph, and had a range of 1,539 nautical miles. The cigar-shaped fuselage was fitted with four 7.7mm Type 92 machine guns, one in the nose, one in a dorsal blister, and one in each of two beam blisters. A 20mm Type 99 cannon in the tail discouraged approaches from behind. Each aircraft was loaded with two 250-kilogram bombs for the attack.

Divided into two *chutais*, the bombers took off from Vunakanau Field on Rabaul at 2:20 p.m. as hundreds of ground personnel lined the runway waving their caps and shouting encouragement. Lt. Cmdr. Takuzo Ito was in overall command of the mission. Lt. Yogoro Seto commanded the first *chutai*; Lt. Masayoshi Nakagawa led the second *chutai*. One plane from the first *chutai* suffered mechanical problems and remained behind. The others lifted off without incident. However, once over the open ocean, they encountered a series of heavy rain squalls. Lieutenant Commander Ito decided to separate the two *chutais* in an effort to improve their chances of locating the enemy. The first *chutai* continued on course, while the second deviated slightly to the north.[87]

U.S. radar began picking up intermittent bogeys as early as 3:42 p.m. At 5:14 p.m. *Lexington*'s radar detected a large bogey 72 miles to the west. The contact vanished from the scopes but reappeared eleven minutes later, now 47 miles away and approaching rapidly. Klaxons sounded as *Lexington* began launching aircraft and clearing the decks.

The approaching aircraft were the nine Bettys from the second *chutai*. Sporting mottled green and brown camouflage, they had closed to within 10 miles of the task force when six U.S. Wildcats tore into them. Over the next several minutes, the fighters sent five of the Bettys, including *chutai* leader Lieutenant Nakagawa, plummeting into the sea.

Waiting impatiently on *Lexington*'s deck, Butch and Duff Dufilho finally got airborne as the four surviving Bettys bored in on the carrier. As Butch clawed for altitude, he saw bombs plummeting toward *Lexington*, which was maneuvering to evade. All fell wide. Bomb bays empty, the Japanese ran for home with the Wildcats in hot pursuit. One more bomber was shot down, but the tail gunner on another shot up one of the Wildcats so thoroughly that the pilot had to bail out. He was quickly picked up. Utah native Ens. John W. Wilson was less fortunate. As he incautiously attacked one of the bombers from directly behind, a 20mm shell from the Betty's tail gun smashed through the Wildcat's windscreen, presumably killing him instantly. His plane splashed into the sea and disappeared.

Jimmy Thach dispatched the Betty that killed Wilson, while other pilots shot down another. That should have left only one bomber, but somehow Lieutenant Nakagawa, last seen plummeting toward the sea, had regained control of his damaged plane. Knowing he would never make it home, he turned toward the *Lexington* at wave-top height, clearly intending to crash into the carrier. Antiaircraft fire zeroed in, knocking pieces off the approaching bomber. The plane wavered and finally smashed into the water and exploded only a few dozen yards from the carrier. The last surviving Betty managed to elude the Wildcats, but the unlucky pilot encountered a U.S. dive bomber returning from an afternoon search mission and was shot down about 80 miles from the task force.

Butch, meanwhile, had once again been left out of the party. By the time he gained sufficient altitude, "there were so many of our fighters, I couldn't get in on the brawl," he said later.[88] As the other Wildcats went chasing off after the fleeing Bettys of the second *chutai*, he and Dufilho patrolled over the task force—the lone remaining aerial defense—but if O'Hare was cursing fate, his luck was about to change.

Only 10 miles to the northeast, the eight bombers of the first *chutai* suddenly appeared. The Fighter Direction Center on the carrier had been so busy dealing with the first attack that it overlooked the new contact, which first appeared on the radar scopes at 4:49 p.m. Now, warned by a visual sighting from the destroyer *Patterson*, Fighter Direction alerted O'Hare and Dufilho, while frantically calling back the Wildcats that had chased off after the survivors of the second *chutai*.

It was too late. The errant Wildcats started back toward the approaching Bettys, remembered Jimmy Thach, "but we all knew we could not intercept them before they reached the bomb-dropping position."[89]

Racing eastward, Butch and Dufilho turned on their illuminated gun sights and test-fired their machine guns. Butch's four .50s all kicked in, but in an incredible stroke of bad luck, none of Dufilho's guns would fire. Apparently, the ammunition belts had jammed, a not uncommon problem with early-model Wildcats. Butch waved him off, but Dufilho refused to leave even after Butch shook an exasperated fist at him.

They intercepted the Japanese formation at 5:06 p.m. just as the bombers began to descend from about 11,000 feet for a stern attack on the ships below. The eight Bettys were flying in a V of Vs—a three-plane V on the left, another in the center, and the final two planes on the right. Butch knew he couldn't wait for help—the enemy formation would be in position to release their bombs within two or three minutes. "Those babies were coming on fast and they had to be stopped," he said later.[90] He had thirty-four seconds' worth of .50-caliber ammunition, a total of 450 rounds per gun.

As antiaircraft fire from the ships blossomed blackly over the task force, Butch swooped down in a high-side pass on the trailing bomber at the far right of the formation, catching the Japanese by surprise. The heavy .50-caliber slugs tore into the Betty's fuselage and ripped open one of the wing fuel tanks. The bomber lurched and fell off to the side, the starboard engine trailing smoke.

Butch pulled up slightly and set his aiming pipper on the next Betty in line, pressing the gun button at a distance of less than 100 yards. Again he holed a gas tank. Trailing vaporized gasoline, the bomber slowed and dropped out of formation.

"I attacked and two of 'em fell out of formation," recalled Butch. "Naturally I was very pleased, and I guess a little surprised, too. That was my first pass at 'em. One was smoking and the other was trailing gasoline."[91]

Pulling up, Butch crossed to the left of the formation and put a burst into the trailing Betty on that side, damaging the left fuel tank and right engine, forcing the bomber to drop out of position. Continuing the run, he put a burst into the next bomber in line, setting it on fire. By now he had lost track of Dufilho, who had accompanied him into the attack in hopes of at least diverting some of the return gunfire from Butch.

Pilots of the returning Wildcats watched developments unfold as they raced to close the distance. "His shooting was wonderful—absolutely deadly," Thach recalled of O'Hare. "At one time as we closed in I could see three blazing Japanese planes falling between the formation and the water—he shot them down so quickly." He considered it a miracle that O'Hare survived the return fire. "Each time he came in, the turtleback guns of the whole group were turned on him. I could see the tracer curling all around him, and it looked to us as if he would go at any second. Imagine this little gnat absolutely alone tearing into that formation."[92]

Butch didn't pause to see if his victims actually crashed—it was enough to break up any kind of coordinated run on the task force below. "When they drop out of formation you don't bother with 'em anymore," he explained. "You go after the next."[93]

Coming around for a high-side pass on what was now the left trailing bomber in the shot-up formation, Butch pressed the gun button. The Betty fell away as the four .50s tore into it, leaving him with an open shot at the lead bomber in the formation. Targeting the left wing, he was surprised when the nacelle exploded. The engine tore free, leaving a gaping hole in the wing. As the plane tumbled out of control, Butch turned his attention back to one of the already crippled Bettys but had to break off when his guns quit after just a few rounds. He had exhausted his thirty-four seconds of ammunition. The entire fight had lasted approximately four minutes.

Aboard *Lexington*, Task Force 11 commander Vice Adm. Wilson Brown and others had watched in awe as the solitary Wildcat took on all eight approaching bombers. "Every moment I expected to see his small craft shot down by Japanese gunners," recalled Brown.[94] Only three Bettys made it close enough to *Lexington* to drop their bombs, and all missed. The nearest bomb struck 100 yards astern, spraying the aft flight deck with fragments. A fourth Betty attacked the cruiser *Minneapolis*, the bombs sending up harmless cascades of water about 100 yards off the port quarter.

In one last bit of excitement, the pilot of Lieutenant Commander Ito's bomber—which had lost its entire port engine—somehow managed to regain control and turned toward *Lexington*. Approaching from astern at low level into a storm of antiaircraft fire, the bomber—probably too damaged to steer accurately—missed the carrier and plunged into the water about a mile off the port bow, leaving a slick of burning gasoline on the surface.

His guns empty, his flight suit soaked with sweat, O'Hare waited to land back aboard the *Lady Lex*. "Naturally you're pretty keyed up," he recalled. "Your mouth and throat get so dry it's hard to talk. Mine was so dry I thought I'd lost my voice."[95] As he finally began his approach, an overeager shipboard gunner cut loose at him with a .50-caliber machine gun, but he managed to set the Wildcat down safely. After instructing the flight deck crew to reload his guns, the first thing he asked for was a drink of water.

O'Hare had made four passes at the *chutai*, firing on seven bombers. He believed he had shot down six, unaware that one of the damaged Bettys had clawed its way back into formation to be counted twice. He was subsequently credited with five kills. Japanese records indicate that only two badly damaged bombers from the first *chutai* made it back to the airdrome at Rabaul. Three were shot down by O'Hare in the vicinity of *Lexington*; another was shot down by another Wildcat pilot about 8 miles south of the task force. The remaining two were so badly shot up during the encounter with Butch or by antiaircraft fire that they had to make crash landings.

O'Hare was written up for a Navy Cross for taking on the entire *chutai* and "preventing the ship from sustaining serious damage or possible loss."[96] Learning he was being put up for a medal, Butch demurred. "I don't want a medal," he insisted to Jimmy Thach. "The other officers in the squadron could have done the same thing and we all know it."[97]

Despite his protests, the paperwork went forward. Admiral Brown noted in a dispatch that Lieutenant O'Hare had shot down six enemy planes—mistakenly bumping the total up by one—and it wasn't long before newspapers in the States picked up the story, noting that O'Hare was the first U.S. Navy ace of the war. Fellow officers began asking him for his autograph—a bit of ribbing Butch took well, but he was in for a still greater surprise. America was in dire need of heroes, and Butch O'Hare certainly fit the bill. As his citation wended its way through the bureaucracy, the proposed Navy Cross was upgraded to the Medal of Honor.

On the morning of Tuesday, April 21, 1942, Butch and Rita found themselves in President Franklin D. Roosevelt's White House office with a gaggle of dignitaries. FDR informed the highly nervous hero that he was now Lieutenant Commander O'Hare, a promotion recognizing his "eminent and conspicuous conduct in battle." Then, as press corps cameras flashed, Rita fastened the Medal of Honor around Butch's neck—a ceremony that required a redo when her face was blocked from the cameras on the first attempt. Other honors followed, including a parade in Butch's hometown of Saint Louis. Ill at ease with all the attention, Butch continued to insist he had done nothing any of his buddies would not have done in the same circumstances. Hauled up to the podium following his parade, he confessed to the admiring crowd, "It is good to get back but it will be a relief to get back to my real job, which is flying and fighting. Looking into machine guns is not nearly as hard as facing cameras."[98]

To Butch's relief, the dog and pony show soon ended as he was ordered back to Pearl Harbor to take command of VF-3, relieving Jimmy Thach, who was heading home. For the next several months, he focused on the business of turning out trained pilots for combat. While exacting, he was no martinet. "Butch was very relaxed, even casual," recalled one of his men.[99] One newcomer to the squadron, who had been excited to learn he would be serving under a Medal of Honor hero, recalled he was "almost disappointed to see [O'Hare] was down-to-earth and almost a slob."[100] On the other hand, "when Butch spoke seriously, you listened because you knew he wasn't going to repeat it," recalled a pilot.[101]

As O'Hare focused on training men, the war ground on. Among the casualties was his wingman in the Medal of Honor action, Lt. Marion Dufilho, who was listed as missing in action on August 25, 1942, after an aerial melee in the Battle of the Eastern Solomons. It was another year before O'Hare returned to the shooting war. In late August 1943 his squadron, now renumbered VF-6 and flying the new F6F Grumman Hellcats, headed into combat aboard the USS *Independence*.

The successor to the F4F Wildcat, the heavily armored Hellcat offered better visibility for the pilot as well as a more powerful 18-cylinder Pratt & Whitney R-2800 "Double Wasp" radial engine. Armament consisted of six M2 Browning .50-caliber machine guns with 400 rounds per gun. Trial combats against a captured A6M5 Zero showed that the Hellcat was faster at all altitudes. It could outclimb the Zero above 14,000 feet, though the Zero could easily outturn the F6F at lower speeds and returned a slightly better climb rate below 14,000 feet.

In a raid on Japanese-occupied Wake Island four weeks later, O'Hare showed he hadn't lost his touch, knocking down an enemy Zero and a Betty on October 5. In the confrontation with the Betty, only one of his six machine guns would kick in, but he managed to shoot up one engine and the wing root on one pass and then finish off the bomber on the second. A week later, upon his return to Hawaii, he was placed in command of Air Group 6 (CAG-6) consisting of Fighter Squadron 6 as well as a squadron of dive bombers and one of torpedo bombers. On November 19, now flying from USS *Enterprise*, his air group supported U.S. landings in the Gilbert Islands. On the first day, CAG-6 flew 173 sorties, most of them against Makin Island, where the Army's 165th Regimental Combat Team was scheduled to land the next day. "Butch seemed in his glory," recalled one of his pilots.[102] He was back in the air.

In addition to his other duties, O'Hare had been grappling with another challenge during the voyage to the Gilberts. The Japanese were increasingly turning to nighttime aerial torpedo raids on U.S. carrier groups in an effort to reduce the losses they had been suffering in daylight attacks. This change in tactics deeply concerned U.S. commanders who had no night-fighter capability to counter the raids. En route to Makin in November, Task Group 50.2 commander Rear Adm. Arthur W. "Raddy" Radford decided to create his own night-fighter capability on the *Enterprise*. The nuts and bolts of that effort fell to Butch as commanding officer of CAG-6.

After some experimentation, Butch and his team came up with a night-fighter element built around three aircraft—a radar-equipped torpedo bomber (TBF) accompanied by two F6F Hellcats. The idea was for the shipboard radar operator to position the TBF in the path of any approaching bogeys. Crewed by a pilot, turret gunner, and radar operator, the TBF would zero in on the enemy aircraft with its own shorter-range radar and guide the night-blind Hellcats to where they could visually pick up the exhaust flames of the intruders and gun them down.

O'Hare nicknamed the new night-fighting teams the "Black Panthers." The first night-fighting mission ever flown from a carrier took place in the early morning of November 23, when two teams launched from *Enterprise*, O'Hare piloting one of the Hellcats. They failed to make contact with enemy aircraft but were ready when the call came again toward evening on November 26.

O'Hare was eating dinner when the alert came at 5:45 p.m. He used the remainder of his steak to make a sandwich but turned down a steward's offer of a dish of strawberry ice cream. "No thanks. Keep it cold until I get back tonight," he replied as he headed for the ready room to grab his flight gear.[103] He would man one of two Hellcats accompanying a TBF aloft. The three night-fighting aircraft launched at 6 p.m. With sunset still almost twenty minutes away, the fighter direction officer (FDO) sent the two Hellcats off after an enemy snooper before the TBF got into the air. This proved to be a serious mistake. As darkness fell, the TBF, with its three-man crew, was in the air, but the two Hellcats were still off by themselves chasing shadows.

They had still failed to join up by 7:05 p.m. when a strike group of fifteen Betty bombers approached the American ships. Nevertheless, the *Enterprise* FDO guided the lone night-fighting TBF, piloted by thirty-three-year-old Lt. Cmdr. John L. Phillips Jr., toward the enemy formation. Phillips's radar operator, Lt. Hazen Rand, picked the flight up on his screen at 3 miles. "We swung in behind them," recalled turret gunner AOM1c Alvin Kernan, "and Rand began calling out the range: three miles, two, one, one thousand yards." At 200 yards, Phillips confirmed, "I have them in sight. Attacking."[104] Phillips squeezed the trigger on his forward-firing .50s, targeting the rear Betty in the formation.

"The two .50-calibers in the wings felt like they were tearing the plane apart," observed Kernan. The surprised Japanese began returning fire from the tail 20mm and top turret, but as the TBF tilted up and away from the firing run, Kernan saw flames licking at the bomber's wing root near the vulnerable gas tanks. He fired at the flames, and the Betty exploded. Trailing fire, the bomber plummeted into the water below, leaving a smear of burning gasoline on the surface.[105]

Meanwhile, *Enterprise*'s effort to direct O'Hare and his partner, twenty-four-year-old Ens. Warren ("Andy") Skon of Saint Paul, Minnesota, onto potential targets was proving an exercise in frustration. Though they fired several times at shadowy shapes, without the benefit of their own radar, they were blind and failed to score any verifiable hits.

The aggressive Phillips was having better luck. Making a wide turn as the *Enterprise*'s FDO once again tried to link him up with the Hellcats, he spotted the exhausts of two Bettys about 1,500 yards ahead. As Phillips maneuvered behind the bomber on the right, O'Hare apparently also caught sight of what he believed to be enemy planes. "Turn on your lights," he radioed Phillips in an effort to be sure he wasn't gunning for the TBF. "I'm going to start shooting."[106]

As Phillips reluctantly blinked his recognition light, the Betty saw the threat. The pilot started to evade, and the gunners opened fire on the TBF. It was too late. Phillips closed to 200 yards and put a burst into the right wing root and cockpit. As the bomber burst into flames, the desperate pilot attempted a water landing, which left a 300-yard trail of burning gasoline before the Betty broke up and sank. An exultant Phillips radioed, "This is duck soup, Butch, if you ride in on their slipstream and then just pick them off one at a time."[107] It wasn't entirely duck soup; a bullet from the doomed Betty had punched through the TBF's skin and hit Rand in the foot. The radar operator's boot was full of blood, and he was in great pain, but Phillips was in no rush to break off now.[108]

O'Hare and Skon were belatedly attempting to link up with Phillips. As they converged on the TBF, Butch radioed Skon, "You take the side you want."

Skon replied, "I'll take the port."

"Roger," acknowledged Butch.[109]

From the TBF's turret, Kernan saw a white light appear to port. As he prepared to fire, he realized it was one of the Black Panther Hellcats—the pilot had turned on the dorsal light. The second Hellcat also appeared, closing on the TBF's starboard wing. As that plane switched off its lights, Kernan noticed a third aircraft just above the other two and crossing to the right. It was a Betty.

He alerted Phillips, who radioed a frantic warning to the Hellcat pilots and told Kernan to open fire. Kernan immediately began shooting. Peering through the small starboard window, Rand saw the enemy bomber above and behind O'Hare. Tracers suddenly emerged from the aircraft's nose to "flash down to the back" of the Hellcat even as Kernan's tracers were "arching over Butch's Hellcat at the Betty."[110] Skon also saw "tracers around [O'Hare's] plane."[111]

As the Betty broke away and disappeared into the darkness, O'Hare's Hellcat abruptly sheared off in a slanting dive to port. Skon, who had not heard from Butch since the last "roger," tried to raise him on the radio, but there was no answer. He started to follow but quickly lost sight of the rapidly descending Hellcat. Phillips also tried to radio O'Hare but received no reply. He saw a flash of white below; whether it was a parachute or the impact of the Hellcat hitting the water, he couldn't be sure. He radioed *Enterprise*, "Butch may be down."[112] Phillips and Skon circled the area while *Enterprise* repeatedly tried to raise O'Hare on the radio. They saw nothing, and *Enterprise* received no response.

Butch O'Hare was gone.

It was later suggested that O'Hare had been hit by Kernan's guns, a victim of friendly fire, but the evidence indicates otherwise. According to Rand, Kernan would have had to practically shoot off the tail of his own plane in order "to have shot Butch."[113] Both Kernan and Rand clearly saw the Hellcats and the Japanese Betty, whose pilot probably thought— at least initially—that he was joining up with other bombers from the strike force. Apparently, the Betty was closing on the exhaust flares of the two Hellcats when the startled nose gunner suddenly realized they were enemy fighters and directed a quick burst toward O'Hare's F6F. From the way the Hellcat went down and the lack of any radio communication, it seems likely that O'Hare was immediately killed or incapacitated.

Admiral Radford subsequently recommended O'Hare for a second Medal of Honor, arguing that his action in organizing and leading the night-fighter effort had saved the task group from serious damage. A review board reduced the recommendation to a posthumous Navy Cross. Phillips, Skon, Rand, and Kernan were also each awarded the Navy Cross for their efforts.

At home, the news that Butch O'Hare was missing in action made headlines around the country. Rita and their daughter, Kathleen, who was only nine months old when her father disappeared, were presented with Butch's Navy Cross the following June. Rita would have to wait a year and a day from the date he went missing to receive the Purple Heart that acknowledged what had already become painfully clear: her hero husband was dead.

There were other honors. On June 22, 1945, the destroyer USS *O'Hare* was launched. Butch's mother broke the bottle of champagne across the bow. Another tribute—though a bit puzzling as Butch had little connection to the city where his father was murdered—occurred on September 18, 1949, when the City of Chicago dedicated Chicago O'Hare International Airport to the fallen hero. Today it remains the most prominent reminder of Butch O'Hare's heroism, though it is likely that few of the hundreds of thousands of airline passengers who pass through its terminals know anything about the man who is honored.[114]

The Doolittle Raid

DEEPLY ANGERED BY THE JAPANESE ATTACK ON PEARL HARBOR, PRESIdent Franklin D. Roosevelt urged his generals and admirals to find a way to retaliate against the enemy's home islands. The question was how. The obvious answer was a carrier raid, but the limited range of carrier-borne single-engine bombers would force the ships to steam much too close to enemy home defenses and remain in peril far too long before making their escape.

Col. James H. Doolittle
Tokyo, Japan
April 18, 1942

As dozens of pilots and B-25 air crewmen crowded into the Operations Office at Florida's Eglin Air Force Base on March 3, 1942, the overall mood was one of curiosity. All had volunteered for a dangerous mission, but none knew just what that mission would entail. They hoped to get some inkling of what lay ahead from the diminutive lieutenant colonel with the receding hairline who had summoned them to this gathering.

What they got was a warning.

"My name is Doolittle," announced the colonel. "If you men have any idea that this isn't the most dangerous thing you've ever been in on, don't even start this training period. You can drop out now."[1]

This then was the legendary Jimmy Doolittle, a giant in aviation, test pilot, racer, aeronautical innovator, the first man to fly coast to coast in less than twelve hours, first to fly an outside loop, first to take off and fly an entire set course solely on instruments, owner of virtually every aviation trophy in existence. This was the legend described years later by a chronicler of his exploits as a "combination [of] laser-sharp analytical intelligence and balls the size of your head."[2]

Some of the volunteers were surprised by Doolittle's small stature—the giant of aviation stood only five feet, four inches tall. "He was such a short little duck," observed an airman. But his outsized personality filled the room. He spoke calmly and directly with no bullshit. "It didn't take but two minutes and you were under his spell," recalled a pilot.[3]

Now forty-five years old, James Harold Doolittle had spent his early boyhood in Nome, Alaska, where his footloose father, a carpenter by trade, took the family in hopes of striking it rich in the goldfields. By 1908, Doolittle's mother had endured enough. She and Jimmy moved back to her native California, settling near family in Los Angeles and leaving the senior Doolittle to his own devices.

Reckless and impulsive by nature, son Jimmy wasn't particularly interested in classroom exercises, preferring more physical activities such as tumbling and acrobatics. Schoolyard bullies soon learned that though small, he was not to be trifled with—the boy was more than willing to resort to his fists if provoked. Noticing his scrappiness, Doolittle's English teacher, who was also a boxing instructor, offered to train him in the finer points of the art. In 1912, at the age of fifteen, weighing in at only 105 pounds, Doolittle won the flyweight division of the Amateur Boxing Championship of the Pacific Coast. Prize money from bouts later helped him pay his tuition at the University of California School of Mines in Berkley, where he enrolled with the intention of earning a degree in mining engineering.

Fate had other plans. Doolittle had yet to finish his senior year in 1917 when the United States declared war on Germany. Responding to the call, he left the classroom behind and enlisted in the Aviation Section of the Army Signal Corps. Flying had long appealed to his daredevil nature. As a youth he had spent long hours constructing a full-sized homemade glider from plans published in *Popular Mechanics* magazine. The glider was smashed to pieces when he tried to get airborne by hitching it to the back of a friend's car, but the would-be birdman and his fascination with flying somehow survived intact. Graduating from flight school on March 5, 1918, he was commissioned as a second lieutenant but, much to his regret, never made it overseas. He spent the war in the States as a flying instructor.

In retrospect, it is surprising he wasn't killed or thrown out of the Army for his aeronautical antics (he later admitted to being "a bit of a mischief maker")—though it might also be said that he was perfectly suited to the "seat of the pants" nature of aviation in those early days of the U.S. Air Service.[4] He was a superb and daring—if sometimes reckless—pilot. He once crashed a plane while chasing a duck; in another incident, he sat on the axle between the wheels of a plane's landing gear as the pilot touched down on the airfield.

Doolittle decided to remain in the Army following the Armistice. As he had married former schoolmate and longtime girlfriend Josephine ("Joe") Daniels (who had shrugged off questions about her sanity from both her mother and his) on Christmas Eve 1917, part of his motivation was the reassurance of "a regular payday," he admitted. "But it was flying that made up my mind," he added.[5] Not only did he love to fly, but he foresaw a great future for aviation and intended to be a part of it.

Probably much to the surprise of his wartime superiors, Doolittle proceeded over the next few years to cut a wide swath in the aviation world, setting speed records and winning numerous competitions on behalf of the Army. In 1922 he became a tabloid sensation when he flew nonstop from coast to coast in twenty-two hours and thirty minutes—a stunning achievement for the time and one that earned him a Distinguished Flying Cross from the Army and the sobriquet the "Lone Pilot" in the press.[6]

As Doolittle matured, he tempered his recklessness. He became a master of the calculated risk, a careful organizer and planner. When he took a chance, he did so because he knew the odds were in his favor. He also demonstrated a flair for the science and technical side of aviation. In 1923, he was awarded one of the Army's coveted slots to do postgraduate work in aeronautical engineering at the Massachusetts Institute of Technology; he eventually earned a doctorate in aeronautical sciences. He experimented with g-forces and contributed greatly to the development of instrument flying. Efficiency reports described him variously as "energetic mentally and physically," "dynamic," "daring and skillful," and "an exceptional combination of very capable engineer and superior pilot."[7]

By 1930, despite national fame, Doolittle was still a thirty-four-year-old lieutenant trying to support a wife, two young sons, his mother, and his mother-in-law on his military salary. Financial considerations persuaded him to reluctantly leave the Army and accept a job as head of the aviation department at Shell Petroleum Corporation. However, he remained in the U.S. Army Reserve and continued to race, winning the coveted Bendix Trophy in 1931 while setting a new transcontinental record of eleven hours and fifteen minutes. However, perhaps one of his most notable accomplishments—though not so flashy as setting speed records—was persuading Shell to produce 100-octane gasoline. Though many in the company referred to the expensive venture as "Doolittle's Folly," he got the last laugh. The 100-octane fuel increased engine performance so much that it became the mandated fuel for military aircraft by the end of the 1930s.[8]

Thanks to his reputation and his work with Shell, Doolittle developed many important contacts overseas. He traveled widely, and by the end of the 1930s, he had grown alarmed at the militarization of Germany. He saw war clouds gathering in Europe and believed the United States would inevitably be swept up in the conflict. Having sat out one war, he wasn't about to miss another. In 1940, he contacted his friend, Air Corps chief Maj. Gen. Hap Arnold, and asked to return to active duty. Soon afterward he was back in the service with the rank of major.

Recognizing Doolittle's organizational skills, Arnold first assigned him to prepare the American automotive industry to switch over to aircraft production as the likelihood of war increased. But following the Japanese attack on Pearl Harbor, Doolittle wanted action. On December 8, he wrote to Arnold, "I respectfully request that I be relieved of my present duties and re-assigned to a tactical unit."[9] Arnold promoted Doolittle to lieutenant colonel and assigned him to his own staff. His initial job was to investigate problems with the new Martin B-26 bomber, a quirky aircraft that had gained a reputation as a widow maker. But in January, Arnold summoned him to discuss what Doolittle later described as "the most important military assignment of my life thus far": a bombing raid on Tokyo.[10]

The assignment, which Doolittle referred to as "Special Aviation Project No. 1,"[11] was simple in concept but complicated in execution. It envisioned a raid on Tokyo by Army bombers launched from a U.S. Navy carrier. The idea came from a Navy captain. Happening to see Army bombers practicing near the painted outline of a Navy carrier used by naval aviators to practice deck landings, the officer got to wondering if it would be possible to launch long-range Army bombers off a carrier to raid the Japanese home islands.

"The purpose of this special project is to bomb and fire the industrial center of Japan," wrote Doolittle. "It is anticipated that this will not only cause confusion and impede production but will undoubtedly facilitate operations against Japan in other theaters due to their probable withdrawal of troops for the purpose of defending the home country. An action of this kind is most desirable now due to the psychological effect on the American public, our allies, and our enemies."[12]

The suggestion was an immediate hit with President Roosevelt, who had been pressing for a strike on the Japanese home islands in retaliation for the attack on Pearl Harbor. A strike by naval aircraft would require the ships to approach within 250 miles of the Japanese coast—far too great a risk to the Navy's precious carriers. But Army bombers—assuming they could take off from the carrier decks—could launch from much further out, reducing the risk to the carriers. Bringing this complicated—some might say harebrained—scheme off would require someone with a talent for thinking things through in advance, someone who could assemble a myriad of details piece by piece into a workable whole. Convinced that Doolittle was that man, Arnold directed him to put together the air component of the strike.

It quickly became apparent to Doolittle that only one Army bomber—the B-25 Mitchell—had a realistic chance of launching from a carrier. With its 68-foot wingspan, it was the only bomber in the U.S. inventory able to squeak by the carrier's superstructure during takeoff. Pilots would have only a few hundred feet of deck to get airborne and, once off, would have no possibility of returning to the too-short runway. The aircraft would have to set down on land—a one-way mission.

Crewed by five men and powered by two 1,700-horsepower Wright Cyclone engines, the twin-tailed B-25B could fly at 272 mph, but its normal 1,350-mile range presented a problem. The plan called for the raiders to launch well off the Japanese coast, bomb their targets, and continue on to friendly airfields in China. Doolittle estimated the overall distance for the twelve-hour flight would be at least 2,000 miles and wanted a margin of safety of 2,400 miles.[13]

The bombers carried 646 gallons of gasoline in two wing tanks. In order to extend their range for the raid, Doolittle needed to find room for more gas. The solution was rubber bladders. One 225-gallon bladder would be squeezed in on top of the bomb bay; another, holding 160 gallons, would go into the crawl space above the bomb bay. The bladders could be moved out of the way after the gas was used up. Still another tank, holding 60 gallons, would replace the belly gun turret in the bomber. That was not much of a sacrifice: the ventral turrets were plagued with mechanical problems and probably wouldn't be needed during a low-level mission. The remainder of the required fuel would be loaded aboard in ten 5-gallon cans. Combined, these expedients boosted the aircraft's gas load to a total of 1,141 gallons. To help compensate for the additional weight, Doolittle ordered the 230-pound liaison radios removed.

As the B-25 was a relatively new bomber, only a handful of units had been equipped with them to this point in the war. The most readily available B-25s belonged to the 17th Bombardment Group based in Pendleton, Oregon. Since he was going to requisition their planes, Doolittle decided to recruit his volunteers from the same unit. Gathering the group commander and squadron leaders, he told them he was organizing a very dangerous mission. Pilots would be required to take off from only 500 feet of runway. "It's strictly a volunteer operation," he added, "and the men must volunteer in the dark. It'll take us away about six weeks, but that's all you can tell your men."[14]

Nearly the entire group volunteered. "The name 'Doolittle' meant so much to aviators that man, we just volunteered like crazy," recalled a pilot.[15] As for the danger, a twenty-four-year-old bombardier from Boston remarked years later, "We were young, and we really didn't give a damn."[16] Not all would get to go. Doolittle needed two dozen crews, a total of 120 men, but a third of those would be backup. Deck space aboard the USS *Hornet*, the carrier that would transport planes and crews to the launch point off the Japanese coast, limited the number of aircraft that could participate in the raid.

The raiders' highly classified training was conducted at Eglin Air Force Base in the Florida panhandle. A Navy pilot with experience in flying heavily loaded planes off carrier decks showed the skeptical Army pilots—who were accustomed to using every inch of their long land runways—how to take off from the much less forgiving carrier deck. The technique consisted of keeping both feet on the brakes, moving the stabilizer back three-fourths, and bringing the engines up to full throttle. The pilot would then release the brakes and pull back on the yoke until the plane almost literally jumped into the air. Despite Army doubts, the technique worked—at least it worked on the ground. Instead of needing thousands of feet to get into the air, pilots were able to horse their B-25s into the air using as little as 294 feet of runway.

Other drills involved low-level approaches and quick bomb release followed by evasive measures, navigation over water, gunnery, target recognition, and gas conservation. None of the crews had any combat experience. Doolittle later reported, "The first pilots were all excellent. The co-pilots were all good for co-pilots. The bombardiers were fair but needed brushing up. The navigators had good training but very little practical experience. The gunners, almost without exception, had never fired a machine gun from an airplane at either a moving or stationary target."[17]

The planes themselves also presented problems. The gun turrets tended to lock up for no particular reason, automatic pilots often malfunctioned, the auxiliary gas tanks leaked, spark plugs tended to foul, and the carburetors kept falling out of tune. More fuel-efficient carburetors were installed. Defensive armament included a top turret with a pair of .50-caliber machine guns augmented by a .30-caliber machine gun in the nose. In order to dissuade Japanese fighters from shooting up the B-25's unprotected rear, black painted "broomstick machine guns" were installed in the tail.

As the mission took shape, Doolittle was determined not to be left out. It was not enough to simply organize the raid; he wanted to lead it. As he later told it, he went up to Washington to make his case to Hap Arnold. The general was not enthusiastic, recalled Doolittle. "I'm sorry,

Jim," he replied. "I need you right here on my staff. I can't afford to let you go on every mission you might help to plan."[18]

Doolittle fervently pressed his case. Finally, Arnold relented. Doolittle could go, he said, as long as he got the okay from Brig. Gen. Millard Harmon Jr., Arnold's chief of staff. Doolittle made a hasty exit and ran down the hall to Harmon's office. "Miff," he gasped, as he caught his breath, "I've just been to see Hap about that project I've been working on and said I wanted to lead the mission. Hap said it was okay with him if it's okay with you."

"Well," said Harmon, taken by surprise, "whatever is all right with Hap is certainly all right with me."

Doolittle later said that as he was leaving Harmon's office, Arnold called in on the chief of staff's intercom. The last words Doolittle heard from Harmon as he hurried away were a plaintive "But Hap, I told him he could go."[19]

In truth, Doolittle was the natural choice to lead the mission and in all likelihood had been Arnold's choice all along. On March 23, twenty-two air crews flew from Eglin to Sacramento, California. From there they went to Naval Air Station Alameda, where the modified B-25s were hoisted onto the USS *Hornet* and secured on the deck for the voyage to Japanese waters. Doolittle had expected to take fifteen bombers, but in the end he managed to squeeze in sixteen and still have room to take off—though the tail of the last bomber in the queue was left hanging over the end of the deck. Now he advised his people to get their financial affairs in order. "And don't in your letters to your folks or to your wives, give any hint where you are going," he added.[20]

The *Hornet* raised anchor at 10:18 a.m. on Thursday, April 2. Commanded by Capt. Marc Mitscher, the carrier was the key element of Task Force 16.2, which included the cruisers *Nashville* and *Vincennes*, four destroyers, and an oiler. The task force would rendezvous at sea with Adm. William ("Bull") Halsey's Task Force 16.1, which included the carrier USS *Enterprise*, cruisers *Northampton* and *Salt Lake City*, four destroyers, and an oiler. *Enterprise* would provide air cover since *Hornet* could not launch fighters with the bombers lashed down on her deck. Halsey would be in overall command.

Doolittle had a scare at the last moment when he was ordered ashore to take a call from Washington. "My heart sank," he admitted.[21] He was sure Hap Arnold had changed his mind and was pulling him off the raid. To his great relief, the caller was Army Chief of Staff Gen. George Marshall, who only wanted to wish him luck. That Marshall would call him personally was gratifying; it also emphasized to Doolittle the great importance Washington attached to the raid.

As the California coast receded into the distance, Doolittle gathered his crews and finally told them what they had volunteered for: "We are going straight to Japan." The Navy would take them in as close as possible; they would then launch from the carrier deck and split up to bomb targets in Tokyo, Yokohama, Osaka, Kobe, and Nagoya. As always, he said, anyone who wanted to back out could do so, no questions asked. No one did.[22]

Mitscher got on the ship's loudspeaker to address all hands. "Now hear this," announced the captain. "This ship will carry the Army bombers to the coast of Japan for the bombing of Tokyo." Mitscher later observed, "Cheers from every section of the ship greeted the announcement. Morale reached a new high."[23] One of the raiders remarked, "The sailors I saw were jumping up and down like small children."[24]

On April 10, the *Hornet* rendezvoused with Halsey's Task Force 16.1, the merger forming Task Force 16. Doolittle's crews continued to prep for the mission, checking and rechecking maps, testing and retesting guns and engines, memorizing landmarks and targets. One target that was strictly off limits was the emperor's palace compound. Doolittle was adamant: he told the disappointed men that bombing the palace would only unite the Japanese people in a nationalistic frenzy. Any psychological advantages of the raid would be lost.[25]

Mechanical problems continued to plague the bombers, now exposed to salt and sea spray. None of the flyers had ever taken off from a carrier. It had been done: during the planning stage two B-25s had been flown from *Hornet* just to ensure it was possible, but neither aircraft had carried a full load; nor had the test been conducted in heavy seas. As *Hornet's* deck was just over 809 feet long and only 127 feet wide, the first bomber to take off—Doolittle's own B-25—would have less than 500 feet of deck to get airborne. More than one pilot nervously paced off the distance between the bombers and the end of the deck. One *Hornet* sailor bet $10 (even money) that fewer than half the bombers would successfully get off.

Each plane would carry four bombs: three 500-pound M-43 high-explosive bombs and one M-43 incendiary, the latter packed with 128 four-pound incendiary bomblets that would spew out to spark multiple fires—or so it was hoped. Doolittle planned to take off three hours before the others, timing the flight so that he arrived over Tokyo at dusk. He would drop his bomb load, all incendiaries, to mark the way for the other bomb crews, who would take off later and arrive over their targets—spread out over a 50-mile front—after dark. Darkness would help conceal them from Japanese fighters and antiaircraft fire. After they dropped their bombs, they would head west to the Allied airbase at Chuchow, China. Located about 70 miles inland and 200 miles south of Shanghai, the airfield was supposed to be ready for them with homing signals and fuel. Once they'd gassed up, the raiders would fly another 800 miles to Chungking.

U.S. intelligence indicated there could be as many as 500 enemy fighters tasked with the defense of Tokyo and environs.[26] One raider pilot asked Doolittle what they should do if the worst happened and they were shot down or forced to land in Japan. It was a legitimate question. "We figured there was only a 50-50 chance we would get off the *Hornet*," recalled twenty-five-year-old Lt. Chase Nielsen. "If we got off, there was a 50-50 chance we'd get shot down over Japan. And, if we got that far, there was a 50-50 chance we'd make it to China. And, if we got to China, there was a 50-50 chance we'd be captured." All were well aware of stories of Japanese brutality toward prisoners. "We figured the odds were really stacked against us," observed Nielsen.[27]

Doolittle replied that each man would have to make his own choices. As for him, he had no intention of being captured. "I'm forty-five years old and have lived a full life," he observed. "If my plane is crippled beyond any possibility of fighting or escape, I'm going to have my crew bail out and then I'm going to dive my B-25 into the best military target I can find."[28] No one doubted he meant every word.

Doolittle hoped *Hornet* could bring them within about 400 miles of the Japanese coast for the launch. If launched from 550 miles, they would have a "remote possibility" of completing the mission. The absolute out-side limit, in his estimation, was 650 miles if they had any hope of making the final 1,200 miles to China after they dropped their bombs.[29]

By 8 p.m. on Friday, April 17, not quite twenty-four hours before the anticipated launch, *Hornet* was approximately 890 miles east of Tokyo. The weather had turned abysmal. Rain squalls swept through, accompanied by high winds. The bombers strained against their lashings on the open deck as the carrier pitched in the rough seas. Unbeknownst to the Americans, they were approaching a Japanese early-warning picket line made up of small radio-equipped vessels. The task force had a scare before dawn when the lights of two enemy surface craft were spotted. Mitscher pressed on, fairly certain the raiding force had not been detected. But that changed hours later. At 5:58 a.m. a patrol plane from *Enterprise* spotted a fishing vessel; the pilot did not attack but suspected he had been seen. Halsey ordered a change of direction to the southwest, but at 7:38 a.m. *Hornet*'s lookouts spotted another enemy vessel only about 8 miles off. It was the 90-ton *Nitto Maru No. 23*, and her lookouts were also awake. A radio message from the vessel alerted Japanese defenses: "Three enemy carriers sighted. Position, 600 nautical miles east of Inubosaki."[30]

Nashville went after *Nitto Maru No. 23* with her big guns, but the damage was done. *Hornet* had picked up the radio message, and it was clear they'd been reported. Halsey, compelled to get his valuable carriers out of harm's way, messaged *Hornet*: "Launch planes. To Col. Doolittle and gallant command, good luck and God bless you."

Aboard *Hornet* the loudspeaker blared, "Now hear this! Now hear this! Army pilots, man your planes!"[31]

Hornet was 624 nautical miles from Tokyo, well outside the optimum distance Doolittle had planned for and on the very edge of his worst-case scenario.

They went anyway. Doolittle called his men on deck. "If there's any one of you who don't want to go, just tell me," he said. "Because the chances of you making it back are pretty slim."[32]

No one balked. One B-25 crewman later said it seemed they were all going forward without thinking—"like automatons."[33] Doolittle ran through the instructions one last time, concluding, "When we get to Chungking,

I'm going to give you all a party you won't forget!"[34] In the scramble that followed, men from the backup crews buttonholed other flyers, offering as much as $150 to trade places with them. There were no takers.

As the lead pilot, Doolittle climbed into his B-25 and peered out at the 465 feet of wet deck before him. Rain pelted against the cockpit glass, and the deck pitched in the heavy seas. Watching the signal officer with his checkered flag, Doolittle stood on the brakes and throttled the engines to a roar. The flag dropped. Doolittle released the brakes, and the B-25 leapt forward, its nose wheel and left wheel hugging the two white lines running down the deck. The lines were there to keep him from drifting into the 6 feet of clearance between his right wing tip and the carrier's superstructure. Doolittle was confident, but in the copilot's seat, twenty-six-year-old Lt. Dick Cole could not help thinking, "It'd be a pretty bad feeling for everybody behind us if we took off and dropped into the water."[35]

The bomber disappeared off the end of the flight deck, and for an instant onlookers thought Doolittle had gone into the drink. Then cheers broke out as the bomber rose up off the bow, circled over the ship to check direction, and headed toward Tokyo. Doolittle looked at his watch. It was 8:20 a.m.[36] Behind him, the fifteen other B-25s lifted off one by one at approximately four-minute intervals and droned off into the overcast.

Cruising along only 200 feet above the water, Doolittle and Cole took turns at the controls, the crew constantly checking the gas gauges and comparing them to estimates. "No one slept or got sick," recalled Cole. "If anyone was scared, it didn't show."[37] They briefly changed course from time to time to avoid revealing themselves to surface craft. "About two hours out we flew directly under an enemy flying boat that just loomed at us suddenly out of the mist," remembered Doolittle. "We don't think they saw us."[38]

They finally made landfall at about noon Tokyo time (1 p.m. ship's time). Crossing the coast some 80 miles north of Tokyo, Doolittle turned south. Flying as low as 30 feet off the ground, they passed over airfields crowded with aircraft. Other planes were in the air. Most seemed to be small biplanes, possibly trainers of some sort, though they also spotted nine fighters in three flights of three. From the copilot's seat, Cole saw people on the ground wave at the bomber. Others were playing baseball.

Doolittle skimmed low over Lake Teganuma northeast of Tokyo and began picking up landmarks as he approached his target—an armory a few miles north of the Imperial Palace. He pulled up to 1,200 feet and banked to the west. "Approaching target," he advised bombardier Sgt. Fred Braemer.

Braemer punched the button to open the bomb bay doors. "All ready, Colonel," he replied as the doors swung open.[39]

Braemer peered through the rudimentary bombsight that had been adapted for the low-level attack. The top-secret Norden bombsight developed for high-altitude missions had been deemed too valuable to risk falling into enemy hands. Ironically, the substitute, devised out of about twenty cents worth of aluminum, turned out to be more accurate for the job at hand.

Doolittle saw the red light on his instrument panel flash. The aircraft lurched as the first bomb fell. The light flashed again, and again, and then again as the first American bombs of World War II fell on the Japanese homeland. It was 12:30 p.m. Tokyo time. President Roosevelt had his small measure of revenge.

Antiaircraft fire blossomed around the bomber as Doolittle turned away. "They're missing us [by] a mile," he announced on the aircraft interphone. A near miss shook the plane. Gunner Paul J. Leonard piped up, "Colonel, that was no mile."[40]

Despite the raiders being forced to attack during daylight hours, contrary to plan, no planes were lost over Japan. Enemy antiaircraft fire was ineffective and the response by enemy fighter planes uncoordinated, with only one B-25 coming under concerted attack. That plane jettisoned its bombs and managed to outrun its attacker. But now, the decision to launch early, well beyond the optimum distance to target, seemed about to exact its price. Most, if not all, of the B-25s were almost sure to run out of gas well before reaching the safety of the Chinese airfields 1,200 miles away. Doolittle's navigator, twenty-three-year-old 2nd Lt. Hank Potter, announced he expected their tanks would run dry 135 miles short of the Chinese coast.

"Fortunately, the Lord was with us," recalled Doolittle.[41] Divine intervention came in the form of a 25-mph tailwind that extended the range of the B-25s. Even so, as they neared China late in the afternoon, Doolittle feared they might not make it. He told Braemer to get the raft ready just in case, adding, "We're going to keep going until we're dry."[42]

Thanks to the tailwind and careful fuel-control measures, they were still in the air as the Chinese coast appeared. But now the weather, which had been clear over Japan, deteriorated. Rain pelted against the windscreen. Doolittle tried to raise the airfield at Chuchow, but arrangements to provide homing beacons had fallen through, and he was unable to get a response. "All we could do was to fly a dead-reckoning course in the direction of Chuchow, abandon ship in midair and hope that we came down in Chinese-held territory," he observed.[43]

As the gas gauges edged toward zero, Doolittle conceded the obvious. "We'll have to bail out," he advised the crew. Leonard would go first, followed by Braemer, Potter, Cole, and finally Doolittle himself. If they all jumped in a straight line, it would be easier to find one another once they were on the ground.

"Get going," Doolittle ordered, setting the controls on autopilot. The men began bailing out, one after another. As Cole stood, his parachute snagged on the seat. Doolittle helped him free it and patted him on the shoulder. "Be seeing you in a few minutes, Dick," he remarked serenely. As Cole disappeared through the forward hatch, Doolittle shut off both gas valves and followed him out into the rainy night. They had been in the air for thirteen hours and traveled 2,250 miles.[44]

As he floated down in the darkness, Doolittle worried about his ankles, which had been badly broken in a mishap years before. He bent his knees in an effort to absorb the impact, only to land in a sitting position in a soggy rice paddy well fertilized with human waste. He clambered out of the stinking muck, unhooked his parachute, and headed toward a nearby light, which turned out to be a small farmhouse. Pounding on the door, he called out, "Lushu hoo megwa fugi," which he had been assured translated to "I am an American."[45]

The occupants were apparently not impressed. He heard movement inside. The light went out, followed by the sound of a bar sliding into place on the door.

Cold and shivering, Doolittle wandered off and found some sort of warehouse. "Inside, two sawhorses held a large box that was occupied by a very dead Chinese gentleman," he recalled.[46] He finally came across a water mill that offered some shelter from the rain, but he was too chilled and miserable to sleep. Setting off at daylight, he hiked down a path toward a village, finally encountering a farmer who led him to a Nationalist Chinese garrison. The major in charge expressed skepticism at Doolittle's claim that he was an American who had dropped out of the sky during the night.

Doolittle offered to show him his parachute as evidence that he was telling the truth about his arrival, but when they arrived at the rice paddy, the parachute was nowhere to be seen. Doolittle suggested that the occupants of the farmhouse could vouch that he pounded on the door during the night, but the Chinese owner and his family blandly denied any such occurrence. "They say you lie," said the major, more skeptical than ever.

To Doolittle's relief, a soldier ducked into the shack and promptly reappeared with the missing parachute. "The major smiled and extended his hand in friendship," recounted Doolittle, "and I was thus admitted officially to China."[47]

Soon reunited with his crew, all of whom had escaped injury, Doolittle learned that their bomber had crashed about 70 miles north of Chuchow. He and Leonard visited the crash site and found the wreckage scattered over acres of mountainside. Locals had already helped themselves to anything of use, including the brass buttons off Doolittle's oil-soaked uniform blouse. The normally indefatigable colonel sat down by a broken wing in near despair. He could only assume all the other bombers had also crashed. There was no telling if anyone else had survived. He felt he had botched his first—and now probably last—combat mission. "I had never felt lower in my life," he confessed.

Leonard broke into his reverie to ask what Doolittle expected when he returned home. "Well," said Doolittle gloomily, "I guess they'll court-martial me and send me to prison at Fort Leavenworth."[48]

Leonard dared to demur. No, he told the colonel. When Doolittle got home, they would pin a medal on him and give him a promotion and another airplane. And when they did, Leonard added, he would be proud to fly with him as his crew chief. Tears came to Doolittle's eyes at this expression of loyalty, but he wasn't convinced.

But Leonard was right. Jimmy Doolittle was about to become one of the most celebrated men in America. He was still in China when he was informed that he had been promoted to brigadier general, skipping an entire grade. While his fears about the other bombers were justified—fourteen crews had either bailed out or crash-landed, and one crew had flown to Russian Vladivostok where they were interned—the majority of the raiders had survived. Two drowned when their bomber crash-landed in the water just off the Chinese coast, and one other died when he bailed out and his parachute failed. Eight raiders were captured by Japanese forces in China. Three of those men were subsequently executed for alleged "war crimes"; another died in captivity, but the remainder were freed after the war.

Doolittle returned to the United States on May 18. The following day he was summoned to the White House to be presented the Medal of Honor—an award he strenuously protested he did not deserve. "Every man on our mission took the same risk I did," he argued upon being told of the award. "I don't think I'm entitled to the Medal of Honor."[49] Seeing that his protests only annoyed Generals Marshall and Arnold, Doolittle wisely clammed up. They were ushered into the Oval Office where a jovial President Roosevelt presented the medal as Doolittle's wife, Joe, proudly looked on.

The physical damage inflicted by the Doolittle Raid, as it became known, had little material effect on the Japanese war effort. About ninety buildings were damaged or destroyed, including targets at the Japanese Diesel Manufacturing Company, the Japanese Steel Corporation, the Mitsubishi Heavy Industrial Corporation, the Nagoya Aircraft Factory, an Army arsenal, nine electric power buildings, and half a dozen gas tanks. Also hit accidently were a temporary Army hospital, six schools, and a large number of private residences. According to postwar Japanese sources, 50 people were killed, and 252 were wounded.

Though Doolittle initially viewed the mission as a failure, his superiors, including the president himself, saw the destruction of sixteen B-25s and even the loss of the crewmen killed or captured as a reasonable price to pay for the propaganda value of the raid—which, after all, had been the primary rationale for the operation. The attack stunned and humiliated the Japanese and heartened an American public that for too many months had had little to celebrate.

Perhaps the most significant benefit of the raid from a military standpoint was that it contributed mightily to the subsequent Japanese effort a month and a half later to seize Midway Island and finish off the surviving American carriers. That decision led the Imperial Navy into disaster and is considered by historians to be a turning point in the war in the Pacific.

Doolittle himself went on to command the Twelfth Air Force operating in North Africa. Promoted to major general in November 1942, he took command of the Fifteenth Air Force in the Mediterranean theater of operations a year later, and at war's end, now a lieutenant general, he commanded the Eighth Air Force in England. He left active service after the war but went on to serve in a variety of important government and aviation-related positions in subsequent years. In 1985, in recognition of his storied service, Congress promoted him to the rank of four-star general on the U.S. Air Force retired list.

Eighty men took off from the *Hornet*'s deck on the morning of April 18, 1942. Of those, sixty-one survived the war. In following years, they held regular reunions until old age finally intervened. The last surviving raider, Doolittle's copilot, Dick Cole, passed away on April 9, 2019, at the age of 103, scarcely a week before the seventy-seventh anniversary of the mission.

Doolittle himself died at the age of ninety-six on September 27, 1993, at his son's home in Pebble Beach, California, after suffering a stroke earlier that month. He was buried at Arlington National Cemetery next to his wife, Joe, who had passed away five years earlier. An admirer once referred to the legendary aviator as the "Leonardo da Vinci of flight." The typically self-deprecating Doolittle laughed at that description, observing, "The guy's wrong. What he meant was I'm the Rube Goldberg of aviation."[50]

But to his fellow raiders, Jimmy Doolittle had no equal. "Young guys like us would go to hell and back for him," said one. "And we did."[51]

3

Coral Sea to Midway

In May 1942, the Japanese set about enlarging their defensive perimeter by moving to seize full control of New Guinea, where they had first landed in March. According to the plan, forces assembled at Rabaul would occupy Port Moresby on the New Guinea coast, along with Tulagi in the Solomon Islands, in an effort to strangle Allied supply lines to Australia. Learning of the plan through radio intelligence, the United States sent carriers *Yorktown* and *Lexington* to intervene. The resulting confrontation, which became known as the Battle of the Coral Sea, was the first action in history between opposing carriers and the first where the opposing ships never sighted or fired directly upon each other. Aboard *Yorktown* was a twenty-nine-year-old dive bomber pilot from New York, Lt. Jack Powers.

Lt. John J. Powers
Coral Sea
May 8, 1942

Jack Powers's mother last heard his voice on December 7, 1941. A Navy dive bomber pilot, he telephoned her at her New York home from Norfolk, Virginia, after news broke about the Japanese attack on Pearl Harbor. What might happen next, neither knew, but for the moment he was out of harm's way.

John James Powers was born on July 3, 1912, in New York City. His father, John Joseph, a Navy veteran of the Spanish-American War, was a postal clerk; his mother, Maria, had immigrated to the United States from

England with her family as an infant in 1883. John was their first child. He was followed two years later by sister Marie, then brother William and another sister, Elizabeth, nine years his junior.

Powers attended George Washington High School and Dwight Preparatory School in New York before entering the U.S. Naval Academy as a member of the Class of 1935 two years before Butch O'Hare's arrival. "Jack" or "Jo Jo," as he was nicknamed by classmates, participated in boxing and apparently demonstrated a mischievous streak. "Never trust him to respect conventionalities, he's a hilarious rebel and his own man," observed the Naval Academy's 1935 *Lucky Bag* yearbook. The yearbook writers went on to note that their classmate made friends easily, had a sense of humor, and possessed "the most stable temperament you've ever seen."[1] His yearbook photo shows a bright-eyed young man with wavy dark hair. He wears a faint smile, as if mildly amused by the process of having his formal photograph taken.

Graduating 228th out of a class of 442, the newly minted ensign reported to the USS *West Virginia* for sea duty. Two years later he transferred to the USS *Augusta* and later to the USS *Utah*. In 1940, now a lieutenant junior grade, he reported to the naval air station at Pensacola for flight training. His decision to enter flight school came as a surprise to his family, who later recalled he had never shown any particular interest in aviation as a youth.[2] Perhaps the "conventionalities" of sea duty had persuaded the "hilarious rebel" that flying was more suited to his temperament.

Receiving his wings as a naval aviator in January 1941, Powers was assigned to Bombing Squadron 5 (VB-5) attached to the USS *Yorktown*. The squadron was equipped with the SBD-3 Dauntless. The "SB" stood for "scout bomber," while the "D" stood for Douglas Aircraft, which manufactured the plane. Crewed by two men—the pilot and a rear-seat gunner—the Dauntless was small and lightweight for a bomber. It mounted two forward-firing .50-caliber machine guns with a twin .30-caliber for the rear gunner and could carry a 1,000-pound bomb. It was not an aircraft for the faint of heart. Diving at a steep angle from 10,000 feet, the pilot would release his bomb over an enemy ship at around 2,000 feet, just high enough to pull up sharply before crashing into the target or the water. Rugged and reliable, the bomber had some drawbacks—its fixed wings, though short, could not be folded, which created some headaches aboard carriers, where space was always at a premium—but the plane was popular among the men who had to fly it.

The *Yorktown* was docked at Norfolk, Virginia, when news of the attack on Pearl Harbor arrived on the afternoon of December 7. Powers and his mates spent much of the following day manning their planes, engines turning over, on the flight deck of the stationary carrier. Whoever issued that directive apparently didn't realize the ship needed to be underway with a wind across the deck in order for the dive bombers to take off. The confusion continued over the next few days as the *Yorktown*'s aircraft were hoisted off the carrier, then hoisted back on and then off again, for no particular reason that the air crews could fathom. Finally, on December 16, with the planes again aboard, *Yorktown* got underway, heading for the Panama Canal and the war in the Pacific.

Combat was only a few short weeks away. On January 31, VB-5 participated in a carrier raid on Japanese forces on Jaluit in the Marshall Islands. Flying in the lead echelon, Powers and twenty-eight-year-old Lt. Johnny Nielsen, who had graduated from the Naval Academy two years after Powers, missed a cargo ship with their bombs, then proceeded to machine-gun a radio station on the four-square-mile coral atoll. "Jo Jo strafed the shack at the foot of the tower, sending his tracer through the window," recalled Nielsen. "He blew it to hell and gone."[3] They also strafed a couple of small vessels in the lagoon but were unable to locate a seaplane base that had been listed as a secondary target. "We'd lost everybody," said Nielsen. "Jo Jo closed up and we headed for the *Yorktown* at 400 feet, trying to hold a fuel-conserving speed. Thirty miles from the ship we contacted it by radio and flew right in to land without circling."[4]

In March *Yorktown* and *Lexington* raided Japanese shipping in New Guinea's Huon Gulf, but the next couple of months consisted mostly of long, tedious patrols to protect supply lines from Hawaii to Australia. "We crossed and recrossed the Coral Sea until we knew the flying fish by name," remarked an SBD pilot.[5] But things were about to heat up as the Japanese seized Tulagi in the Solomon Islands on May 3 to support operations in the Coral Sea area. At the same time, radio intelligence indicated that the Japanese were about to launch an amphibious assault—code-named Operation Mo—to seize the Allied base at Port Moresby on the coast of New Guinea less than 1,500 miles from Australia.

Commanding Task Force 17, consisting of *Yorktown* and *Lexington*, Rear Adm. Frank Fletcher was directed to intercept the enemy naval force as it headed for Port Moresby. As a preliminary, on May 4, Powers and his dive bomber squadron attacked Japanese shipping at Tulagi. Powers claimed two hits on enemy vessels. The raid was a success, though pilot claims—destruction of two destroyers, a transport, four gunboats, immobilization of a cruiser, and damage to another destroyer and a seaplane tender—far exceeded the actual damage inflicted.

Dawn on May 7 found Fletcher's task force just south of Rossel Island, the easternmost island of the Louisiade Archipelago at the southeastern tip of New Guinea, as he awaited the appearance of the enemy armada. U.S. intelligence indicated the MO Striking Force included transports, cruisers, and destroyers, but Fletcher's primary target would be the three Japanese carriers assigned to protect the Port Moresby landing and the associated operations at Tulagi. The carriers included two Pearl Harbor veterans, *Shōkaku* ("Soaring Crane") and *Zuikaku* ("Auspicious Crane"), operating as the strike force, along with the light carrier *Shōhō* ("Happy Phoenix") supporting the Port Moresby invasion force.

Fletcher did not have long to wait. At 8:15 a.m. a scout from *Yorktown* spotted two enemy cruisers 200 miles northwest of Task Force 17. Due to a ciphering error, the report misidentified the vessels as carriers. *Lexington* began launching planes at 9:26 a.m., and *Yorktown* soon followed. The scout's error was not recognized until planes were already on their way. Fortunately, at 10:12 a.m. a report arrived that Army scout planes had spotted a carrier, ten transports, and sixteen other warships only 30 miles from the previously reported location.

The attack aircraft were rerouted and twenty-eight minutes later spotted the 11,262-ton *Shōhō*, accompanied by two or three heavy cruisers and one or two destroyers. *Lexington*'s dive bombers and torpedo planes arrived first and pummeled the enemy carrier, hitting her with 1,000-pound bombs and at least five torpedoes. By the time *Yorktown*'s dive bombers arrived, the *Shōhō* was doomed, but they hastened her demise with as many as eleven more hits.

As the last VB-5 crew to attack, Powers and his backseat gunner, twenty-one-year-old ARM2c Everett Hill of Oakland, California, planted their 1,000-pound bomb on *Shōhō*'s blazing flight deck, doing their part to make her "one of the most sunk ships in the history of naval warfare," as one *Yorktown* pilot wryly observed.[6] At 11:31 a.m. the surviving Japanese crewmen were ordered to abandon ship. Less than four minutes later, *Shōhō* disappeared beneath the waves, the first Japanese carrier to be sunk by American forces since the war began. Only about 200 of her 800 crewmen were rescued. Total American losses were three SBDs, two from *Lexington* and one from *Yorktown*.[7]

Despite the loss of *Shōhō*, the MO Striking Force continued on course for Port Moresby. That evening, addressing VB-5's aircrews in his capacity as squadron gunnery officer, Jo Jo Powers reviewed point-of-aim and diving techniques with his Dauntless pilots. He stressed the importance of descending to the lowest possible release point in order to ensure a hit. The lower the better, he reiterated.

The pilots understood the logic of his admonition. They also realized that very low bomb-release points left the aircraft more vulnerable to close-range enemy fire, it was more difficult to recover from the dive, and there was greater chance of being caught in one's own bomb blast. None of that seemed to deter Powers. Talking things over with roommate Johnny Nielsen that night, he vowed, "I'm going to get a hit tomorrow if I have to lay it on their flight deck."[8]

Despite the victory over *Shōhō*, the mood in *Yorktown*'s ready room the next morning was subdued. The pilots were on edge, knowing there would be no element of surprise. This time the Japanese would be expecting them. Powers delivered a pep talk, repeating his vow to get a hit if he had to lay it on the enemy flight deck. As the announcement came over the speaker, "Pilots, man your planes!" and the men started from the ready room, he called out a final admonishment, "Remember, the folks back home are counting on us!"[9] S1c Lynn R. Forshee, a nineteen-year-old VB-5 gunner—one of the backseat boys along for the ride—heard about Powers's "lay it on the deck" promise later. "I'm quite sure that his rear seat man, Hill, would not have found much reassurance in that," he remarked grimly.[10]

Bucking heavy cloud cover and intermittent squalls, a scout from *Lexington* spotted the MO Striking Force at 8:20 a.m. *Yorktown* began launching planes at 9 a.m.: six Wildcats from Fighting Squadron 42, seven SBD-3s from Scouting Squadron 5 (VS-5), nine TBD-1s from Torpedo Squadron 5, and seventeen SBD-3s from Powers's VB-5, for a total of thirty-nine aircraft. *Lexington* began launching only minutes later, putting up another thirty-six fighters, dive bombers, and torpedo planes.

Powers, with Everett Hill manning the backseat, led the third division of VB-5 dive bombers. Their Dauntless #4597 carried a single 1,000-pound bomb. An hour and fifteen minutes after takeoff, the dive bomber crews spotted what they believed to be two carriers, a battleship, three heavy cruisers, and four light cruisers or destroyers. Using the clouds for concealment, they waited impatiently for the slower torpedo planes to arrive so that they could launch a coordinated attack on the nearest flat-top, the *Shōkaku*. A handful of Japanese fighters circled lazily over the carrier, momentarily oblivious to the presence of the dive bombers above.

Finally, at 10:57 a.m., the torpedo planes were in place, but the delay proved ill-advised. By now the Japanese had recognized their peril and scrambled their fighters. As the first echelon of seven dive bombers from VS-5 hurtled down toward *Shōkaku*, "it sounded like rain on the roof, the Zeros were pouring so many bullets into us," recalled an SBD pilot.[11] Adding to their problems, as the dive bombers descended below 8,000 feet and encountered warmer, moister air, their windscreens and bomb-sights fogged up. Unable to see, the pilots "bombed from memory," as one put it.[12] "I had to put my head out over the side of the cockpit," said another.[13] The results were unimpressive. The first seven bombers scored some close misses on *Shōkaku* as she maneuvered wildly to evade but no hits.

The seventeen SBDs from VB-5 now swung in for their turn. Johnny Nielsen looked out over his left wingtip to see the irrepressible Powers, not more than 50 feet away, "making monkey faces" at him through the cockpit glass.[14] "When I glanced at him, he gave me a big grin and a silly sort of wave with his arm. He was set to make a determined attack, but he wasn't thinking any more about committing suicide than I was," Nielsen observed.[15]

Then they went in. Japanese fighters hit the rear of the formation as the first bombers started down. Again, fogged windscreens and gunsights plagued the SBDs. One after another, the dive bombers hurtled down, pulling up at between 1,500 and 2,000 feet as they released their bombs. Close misses threw up geysers of water around the enemy carrier. At about 11:05 a.m., one of the 1,000-pounders finally scored a hit near Shōkaku's bow. The blast tore up the flight deck, knocked out the forward elevator, and ignited an intense fire.

Nielsen released his bomb and pulled out of his dive at a safe altitude. He wasn't sure he had scored a hit, but he could see explosions. "As I looked at the carrier, I could see an airplane directly over the center of the flight deck—about 300 feet—and nosed down at almost 45 degrees," he recalled. "It was headed into an area of smoke and debris which covered the whole after part of the Jap carrier. It must have been Jo Jo. It couldn't have been anyone else. In the position he was in, it would have been impossible for him to pull out."[16]

Other pilots also saw Powers as he dove on Shōkaku. The SBD was hit repeatedly by antiaircraft fire, which threw it off course. One of the Zeros also apparently scored a 20mm hit as the dive bomber descended. Flaming gasoline streamed from the fuel tanks. Powers radioed that both he and Hill had been wounded, but he guided the burning dive bomber back over the Shōkaku's deck.

Down he went, lower and lower—past the 2,000-foot ordinary recovery point, past 1,500 feet. Finally, well below 1,000 feet, he pulled the release handle for his 1,000-pound bomb. He may have been no more than 200 feet over the target when the bomb tore through the carrier's flight deck. Fellow pilots saw the SBD stagger as Powers tried to pull out. Then the plane disappeared in a pillar of flame and debris as the bomb exploded on the starboard side near the carrier's island, killing over a hundred Japanese sailors and igniting fierce fires on the flight deck and upper hangar deck. The damage was so severe that the carrier was no longer capable of further flight operations, but Powers and Hill were doomed. Their Dauntless smashed into the sea not far away from burning carrier.

"There is no question that John knew what he was doing," observed a fellow pilot. "He knew that if you go below about 700 feet in your recovery, the blast from a 1,000-pounder will get you every time. To stay above 700 feet means you must release your bomb not lower than 1,000 feet. He held his to 500 and was probably below 300 when the explosion came. He just decided not to miss, God bless him."[17]

Though hit at least once more by *Lexington* dive bombers, *Shōkaku* was still afloat as the American strike force headed for home. She would survive, but she was out of the battle. Unable to recover aircraft, the carrier could not throw her full weight into the Japanese air attack on Task Force 17—an absence that may well have spared Fletcher from disaster. She was also unavailable for the pivotal battle of Midway a month later.

Back in New York, Powers's parents received a telegram on June 23 reporting that he was missing in action. In Oakland, California, Everett Hill's parents were notified of his loss. Hill, an amateur radio buff and former track star at Fremont High School, had enlisted in the Navy after graduating in 1939. A letter from his squadron commander, Lt. Wallace C. Short, commented on the youth's "cheerful personality" and "splendid character" and offered his parents a ray of hope:

> There is a possibility that his pilot made a forced landing in the water and that your son may now be a prisoner of war of Japan, for, inasmuch as the action took place over enemy waters, it was impossible to conduct a search for the missing planes. While I do not want to unduly raise your hopes, I can say that each plane of our squadron is equipped with a rubber boat and emergency rations. We all hold to the faint hope that the pilot of the plane managed a safe landing in the sea and will eventually reach a group of nearby islands.

However, another source was less encouraging, telling the Hills that it appeared their son's plane had been destroyed in the blast of its own bomb. In fact, there was little chance either Powers or Hill had survived.[18]

And so things stood until the evening of September 7, 1942, when Jo Jo Powers's mother, like millions of other Americans, turned on her radio to listen to President Franklin D. Roosevelt's latest fireside chat. The president called on the nation to be worthy of the men fighting its battles. He then cited an example of those men, relating how Lt. John J. Powers dove his plane onto a Japanese carrier and dropped a bomb on the flight deck so close that his own plane was destroyed in the explosion. "I have received a recommendation from the Secretary of the Navy that Lt. Joseph James Powers of New York City, missing in action, be awarded the Medal of Honor. I hereby and now make this award," he announced.[19]

As newspaper reporters descended on the Powers family's apartment the next day, Mrs. Powers, described as "a sixty-year-old woman, her hair streaked with gray," sobbed softly but attempted a brave front. "My boy hasn't given his life in vain. He did his duty to his country," she managed. Even so, she and Jo Jo's two sisters continued to express the forlorn hope that he might yet turn up safe.[20]

That was not to be. Powers and Everett Hill were officially declared dead a year later, on May 3, 1943. On September 17, five hundred officers and men at the Naval Receiving Station in New York stood at attention as Adm. Royal E. Ingersoll, commander in chief of the Atlantic Fleet, draped the blue-starred ribbon of the Medal of Honor around Mrs. Powers's neck. Her husband had passed away the previous July only two months after Jo Jo's death in action, but she was accompanied by her younger son William, a member of the Merchant Marine. A newspaper reporter observed that "her face betrayed no emotion as she accepted her country's highest decoration."[21]

Jo Jo Powers's war had lasted just five months.

"JACK Powers,—you mean Jo Jo? Sure we know him, who doesn't? Even the kids in the streets grin when they tell you this. That 'certain something' that makes everybody his friend on sight is Jo's most notice-able trait."

—U.S. NAVAL ACADEMY *LUCKY BAG*, 1935

The loss of *Shōhō* and damage inflicted on *Shōkaku* persuaded the Japanese to abandon Operation Mo. Port Moresby would be spared, but the Battle of the Coral Sea was not yet finished. Even as U.S. aircraft attacked the invasion force, Japanese planes were converging on *Lexington* and *Yorktown*. Barring the way was a handful of F4F-3 Wildcats backed up by SBD Dauntless dive bombers that had been pressed into service as an antitorpedo plane screen. It would prove to be an ill-advised arrangement, as a *Lexington* SBD pilot by the name of Bill Hall was about to discover.

Lt. (j.g.) William E. Hall
Coral Sea
May 8, 1942

Less than 200 miles away from the burning *Shōkaku*, 28-year-old Lt. (j.g.) William E. "Bill" Hall of *Lexington's* Scouting Squadron 2 (VS-2) patrolled in his Dauntless dive bomber, awaiting the inevitable arrival of Japanese torpedo and fighter planes over Task Force 17. Considering that the SBD was not designed as a fighter plane, it was an encounter he was unlikely to survive.

Standing only five feet, five inches tall, the soft-spoken redhead, known to his squadron mates as "Pappy," had been born in Storrs, Utah, on Halloween Day, October 31, 1913. He grew up in Hiawatha, a small coal-mining town about 12 miles southwest of Price. His father was a mine company clerk; his mother served as the local postmistress.

The attending physician joked that Bill, having been born on Halloween, would likely be a "little devil." Instead he turned out to be "a quiet, scholarly fellow who liked to fish and fool around with radio equipment," his parents later told a newspaper reporter. He loved music and could play "most any instrument."[22] Those parental recollections notwithstanding, it appears that young Bill wasn't completely immersed in scholarly pursuits: some of the locals observed that he seemed to figure prominently in a lot of fights as a youngster, usually coming out on top, despite his small stature.

Hall attended Wasatch Academy, a boarding school in Mount Pleasant, Utah, before heading off to college at the University of Redlands in

San Bernardino, California, where he majored in music. Considered "too light for football," he was a star hurdler on the track team. He received a bachelor's degree in music in 1936.[23] Returning to Hiawatha after graduation, he taught music at the nearby Consumers School for a year but moved on in August 1938, joining the Navy in hopes of becoming a naval aviator. "When I signed up ... they weren't going to take me because I had no mathematics, but I showed them my degree," he recalled. "They had to take me then, but they said I probably couldn't make a go of it."[24]

Hall was assigned to flight training at Naval Reserve Aviation Base, Long Beach, California, and then Naval Air Station Pensacola in Florida. An evaluation by an instructor at Pensacola was less than encouraging, noting, "He is never quite certain of having conducted himself well enough. This apparent lack of confidence handicaps his abilities somewhat."[25] Nevertheless, Hall successfully made it through flight training and received his wings in September 1939. Commissioned as an ensign, he was assigned to Scouting Squadron 5 aboard the USS *Yorktown* flying SBD dive bombers. Following the attack on Pearl Harbor, he participated on February 1 in *Yorktown*'s strike on Makin Island. Later loaned out to USS *Enterprise*, he flew in raids on Wake and Marcus Islands. In April he was reassigned to Scouting Squadron 2 on the *Lexington*. Now a lieutenant junior grade at the ripe old age of twenty-eight, he arrived with the most combat strike experience of any of the pilots in the squadron. In recognition of his exalted stature and advanced age, his new squadron mates promptly dubbed him "Pappy."

On May 7, 1942, as *Lexington* and *Yorktown* moved to block the Japanese attack on Port Moresby, Hall and his gunner, twenty-two-year-old ARM3c Doyle C. Phillips of Madison, Indiana, joined in the bombing attack on the light carrier *Shōhō*. Attacked by enemy fighters, their SBD was hit in the gas tanks, but the self-sealing tanks absorbed the damage without leaking or catching fire. Another bullet smashed through the side panel of the windshield and hit Phillips in the shoulder. The distraction spoiled Hall's aim, and his bombs went wide. He would not get another chance.

The next morning, he had scarcely returned from a scouting mission in search of enemy ships, when word came of an inbound Japanese strike.

"We refueled, checked our armament and took off on an anti-torpedo defense flight," he recalled.[26] The alert turned out to be a false alarm, but the real thing was soon to follow. At 10:55 a.m., radar operators aboard both *Lexington* and *Yorktown* picked up a large formation of aircraft only 68 miles away. It was the Japanese strike force: sixty-nine planes from *Shōkaku* and *Zuikaku*, consisting of thirty-three Aichi Type 99 carrier dive bombers (code-named Vals), eighteen Zero fighters, and eighteen Nakajima B5N2 torpedo aircraft (code-named Kates).

Pappy Hall and nine other SBDs from *Lexington*, along with eight from *Yorktown*, were still in the air following the previous alert. Now *Lexington* launched five more SBDs and five Wildcats. *Yorktown* contributed four more Wildcats. The Wildcats were designated to deal with dive bombers and enemy fighters at higher altitude, while the Dauntlesses tackled the low-flying Japanese torpedo planes. The use—many would say misuse—of the dive bombers as fighters resulted both from hard reality and ignorance. The hard reality was that due to organizational tables at that point in the war, there were not enough Wildcats aboard the carriers to fulfill both offensive and defensive roles.

The ignorance—really an intelligence failure—was the lack of appreciation for the capabilities of Japanese aircraft. The single-engine carrier-based Kates had a three-man crew—pilot, navigator/bombardier, and radio operator/gunner—and could carry either one torpedo or a bomb load. American tacticians wrongly assumed the aircraft were comparable in performance to the sadly out-of-date U.S. Douglas TBD Devastator torpedo plane. In fact, the Kates were much faster and could attack from higher altitudes than believed. Worse yet, the slow SBDs were no match at all as fighter planes against the fast and agile Japanese Zero with its two 20mm cannons and two 7.7mm machine guns.

At 11:09 a.m., the fighter director aboard *Lexington* reported enemy torpedo planes only 35 miles out. Hall, having lost Doyle Phillips to a bullet wound the day before, was flying with eighteen-year-old S1c John A. Moore of Newport, Kentucky, as backseat radioman/gunner. Due to the overcast, Hall had been circling at an altitude of 800 to 900 feet, much lower than he would have liked. "There were four planes in my flight and we were flying in two-plane sections," he recalled. He could feel the adrenalin building as they waited for the enemy formation to come within sight. "There is more a feeling of anxiety than of fear," he said later. He likened the feeling to preparing for an important football game. "The difference lies in that we trade slugs for life instead of a ball for yards," he added pensively.[27]

As Hall waited, eight SBDs from *Yorktown*, flying at 1,500 feet, headed out toward the approaching torpedo planes. Their first indication that the U.S. defense plan was ill conceived arrived as the Kates came in higher and faster than anticipated and flashed right past the waiting SBDs. The Kates were followed by Zeros, which tore into the slower Dauntlesses. SBD section leader Lt. (j.g.) Swede Vejtasa shouted, "Turn! Turn! Turn!" into the radio, but the other pilots in the four-plane section failed to react in time. As Vejtasa maneuvered for his life, his wingman plummeted toward the ocean in flames. A second Dauntless also went down; then a Zero blew the tail section off a third, sending the pilot and gunner to their deaths. "The SBD is not a fighter plane," one of the surviving pilots observed later. "[It was] disastrous to even have us out there."[28]

"Shortly before 11 a.m. [we] saw several attacking aircraft coming in a line of attack formation," recalled Hall.[29] There were ten all together: a group of four to his right and another flight of six to his left. Hall's wingman, Ens. Robert Smith, lit out toward the group of four. Hall turned toward the other six. He admitted to feeling less than heroic. *This is like suicide, taking on this whole bunch*, he thought to himself. *But here they come. This will be a real rooster fight.*[30]

As the Nakajimas approached *Lexington* from the port side at an altitude of 600 feet, Hall rolled sharply left and dived at the nearest torpedo plane racing toward its drop point. Postwar records indicate the three-man crew included Warrant Officer Saburo Shindo as pilot and second *shotai* (flight) leader Lt. Norio Yano. Hall got into position and opened up with his two forward .50-caliber machine guns. "I attacked the first plane and in a few moments we saw the right wing of the enemy craft start to smoke," he said.[31]

Hall pursued the stricken Kate at wave-top level past a U.S. destroyer and through a hail of antiaircraft fire as Shindo remained on course. The

Japanese crew finally dropped their anti-torpedo but continued to race toward *Lexington*, the right wing now streaming bright flames. Suddenly, recalled Hall, "the plane went into a left rolling turn, plunging toward the water." It crashed into the sea and exploded only 100 yards off *Lexington*'s starboard bow.[32]

Hall didn't pause to celebrate. "I was just trying to keep myself in the air," he recalled.[33] A few moments later, his engine began to miss. "After taking off, I [had] switched my gas line to the right tank to save the main tank's fuel for combat," he recalled.[34] The right tank had now run dry. He quickly shifted to the main tank, but the oversight cost him altitude. At the same time, he caught the attention of five Zeros flying escort for the torpedo planes. In the rear cockpit, Moore began rattling away with his .30-caliber machine guns as they closed in.

Swooping in from behind, the lead enemy fighter cut loose. Hall heard a loud pounding as slugs riddled the SBD's aluminum skin. One bullet punched into the cockpit so close it severed the headphone cord to his flight helmet. But the pilot of the Zero then made a fatal mistake. Passing under the slower SBD, he remerged in a shallow climbing turn in front of Hall's forward .50s. Hall riddled him. "I was able to get on his tail and he never pulled out of the shallow turn and went in," he recalled.[35]

Firing from the rear cockpit, Moore thought he set one Zero on fire and damaged another in the fast-paced action. As Hall clawed for altitude, yet another Zero came at him head-on, guns winking. "I returned fire and did not run away as we neared," he recalled.[36] Apparently hit, the Zero broke off to the left, slanting down toward the water.

Climbing to the right, Hall was watching his victim's descent when another Zero roared up on his tail and put a 20mm shell into the dive bomber just forward of the cockpit. The explosion knocked out the hydraulics and sent a spray of metal into Hall's right leg, nearly tearing his foot off. Another fragment hit him in the back of the head. "There was no pain, but a sudden pressure on my foot," he said later. "I looked down and saw the blood. They apparently were explosive shells and the only reason I can figure I wasn't more seriously injured was that the shells penetrated into a hydraulic reservoir."[37]

Somehow Hall managed to stay aloft. Unable to press the rudder pedals with his mangled right foot, he steered with his left foot and the rudder trim tabs as Moore continued to fire the rear machine gun. The Zeros finally broke off, and Hall guided the SBD into the temporary refuge of the overcast.

Though the SBD crews managed to disrupt the Japanese attack, they were unable to stop all the torpedo planes. *Lexington* was hit twice on the port side at 11:20 a.m. Shortly afterward, nineteen Aichi Type 99 Val dive bombers appeared overhead. One scored a hit on the port forward five-inch ready ammunition locker, wiping out the crew of a five-inch gun and starting several fires. Another bomb struck the funnel. Two others detonated alongside the ship, flooding two compartments.

Fumbling around in the blood-spattered cockpit of his SBD, Hall took the radio cord that had been severed from his helmet and knotted it around his shattered right leg as a makeshift tourniquet. Drenched in blood and now in great pain, he turned toward the *Lexington*. It was 11:39 a.m., less than twenty minutes after the first torpedo smashed into the carrier. The ship had taken on a slight list due to the torpedo and bomb damage but was still operational as Hall approached in his riddled dive bomber. He fired a red flare in hopes of identifying himself to jittery antiaircraft gunners who at this point were likely to view anything in the air as hostile.

"I tried to drop my landing gear, and only one wheel came down, as I had no hydraulic action," he remembered.[38] Despite the precautionary flare, antiaircraft gunners on one of the screening destroyers opened up on him as he flew by. A shell punched through one side of the cockpit and out the other side, passing so close to Hall that it tore the leg on his flight suit. Fortunately, the projectile had apparently not traveled far enough to arm; otherwise it might have exploded in the cockpit. It occurred to Hall that he might have escaped death at the hands of enemy Zeros only to be gunned down by his own people.

Descending to the wave tops, he swung around and made an emergency pass over *Lexington* to indicate he needed to land immediately. He had one bit of good luck: by shaking the plane violently, he managed to coax the balky wheel to descend. However, the lack of hydraulics prevented him from engaging the landing flaps to reduce his air speed during the descent to the carrier deck. Using the hand tab controls, he brought the heavily damaged SBD in, descending some 30 knots faster than the normal landing speed. The control officer attempted to wave him off, but Hall stayed on course. "I knew I could not last another round, as my engine had long since exceeded the danger heat point," he observed.[39] Weak from loss of blood, he was also becoming incapable of performing the most routine operations. Cutting the engine, he dropped onto the deck.

The SBD's tail hook snagged the second arresting wire but was going so fast it ripped the wire out of the deck. The aircraft passed over the next several wires before finally hooking the ninth and final wire, coming up just short of the crash barrier.

Safely down, Hall surveyed his wreck of an aircraft, which "had been so thoroughly riddled, it was a wonder it didn't break its back while we were landing."[40] Thanks to the armor plating protecting the rear cockpit, Johnny Moore had escaped injury—bullet dents in the steel bore testimony to the quality of American metallurgy. Hall was pulled from the blood-soaked front cockpit and hustled down to sick bay. The SBD was beyond salvage. Deck crews hastily stripped the plane of its prop and accessible parts and pushed it overboard.

Of the twenty-three SBDs sent aloft on antitorpedo patrol, six were shot down. Two others, including Hall's, were jettisoned due to battle damage. Eleven pilots and radiomen were killed; at least three others, including Hall, were wounded. VS-2 pilots and gunners claimed seven torpedo planes and six fighters destroyed, with another fighter listed as probably destroyed for a total of fourteen. Other reports for the squadron are incomplete due to subsequent events but list nine torpedo planes and two fighters shot down.[41] Other SBDs from Bombing Squadron 2 and *Yorktown's* Bombing Squadron 5 claimed four enemy fighters, one torpedo plane, and one dive bomber. Wildcats claimed ten fighters, four dive bombers, and one torpedo plane.

Japanese records indicate those claims were somewhat exaggerated, listing total losses as twenty-three aircraft: one fighter, thirteen carrier bombers, and nine torpedo planes shot down, missing, or ditched. It is estimated that the SBD antitorpedo patrol accounted for five or six torpedo planes and one dive bomber. At least five aircraft that tangled with the SBDs made it back to *Zuikaku* but were so badly damaged they were immediately pushed over the side.

Meanwhile, Hall's travails were far from over. At 12:47 p.m. *Lexington* was rocked by a massive explosion as gasoline vapors from the damaged port avgas tanks ignited. Less than two hours later another explosion started massive fires in the hangar and knocked out power to the forward half of the ship. A third blast at 3:25 p.m. knocked out water pressure in the hangar. Burning and listing, *Lexington* drifted to a halt. Efforts got underway to evacuate the wounded.

His foot cleaned and bandaged, Hall made his way to the air group abandon-ship station. "They brought out all the ice cream aboard for the men and everyone was eating ice cream from helmets until it came time to abandon ship," he recalled.[42]

The order to abandon ship came at 5:07 p.m., and the aviators began climbing down lines and dropping into the ocean. Hall somehow made it down a line and into the water where he clung to the side of a life raft for two hours before a whaleboat from a cruiser picked him up. A total of 216 *Lexington* crewmen were killed, and 2,735 were rescued. Adrift and on fire, the doomed carrier was finally sent to the bottom hours later by five torpedoes delivered by the USS *Phelps*. *Yorktown*, though also hit during the Japanese attack and trailing oil, survived the battle.

Hall ended up at Balboa Naval Hospital in San Diego, where he began the long rehabilitation for his shattered foot. Among those tending to the wounded aviator was the twenty-six-year-old head nurse on his floor, Leah Christine Chapman. A redheaded farm girl from tiny Anderson, Missouri, "Chris" Chapman stood three inches taller than the diminutive dive bomber pilot, but that didn't dissuade Pappy Hall. When he was finally mobile enough to ask her out, she showed up wearing a hat and her tallest high heels in an apparent effort to discourage his attentions. Hall only laughed. "Don't you think I know you're taller than I am?" he responded. "Take off that silly hat and let's go out!"[43]

The two were married on September 20, 1942, in Price, Utah. Spending a weekend at Bright Angel Falls at the Grand Canyon, the newlyweds missed an announcement by President Franklin D. Roosevelt. The president said he intended to award the Medal of Honor to Lt. William E. Hall for his actions during the Battle of the Coral Sea.

Returning to duty at the naval air base in San Diego, Hall was confused when his commanding officer began offering what seemed to be rather excessive congratulations. "Everybody must get married sometime," replied the bemused pilot, assuming the officer was referring to his recent wedding. His CO then explained that the congratulations were for earning the nation's highest decoration for valor. "I thought some mistake must have been made and I was afraid to show my face until word finally came from the personnel center and verified the action," remembered Hall.[44]

The medal was presented in a ceremony at Hall's air base. Rear Adm. Ralston S. Hughes of the Eleventh Naval District did the honors. The hero—described in newspaper accounts as "unassuming and genuinely likeable"—confessed to being "surprised by all this fuss," adding, "All I did was my job, no more than anyone else."[45] He had little to say about the medal, then or later, and never saw combat again. Recovered from his wounds, he spent the next year as an instructor at Naval Air Station Daytona Beach, in Florida, teaching new dive bomber pilots the ropes. Ironically, he was nearly killed while serving as a flight instructor when his plane caught fire, forcing him to crash-land. Once again, his luck held good, and he survived.

John Moore, the rear gunner who had shared those tense moments over the Coral Sea on May 8, 1942, did not survive the war. The twenty-one-year-old Kentuckian was killed in a dive bomber crash during night exercises in Nevada on September 11, 1944. The pilot, the son of a rear admiral, was also killed. Their bodies, completely incinerated when the aircraft burned, were not recoverable, but Moore's death was verified by two witnesses who saw him climb into the airplane prior to takeoff.

Bill Hall was released from active duty in October 1946 with the rank of lieutenant commander. He took a job with the Veterans Administration but remained in the Naval Reserve for another fourteen years, finally retiring in November 1960. He and his wife had two daughters,

Gwendolyn and Linda Kay. Hall passed away on November 15, 1996, in Kansas City, Kansas, at the age of 83 and is buried in Fort Leavenworth National Cemetery. Wife Chris passed away in 2001 and is buried with him. As for the Medal of Honor, Hall insisted to the end that he was only doing his job.

— ❦ —

Stung by the Doolittle Raid and the show of American resolve at the Coral Sea, the Japanese now decided to expand their defensive buffer and at the same time lure the remaining U.S. aircraft carriers into a trap by seizing Midway Island 1,137 miles west of Hawaii. The principal striking force would be Adm. Chuichi Nagumo's First Air Fleet: four fleet carriers, along with two fast battleships, two heavy cruisers, a light cruiser, and a dozen destroyers. The occupation of Midway would be accomplished by 5,000 troops crowded aboard a dozen transports and supported by a light carrier, two battleships, and an array of cruisers and destroyers. It was assumed the U.S. Navy would feel compelled to respond to the threat to Midway and would sally out to be destroyed. This defeat and the subsequent threat of further attacks on Fiji, Samoa, and even Hawaii itself would then presumably persuade the U.S. government to agree to a negotiated peace, leaving Japan with the spoils of its early conquests.

There was only one problem. The Americans knew they were coming. Having broken the Japanese naval code, U.S. intelligence became aware of the Japanese plan and laid an ambush with three carriers and air elements stationed on Midway itself. Tragically, many of the American pilots would go into battle flying obsolete aircraft that were no match for Japanese planes. These included the obsolete Brewster Buffalo and the equally obsolete Chance-Vought SB2U-3 dive bomber, the so-called Vindicator. The men who climbed aboard these planes that June knew they were probably doomed. They took to the air anyway. One of them was Capt. Dick Fleming.

Capt. Richard E. Fleming
Midway Island
June 4–5, 1942

Dick Fleming was afraid the war would pass him by.

The twenty-four-year-old dive bomber pilot with Marine Scout Bombing Squadron 241 (VMSB-241) had been on a training run with the carriers when the Japanese attacked Pearl Harbor on December 7, 1941. He spent the following months patrolling empty ocean around Midway Island, fretting that he had been consigned to the war's backwaters.

Born in Saint Paul, Minnesota, on November 2, 1917, Richard Eugene Fleming was the son of an English immigrant who had arrived in the United States in 1884 and risen to the vice presidency of a wholesale coal company. Both his father, Michael, and mother, Octavia, who had been born in Nebraska to French Canadian parents, were devout Catholics. Richard—everyone called him Dick—was their second son, preceded by Ward, who was a year older. A third son, James, was born five years after Richard.

Fleming was a good student and showed a stern sense of responsibility at an early age. He enrolled at St. Thomas Military Academy in 1931. Three years later he was promoted to captain of cadets, the school's highest student military rank. His 1935 yearbook entry described him as "the dashing and fiery captain of 'C' company. A debonair man-about-town. . . . His magnetic personality and merry wit make him welcome the school over by his classmates."[46] Active in a variety of school organizations, including the debate team and yearbook staff, he was also named president of the prestigious Tusculanum Club, made up of exceptional Latin students. Graduating cum laude in 1935, he enrolled at the University of Minnesota, where he majored in journalism and was chapter president of his fraternity, Delta Kappa Epsilon.

Somewhat curiously in light of later events, the young student developed a keen interest in Japanese art. He collected oriental pipes and struck up a warm relationship with a Japanese merchant in Saint Paul, recalled friends.[47] He was also a member of the Reserve Officers' Training Corps (ROTC), and toward the end of 1938, he queued up with about 200 other students for an interview with visiting Army Air Corps recruiting officers looking for potential flying cadets. His interest surprised his friends and family; he had never talked much about flying and had shown little interest in pursuing a military career.

Though doubtful of his chances, the tall, lanky youngster—he was six feet, two inches tall and weighed an unimpressive 140 pounds—was one of only nine applicants to pass the rigorous examinations. Returning home for the Christmas holidays, the normally levelheaded youth told his mother he might join the Army Air Corps as a flying cadet. He was considering quitting college in order to enlist. This sudden revelation took Octavia Fleming by surprise. Dick's older brother, Ward, was the one who had always talked about becoming a flyer. As for quitting school, she quickly disabused him of that possibility. Come what would, Dick was going to finish his last year of college, she told him firmly.[48]

In June 1939 Fleming graduated from the University of Minnesota with a bachelor's degree and a commission in the Army Reserve. In the meantime, he had learned that the Marine Corps had an aviation arm. He told his brother Ward he was thinking of becoming a Marine flyer. Ward pointed out that he was already in the Army Reserve; why didn't he just sign up for the Army's flying program?

"I've always wanted to be a Marine," said Fleming. "Did you know they were the original dive bombers, down in Haiti?"

"You've got an Army commission," reiterated Ward, unimpressed.

"I could resign," replied Fleming.[49]

And he did. Signing on as an aviation cadet after graduation in 1939, he began training at the Naval Reserve air base in Minneapolis. When not mastering the open cockpit trainers, the would-be falcon appears to have devoted himself to accumulating as much sack time as possible. "Gets his exercise swabbing out the head and fighting mice for possession of his bunk," commented the class scrapbook.[50]

Completing "Elimination Base" training, Fleming entered flight training at Pensacola in January 1940. Though he fell behind early and worried that he might flunk out, he rebounded and graduated on December 6, 1940. Opting for a commission in the Marine Corps, he was assigned to an SB2U-3 two-man bomber. Known as the "Vindicator," the slow and cumbersome craft, part metal and part fabric and already obsolete by the outbreak of the war, was derisively referred to by some pilots as the "Wind Indicator."[51]

Ten days after Pearl Harbor, Fleming led a flight of seventeen SB2U-3s from Oahu to Midway, a distance of 1,137 nautical miles. For the next six months, his squadron (VMSB-241) flew long patrols out of Midway, never making enemy contact. By now, he had been promoted to captain. VMSB-241 pilot 2nd Lt. Sumner H. Whitten recalled him fondly. "Captain Fleming was a laughing, slightly sardonic character, and had the only library or collection of books," he observed. "I can remember borrowing some of them—mostly modern classics. He was the squadron repository of all the dirty jokes, ribald songs, and always knew how to get recreational activity going."[52]

In letters home, Fleming chaffed at spending the war in the "backwaters."[53] Many of his letters went to Peggy Crooks, his longtime girlfriend back in Saint Paul. They met in a diner when they were teenagers, she a student at Summit School and he a high school student at St. Thomas. A serious relationship had blossomed. "I don't know what you would call it," she said of their relationship years later, "whether it was understood that we'd get married or whether we'd decide later."[54] In one of his letters to Peggy, written toward June 1942, Fleming wrote that he hoped she would go on with her life if something happened to him. "He must have been fairly certain about his chances," observed Jack Kolb, a retired Minnesota agronomist who spent years compiling material on Fleming's life. "He knew there were good odds that he wouldn't be coming home."[55]

Fleming's pessimism may have been due in some degree to the aircraft he piloted. Though the squadron received eighteen SBD-2 Dauntless dive bombers in late May, it also continued to fly its obsolete Vindicators. The SB2U-3 was only one of several types of U.S. aircraft that were hopelessly outclassed by the Japanese in the opening months of the war. The two-seater—manned by the pilot and a rear-seat gunner with a .30-caliber machine gun—was slow, difficult to maneuver in a dive, and generally a lousy bomber. Some of the Vindicators at Midway were so decrepit their fabric had been patched with wide bands of medical tape.[56] Whatever their dedication, the pilots could entertain few illusions about their chances if they ran up against the more sophisticated Japanese fighters.

That day was fast approaching. Even as Fleming endured seemingly endless patrols, the Japanese invasion force was steaming for Midway. Patrol planes spotted the enemy naval force on June 3, 1942, but initial attacks by land-based aircraft from Midway had little effect on the Japanese, now about 570 miles from the island. The following day, enemy planes pounded Midway, knocking out the command post and mess hall, damaging the powerhouse on Eastern Island, destroying the oil tanks on Sand Island, damaging the gasoline system, and setting the hospital and storehouses on fire.

Few men were killed on the ground, but Marine pilots who contested the raid in their aging Brewster F2A-3 Buffalo fighters were murdered in the air. Out of twenty Buffaloes and six Wildcats, seventeen failed to return, and seven others were severely damaged. So slim were their chances that an officer observed darkly of the pilots of the obsolete Buffaloes that they "were lost before leaving the ground."[57]

Fleming's opportunity for action arrived the morning of June 4 when dive bombers, torpedo planes, and even Flying Fortresses from Midway were ordered to attack an enemy carrier "bearing 325 degrees, distance 180 miles on course 135 degrees."[58] Piloting an SBD-2 Dauntless dive bomber, Fleming took up position on the wing of attack leader Maj. Lofton Henderson. His backseat gunner, twenty-four-year-old Cpl. Eugene Card of Oakland, California, was glad to be flying with calm and collected Fleming—the captain was so cool he had actually taken a nap during the hectic confusion preceding takeoff that morning.[59]

Shortly before 8 a.m., Fleming, serving as navigator for the sixteen dive bombers, suddenly broke in on the plane's intercom: "We've made contact. There's a ship at 10 o'clock."[60] Card looked down and spotted a long black ship on the water. Because the squadron had only received SBDs in late May and had no practical experience in dive-bombing tactics, Henderson decided to resort to the more familiar glide-bombing attack. While he may have had little choice, it was a poor decision as it left the formation far more vulnerable both to air attack and antiaircraft fire.

As the dive bombers moved into position with eleven of the old Vindicators trailing behind, enemy Zeros winged toward them. "Here they come!" Fleming shouted into the radio.[61] Card saw a fighter flash by their starboard wing. White smoke rings appeared as the Japanese guns hammered away. The wing of Henderson's dive bomber burst into flame. He fought to stay in the air but quickly lost control and plunged into the sea. Card saw fragments of another plane drifting down like leaves, then a parachute. Fleming flew on. "We got into a cloud and from a hole in it we spotted a carrier and started our dive," said Card.[62] Their target was the 17,300-ton *Hiryū* ("Flying Dragon"), a veteran of the Pearl Harbor attack, sporting a huge rising sun painted on her deck.[63] As they approached, Card became aware of a peculiar "wuf-wuf" sound as antiaircraft shells blossomed blackly around them.[64]

Jockeying through a hail of fire from enemy fighters and antiaircraft batteries, Fleming pressed his glide-bombing attack, machine-gunning an enemy gun crew as he descended to within a few hundred feet of the deck before finally releasing his bomb. His perseverance went unrewarded as the bomb missed close astern. To Card, facing rearward, the antiaircraft fire hitting the dive bomber sounded like "buckets of bolts" being thrown into the propeller. The plane lurched, and small punctures suddenly appeared all over the cockpit. Parts of the instrument panel disintegrated. Card took a spray of metal in his legs. Fleming suffered cuts to his arm as the compass shattered. "The captain told me later he was spitting glass and alcohol for five minutes," said Card.[65] As they raced away at wave-top height, it appeared to Card that "the whole side of the carrier was in flames." In fact, though the attackers bracketed the carrier with numerous near misses, *Hiryū* remained unscathed.[66]

Not so the dive bombers. Eight of the sixteen SBDs failed to return from the attack. It appeared that Fleming's SBD could well be number nine. "We may have to sniff our way home," he informed Card over the intercom, still unflappable, despite the loss of the compass.[67] Miraculously, they made it safely back. "For 15 miles three Jap Zero fighter planes pursued us, but gave up the chase near Midway," related Card. As they approached the airfield, a fire broke out on one side of the fuselage, but Fleming managed to bring them down, staying on the runway despite the flames and a flat left tire. "One whole side of our ship was ablaze when we landed," noted Card.[68]

Rolling to a stop, Fleming helped his wounded gunner out of the rear cockpit. "Boys, there is one ride I am glad is over," Fleming exclaimed in relief to the ground crews who ran out to help.[69] He shook hands with Card before the gunner was transported to the hospital, dismissing two minor wounds to his own arm as inconsequential. Mechanics later counted 179 holes in Fleming's dive bomber. Of the sixteen SBDs and eleven SB2Us that left that morning, eight SBDs and three SB2Us were lost. Only six SBDs and six SB2Us remained operational.[70]

Though land-based air attacks had been relatively ineffectual, U.S. carrier planes succeeded in knocking out four Japanese carriers during the day. Fleming, the cuts to his arm patched up, made another flight before day's end, searching without success for one of the crippled enemy carriers. He had managed to catch only four hours of sleep when the exhausted pilots were alerted yet again in the early morning hours. The Japanese were withdrawing.

At 6:30 a.m. the remaining dive bombers and SB2U-3 Vindicators of Fleming's squadron were ordered to attack "two enemy battleships, one damaged, bearing 268 degrees, distance 170 miles from Midway."[71] The "battleships" were actually the heavy cruisers *Mikuma* and *Mogami*, which had collided during the night. *Mogami*'s bow had been partially sheared off, and *Mikuma* was trailing a 30-mile-long oil slick, making the pair easy to track. With his Dauntless wrecked the day before, Fleming led a flight of six Vindicators. Replacing the injured Card as radio gunner was PFC George Albert Toms of St. David's, Pennsylvania. The tall, dark-haired nineteen-year-old, a country club golf caddy in more peaceful times, had been in the Navy just under a year.

Joined by six of the squadron's SBD-2s, they soon located the telltale oil slick and followed it to the two cruisers. The squadron's more modern SBDs went first, attacking *Mogami* at 8:05 a.m. The dive bombers bracketed the ship with their bombs and inflicted extensive topside damage but scored no direct hits. Three minutes later, Fleming led his six Vindicators against the 13,668-ton *Mikuma*. Approaching out of the sun in a long, slow glide from 4,000 feet, he came in over the cruiser's stern. Heavy antiaircraft fire from *Mikuma*'s impressive array of defensive weapons—including multiple 127mm, 25mm, and 13.2mm guns—blossomed around the approaching planes. Black smoke suddenly burst from the engine of Fleming's plane, followed by licking flames. As the fire spread, Fleming doggedly maintained his approach. At 500 feet, he finally released his bomb.

The 500-pound bomb apparently missed astern, but what happened next remains in some dispute. It is now generally agreed that the stricken Vindicator crashed in flames in the water alongside *Mikuma*. Eugene Card said he was told by squadron mates that Fleming's plane "hit the sea just off the bow of the target ship."[72] However, Capt. Leon Williamson, who was flying immediately behind and to Fleming's left, reported that the stricken SB2U-3 crashed into the cruiser. Williamson's account is supported by Capt. Akira Soji, commanding the *Mogami*, who said the plane crashed directly into *Mikuma*'s aft gun turret. "I saw a dive bomber dive into the last turret and start fires," he reportedly told interrogators after the war. "He was very brave."[73] Soji suggested the crash—if in fact there was a crash—was a "suicide" attack, but most Americans doubted that Fleming would intentionally crash into the cruiser. "He simply couldn't pull out of his dive," observed Jack Kolb.[74]

Wherever Fleming's plane actually crashed, it was the only aircraft lost in the attack. The remainder of the flight survived, though all also missed with their bombs. *Mikuma* remained afloat, but her respite would be measured in hours. She was finally finished off by U.S. carrier planes the next day.

Capt. Dick Fleming and PFC George Toms were declared missing on June 6. The designation was changed a year later to killed in action. "Fleming was a popular officer, a good pilot and flight leader," said VMSB-241's 2nd Lt. Sumner Whitten. "We all missed him."[75]

On November 24, 1942, Octavia Fleming traveled to Washington, DC, to accept her son's Medal of Honor from President Roosevelt. It was the only Medal of Honor presented for action in the battle of Midway, and Fleming was the first Marine Corps Reserve pilot to receive the honor in World War II. PFC Toms was awarded a posthumous Distinguished Flying Cross.

In 1943, the destroyer USS *Fleming* was named in honor of the gallant pilot. More than two decades later, in 1965, after being referred to for years by pilots as "Fleming Field," the airport in South St. Paul, Fleming's hometown, was officially named South St. Paul Municipal Airport/ Richard E. Fleming Field. Citizens of Saint Paul have made an effort to keep Fleming's memory alive. Exhibits have been mounted about his life, and in 1998 he was one of seven Minnesota aviators inducted into the Minnesota Aviation Hall of Fame. Every year the "Fleming Sabre" is ceremoniously awarded to an outstanding military student at St. Thomas Academy.

Peggy Crooks, "the girl back home," never married. "Once I knew a fellow like Dick, it wasn't easy to get seriously interested in another man," she confided to a friend years afterward. "I had dates with other men later on, on again and off again, most mostly off again." But neither would she characterize her life as a tragedy. "I was heartbroken for years," she admitted, "but it wore off and my life has had more than enough satisfactions."[76] After working more than forty years for Saint Paul's United Way, she died in the late 1990s, having outlived not only Richard Fleming but all the members of his family, including his two brothers.

Among the items she left for posterity was twenty-four-year-old Dick Fleming's last letter, dated May 30, 1942, which he left behind at Midway, to be mailed in the event of his death.

Dear Peggy,

I have had Dr. Forrester, our flight surgeon, hold this letter and package until he felt it should be sent. I had rather hoped to give it to you myself (the package, I mean), but it seems that other ideas prevented it.

I've had the wings over a year, but didn't send them because I wanted to get some changes made in them and then planned in my own quaint way, to pin them on myself. They're the promised exchange for the other ones sent last year.

Aside from that, Peggy darling, there's nothing to be said. Letters like this should not be morbid nor maudlin, and we'll let it suffice to say that I've been prepared for this rendezvous for some time. I hope that you will not entirely forget me, but I also hope that you don't let this cause you any lasting sorrow. You're the finest girl I ever knew . . . and I know that the future years hold much for you. This is something that comes once to all of us; we can only bow before it.

And so good-bye my darling, with the knowledge that despite the pains and crazy stunts of "growing up," we really had something. Always regard it as such and don't let any of it cause you sorrow.

All my Love,
Dick[77]

The failure of the MO Striking Force to carry out a landing at Port Moresby in May was a welcome development for U.S. Army Air Forces in the Southwest Pacific, which had found little cause for celebration since the war began. Resistance to the Japanese invasion of the Philippines had for all practical purposes ended in early April 1942 with the fall of Bataan, though Corregidor would hold out for another month. The survivors of the largest mass surrender in U.S. history were now entering a hell beyond belief at the hands of their captors. The remnants of some air units had escaped to Australia to regroup and continue the fight. Eventually those efforts would result in the organization of the Fifth Air Force, but for now the air war against the enemy had to be conducted largely on a shoestring. In August plans were hatched for the largest raid yet on Rabaul, which the Japanese were transforming into a major bastion to support offensive operations in New Guinea. By the standards soon to be seen in Europe, where bomber formations would number in the hundreds, the Rabaul operation was almost laughable. The strike would be carried out by approximately twenty B-17 Flying Fortresses. One of those heavy bombers would be piloted by a twenty-four-year-old from the White Mountains region of New Hampshire. His name was Harl Pease.

Capt. Harl Pease Jr.
Rabaul
August 6–7, 1942

At 11 p.m. on March 13, 1942, airmen at Del Monte Field—a rudimentary bomber strip carved out of a meadow at the Del Monte pineapple plantation on the southern end of the Philippine island of Mindanao—detected the sound of aircraft engines.

For weeks, the beleaguered Americans had been under near-constant attack during the daylight hours by enemy fighters and bombers as the Japanese tightened their grasp on the Philippines, but this particular aircraft, still invisible in the night, had been expected. Ground crews snapped on the landing lights, and the shadowy bulk of a B-17 Flying Fortress materialized out of the darkness, touched down on the dirt airstrip, and cut its engines.

Piloted by 1st Lt. Harl Pease Jr., a lanky twenty-four-year-old from Plymouth, New Hampshire, the B-17 had arrived on a special mission: to rescue Gen. Douglas MacArthur from the Japanese onslaught and transport him back to Australia. Pease's B-17 was one of four dispatched from Batchelor Field near Darwin to evacuate MacArthur, his family, and key staff, but the mission seemed jinxed from the start. One plane never got into the air due to engine trouble; another experienced mechanical difficulties and turned back after only 50 miles; the third, searching in vain for Del Monte Field, crashed into the water just offshore. Two crewmen died. Pease had continued on despite problems with his hydraulic system, which knocked out his superchargers and brakes. Touching down at Del Monte in the darkness, the lack of brakes forced him to ground-loop the big bomber to keep it on the airstrip.

Now Pease found it had all been for nothing. The general was not there. Evacuated from Corregidor by PT boat, he was not expected for another twelve hours. As far as Maj. Gen. William F. Sharp, senior commander on Mindanao, was concerned, that delay might have been providential. Pease's battered B-17 did not inspire confidence; nor was General Sharp reassured by the pilot's youthful appearance.

Pease was not inclined to argue. Despite his youthful demeanor, the New Hampshire native was considered one of the most capable pilots in the 19th Bomb Group, and he knew his enemy. With daylight, Japanese fighters were sure to put in an appearance, and Pease preferred not to be sitting helplessly on the ground when they arrived. With General Sharp's blessing, as dawn approached with no sign of MacArthur and his entourage, he loaded the bomber with sixteen stranded U.S. airmen eager to escape the Philippines, lifted off, and returned safely to Australia.[78]

And so Harl Pease missed his chance to go down in history as the savior of the great Gen. Douglas MacArthur. The general and his party would be successfully picked up by two other B-17s two days later. But, as it turned out, Pease would be granted another opportunity for fame—one he would follow through to a tragic conclusion.

By the time of the aborted MacArthur rescue, Harl Pease had been in the service just over two years, having signed on as an air cadet in September 1939, apparently looking for a little excitement. He came from a solid family. His father, Harl Sr., owned a successful automobile dealership; his mother was an organist in Plymouth's Congregational church. Several ancestors on his mother's side had fought in the American Revolution, which was a source of family pride.

Growing up in Plymouth, Harl was an outgoing boy with a reputation for being a bit of a prankster. He played trumpet in the high school band; a friend recalled one icy morning when young Harl flew down a hilly town street using his trumpet case as a sled. A good student, he was also athletic and played on the high school baseball and football teams. He loved to fish as well. Summers he spent working as a grease monkey in his father's car dealership where he was said to be "chief story-teller supreme."[79]

A college friend recalled Pease's aplomb—or perhaps it was his waggish humor—as a freshman at the University of New Hampshire at Durham. Freshmen were required to wear a green beanie at all times or face dire consequences from upper classmen. The classmate related how Harl, naked except for the required beanie, emerged from the shower area and unexpectedly encountered the female proctor charged with maintaining order in the building. Undaunted, Harl promptly swept off the ever-present beanie, covered himself as judiciously as possible, and has-tened back to his dorm room.

Pease threw himself into school activities, playing in the university band and participating in cross-country and winter track. He was a mem-ber of ROTC but was apparently not especially interested in a commis-sion as he opted out after two years. During his senior year he served as editor in chief of the school yearbook. Graduating in 1939 with a bach-elor's degree in business administration, he worked that summer for his father, but if his father hoped Harl would join him permanently, he was to be disappointed. His son had no intention of staying permanently in small-town Plymouth. Harl's avenue to the larger world was to enlist as a cadet in the Air Corps. He received his wings and was commissioned as a second lieutenant in June 1940 at Kelly Field in Texas. His mother and sister traveled to San Antonio to attend his graduation.

Pease was assigned to the 93rd Bombardment Squadron, 19th Bomb Group, piloting B-17s, then the state-of-the-art bomber in the American military. Developed during the 1930s as a strategic bomber to be used for precision, high-altitude daylight bombing, the four-engine, heav-ily armed B-17—aptly nicknamed the "Flying Fortress"—had a nearly 104-foot wingspan, a cruising speed of 182 mph, and a range of 2,000 miles with a 6,000-pound bomb load. It was typically crewed by ten men: pilot, copilot, navigator, bombardier, top turret gunner/engineer, radio operator, two waist gunners, a ball turret gunner, and tail gunner. Armament consisted of ten to eleven .50-caliber M2 Browning machine guns, including two in a top turret, two in a belly turret, two tail guns, two waist guns, and two forward-firing guns. Earlier models included another gun at the radio operator's station. It was originally anticipated that the heavily armed B-17 would be invulnerable to fighter attack, a preconception that proved sadly misplaced. Nevertheless, the big bomb-ers were far from helpless.

In October 1941, with war clouds gathering, Pease's bomb group was sent to the Philippines, assigned to Clark Field on Luzon, about 40 miles from Manila. The Japanese attack on December 8 caught many of the B-17s on the ground, but Pease's bomber apparently escaped destruction. Two days later he participated in one of the first bombing attacks of the war on the Japanese, a sortie against enemy forces on the northern tip of Luzon. Subsequent weeks were a hellish grind for the bomber crews as they tried to stem the Japanese onslaught. Attrition was severe. By the end of December, Pease's 19th Bomb Group had only eleven B-17s remaining. Twenty-two of the big bombers had been destroyed in only three weeks.[80] The survivors operated briefly out of the rudimentary Del Monte Field on Mindanao but were soon withdrawn to Australia.

Promoted to captain, Pease served as operations officer for the 93rd Squadron based at Mareeba in Far North Queensland but continued to fly missions. The outgoing New Englander was popular among the officers and men. "He had many friends," recalled a fellow pilot. "They were drawn to him by the warmth of his personality."[81] In June he and his crew members each received the Distinguished Flying Cross for their effort to rescue General MacArthur in March, but by now attention was increasingly focused on Rabaul, which was being transformed by the Japanese into a fortress and major base of operations.

Allied bombers had been conducting periodic raids on Rabaul for months, but the mission planned for August 7 was to be the biggest yet, an effort to disrupt Japanese operations while the First Marine Division landed on Guadalcanal in the Solomon Islands, just over 650 statute miles southeast. The hope was to send twenty B-17s—a substantial number, considering the limited resources in those days—but in the end only sixteen were deemed operational. The bombers left Mareeba in North Queensland, Australia, on the night of August 6, bound for Port Moresby, where they would refuel before departing early the next morning for the 500-mile flight to Rabaul.

Pease's copilot was twenty-year-old F/Sgt. Frederick W. Earp of Penrith, New South Wales, one of a number of Australians who had been integrated into the various bomber crews. The remainder of his regular crew consisted of bombardier 1st Lt. Robert B. ("Bruce") Burleson of Hamilton, Alabama; engineer S/Sgt. Rex E. Matson of Elletsville, Indiana; radioman Sgt. Alvar A. Liimatainen of Marquette, Michigan; navigator 2nd Lt. Richard M. Wood of Tulsa, Oklahoma; gunners Sgt. David W. Brown of Childress, Texas, and Sgt. Chester M. Czechowski of

Chicago, Illinois; and Sgt. Fred W. Oettel of Los Angeles, California, as crew sergeant.

Though a regular member of Pease's crew, Liimatainen was a last-minute addition for the Rabaul mission. Temporarily hospitalized, the twenty-two-year-old former hotel bellhop had been replaced on the roster by Pvt. Edmond Troccia, a former college student from Poughkeepsie, New York. However, as the truck was bringing the crew out to the plane, Liimatainen ran out on the field and waved them down. He insisted he could make the flight, so Troccia was moved over to another aircraft, and Liimatainen took his usual place at the radio.

It soon appeared Liimatainen could have stayed in the hospital. Their B-17E was scarcely an hour from New Guinea when one of the engines failed. Knowing that repair facilities at Port Moresby were rudimentary, they turned back to the airfield at Mareeba on the three remaining engines. Pease could have honorably stood down at that point, but he was unwilling to give up that easily. His friend and fellow pilot Ed Jacquet noted later that Pease, whom he described as "very energetic and dedicated to winning the war," had done all the planning and briefing for this big mission.[82] He did not intend to be left behind if he could avoid it.

Scouring the field at Mareeba, Pease found there was only one other B-17 available. It was flyable but had been removed from combat service after aborting several missions due to electrical problems and underperforming engines. The orphan had no official name, but some wag had scrawled under the pilot's window "Why Don't We Do This More Often"—a title B-17E #41-2429 was destined to carry into the history books. In an odd twist, this same B-17 was one of three that had participated in the successful rescue of General MacArthur from Mindanao on March 17 following Pease's failed attempt.

Requisitioning the bomber, Pease and the crew took off again for the three-hour flight to New Guinea, finally arriving at Seven Mile Strip at Port Moresby at about 1 a.m. There Pease encountered the 93rd Squadron's engineering officer, Lt. Vincent Snyder. All too familiar with the multitude of mechanical issues plaguing *Why Don't We Do This More Often*, Snyder "raised hell in no uncertain terms" over the idea of taking the aircraft to Rabaul.[83] Pease's arguments were not strengthened by the fact that an electric fuel pump had already failed on the tired B-17. The crew had to borrow a manual pump from another bomber. Undaunted, Pease appealed to squadron commander Maj. Felix Hardison. Over Snyder's objections, Hardison agreed to let him go on the mission.[84]

Snyder urged Hardison to at least assign Pease and his trouble-prone aircraft to a spot inside the formation where he would have more protection should things go bad. Again he was turned down. The slots had already been determined, and the planes were parked in their assigned positions. Pease ended up as "tail end Charlie" in the right wing position of the three-plane element led by Capt. Edward M. Jacquet. Rather than a more protected position as Snyder had suggested, *Why Don't We Do This More Often* would occupy one of the most vulnerable spots in the formation.[85]

At 7:30 a.m. the first B-17s began to lift into the air for the long flight to Rabaul. Sixteen quickly became fifteen as *The Queen of the Skies*, suffering a runaway supercharger, went out of control. Lt. R. B. Gooch, the bombardier, recalled, "Our B-17E, carrying a full load, veered off the runway and crashed into a rock pile. The plane was a total wreck, but all the crew escaped with only a minor injury to our navigator's leg. The bombs were torn from their shackles, but fortunately none detonated."[86]

Gooch's good pal, 1st Lt. Bruce Burleson, ran over to check on his friend. "After seeing I was all right," recalled Gooch, "he said, as only Bruce Burleson could say it, 'Gooch, you have used up all your luck.'" With that, Burleson climbed back aboard Pease's plane and took off into the night, leaving Gooch behind.[87] As it turned out, Gooch's plane wasn't the only casualty that night: two other B-17s aborted soon after, one with engine trouble and the other due to electrical failure, but *Why Don't We Do This More Often* wasn't one of them.

Some three hours later, at about 11:45 a.m., the thirteen remaining B-17s began to close on Rabaul at 22,500 feet. Skies were clear. The target was Vunakanau airdrome, the former Australian airfield situated on a plateau just outside Rabaul township. Recent reconnaissance photos had revealed as many as 150 bombers and fighters at the airfield, possibly in transit to the new airfield the Japanese were building on Guadalcanal. The B-17s approached in a "V of Vs," with Jacquet's three-plane element to the right and slightly above Major Hardison's element. Pease maintained position on the outside just off Jacquet's starboard wing.

In an effort to avoid detection, the bomber crews had maintained radio silence throughout the flight, but Japanese radar was good out to 90 miles, and numerous observation posts and listening stations had been positioned to give warning of approaching aircraft. The first Japanese fighters—over two dozen in all—arrived on the scene shortly after the B-17s opened their bomb bay doors still some fifteen minutes from the drop point. No B-17s were downed, but as the formation pressed on over Rabaul's spacious Simpson Harbor, dozens of antiaircraft batteries from ships and from shore positions laced the sky with flak. A 20mm shell smashed into Lt. Vince Snyder's *Queenie*, knocking out the oxygen system. Snyder pressed on, maintaining formation despite increasing lightheadedness from lack of oxygen.

The formation remained intact during the bomb run over the enemy airdrome, but Japanese fighters stepped up their attacks as the B-17s turned toward home. At the point of the arrowhead formation, Maj. Richard H. ("Dick") Carmichael's *Suzy-Q* was hit by enemy fire that killed one of his side gunners, wounded another, and knocked out his oxygen system. Carmichael radioed Hardison on the command radio that he had to reduce his altitude and quickly put *Suzy-Q* into a dive. Hardison followed, as did Snyder in *Queenie*, which had its own oxygen problems. The hasty descent by the lead B-17s broke up the previously tight formation as the Zeros pressed their attack.

Flying to Pease's left in *Tojo's Jinx*, Capt. Ed Jacquet had already lost one gunner killed and another wounded to the Zeros. Now he noticed that Pease had feathered the prop on one of his inboard engines and was falling behind. "We hollered and screamed for the formation to slow down to protect Harl," he said later. "We broke silence on our radios but of course they were very unreliable radios. Later the other pilots said they never heard us."[88]

Watching from another B-17, Maj. John D. Bridges saw Pease's bomber descend about 1,000 feet with the left inboard engine out. Japanese fighters swarmed over the crippled aircraft. Flames suddenly erupted from the bomb bay as the auxiliary fuel tank caught fire. The 400-gallon tanks were needed to make the long flight to and from the target area. Major Carmichael later observed that Pease's plane had an older-model auxiliary tank that lacked a self-sealing liner. "I guess nobody knew it, maybe he didn't pay much attention to it, or at least he didn't change it. We had to have a bomb-bay tank to get to Rabaul and back. So I think that's what did him in on the way back. He was hit and caught afire."[89]

Bridges saw the flaming auxiliary tank fall from the bomb bay, but the bomber was doomed. Manning a waist gun aboard *Queenie*, Ed Troccia, who had been bumped from Pease's crew when Liimatainen showed up from the hospital, witnessed what appeared to be the plane's final moments. "The Zeros swarmed all over him and I saw him going down with both inboard engines on fire," he reported. Losing sight of the crippled B-17, Bridges called out over the interphone to his turret gunner, "Where's Pease? What happened to Pease?" The gunner was too busy fending off enemy fighters to respond.[90]

Twenty minutes after releasing their bombs, the twelve remaining B-17s ducked into cloud cover and started the long return to Port Moresby. Reports to 19th Group Headquarters optimistically claimed heavy damage to Vunakanau airdrome and the destruction of six or seven of the Zeros that had attacked the formation. In fact, there was little damage to the airfield, and no Zeros had been lost. The reports indicated that Pease's bomber had gone down in flames, and the entire crew was presumed to have perished though no one had actually seen the plane crash.

Learning of Pease's dogged insistence on accompanying the mission and his apparent death in action, Maj. Gen. George C. Kenney, who had arrived in theater to take command of the soon-to-be-designated Fifth Air Force, set the wheels in motion to recommend him for the Medal of Honor. Kenney confided to his diary that Pease probably "had no business in the show," but he felt his sacrifice deserved recognition.[91] Bessie and Harl Pease Sr. accepted their son's medal from President Roosevelt at the White House on November 4, 1942. The other crew members of the missing B-17 were awarded posthumous Distinguished Service Crosses.

Unbeknownst to those writing his epitaph, Harl Pease had survived. After falling from formation apparently enveloped in flames, *Why Don't We Do This More Often* had somehow remained airborne, finally crashing by the Powell River 40 nautical miles south of Rabaul. At some point during that flight, Pease, tail gunner Chester Czechowski, and a third crewman had parachuted into the jungle.

A belated indication that Pease had survived surfaced on February 9, 1943, when a Japanese radio broadcast monitored by the Australian Broadcast Company referenced the capture of a Captain Peace (*sic*) shot down during an air attack.[92] No further information was forthcoming. Neither Pease nor any other member of his crew was officially reported by the Japanese as a prisoner of war; nor did any of them emerge from captivity when the war ended three years after their plane went missing.

In late June 1946, ten months after the Japanese surrender, a search party from American Graves Registration Services looking into reported crash sites on New Britain found wreckage by the Powell River south of Rabaul. The wreck turned out to be the missing *Why Don't We Do This More Often*. A large section of the fuselage lay in the river. In the cockpit section, which had come to rest some distance away, searchers recovered two complete sets of remains, some coins, and a diamond ring. With the help of dental charts, the remains were eventually identified as copilot Frederick Earp and radioman Alvar Liimatainen. Natives reported that three more bodies had been seen lying alongside the wreckage immediately after the crash but were apparently later washed away by the river.

Members of the 604th Quartermaster Graves Registration Company revisited the crash site in December 1948. They questioned a native who said he had witnessed the crash and seen a parachute descending before the plane exploded. He showed the team where the parachute had come down, and the investigators found scattered human remains, a billfold, two shoes, and a trinket with a crown on it. They could not identify the remains, but circumstances suggested that whoever it was had been killed during his descent or succumbed to wounds shortly afterward.

Harl Pease was not found, and the details of his fate would not emerge for some forty years. In the 1980s, author John H. Mitchell, who had long been interested in the actions of the 19th Bomb Group, was contacted by an elderly priest, Father George W. Lepping. Father Lepping had seen an article by Mitchell in a flight magazine published by Air Niugini, based in Papua New Guinea, and thought the writer/historian might be interested in his experiences as a prisoner on Rabaul during the war—most specifically in his information about Harl Pease.

A Catholic missionary ordained in 1938, Father Lepping had arrived at the prison camp on Rabaul on September 7, 1942, after the Japanese took a number of civilian residents into custody. Among the military prisoners already there were Pease and his tail gunner, twenty-four-year-old Chester Czechowski, who had been brought into camp around August 10. "I remember Captain Pease had been wounded, the Japanese pilots who shot down his B-17 had machine gunned the crew as they were parachuting down and Captain Pease had taken a bullet through the calf of his leg," recalled Lepping. When Pease asked for medical attention, the Japanese laughed and replied, "We don't treat American airmen!"[93] Fortunately, one of the civilian prisoners had retained some medical supplies and treated the wound daily until Pease was able to walk again.

According to Lepping, Pease was widely respected, even by the Japanese guards who seemed somewhat in awe of him as the captain of one of the vaunted B-17s, which they called "Boeings." The younger guards would ask Pease in broken English, "You, you, ah Captain Boeing?" whereupon Pease would draw himself up proudly and reply to his admirers, "Me, me, Captain Boeing."[94]

Still irrepressible despite his situation, Pease was full of stories about his experiences in the Philippines and in Java, recalled Lepping. Pease told how the air crews would stow warm beer in their planes so that it would chill at high altitudes, allowing them to enjoy cold brew when they returned to base. He mischievously came up with names for the various Japanese guards, including one he called "Tanglefoot" for his odd way of walking and another nicknamed "Brains" since he apparently didn't have any.[95]

But on the morning of October 8, Father Lepping recalled, Pease, Czechowski, two other captured airmen from a downed B-26, and two Australian Coastwatchers were handed picks and shovels and told they were being transferred to another camp to work on a new airfield. Some of the other prisoners gave them a few articles of spare clothing, and the six were ushered away. Later in the afternoon, the Japanese returned with the picks and shovels and gave back the items of clothing the others had provided. "We never saw the six men again," said Lepping, but the implications were obvious to all.[96]

Details of their fate were later provided by WO Minoru Yoshimura, a platoon leader in the 81st Naval Garrison Unit. He testified that the six military prisoners, along with two native prisoners, were brought to an area near Rabaul's volcanic Tavurvur crater. A number of officers watched as the prisoners, blindfolded and with their hand tied behind their backs, were lined up by a large pit that had been prepared by native laborers. Yoshimura said he was surprised to see an Army medical officer arrive on a motorcycle with an attached sidecar.

Yoshimura ordered the naval guards to bayonet the prisoners, but the sailors made a bad job of it. The two natives and one of the white prisoners collapsed into the hole, but the others fell to the ground writhing in agony. At this point the medical officer stepped forward. "I asked him what he was going to do," recalled Yoshimura. "He did not reply, but laughed and produced some medical instruments." The doctor cut the jugular vein of one of the prisoners, then opened the man's abdomen and extracted "some dark-looking object," presumably his liver, which he handed to his NCO. He then repeated the process on another prisoner "who was still alive and writhing on the ground." The whole process took five or six minutes. Taking the extracted body parts, the medical officer and his driver climbed onto their motorcycle and left. The bodies were shoved into the hole, and Yoshimura stabbed each one in the throat to ensure there were no survivors.[97]

The remains of Harl Pease and Chester Czechowski were never recovered. Harl Pease Sr. died in 1964, followed by wife Bessie ten years later. The last member of the family, Harl Jr.'s sister Charlotte, never married. She passed away in 1982 and was buried in the Pease family lot at Trinity Churchyard in Holderness, New Hampshire. The lot includes an impressive memorial to her brother, who was also honored in 1957 when the Portsmouth Air Force Base in his home state was renamed Pease Air Force Base. The base was closed in 1991, but part of the site remains in operation as Pease Air National Guard Base.

Harl's parents and sister never knew what actually happened to him. "In a way it was good Harl's parents didn't know the terrible ending that he had," said Harl's cousin Fay Benton in 2009. "I don't think they could have taken it."[98]

4

Cactus

THE ATTACK ON RABAUL BY HARL PEASE'S BOMB SQUADRON COINCIDED with the landing of the U.S. First Marine Division on Guadalcanal. The war in the Pacific was pretty much all about airfields; the Japanese were building one on Guadalcanal, and the United States wanted it. With little opposition from the Japanese garrison—which consisted mostly of labor troops—the landing was successful but soon came under intense pressure from enemy naval forces. U.S. naval support was forced to retire, and the Japanese began landing reinforcements to eradicate the beachhead. On August 20, nineteen U.S. Wildcats and twelve Dauntless dive bombers touched down on the former Japanese airfield—now renamed Henderson Field in honor of Maj. Lofton Henderson, the Marine squadron commander shot down at Midway—and an intense struggle began for control of the air over the island. Whoever owned the air controlled the sea lanes and the influx of reinforcements and supplies. For the next two months, while Marine infantry battled repeated Japanese ground assaults on the airfield perimeter, Marine pilots fought for control of the skies. Conditions were primitive, food scarce, the supply of gasoline a constant worry. They were short of everything except guts.

Maj. John L. Smith
Solomon Islands
August–September 1942

John Lucian Smith had planned to become an accountant. Fate decided that his balance sheet would consist of other men's lives.

Born the day after Christmas 1914 in Lexington, Oklahoma, Smith was the youngest of three sons of a rural mail carrier. Located about 40 miles south of Oklahoma City, in 1940 Lexington had a population of only 1,084. Young Smith, known to friends as "Johnny," attended public schools and played football in high school. Originally aspiring to a career in business, he enrolled at the University of Oklahoma, where he majored in accounting. He graduated in 1936 with a bachelor's degree in business administration and passed Oklahoma's certified public accountant examination, but as it turned out, a business career was not in the books.

Like so many other students on a tight budget, Smith had joined the Reserve Officers' Training Corps (ROTC) to supplement his college tuition. After graduation, he was commissioned as a second lieutenant in the field artillery. After a brief stint at Fort Sam Houston in Texas, he resigned his Army commission in order to join the Marines. Appointed second lieutenant on July 1, 1936, he served two years with the artillery before testing for naval aviation school. He began flight training at Pensacola in July 1938, earned his wings, and subsequently served at bases in Guantánamo Bay, Hawaii, and San Diego.

While stationed in Virginia, Smith met twenty-one-year-old Louise Maddox Outland, the daughter of a prosperous insurance company executive with family roots dating back to the American Revolution. A graduate of the College of William and Mary with a master's degree in English literature from Old Dominion University, Louise was working as a public school teacher. "She was not only a very well-educated woman," family members later observed, "but she also possessed a sharp mind and loved to converse about all things, whether it be Jane Austen novels, the United States Constitution, genealogy, historical events, or matters of the day."[1] She and Smith were married in Norfolk, Virginia, on June 21, 1940.

Smith was "a more quiet type than his peers," remarked an acquaintance, "a large sinewy man with a thick neck on square shoulders [and] the steadiest eyes I have ever seen."[2] Just before the Battle of Midway, now a captain, he was selected to lead the newly created Marine Fighter Squadron 223 (VMF-223) in Hawaii. Described by one of his pilots as "an ambitious, no-nonsense officer,"[3] he arrived with a reputation as a top-notch tactician. Pilots found him to be somewhat moody, a tough disciplinarian who pushed relentless training as he prepared his inexperienced squadron for what lay ahead. Pilot Joe Foss, who would go on to become the top Marine Corps ace of the war and was as gregarious as Smith was taciturn, recalled him as "a self-contained guy more or less." While he admired and respected Smith for his abilities—he had "the right stuff"—he also struck Foss as "really a deadpuss" who seemed unable or unwilling to adopt a familiar way with his peers. Even when he smiled—which according to Foss was a rare event—it seemed forced. "Smitty, he was really all business," observed Foss.[4]

"It was peculiar how he was usually called by his full name, like J. Edgar Hoover, although some of us called him 'Smitty,'" remarked Marion Carl, who flew with Smith at Guadalcanal. "But whatever anybody called the C.O., or whatever they thought of him, one thing became certain: John L. Smith may have had his faults, but combat leadership was not among them." Years later, Carl, another top ace of vast experience, would rate Smith as "perhaps the strongest squadron commander and finest combat leader I had ever known."[5]

The First Marine Division was hanging on by its fingernails when Smith's squadron—the first American air support to arrive—landed on primitive Henderson Field on August 20. Smith's nineteen F4F-4 Grumman Wildcats and the accompanying squadron of twelve Douglas SBD Dauntlesses flew in from the escort carrier USS *Long Island* 200 miles offshore. The F4F-4s were a step up from the F4F-3s lost at Wake, having six .50-caliber M2 Browning machine guns in the wings as opposed to four. The air support was desperately needed, a fact impressed on Smith when a bedraggled infantry sergeant approached him, saluted smartly, and blurted, "Christ, Captain, we're sure glad to see you. The guys sure have been prayin' for this day."[6]

The squadron's first aerial combat occurred just after noon the next day when Smith, leading a routine patrol of four Wildcats, bumped into six Japanese Zeros near Savo Island just north of Guadalcanal. Neither he nor the other three Americans had ever seen a Zero before, but Smith immediately recognized them for what they were. The Wildcats were at 14,000 feet. The enemy fighters were 500 feet higher and on a reciprocal heading. Though the Japanese had the advantage of altitude, Smith didn't hesitate. "Pick your target and attack," he radioed. "All right, boys, let's get 'em."[7]

Climbing quickly, the Marine pilots met the Zeros head-on. Smith fired on the lead Zero as they closed in a deadly game of chicken. Smith's mouth had gone dry, and his heart was pounding, but he concentrated his attention on the enemy. The Japanese pilot broke off first. As the Zero pulled up, Smith sent a burst into its blue-green underside. Before he could follow up, two Zeros latched onto his tail. He dove away and was lucky to escape with only a few bullet holes in his Wildcat. The Zero pilot he had fired on was less fortunate. Mortally hit, the Zero crashed into the water just off Savo Island. The victory, Smith's first, was also the first American air-to-air kill of the Guadalcanal campaign, but Smith nearly didn't live to celebrate. Joining up with two of his F4F-4s, he went after a group of five Zeros. The Japanese shot them up so badly that the two other pilots had to make deadstick landings on Henderson Field. Smith got his Wildcat down in one piece, but it took mechanics days to make it flyable again.[8]

Five days later Smith shot down two bombers in a melee over Henderson Field involving sixteen twin-engine Bettys and an estimated fifteen Zeros. Exhausting his ammunition in firing on the second bomber, he closed in to look it over and saw that the gunner in the top turret was apparently dead. He could not see a pilot in the front compartment. There seemed to be no one at the controls as the aircraft, smoking heavily, descended in a long glide toward the sea. It appeared that everyone was dead or incapacitated with the exception of the tail gunner, who was frantically trying to get out of the glassed-in rear compartment. He did not succeed. Continuing its glide, the plane finally slammed into the sea.[9]

Smith shot down two more Bettys over Henderson on August 29 during a Japanese raid conducted by eighteen bombers escorted by twenty-two Zeros. Other pilots knocked down a bomber and five Zeros, though the Japanese managed to hit the field hard, destroying two Wildcats on the ground and "causing sizeable loss to aviation material."[10] The squadron had been in combat just nine days and had already lost six of the original nineteen fighters.

The next day, August 30, the squadron spent a muggy morning waiting on standby. The pilots remained on alert until thirty minutes after dawn, but no Japanese aircraft showed up. As the sun rose over the air-field, the pilots retreated to the Japanese-built operations shack—known as the "Pagoda"—to kill time playing cards while awaiting developments. Finally, around 11:30 a.m. the phone rang in the operations shack. Coast-watchers had spotted a large flight of Japanese bombers and Zeros head-ing toward Henderson Field from Rabaul. Dropping their cards, the pilots scrambled for their planes.

Eight Wildcats and seven Army P-400 Airacobras took off at 11:45 a.m. to await the enemy formation. The Wildcats settled in at 15,000 feet, while the P-400s, lacking the oxygen systems and an efficient supercharger necessary for higher altitudes, waited below. Introduced just before the war, the P-400 Airacobra, with its engine located just behind the pilot, was the export version of the P-39. The short wings gave the plane poor climb performance; it was virtually a duck at anything over medium altitude. Armament was also poor, consisting of a 20mm cannon and two .30-caliber machine guns in the wings. It was not a good match for a Zero at any altitude.

The first indication of trouble came about forty minutes after takeoff when a frantic voice broke in on Smith's radio. "Zeros on us! Jumping us! We're just north of the field!"[11] It was one of the P-400 pilots. Scan-ning the sky north of the field, Smith saw the Zeros tearing into the Airacobras. Two parachutes were visible. Four of the Army fighters were shot down in a matter of minutes. The others ran for the airstrip, where friendly antiaircraft fire might give them a chance of survival.

Smith and his wingman were already on their way into the fracas, rac-ing toward twenty-two black-and-brown-painted Zeros 3,000 feet below. The enemy pilots were making about 230 knots, banking slowly to the left, apparently oblivious to the danger from above. Smith slid in behind a flight of four enemy fighters. As he closed to 700 feet and the nearest plane's wingspan filled his fixed gunsight, he pressed the trigger button. Chunks of metal hurtled off into space followed by a sudden flash as the Zero burst into flame. Trailing black smoke, the doomed plane winged over slowly and plunged toward the ground. "The first one never knew what hit him," recalled Smith.[12] Plumes of smoke marked the demise of other Zeros as Smith's fel-low Wildcats also took a toll on the surprised enemy. The survivors scattered.

Joined by three other F4F-4s, Smith began a slow climb, searching for the enemy. He noticed a small dot emerging from a cloud at his ten o'clock. The dot resolved itself into a Zero. Smith gunned his Wildcat after the enemy pilot, who made a futile effort to climb away. Seconds later Smith was within range, and he pressed his gun button. Pieces began to tear away from the fleeing Zero as the heavy slugs chopped through thin aluminum. The cowling broke free, part of it hitting Smith's canopy. Flames flickered on the enemy plane as the pilot desperately tried to evade. Smith gave him another burst, and the Zero exploded. In less than five minutes, Smith had knocked down two Japanese planes.

There was more to come as Smith and the other Wildcats scouted to the north, then turned back toward Henderson Field. "In a few minutes a third [Zero] came climbing up under the belly of my Wildcat," recalled Smith. "He was sewing bullets up and down the fuselage. I dropped the nose of my plane and came at him head on. One of his bullets shattered my windshield, but missed me. By this time my .50-caliber slugs were tearing great chunks off his plane. I could see pieces dropping all over the place."[13]

Smith's burst of .50-caliber shattered the Zero's propeller and motor and lit up the enemy plane like a torch. He caught a quick glimpse of the Japanese airman as the burning plane hurtled by. "We tore past each other less than 15 feet apart." The enemy pilot was slumped over the controls, his hair in flames. "I suppose it was one of those days when nothing you do is wrong," said Smith. "He blew some holes in my windshield, but that was my lucky day, I guess."[14]

Short on gas and ammo, Smith descended through the clouds, leveling out at 800 feet. Two aircraft came into view to his left. Thinking one might be his wingman, Smith closed to within 500 feet of the pair and realized they were Zeros. The Japanese pilots hadn't seen him. "I sat back at 50 feet, with my nose practically on the second one's tail, sending tracers into his wing tanks and cockpit," recalled Smith. As Smith's guns went dry, the Japanese pilot pulled straight up, then nosed over into a dive and crashed into a field near the beach below. "It wasn't even a fight," remarked Smith. The second enemy pilot "looked back, then climbed his Zero like an express elevator" and fled for home.[15]

Landing at Henderson Field, Smith pushed open his canopy. "How many?" one of his ground crew called up to him over the engine noise. With a wide smile, Smith held up four fingers to the cheering crews.[16] He landed without a cartridge in his belts, having shot down four enemy planes in about a quarter of an hour. With a total of nine kills, he was now the leading Marine Corps ace. "He's a quiet, modest man," wrote a news correspondent as Smith's fame spread. "He wears a red baseball cap and has to be urged before he'll tell much about what he has done."[17]

By mid-September Smith had racked up a dozen victories, leading squadron mate Lt. Marion Carl, who had eleven. The official tally for the squadron was twenty-eight. But Smith was more than just a hot-shot fighter pilot: he was a thinker, carefully assimilating and refining the tactics that would allow his hard-pressed squadron to most efficiently counter the Japanese air assault on the Guadalcanal beachhead—to best approach the fast-moving, well-armed Betty bombers, deal with the agile Zeros, and survive to do it again and again and again.

He admitted he had been scared when he first encountered the "redoubtable Zeros."[18] Experience convinced him the Zero was not invincible and tempered his fears but not his caution. "The Japanese are excellent fighters," he explained. They flew good planes. Their weakness was that they "lack the proper thinking process to analyze a situation, then attack or run, whichever seems most intelligent," he observed. "They plunge into any fight, often losing planes and pilots unnecessarily." By contrast, the American pilots were more practical about the odds. "We have to hit and run, knocking out as many planes as we can at the first onslaught, then getting away. It isn't smart to dogfight with the Zeros since they can maneuver faster."[19]

Civilians back home reveled in the exploits of the fighter pilots, but the terse language of the squadron's war diary paints a grimmer portrait of the life-and-death struggle in the skies over Guadalcanal:

September 5: "Major Morrell, Lieutenants McLennan, Jeans, Pond, Ramlo, Frazier, Hughes and Reed took off on alert, attacked 26 twin engine enemy bombers and an estimated 20 Zero fighters. Major Morrell and Lt. Pond each shot down one enemy bomber. Lt. Pond had his own engine shot up by a Zero fighter and was forced to land dead stick with a slight bullet graze in his left arm. Major Morrell received shrapnel wounds in both legs from a 20mm explosive shell fired from a Zero fighter and although badly wounded and with his engine running poorly and spraying oil into his cockpit he brought his plane back to a safe landing on the field. He was taken to the Division Field Hospital."

September 9: "Attacked 26 twin engine bombers and an estimated 20 Zero fighters. Lt.s. Trowbridge and Canfield each shot down a bomber, and Lt. Kendrick shot down a bomber and a Zero. Captain Carl . . . is missing in action. Lt. Winter . . . crash landed on the field with no aileron control and ran into a parked SBD-3 causing damage to his plane, engine and propeller. Lt. Canfield . . . was attacked by Zeros after making his runs on the bombers. He was forced down to an altitude of 20 feet with a Zero on his tail firing at him. He managed to avoid serious damage until close by a friendly destroyer when his engine froze up and stopped. He crash landed in the water and manned his rubber boat until the destroyer picked him up. . . . His plane sank within 30 seconds and is permanently lost."

September 13: "Scattered force of 15 Zero fighters were contacted. Major Smith and Lt. Phillips each shot down one Zero. Lt. McLennan missing in action. Lt. Haring killed in action. . . . Plane Bu. No. 03501 manned by Lt. Phillips badly shot up. Pilot uninjured."[20]

On the afternoon of October 2, Smith became a victim himself when his flight was surprised by Japanese fighters pouncing out of the sun. Smith was engrossed in shooting up a Zero in front of him, when two others slipped onto his tail and riddled his Wildcat. Aircrews listening to radio traffic back on Guadalcanal heard one of the Marine pilots call out to Smith, "John, you've got a Zero on your tail!"

"I know, I know," Smith exclaimed. "Shoot the SOB if you can!"[21] Then the radio went silent.

The Zero in front of Smith's Wildcat started down.[22] Then his own damaged engine quit. As the aircraft lost altitude, Smith managed a dead-stick landing in a rough jungle clearing some four to six miles southeast of Henderson Field. Escaping injury, he climbed out of the plane and made his way into the trees as other Wildcats circled protectively overhead. As he started back toward Henderson field, he saw another fighter crash into a ridge just to the east, one of six Wildcats lost that afternoon. Pushing through the dense jungle, Smith made his way across the Tenaru River without encountering any Japanese patrols. He finally reached the American perimeter that evening, meeting up with a Marine patrol that had been sent out to look for him. "It was just like taking a hike," he remarked with studied nonchalance.[23] The Marines later sent out a patrol to recover Smith's trademark red baseball cap and destroy the crashed Wildcat.

By October 3, Smith's squadron had suffered six killed in action. Others were ill or had been wounded. Only nine of the original eighteen pilots remained, and they were feeling the strain. "The lines around Smith's eyes tightened and his eyes became hard," observed a news correspondent.[24] It appeared that VMF-223 was headed for extinction. But the process was already getting underway to relieve the battered squadron. On October 16, the handful of survivors left Guadalcanal. The squadron claimed 111.5 kills, including 51 Zeros and an equal number of bombers.[25]

A major now, Smith left Guadalcanal as the Marine Corps's leading ace with nineteen victories. News correspondents celebrated him as "the hottest pilot in the Solomons." Back in the States, he and several other Marine aces went on tour to help sell war bonds, attending a dizzying round of rallies and public receptions. His photograph appeared on the cover of *LIFE* magazine on December 7, 1942, and he found himself hailed as a national hero. If any of this went to his head, it didn't show. "I haven't done anything more than others have done and are doing every day," he protested. "That's all there is to it." A news reporter found the hero to be "a tall and tired young man who isn't particularly impressed by the exploits of Major John L. Smith."[26]

Not quite four months later, on February 24, 1943, accompanied by wife Louise, John Smith received the Medal of Honor in a ceremony in President Franklin D. Roosevelt's office in Washington, DC. His citation was not for a single act but for his leadership and accomplishments during August and September 1942, when his squadron played a crucial role in keeping Guadalcanal in American hands. "Repeatedly risking his life in aggressive and daring attacks, Major Smith led his squadron against a determined force, greatly superior in numbers, personally shooting down 16 Japanese planes between 21 August and 15 September, 1942," noted his citation. "In spite of the limited combat experience of many of the pilots in his squadron, they achieved the notable record of a total of 83 enemy aircraft destroyed in this period, mainly attributable to the thorough training under Major Smith and to his intrepid and inspiring leadership."[27]

Visiting his hometown, the hero was greeted with a grand celebration and presented with a $100 watch. But his thoughts seemed far from Lexington. "He has that faraway look in his eyes . . . and seems anxious to get back and start out again," remarked a family acquaintance.[28]

Smith did want to return to combat, but his abilities as an instructor and organizer were considered too valuable to risk. "Not until you have trained 150 John Smiths," he was told.[29] Promoted to lieutenant colonel, he went overseas again in 1944 as executive officer of Marine Air Group 32 in the Philippines, but he never again saw air-to-air combat. With nineteen victories at Guadalcanal, he finished as the sixth ranking Marine Corps ace of World War II.

Smith stayed in the Marines after the war, serving mostly in staff positions. He and Louise had four children. "Based on his previous record, everyone figured he would easily make brigadier general," observed Marion Carl. "Unfortunately, while at Marine Corps Headquarters, he alienated some of the ground officers." He paid the price when he was passed over for promotion. "He was a proud type and getting passed over hit him pretty hard," noted Carl, who eventually became a major general. "His career in the Marine Corps was effectively over."[30]

The onetime fighter pilot retired as a full colonel in 1961. He moved to Encino, California, and took a job as an executive in the aerospace industry. Laid off from his position as director of foreign sales with Rocketdyne, Smith found that no one would hire him because of his age. Despondent, he walked into his backyard on June 9, 1972, and shot himself.

A spokesman for the Los Angeles City Council expressed the widespread shock and dismay over the war hero's suicide. "I think it is a sad commentary on our society that someone who has reached the age of 57 is no longer useful to us and simply ought to be pushed off to a garbage heap," he observed in a statement from the council.[31]

Colonel Smith is buried in Arlington National Cemetery. Twenty-seven years after his death, on December 3, 1998, a monument was dedicated to the heroic pilot in his hometown of Lexington, Oklahoma, population now 2,086. "It's a neat monument," observed a member of the town's park advisory board. "We're real proud of it. We're proud of him, too."[32]

Maj. Robert E. Galer
Solomon Islands
August–September 1942

Robert Galer's boyhood friends used to say he was blessed with luck—the sort of guy who was born with a rabbit's foot in every pocket. They may have been right: few pilots could have survived being shot down as many times as Bob Galer.

Born October 23, 1913, in Seattle, Washington, Robert Edward Galer came from a long-established local family. His father, Fred, was a captain in the Seattle Fire Department—a street near a local fire station is named in his honor. His mother, Mary, was a slight, cheerful woman familiarly known around the neighborhood as "Mame." Bob earned a reputation as a standout athlete while attending Queen Anne High School, where classmates nicknamed him "Bubble Eyes." Despite the implications, there was nothing wrong with his eyesight. Standing five feet, ten inches tall and weighing in at about 155 pounds, he set record scores on the all-city basketball teams. He also played football, baseball, tennis, and track and joined the Boy Scouts and the YMCA.[33]

Galer continued his athletic glory at the University of Washington as an outstanding forward on the basketball team. In 1934 he set a new scoring record with 176 points. Now known to his teammates as "Goose," he captained the team in 1935 and was All-Coast in 1934 and 1935. Galer enrolled in the Naval Reserve Officers Training Corps (NROTC) at the university and was president of the Compass & Chart, the NROTC honorary society. In addition to all the rest, he held down various jobs to pay his college tuition.

But Galer's driving ambition was to fly. Two years before graduation, he was already infatuated with airplanes. "I don't know where he got the bug," remarked his college basketball coach, "but he sure was crazy to fly. The only time I ever saw him ruffled or upset was when he got his teeth banged up in a game. He wanted to know if it would hurt his chance of passing the physical for the Navy."[34]

In 1935 Galer graduated with a degree in industrial engineering. The following January he headed to Pensacola as an aviation cadet. "All I thought then was that it might be fun to take a plane up occasionally," he explained; "nobody was talking about a war." He earned his wings and accepted a commission in the Marine Corps because he liked the Marine officer in charge of his training program. He was promoted to first lieutenant in July 1939 and to captain in March 1941. He couldn't have been happier. "The thing was, I liked flying, and if you like flying you don't think too much about what's coming tomorrow," he observed.[35]

As war approached, Galer was flying fighters with Marine Fighter Squadron 211 (VMF-211), later to become the famed "Lost Squadron of Wake." But once again Galer's famous luck held good. To his great disappointment, when much of the squadron, including Henry Elrod, went to Wake, he was ordered to stay behind on Oahu. "They had just discovered I was the only spare landing signals officer in the Pacific," he recalled.[36] As a result of being qualified to direct planes landing on aircraft carriers, he escaped the fate of his squadron when Wake fell to the Japanese.

Present for the Japanese attack on Pearl Harbor on December 7, he never got into the air. "We didn't have one operational airplane, and we were running around like chickens with their heads cut off," he recalled. Someone handed him a rifle and pointed him toward what he described as a half-finished swimming pool. "There was a hole, and there were about a dozen Marines in there. We'd shoot volleys at the strafers going by." It was like shooting popguns in a carnival gallery, he admitted, but "what else could you do?" Galer had never given the Japanese much thought, but Pearl Harbor changed everything. "Every man I knew wanted to get a shot at the bastards," he declared.[37]

Promoted to major and given command of Marine Fighter Squadron 224 (VMF-224), Galer led his squadron onto Henderson Field on August 30, 1942. The Wildcat pilots landed in the middle of an alert, which was an indication of what little respite they would have in coming weeks. Japanese planes threatened from the air. Japanese naval forces threatened from the sea. Japanese infantry continued to battle tenaciously for Henderson Field on the ground. "My squadron spent one night on the runway with our .45s drawn in case they broke through the lines," he recalled. "They were that close."[38] Japanese warships and aircraft bombarded the field by night. "In fact, right next to each of our tents we had slit trenches," remembered Galer. "I was next to mine one night, and they dropped a 500-pound bomb just the other side of it. It blew away the tent, but it didn't break the mosquito netting on my cot."[39]

Galer scored his squadron's first victories on the afternoon of September 2, knocking down a Betty bomber. "I saw it coming and dived for it [in] what we call an 'overhead' pass," he recalled. "It burst into flames and dropped into the water. But a Zero had me bore-sighted and riddled my fighter." Galer knew his Wildcat was finished, but he hoped to stay in the air long enough to get some revenge. "So I headed into a cloud and instead of coming out below as the Jap expected, I came out on top and let him have it. Then we both fell—but he was in flames." Galer managed to get his Wildcat—*Barbara Jane*, named in honor of a college sweetheart—down in a field and walked away.[40] Back in the air, he knocked down another Zero on September 5.

Six days later, Galer's flight tangled with another bunch of enemy bombers. Galer knocked one of them out of the sky and set out after a Zero. "But I didn't pull around fast enough, and his guns knocked out my engine, setting it on fire." At 5,000 feet, Galer laid the Wildcat on its back and dived for some clouds. "Coming through the clouds, I didn't see any more Japs, and leveled off at 2,000 feet," he recalled. "I set down in the drink some 200 or 300 yards from shore and swam in, unhurt."[41]

Shot down twice in a matter of days, Galer—described by a visiting news correspondent as "a likeable young man with brown hair, brown eyes, and an agreeable smile"[42]—remained unfazed. His attitude impressed Joe Foss. Galer, he recalled, was "a little guy. I'd say he weighed about 140 pounds or so, and moved like a piece of greased lightning." Perhaps more importantly, observed Foss, "he had the right attitude."[43] Part of Galer's charm was his wry, somewhat self-deprecating sense of humor. Asked once what happened to his plane after he survived a crash landing in the water, he observed blandly, "Well, that was *Barbara Jane* and she couldn't swim."[44]

On October 2, Galer was shot down again—for the third time in three weeks—again bailing out over the water after knocking down two Zeros in a melee with a mixed force of Japanese bombers and fighters. This time, cruising at about 20,000 to 25,000 feet, he and six other Wildcats were jumped by eighteen Zeros from out of the sun. As they scattered, Galer heard slugs punching into his aircraft, "but none stopped me."[45]

He and 2nd Lt. Dean Hartley went after a cluster of seven Zeros hovering above. "In about four minutes, I shot down two Zeros and Hartley got a possible," recalled Galer. "The other four were just too many and we were both shot down." Hartley horsed his plane to a field, but Galer couldn't make it. "The Jap that got me really had me bore-sighted," he recalled. "He raked my ship from wingtip to wingtip. He blasted the rudder bar right from under my foot. My cockpit was so perforated it's a miracle that I escaped. The blast drove the rivets from the pedal into my leg."[46]

Galer pancaked into the water near Florida Island and managed to clamber out of the aircraft. "You didn't parachute because they'd shoot you down," he said.[47] But water landings had their own perils. "When you land in the water, it feels like you've just hit a brick wall," he remarked.[48] It took him an hour and a half to swim ashore. "I worried not only about the Japs but about the tide turning against me, and sharks," he recalled. Finally reaching shore, Galer, pistol in hand, encountered four natives armed with machetes and spears. The confrontation ended happily as one of the natives announced in broken English, "Me Christian! Me friendly! Me Charlie!" They took him to their village, then escorted him to a Marine camp on a beach about five miles away.[49]

Back at Henderson Field, Galer got a new Wildcat, painted *Barbara Jane* on it, "put a St. Chris in [his] helmet," and went up again.[50]

"Our F4F was an excellent airplane, very tough," he observed. "It would absorb a lot of punishment. The Japanese Zero could outperform it, but couldn't take the punishment. If you got some ammunition into a Zero, it would usually explode."[51] Even those Zeros that didn't go down right away were probably doomed. "The odds were that if you put holes in them at all, their making it back all the way to their base was very problematical."[52]

Despite the home advantage, Guadalcanal was no cakewalk. Normal routine pitted four or six fighters against as many as two dozen bombers. "They kept coming," Galer said of the Japanese air effort to neutralize Henderson Field. "It was a very tough couple of months."[53]

By the end of the Solomon Islands campaign, Galer had officially shot down a total of 11.5 enemy planes—though his unofficial tally was reportedly 27—in a period of only twenty-nine days. "Everybody says, 'How in the hell did you shoot down half an airplane?'" chuckled Galer. "That really means that my wingman and I both shot at the same airplane [that went down]."[54] His squadron was credited with downing seventeen Zeros, thirty-four bombers, and nine seaplanes. Six of VMF-224's pilots were killed in action.

A correspondent later asked Galer how a pilot feels in the chaos of air combat. "I think it's a combination of everything," replied Galer thoughtfully. "You're hot and cold at the same time—just plain scared, I guess. You realize that to hurry is fatal. And then your training calms you down. You do it just like you were taught, just like you've done it hundreds of times in practice. That sick feeling every pilot knows just before engaging in combat disappears as he mixes with the enemy."[55]

Adm. Chester Nimitz awarded Galer the Navy Cross during a visit to the Solomons in the Fall of 1942. On the recommendation of the Secretary of the Navy, the decoration was upgraded to the Medal of Honor. President Franklin D. Roosevelt presented Galer with the medal on March 24, 1943, in recognition of his personal combat performance and his daring and aggressive leadership against superior enemy forces. Galer's mother, an ardent Democrat and avid Roosevelt fan in a family of Republicans, was probably more excited than her son, he admitted later. She attended the ceremony in Washington and met the president, which "made her day," laughed Galer. "When she went back to Seattle, she was a real celebrity for a couple of days."[56]

Promoted to lieutenant colonel in 1944, Galer was assigned to help organize radar teams and figure out how the technology could assist with close air support and with guiding aircraft back to base. The idea was to keep him out of danger. Instead he ended up on the beach at Iwo Jima on the afternoon of the landing, February 19, 1945. "We got to about the high tide [line] and dug a hole in the sand. That's as far as we got the first day," he recalled.[57] Galer survived thirty-five days on Iwo Jima; then the radar team went to the Philippines and later still to Okinawa to provide forward air control.

Galer stayed in the Marine Corps after World War II and again flew in combat in the Korean War. On August 5, 1952, he lost the fifth plane of his career when his Corsair was shot down by North Korean antiaircraft fire 100 miles behind enemy lines. "I did a dumb thing," he told a reporter years later. "We were bombing, and when we finished, I went back to take a picture. And this anti-aircraft gun, he nailed me."[58]

As he bailed out of the crippled Corsair, his foot caught in a cockpit strap, leaving him dangling head down as the plane hurtled toward earth. Somehow he freed his foot, but as he fell he struck the Corsair's rear stabilizer, banging up his left shoulder and breaking several ribs. His parachute opened 150 feet from the ground. "I floated down through the smoke of the crash and landed within 10 feet of the wreckage," he recalled. "The plane was burning and some of the ammo was exploding. While getting out of my chute I heard small arms fire, but I don't know what they were shooting at."[59]

Galer ran through a cornfield and followed a dry streambed to higher ground. Breathing was difficult, and his left arm was practically useless. He saw several men creeping up on the wreckage and heard voices as people, including three men with rifles, searched for him. The legendary Galer luck held firm. He sent out a call for help on his portable radio and took shelter in a cave. An hour later a Navy helicopter appeared over a low ridge. Galer made it into the dangling sling on the fourth pass and was pulled aboard. En route home, the helicopter was hit by antiaircraft fire three times, once so hard that it momentarily spun out of control, but they made it. Four hours after being shot down, Galer stepped onto the deck of a ship off the east coast of Korea.

Bob Galer retired from the Marine Corps in 1957 as a brigadier general and went to work for Ling-Temco-Vought as general manager of the aeronautical and missile division. He and his first wife had two sons but later divorced. Galer subsequently worked as a real estate broker and appraiser and for LaCreme Coffee and American Cold Storage commercial warehouses in Texas, where he and his second wife made their home. He also served on several museum boards. His oldest son, Robert T. ("Tip") Galer, also became a flyer, eventually retiring from the Air Force with the rank of colonel.

Bob Galer died June 27, 2005, at the University of Texas Southwestern Medical Center in Dallas, two days after suffering a stroke. His ashes were interred in the Texas State Cemetery in Austin. Son Robert (fondly described by Galer as a "smart aleck") used to joke that his father had been shot down so many times he qualified as an enemy ace.[60] Galer himself frequently observed he was "the luckiest old Marine around."[61] Or maybe it was more than just luck. In later years, the man they said was born with a rabbit's foot in every pocket attributed his success—and his survival—to a higher power. "I've been shot up and shot down four times," observed the aging fighter pilot. "God always had someone there to help."[62]

Lt. Col. Harold W. Bauer
Guadalcanal
May 10–November 14, 1942

Joe Bauer first earned fame on the football field, playing for Navy. Though a big man, he didn't rely on size to carry the day on the gridiron; he used his brains. "They say he was always breaking out into the open by doing the unexpected, but what seemed improvised on the spot had been charted and planned long before," remarked an acquaintance.[63]

It was a gift that would serve him well in the skies over the Pacific.

Born in Woodruff, Kansas, on November 20, 1908, Harold William Bauer was the third child of John and Martha Bauer, both Volga Germans who had emigrated from Russia. John Bauer worked for the

Chicago, Burlington, and Quincy Railroad as a stationmaster. He and Martha instilled in their five children a strong work ethic and an appreciation of the value of a good education. All three Bauer boys would go on to attend the Naval Academy; the two girls graduated from the University of Nebraska.

Due to John Bauer's job as a stationmaster, the family moved around a lot in the early years, often living above the station itself in whatever town they landed in. The end of World War I found them in their first real house in Alma, Nebraska, where the oldest children attended high school. Harold and his brother Dale gained recognition as star athletes, playing both football and basketball. Harold was also a top-notch student, accumulating 29 A's and three B's during his years at Alma High. That academic record and his athletic abilities earned him an appointment to the Naval Academy in 1926. Taking note of his dark complexion and prominent cheekbones, his classmates promptly dubbed him "Indian Joe"—a misnomer encouraged by Bauer himself, who delighted in telling people he was part Indian. The name stuck, and from then on Bauer was known to all as "Joe."[64]

Bauer joined the boxing and track teams at the academy. He also played football. "I didn't know what football was until I started the season here," he wrote home. "It sure is a big, bad, rough game. I twisted an ankle, two knees, a neck and captured a charley-horse. But I'm still going strong."[65] As a sophomore, in a game broadcast on nationwide radio, he broke a 6–6 tie against Penn State when he caught a pass and carried the ball the length of the field for a touchdown. Academically, in his senior year he ranked 135th in a graduating class of 405.

Graduating from the Naval Academy in 1930, Bauer took a commission in the Marine Corps, mostly because he thought there would be more opportunity to play football. He was right. He coached outstanding teams at Quantico, then joined the coaching staff for the basketball and lacrosse teams at the Naval Academy before assignment to the San Diego Naval Base. While at San Diego, he met nineteen-year-old Harriette Hemman, who had come to California from Texas with her mother in hopes of becoming a movie actress. She and Bauer were married on December 1, 1932. Their son, William Dale, was born in 1936.[66]

Meanwhile, Bauer had traded athletics for aviation. He reported to the naval air station at Pensacola for flight training in December 1934 and received his wings in February 1936. By the time war broke out, the former football star, now a captain and squadron executive officer, had already earned a reputation as an outstanding pilot. "Before the war he used to do some funny flying in target practice, and he put so many shots into the sleeve that nobody could believe it," recalled Maj. Ross Jordan, who had been involved in the training program. "They suspected he was using extra ammunition, but when they gave his ammunition a close check, they found he was still getting the same results. After that, they were willing to listen to what he said about gunnery."[67]

With the outbreak of war, it appeared that Bauer's career as a fighter pilot was likely to be brief. Smoke was still rising over Pearl Harbor when his squadron, Marine Fighter Squadron 221, set out aboard the USS *Saratoga* to reinforce beleaguered Wake Island. Convinced that the mission was a veritable death sentence, Bauer wrote a "last" letter to Harriette telling her how much he loved her and urging her to move on with her life. "You have been the most wonderful wife a man could ask for," he assured her.[68]

To the squadron's good fortune, the Wake mission was canceled. Promoted to major, Bauer was named to command Marine Fighter Squadron 212 (VMF-212). In May the squadron was sent to New Caledonia and then to Efate in the New Hebrides. Bauer's duties there consisted of training flyers and developing airfields. His men referred to him as "Coach," a tribute to his former coaching days, his frequent pep talks to the younger men, his advanced age (he was thirty-four), and his constant emphasis on aerial tactics.[69]

A news correspondent later described Bauer as "a tall two hundred-pounder with the quick, alert ways of a little man" and a cheerful, upbeat personality. A terrific flyer and intensely competitive, Bauer practiced dogfighting with his men, offering a dollar to any pilot who could get on his tail. He emphasized taking the initiative: "Always be aggressive; never hang back; get hold of the other fellow in the air and never let go of him until he's dead or gone," recalled one of his pilots who had come out on the short end of an in-air tutorial.[70]

It was Bauer's contention that the highly maneuverable but unarmored Zero was vulnerable if the heavily armored Wildcat ignored acrobatics and just kept turning into an opponent head-on. "A Zero can't take two seconds' fire from a Grumman and a Grumman can take sometimes as high as fifteen minutes' fire from a Zero," explained the wing's assistant operations officer, Maj. Joseph N. Renner.[71] Lt. Jefferson DeBlanc recalled Bauer's exhortation about dealing with the legendary Zero: "Dogfight them, for they are paper kites," declared the colonel.[72]

Bauer focused especially on gunnery, teaching the beam, the highside, and—above all—the overhead pass. "Either Bauer invented the overhead pass or else he was the first to show what really could be done with it," recalled Maj. Ross Jordan.[73] This difficult-to-counter maneuver consisted of approaching the enemy plane from superior altitude and an opposite course, then rolling inverted above the target to pull down vertically into the attack. It was especially deadly against the Japanese Betty as it negated the effectiveness of the 20mm gun in the bomber's tail.

No martinet, Bauer had a sense of fun and was popular with the enlisted men. One of his sergeants recalled finding a couple of ancient tuxedos on Efate. He and a buddy prankishly buttoned them on and were headed down the road to get some laughs at the mess hall when they spotted Bauer striding toward them. The sergeant figured they were in for a tongue lashing, but as Bauer came abreast, he merely glanced at them, remarked, "Good evening, men," and proceeded on his way as if it were the most normal thing in the world to encounter a couple of Marines wearing tuxedos in the jungle. "He was quite a man," observed the sergeant.[74]

With the American seizure of Henderson Field in August, Bauer's responsibilities at Efate evolved into an important support role, supplying planes and replacement pilots for the defense of Guadalcanal only 680 nautical miles to the north. But what Bauer really wanted was combat. Expanding on his support role duties and recently promoted to lieutenant colonel, he fastened on any excuse to drop in on Henderson Field, where the action was. On his first visit on September 28 to "clear up a few administrative problems," he was hanging around at Henderson chatting with Bob Galer and some other officers—looking at the sky "like a wild duck with a clipped wing," one recalled—when the air alarm went off.[75] Bauer wrote later he had already "talked them into giving [him] a plane for any air raid that might materialize." He ran to the waiting plane and took off with the others for his first air-to-air combat. He later remarked that rising to do battle with the enemy felt like the old days on the athletic field, waiting for the kickoff.[76]

Picking out a Japanese twin-engine bomber, Bauer gave it a burst and set it on fire. He continued to follow the plane as it descended, shooting all the way, until it slammed into the side of a mountain. "He just got up there to Guadalcanal, popped into a plane, shot down a Jap, landed, and grabbed a transport plane back to Efate," recalled Galer's exec, Maj. Frederick R. Payne. "It was a real Bauer stunt, a sort of game, a sort of joke, and I'll bet he was grinning all the way back to the New Hebrides."[77]

That wasn't far from the truth. "We shot down 23 bombers and 1 Zero," Bauer noted in his diary. "I got credit for one Jap bomber. Am going to return in a couple days and try to increase said total. . . . It was the greatest sight of my life to see the Jap bombers fall out of the sky like flies."[78]

Receiving permission to bring four pilots a week to Guadalcanal for combat experience, Bauer's next opportunity came on October 3 when Coastwatchers reported a large flight of Japanese bombers headed for Henderson Field. Bauer was not supposed to be in the air, but there was no denying him. "We got 3 in the first pass," he exulted in his diary.[79]

Bauer smoked a Zero, then climbed and knocked down a second. With five of his six guns refusing to operate, he suddenly found the rest of his flight had disappeared, "leaving me to play with the Zeros all by myself." Undeterred, the Coach went after a trio of Zeros with his remaining gun. One fled, and Bauer shot down the other two. "I definitely shot down four and might have got more," he exulted.

Retreating to the clouds, he was attempting to clear his guns when he noticed a parachute floating down toward the water. "Suddenly a Zero came out of nowhere and opened up with a very long burst on the parachute," he said later. "This infuriated me." Still with only one operable gun, Bauer charged after the Zero. "I know I got several hits on him and chased him away smoking," Bauer noted in his diary. "I'm positive he didn't get his plane back to his base. I returned to the field nearly out of gas—jumped in another plane and went back to locate the parachutist for rescue." The downed aviator, twenty-two-year-old Capt. Ken Frazier, survived to be picked up by an American destroyer.[80]

Bauer's four kills on October 3 elevated him to ace. In his excitement, upon landing back at the "Fighter One" airstrip, he clambered out of the cockpit still wearing his parachute instead of leaving it in the plane as was standard procedure. "We were terribly happy because of what he'd done, but we couldn't help laughing a little to see him so excited," recalled a member of the ground crew. "He didn't think he was. In fact, he explained to us that he was as calm as he'd ever been in his life." At that point another mechanic remarked that the colonel had landed with his high-altitude supercharger on, as well as the auxiliary fuel pump—both of which should have been cut off under 15,000 feet. The result was an engine fire that had to be put out with fire extinguishers. "The Coach didn't excuse himself. He just laughed about it," recalled the mechanic.[81]

Less than two weeks later, on October 16, Bauer left Efate to take up permanent residence at Guadalcanal, charged with synchronizing fighter operations. The new job was likely to keep him more or less ground bound. But first he had to land. As the VMF-212 pilots, low on fuel, came into Guadalcanal's Fighter One airstrip at about 5:30 p.m., nine Japanese dive bombers materialized over the anchorage off Lunga Point and scored a hit on the USS *McFarland*, which was loaded with gasoline and munitions for the air squadrons at Henderson.

Waiting to land, Bauer saw smoke and flame rising into the sky over the anchorage. Ignoring his nearly empty gas tanks, he turned away from the airstrip and raced alone toward the Japanese formation, which was now winging away from the *McFarland*. A two-seat, single-engine, carrier-based dive bomber, the Val could carry a 550-pound bomb under the fuselage and smaller bombs under the wings. Two 7.7mm machine guns were mounted over the engine with another 7.7mm manned by the rear-seat gunner. It had a top speed of 270 mph but was poorly armored and lacked self-sealing gas tanks.

In what seemed like only seconds, Bauer sent four of the Vals plunging into the water in flames. Watching from a hill overlooking the anchorage,

Assistant Operations Officer Joe Renner saw Bauer down three of the dive bombers in quick succession. "They were so determined to get away at full throttle that they were just right down over the water going as fast as they could," recalled Renner. "He came right behind them and let them have it. One would blow up; he'd jump over its wreckage and get the next one. He shot down four that day. He said he probably could have got all nine, but he had just come up from Espiritu Santo and was a little short on gasoline. He was afraid to chase them any farther for fear he couldn't get back."[82]

Clambering out of his Wildcat at the airstrip, adrenalin still pumping, Bauer excitedly called to Lt. Clair Chamberlain, the first pilot he saw, "Chamberlain, where the hell were you? There was the table all set, and enough for two of us! The least you could have done was count 'em for me!"[83] One of Bauer's men recalled, "After a fight he was always a little crazy with excitement. I never saw a man who loved a fight the way he did."[84]

Over the next weeks, the Marine pilots were heavily engaged. Bauer did his job and stayed on the ground, organizing air strikes and overseeing operations. "As flight director of VMF-212, Bauer was one of the top strategists in determining which squadron would be on scramble alert, who would give air ground support, and who would carry out search missions," recalled Capt. Joe Foss. "We all worshipped him. 'Put me on the team, Coach,' pilots would plead when they wanted to go on a strike."[85]

Bauer's main criterion was pilot aggressiveness. He wanted fighters. Pilot Marion Carl thought bachelors tended to be more willing to mix it up with the enemy, but Bauer was a notable exception. "Joe Bauer was a husband and a father and he was as aggressive as they come," admitted Carl.[86] A hard-charger himself, Bauer expected his pilots to get in there and fight no matter what—no excuses. "There was still a theory that in the air a pilot should only fight when he saw some advantage, but the colonel said that anything that wore a red dot on it was enemy and must be fought with," recalled 2nd Lt. Charles M. ("Mel") Freeman.

He well remembered Bauer's displeasure one day when some pilots—including Freeman himself—found themselves out of position in an encounter with a group of Zeros and failed to engage. "He was so mad he was boiling." As he stalked out through the ready room, he didn't say a word to anyone except to toss over his shoulder, "If you boys don't want to fight, I'm going to start weeding you out and sending you home." Freeman felt sick about what had happened. "His opinion meant more to me than any medal the president could pin on me," he admitted.[87]

While adhering to his administrative duties, Bauer chaffed at being stuck on the ground. Finally, on November 14, as VMF-212 began to rotate home, he scheduled himself to lead a fighter escort accompanying an afternoon dive bomber/torpedo plane strike on Japanese transport ships. Also flying the mission was Capt. Joe Foss. "He said I wasn't going to get all the fun alone, so we all took off," observed Foss.[88]

Upon arriving at the target area some 15 or 20 miles north of the Russell Islands, they found several damaged enemy transports dead in the water and smoking. Some ships had heaved to in order to pick up survivors. There were no enemy aircraft in view, so the Marine fighters circled lazily overhead as the bombers and torpedo planes conducted their attack. The fighters concluded the mission by dropping down to strafe the enemy vessels. As they finally turned for home, Foss was startled to see tracers zipping over his canopy. He swiveled his head to find two Zeros closing in. Bauer immediately "just put that plane on its tail," recalled Foss, and headed straight for one of the Zeros. "Both he and the Jap were shooting everything. Then—bang! And the Zero blew up."[89]

Foss and another pilot chased the second Zero but couldn't catch him. They returned to the scene of the first shoot-down, but Bauer's Wildcat was nowhere to be seen. Foss spotted an oil slick about a mile from where the Zero had gone into the drink. He circled and saw Bauer swimming with his life jacket on. Foss buzzed down for a closer look, and Bauer waved him toward home. "He was in good shape—no visible cuts," recalled Foss. "I tried to give him my life raft, but it wouldn't come out, so I gave full throttle and flew toward home."[90]

Back at the field, Foss rounded up an amphibious aircraft, but takeoff was delayed by the arrival of some fuel-starved bombers. The amphibian finally got airborne and headed out after Bauer, but darkness was already closing in. "By the time we got to where the enemy fleet was, it was pitch dark. Absolutely black," recalled Foss.[91] They had no choice but to abort.

At daybreak the next morning, they were out again with a flight of aircraft and the amphibian. They came across two Japanese planes, which they promptly shot down, but there was no sign of Bauer.

The pilots held out hope the Coach had made it to Baraku Island about ten miles away, but four days of intense searching by planes and Russell Islands natives failed to locate any trace of the missing flyer. "We searched the area but no sign of a soul," wrote Foss soon afterward. "So in my way of thinking one of the following two things happened—either the Japs happened upon him and took him prisoner or the sharks got him." Any remaining hope evaporated when the war ended and no Joe Bauer emerged from Japanese custody.[92]

Wartime records credit Bauer with eleven victories (revised lists credit him with ten). He was decorated posthumously with the Medal of Honor for his actions on October 16 when he ignored his nearly dry gas tanks to single-handedly shoot down four Japanese bombers attacking the *McFarland*. The award was approved in 1943, but Harriette Bauer deferred an invitation to come to the White House and receive the decoration from President Roosevelt. "No, save it for Joe, he'll pick it up in person," she insisted.[93]

Bauer's ten-year-old son, accompanied by Harriette, finally accepted the medal on behalf of his father from Gen. Field Harris in a ceremony at Naval Air Station Miramar in San Diego on May 11, 1946. William D. Bauer was destined to follow in his father's footsteps as a Marine aviator, becoming a colonel and commanding, among other units, VMF-212, in a distinguished career that included duty in Vietnam. The Medal of Honor awarded to his father is currently on display at the air museum in Quantico, Virginia.

Soon after Joe Bauer disappeared, Joe Foss wrote to Harriette Bauer about the circumstances of that last flight. "To me, Marine Corps Aviation's greatest loss in this war is that of Joe," he concluded. "He really had a way all his own of getting a tough job done efficiently and speedily, and was admired by all, from the lowest private to the highest general. . . . I am hoping that someday Joe will come back—I'll never lose hope, knowing Joe as I did."[94]

Unfortunately, that was not to be. But Joe Bauer left a legacy of leadership to be emulated by generations of Marine pilots yet to take to the air—including, as it turned out, his own son.

Capt. Joseph J. Foss
Guadalcanal
October 9–November 19, 1942

Joe Foss once said he couldn't remember a time when he didn't want to fly. As a boy, he used to watch the open-cockpit Lockheed Vega mail plane drone low overhead on its regular route past his family's South Dakota farmhouse and wonder what it would be like to be free of the ground. He intended one day to find out.

For a less tenacious individual, becoming a pilot would have remained an unrealistic dream. Born on April 17, 1915, Joseph Jacob Foss was one of three children of Mary and Ole Frank Foss, who eked out a living on the family farm near Canton, South Dakota. There were few amenities for the Foss clan, which claimed Norwegian-Scottish ancestry. "We lived as simple as you could get," recalled Foss. "When it was 40 degrees below zero outside, it was 40 degrees below zero inside where we slept."[95] As late as 1943, the farmhouse lacked electricity.

Joe, who stood six feet tall and weighed 175 pounds, spent his after-school hours pumping gas and working on cars at the local service station in an effort to make ends meet. He took odd jobs with other farmers in the area and later worked as a butcher in a supermarket and as a laborer in a packing house. Somehow he also found time to blow baritone sax in the Washington High School Band, though he admitted he didn't play very well due to severe bouts of stage fright.

He took his first airplane flight in the Spring of 1931, paying $1.50 for a ride in an all-metal Ford trimotor. The experience was everything he had hoped for and more. "Now I knew I had to become a pilot," he recalled years later.[96] Five years after that first flight, Foss made his way to the Sioux Falls airport to inquire about flying lessons. The cost for lessons was $64—exactly the amount he had made in an entire month working at the gas station. Foss never hesitated. The next day he returned to the airport and paid the money. Several lessons later, he soloed.

A month before Joe's eighteenth birthday, Ole Foss was killed when he got out of his car during a storm and came into contact with a downed power line on the roadway. Joe already knew that farming was not for him, but his father's death put even greater financial pressure on the family. Graduating from high school, he attended a Lutheran college in Sioux Falls but had to take time off to help with the farm. He subsequently enrolled at the University of South Dakota, mainly because the school offered a government flying course. He worked his way through school waiting tables, washing dishes, sweeping the floor at a fraternity house, and working as a janitor. He joined the National Guard, primarily to get some extra money, but found he enjoyed the drilling and the discipline. Another turning point came during Foss's junior year when his roommate left to join the Marine Corps. Some months later, the newly minted Marine came home on leave, and Foss saw him in his uniform. At that point, he later said, "I knew it was the Corps for me!"[97]

In February of his senior year, Foss hitchhiked 300 miles to Minneapolis, the location of the nearest Marine Corps recruiting station. He already had his pilot's license, and the Marine Corps agreed to accept him for flight school. Graduating from the University of South Dakota in June 1940 with a degree in business administration, Foss immediately reported for duty at World Chamberlain Field in Minnesota. On March 15, 1941, after seven months of training, he was commissioned as a second lieutenant in the Marine Corps.

Foss proved to be a natural pilot—in fact, he proved to be a natural *fighter* pilot. An ophthalmologist later discovered the blue-eyed ex–farm boy had 20/10 vision, which meant he could see the detail at 20 feet that most people saw at 10. But Foss was about to endure a lengthy bout of frustration. To his profound disgust, he was assigned to duty as a flight instructor. His dissatisfaction only deepened with the arrival of war with Japan and his inability to escape the training station. "I was devastated," he recalled. "I had my heart set on action. I wanted to get into combat. Instead, my career as a fighter pilot appeared to be over before it started."[98]

Part of the problem was his age. At twenty-six, Foss was years older than most of his fellow pilots and "the military wanted young bucks as fighter pilots—the 21-year-olds," he noted.[99] But by volunteering for virtually anything that came along, Foss finally managed to wrangle his way into a combat outfit as operations officer. In August 1942 he was promoted to captain and made executive officer of Marine Fighter Squadron

121 (VMF-121). Married that same month to his college sweetheart, the former June Shakstad, he left for the war zone on September 1.

Four weeks later VMF-121 arrived at Henderson Field to reinforce the weary pilots of the so-called Cactus Air Force. Dubbed "Smokey Joe" by virtue of his incessant cigar smoking, the slow-talking, good-natured Foss flew his first combat mission on October 10. Three days later, during an enemy bombing raid on Henderson Field, a Zero jumped Foss's Wildcat. In his haste, the overanxious Japanese pilot overflew the F4F-4, making himself an easy target. Foss cut loose with his six .50-caliber machine guns and "blew him to hell." Three other Zeros took quick revenge, shooting up Foss's Wildcat so thoroughly—mechanics later counted 258 holes—that he had to make a deadstick landing on the field. "Afterwards, I realized that I had been a little excited," he admitted. After that close call, he spent so much time looking around in the air that his squadron mates started calling him "Swivel Neck Joe."[100]

Foss got his second victory on October 14 when he shot down a Zero pursuing another Marine pilot. His first burst knocked the Zero's wing off. The doomed plane plunged into a hillside above Henderson. "I never had an easier kill," he remarked.[101] The next day Foss led his flight out to intercept a group of Japanese bombers heading for Henderson. Climbing for altitude, he looked down and saw that the last two planes of his flight had grown to five. Three Zeroes had come in behind the two Wildcats below him. Foss dove on the Zero farthest to the left and opened fire. Flames erupted from the enemy plane. It fell into a spin and crashed into the ground. Foss quickly crippled a second enemy fighter, then went after the third. His first pass had no effect, but as Foss came back at the Zero, the enemy pilot opened fire from hundreds of yards away. Foss flew directly at him. The Zero pilot lost his nerve and pulled up, and Foss shot him down in flames.

Looking over his right shoulder, Foss now spotted the reason he had taken to the air in the first place—eight twin-engine Betty bombers flying in a V formation. With seven crew members and 600-gallon gas tanks, the Betty had a long range and a respectable payload. Foss made a run on the right rear bomber, but as he drew near, the enemy plane exploded, falling victim to another Marine fighter. Foss turned and went for the underside of the last plane on the left wing of the V formation. Pulling his nose straight up, he pressed the trigger. "It was impossible to miss," he recalled. "It was like pointing a pistol straight up in a room—you cannot help hitting the ceiling." Flames erupted from the Betty's gas tank, flashing back so intensely he could feel the heat on his face through the Wildcat's canopy. The left wing suddenly separated from the bomber's fuselage, and the plane tumbled into the ocean. Kill number 5—Capt. Joe Foss was now an ace.[102]

Foss was back in the air on October 23, again to intercept a formation of Betty bombers escorted by Zeros. Five of the fighter escorts immediately dove toward Foss and his flight, with twenty more Zeros close behind. Diving to gain speed, Foss riddled a Zero chasing a Wildcat, then looped, came up behind another Zero, and knocked it down too. As he came out of the loop, Foss nailed a third enemy fighter. Before the melee was over, he had shot down yet another for a total of four. The following day, he intercepted another enemy raid and shot down two planes. Later in the day, he shot down three more Zeros, giving him a total of five victories in a single day for a grand total of sixteen. "Not bad for twelve days work," he remarked laconically.[103] His nine-plane flight soon became known around Henderson Field as "Foss's Flying Circus" in recognition of their aerial exploits.

Though supremely efficient behind the guns, Foss became notorious for yakking on the radio with a running commentary during air-to-air combats. Bob Galer remarked that some people might think Foss talked too much. "I guess he did," conceded Galer, "because he made it hard for the rest of us to say anything, but he got results. He wasn't faking it for a minute."[104]

"Skilled fighter pilots have one thing in common: They are fast," Foss explained later. "The airplane becomes an extension of your body, like an arm or a leg. If somebody's coming at you with a red-hot poker, you instinctively get out of the way. You don't have to think about it. You just do it. In the air, whoever acts smartest and fastest is going to be the survivor."[105]

The kills were often spectacularly violent. "Because I usually shot from very close range, the Zeros almost always exploded, which was quite a sight," he observed. "There was a bright flash when the gas tanks blew and the engine would spin off by itself in a lopsided whirl. The pilot, usually still buckled in his seat, popped out of the cockpit and the air was showered with thousands of little pieces of the plane. What was left of the wing fell like a giant burning leaf. When a Zero blew up in front of you there was nowhere to go except right through the debris. All you could do was duck and hope you missed any big pieces."[106]

Smokey Joe's hot streak nearly came to a permanent end on November 7 as he led eight VMF-121 Wildcats equipped with 250-pound bombs to attack enemy ships sighted near Florida Island north of Henderson Field. As they searched for the enemy vessels, Foss spotted six floatplane Zeros crossing from right to left and descending. He radioed the others, jettisoned his bombs, and raced in toward the unsuspecting enemy fighters.

Foss closed on the Zero farthest to the left. The enemy pilots seemed oblivious. As the gray-green wingspan loomed in his gunsight, Foss pressed the trigger, making a 60- to 70-degree deflection shot. For a moment nothing seemed to happen as the .50-caliber slugs hammered the Zero. Then the plane exploded. Foss maneuvered away from the debris, surprised to see a parachute opening below. More parachutes blossomed as the other five Zeros fell, blasted from the sky by the Marine Wildcats. The enemy pilots had managed to bail out. The question, as it turned out, was why? Foss noticed that five of the parachutes were empty. "When I spotted the sixth, it was about 2,000 feet above me, and the Japanese pilot was struggling out of the harness," he recalled. "Pulling free, he plunged past my plane, falling headfirst into the sea."[107]

Minutes later, Foss almost joined him. Forming up for a run on the enemy warships now visible on the waters below, he spotted a slow enemy float biplane—a two-seat reconnaissance aircraft known as a "Pete." Lining up for what should have been an easy kill, he was taken by surprise when the enemy pilot cut the throttle, letting his rear gunner get a good shot at the pursuing Wildcat. The burst "pierced the left side of my engine cowling and shattered on through the left side of the canopy three or four inches from my face—right across and out the other side," recalled Foss.[108]

As wind shrieked through the broken canopy, Foss checked his instruments and found no indication of serious damage. He maneuvered for a belly shot on the Pete, directing a stream of slugs into the base of the right wing. The aircraft burst into flames almost immediately. "As the smoking plane spiraled toward the sea, I spotted a second scout, its pilot apparently unaware his companion had been knocked out of the clouds," observed Foss. "Circling behind him, I pulled up for an unhurried belly shot, and sent my nineteenth victim to join his buddy in the drink."[109]

But Foss was not home free. As he searched for the rest of his flight, his engine began to cut in and out. "Soon the stops got closer than the starts and I realized I wasn't going to make it back to Henderson," he recalled.[110] The engine finally quit for good, and he glided down through a squall toward the sea 3,500 feet below. Opening the shattered canopy, he could see an island and a village of some sort about five miles off. Then the plane smashed into the water, the canopy slammed shut, and water poured into the cockpit. The Grumman manual claimed the Wildcat would float at least thirty seconds. Foss's aircraft went down like rock.

The one test Foss had failed during flight school was the skill he now needed most: the South Dakota farm boy had never learned to swim. He found himself in utter darkness as the Wildcat plunged below the surface. Somehow he managed to push the canopy open and unhook the leg straps of his parachute harness. Pulled toward the surface by his parachute pack and life preserver, he jerked to an abrupt halt as his left foot caught under the cockpit seat. "The need to breathe was almost uncontrollable," he said later, "but I tapped the last of my strength to free my foot."[111] He shot to the surface and lay there gasping for air.

For the next four or five hours, Foss paddled haplessly around, dodging sharks and fervently praying. At long last he heard voices, and a "war canoe" manned by a missionary and some natives from the Catholic mission on nearby Malaita Island emerged from the night. Hearing one of the occupants speaking English with an Australian accent, Foss yelled, "Hey, over here!" Moments later they plucked him from the sea. The men told Foss that the jut of land he had been swimming toward was overpopulated with man-eating crocodiles. "If somehow I'd made it to land, I'd probably have been somebody's supper."[112] The next day searchers spotted his parachute spread out on the beach, and a PBY dropped in to bring Foss home.

Back in the air again on November 12, Foss took a flight up to 29,000 feet to ambush an enemy bomber formation reported by Coastwatchers. Nineteen Bettys came out of the clouds at about 500 feet and headed for the ships in the harbor off Henderson Field. Foss got into position about 100 yards behind a Betty and cut loose. The right engine caught fire; the plane cartwheeled, "then plopped into the water on its belly." Foss was lining up another bomber when a Zero suddenly materialized out of nowhere. Foss let the plane speed by, latched onto its tail, and put a burst into the wing mount area. The plane exploded only a few feet above the water. Turning back to the bomber, Foss missed on his first pass, "probably because I was swiveling around like crazy, watching for more maverick Zeros." On his second pass he hit the base of the bomber's wing, flaming the left engine to bring the plane down. The day's victories, bringing his total to twenty-three, made him the top American ace of the war and the first to surpass twenty kills.[113]

A week later VMF-121 pulled out for rest and recuperation on New Caledonia and then in Australia. Foss needed the break. He had contracted malaria on Guadalcanal, and the disease was wearing him down. He left Guadalcanal with a temperature of 104 degrees and spent the next month on sick leave, losing 37 pounds. He would continue to fight malaria in the future, always afraid he would be shipped out of the combat zone if doctors learned how sick he really was. "When the doctors inquired about my health, I just plain lied," he said later. It was typical Joe Foss. Years later a friend remarked, "If I had to pick out one trait that stands out through all the years I've known Joe, it would be tenacity—in everything he does."[114]

In combat, Foss was "slam-bang and energetic in his methods," observed fellow officer Walter Baylor. "He was an energetic, determined seeker-out of enemy planes; when he located a flight he would smash headlong into it without hesitation and with little attempt at finesse. He would just shoot down everything that came into his sights."[115] This was somewhat of an exaggeration in that it lauded Foss's aggressiveness while underestimating his intelligence. Foss was tenacious and aggressive but far from stupid. Once, asked by some green Australian Spitfire pilots how to "handle a Zero one-on-one," Foss replied candidly, "We have a saying on Guadalcanal. If you're alone and you meet a Zero, you're outnumbered. Run like hell is my advice." The Aussies were disdainful. Foss dismissed them as idiots.[116]

By January 1, 1943, Foss was back on Guadalcanal, where he was given command of VMF-121. Two weeks later, on January 15, he knocked down three Zeros in a brawl north of the island. The first dove right in front of him, and Foss exploded it in a ball of fire. The second was glued to the tail of a diving Wildcat. "I easily lined up for a shot at almost point-blank range and sent the enemy in a slow, flaming spin toward the water," he recalled. The third Zero flew straight at him. Both planes were firing, the tracers skimming just overhead. At the last moment they broke off, both maneuvering for another pass. "Everything was pumping inside me, my heart beating rapidly, my mouth dry," admitted Foss.[117]

On the second pass, Foss managed to put some slugs into the cockpit area, but the enemy pilot doggedly circled back for a third attack. As more enemy fighters approached, the persistent Zero finally spewed smoke, burst into flames, and fell toward the sea. Foss ran for home. The victories brought his score to 26—tying the record Eddie Rickenbacker had held since 1918. The World War I ace sent Foss a congratulatory cable and a case of Scotch. "Both disappeared in transit, and I never received them," Foss observed ruefully.[118]

Ironically, Foss won what he considered his greatest personal victory without firing a shot. As the tide of the aerial struggle turned against the Japanese, attacks on Henderson Field dropped off. "Daily dogfights over the fighter strip were a thing of the past," observed Foss.[119] In response, Maj. Gen. Francis P. Mulcahy, who had taken over in December as commander of land-based aircraft, insisted that virtually all available planes be sent out on offensive operations. Foss believed Mulcahy's disregard for airfield defense was premature. He was convinced the Japanese would eventually mount a major air raid on the field and wreak havoc on the neat lines of parked aircraft. As a precaution, he proceeded to "hide" eight Wildcats, ready to go, in some palm trees at the end of the fighter strip.

When Mulcahy found out about Foss's secret Air Force, he hit the roof. Foss was censured, and the general told him he was through. Perhaps providentially, the very next day, January 25, the Japanese came, just as Foss had expected, and his cached Wildcats were the only planes immediately available to stop them. Climbing for altitude over Henderson, Foss saw "a sky black" with enemy planes. "There were sixty-plus Zeros, at least two dozen Betty bombers, and eighteen dive bombers, and in the far distance another whole swarm heading toward me," he recalled.

As about a dozen Zeros tried to suck the handful of Wildcats into a fight, Foss ordered his pilots to hang back and wait. Hopelessly outnumbered, he thought maybe he could bluff the Japanese into thinking they were heading for a trap, giving them pause and allowing the ground crews time to move planes off the strip and get more fighters into the air. His scheme was helped by the presence of heavy clouds that, for all the Japanese knew, might conceal scores of waiting enemies. The Americans did not attack, but neither did they flee. "By refusing to run away when the odds were clearly and overwhelmingly against us, we instilled the deep suspicion that we must have many more planes in the air," Foss explained later. "When another squadron managed to get into the air and engage a group of twenty Zeros in between two other cloud layers, the idea was firmly implanted."[120] To his amazement, the Japanese armada abruptly turned away and headed toward home. Having every advantage, they had failed to follow through. It was, the poker-playing Foss admitted, "the greatest empty hand" of his life.[121]

Forgiven for his previous display of disobedience, Joe Foss remained in the combat zone until February 17, when he was ordered back to the United States. The publicity attending his combat record had made him a national hero. He was pictured on the cover of *LIFE* magazine, and an article in the *Saturday Evening Post* referred to him as "America's greatest fighter pilot of all time."[122] In recognition of his cumulative achievement, he was awarded the Medal of Honor at the White House on May 18, 1943. Though he went overseas again in early 1944, Foss did not score any more air-to-air kills. Nevertheless, with twenty-six victories, he finished as the leading Marine Corps ace of the war.

After the war, Foss served two terms in the South Dakota Legislature. In 1954 he was elected governor of South Dakota. At age thirty-nine he was the youngest man to hold that position up to that time. In 1959 he became the first commissioner of the American Football League. An avid hunter and fisherman, he hosted the *American Sportsman* television program in the 1960s and produced and hosted the syndicated TV series *The Outdoorsman Joe Foss* from 1967 to 1974. A lifetime member of the National Rifle Association, he served as its president from 1988 to 1990.

There were disappointments. Foss's marriage to his college sweetheart did not last; they separated in 1959, a failure he later blamed largely on himself for not spending more time with his wife and children, including a daughter born with cerebral palsy. He remarried in 1967, and in the 1970s he became involved in the Campus Crusade for Christ International. "The greatest thing that's ever happened to me was the day I accepted Jesus Christ as my Lord and Savior," he avowed.[123]

Joe Foss died on New Year's Day in 2003, two months after suffering an aneurysm and lapsing into unconsciousness. He was survived by his second wife, Didi, a son and daughter, and a stepson and stepdaughter. The old warrior was laid to rest in Arlington National Cemetery.

Years after the war, Foss remarked that he didn't let much bother him. "When I was a kid I used to hear people ask, 'Is that a life-or-death decision?' and it almost never was. A decision may affect life, but it probably doesn't affect the breathing process—which is number one," he observed. "Because of that I don't get too lathered up about most things."[124]

As for the Medal of Honor, a reporter once asked him if his medal had helped him in his postwar career. Foss replied that the award had certainly opened many doors for him, then added, "Once inside, it was up to me to prove myself."[125]

ACOM John W. Finn (U.S. Navy).

A PBY patrol bomber burns at Naval Air Station Kaneohe, Oahu, during the December 7, 1941, attack (U.S. Navy).

Capt. Henry T. Elrod (USMC).

F4F-3A Wildcats flown by Lt. Cmdr. John Thach (F-1) and Lt. Butch O'Hare (F-13) during an aerial photography flight on April 11, 1942 (U.S. Navy).

Wreckage of VMF-211 Grumman Wildcats following the fall of Wake. The Wildcat in the foreground was flown by Henry Elrod when he sank a Japanese destroyer (USMC).

President Franklin D. Roosevelt presents Butch O'Hare with the Medal of Honor on April 21, 1942: President Roosevelt, Secretary of the Navy Frank Knox (behind FDR), Adm. Ernest King, Edward O'Hare, and his wife, Rita (U.S. Navy).

Lt. Edward H. ("Butch") O'Hare (U.S. Navy).

Lt. Col. James H. ("Jimmy") Doolittle wires a Japanese medal to a bomb aboard USS *Hornet* for "return" to the empire prior to the famous raid (U.S. Navy).

One of the sixteen B-25 bombers aboard USS *Hornet* for the Doolittle raid lumbers off the deck after the task force was spotted by an enemy picket ship (U.S. Navy).

Lt. John J. Powers (U.S. Navy).

SBD Dauntless dive bombers in flight. Dive bombers such as these were piloted by two Medal of Honor recipients during the Battle of the Coral Sea, Lt. John Powers and Lt. William Hall (U.S. Navy).

Lt. (j.g.) William E. Hall
(National Archives).

Capt. Richard Fleming
(public domain).

The Japanese heavy cruiser *Mikuma*, its deck shattered by bombs, was sunk by carrier planes on June 6, 1942. Dick Fleming was killed in an attack on the crippled ship on June 5 (U.S. Navy).

The Voight SBU2 Vindicator flown by Richard Fleming on his last mission was already obsolete by the time of the Battle of Midway (U.S. Navy).

Capt. Harl Pease
(U.S. Air Force).

Aerial photo of the harbor area at Rabaul depicts two of the prominent volcanoes on the edge of the caldera, the South Daughter on the right of the frame and the Mother Peak to the left on the other side of the gap (U.S. Air Force)

Maj. John L. Smith (USMC).

Here sporting their newly awarded Navy Crosses, Maj. John L. Smith, Maj. Bob Galer, and Capt. Marion Carl played a key role in turning back the Japanese air threat during the long battle for Guadalcanal (U.S. Navy).

F4F Wildcat fighters on Henderson Field on Guadalcanal, Solomon Islands, January 1943 (National Archives).

Maj. Robert Galer (USMC).

Lt. Col. Harold W. Bauer (USMC).

Joe Bauer re-creates one of his victories for the ground crew at Henderson Field (USMC).

Capt. Joseph Foss (USMC).

Gen. Kenneth N. Walker
(U.S. Air Force).

The B-17 *San Antonio Rose*. The bomber, carrying Gen. Kenneth Walker, disappeared during a mission over Rabaul on January 5, 1943 (U.S. Air Force).

B-17s of the 43rd Bombardment Group (Heavy) in their revetments at Jackson Airfield (7 Mile Drome) at Port Moresby, New Guinea, on December 31, 1942, less than a week before General Walker's fatal mission (U.S. Air Force).

1st Lt. Jefferson DeBlanc
(USMC).

Capt. Jay Zeamer
(U.S. Air Force).

Gen. Hap Arnold presents Jay Zeamer Jr. with the Medal of Honor as parents Jay and Margery Zeamer look on (public domain).

Only known photo of Jay Zeamer's B-17 *Old 666*. The bomber is parked at 14 Mile Drome (Schwimmer Airfield) near Port Moresby, New Guinea, and appears in the last few seconds of a military film from the 8th Photographic Reconnaissance Squadron (U.S. Air Force).

Sgt. (later 2nd Lt.) Joseph Sarnoski (U.S. Air Force).

The "Eager Beavers" of *Old 666*. Front row: William Vaughan, George Kendrick, Johnnie Able, Herbert Pugh. Back row: Bud Thues, Jay Zeamer, Hank Dyminski, Joe Sarnoski. Just prior to the June 16 Medal of Honor mission, Forrest Dillman was added to the crew, and John T. Britton and Ruby Johnston replaced Dyminski and Thues, who had contracted malaria (National Archives).

The General, the Agitator,
and the Screwball

By January 1943 the situation of Allied forces in the Pacific had markedly improved. The Japanese were about to concede defeat at Guadalcanal and began to evacuate surviving troops in mid-January. The U.S. brass would declare victory on the bitterly contested island in February, their eyes already turning toward the Northern Solomons and Bougainville. In Australia, the Fifth Air Force, commanded by Gen. George C. Kenney, was girding for a concerted effort against Japanese bases on northern New Guinea and the much-vaunted bastion at Rabaul. In January, two U.S. airmen—one of them a headstrong brigadier general, the other a Marine lieutenant blessed with what might charitably be described as more guts than sense—would perform actions that resulted in the award of the Medal of Honor. Five months later, a "screwball" Army captain would earn a third.

Brig. Gen. Kenneth N. Walker
Rabaul
January 5, 1943

Army Brig. Gen. Kenneth N. Walker arrived in the Southwest Pacific in June 1942 with a troubled personal life and an oversized reputation as a strategic bombing expert. Just shy of his forty-fourth birthday when he arrived in the war zone, Walker had been born on July 17, 1898, in Los Cerillos, New Mexico, a small town south of Santa Fe, the only child of

Wallace and Emma Walker. His father was a linotype operator in the printing industry; his mother had grown up in Nebraska, one of nine children of a Civil War veteran who had taken up farming. Their marriage was short-lived. The couple divorced when Kenneth was still a boy, and he was raised by his mother in Denver, Colorado.

Intelligent and ambitious, Walker took college-level courses in business administration and was enrolled in a management training program when the United States entered World War I in 1917. Six months later he enlisted in the Army and was accepted for flight training. Though he received his commission as a second lieutenant only about a week before the war ended and never got overseas, Walker found a home in aviation. He stayed in the fledgling air arm as a flight instructor and, over the next decade, served in a variety of billets, including a tour in the Philippines and a stint as commander of a bombardment squadron.

However, it was not until Walker was sent to Air Corps Tactical School in late 1928 that the quality of his intellect and his single-mindedness began to attract serious attention. There he became a fervent disciple of strategic bombing, joining a coterie of similarly minded officers who became known as the "Bomber Mafia." Walker and the Bomber Mafia argued that "bombardment aviation is the basic arm of the Air Force" and all other elements—fighters, reconnaissance, and so forth—were subordinate. The chain-smoking Walker argued his case with a narrow-minded passion that was described in some quarters as almost "rabid" in its intensity, earning him notoriety as the "high priest" of strategic bombing.[1]

During the 1930s Walker worked on formalizing bombardment strategy and solidified his reputation with published articles and studies promoting Bomber Mafia dogma. The Walker school of thought held that fighters—those romantic knights of the sky during the recently concluded world war—could not defeat a well-organized bombardment attack: modern bombers could fly too high and too fast and were too heavily armed to be seriously challenged. "The well-organized, well-planned, and well-flown Air Force attack will constitute an offensive that cannot be stopped," he argued.[2] Daylight precision-bombing campaigns against critical industrial targets would bring the enemy to his knees—potentially avoiding the need for prolonged land battles.

On the social scene, women tended to find the up-and-coming officer handsome, despite his prominent nose and thick glasses. He was slender but with an athletic build; he paid close attention to his dress, had a flair for the social graces, and was a good dancer. A wandering eye would eventually lead him into trouble, but in 1922 he married Marguerite Potter, a University of Oklahoma graduate with a degree in sociology. Described as "beautiful and lively," she had one year been named "Sooner Queen" at the university. She and Walker had two sons, Kenneth in 1927 and Douglas in 1933, but the marriage ended in divorce in 1934 after Marguerite learned her husband was having an affair. Walker remarried and had another son, but this marriage also ended in divorce. Later, in an apparent reference to his personal life, he conceded to a boyhood friend before heading overseas that he had "made a terrible mess of things."[3]

Despite his marital issues, Walker's consuming passion was always his career. An acquaintance remembered his "near total involvement with himself and his ideas." Those who knew him described him as "single-minded and high strung" and "totally dedicated to his work," though he was affable and relaxed in social situations.[4] The rewards came slowly. Referred to in some quarters as the oldest first lieutenant in the Air Corps, he graduated from Command and General Staff School in June 1935 and was promoted to captain in August. Just over a year later, he was made temporary major, a rank that did not become permanent until 1940. In 1941, now a temporary lieutenant colonel, he was named to the Air War Plans Division, joining former fellow instructors from the Air Corps Tactical School and card-carrying members of the Bomber Mafia.

By now, developments in Europe seemed to cast some doubt on the Bomber Mafia's insistence that bombers could operate without fear of fighter interference. German bombers over England were shot down in large numbers. Similarly, the British suffered so many losses over the Continent during daylight bombing attacks that they switched to nighttime raids. Undeterred, the Bomber Mafia insisted that the new generation of more heavily armed and armored U.S. bombers—such as the B-17 Flying Fortress introduced in 1935—were in a different category. Walker never backed off from his contention that bombers would prevail. "Each of us scoffed at the idea that fighters would be needed to protect bombers, to enable bombers to reach their objective," recalled fellow War Plans Division officer Laurence S. Kuter.[5]

Following the Japanese attack on Pearl Harbor, Walker was anxious to get overseas and put his theories into practice. He made full colonel in February 1942, but it was not until June, now sporting the single stars of a brigadier general, that he got his wish and was dispatched to Australia to serve under Maj. Gen. George Kenney, then organizing the nascent Fifth Air Force. Kenney, a short bulldog of a man and a combat veteran of World War I, had known Walker for years. "Ken was the serious, studious type," he recalled. "In his early forties, of medium height, slight build, with dark hair and eyes and an intelligent face, he was a likable, hardworking asset to a command."[6] Based on Walker's reputation, Kenney named him to lead V Bomber Command.

Headquartered in Townsville, Australia, V Bomber Command staged planes through Port Moresby on New Guinea for bombing missions targeting Japanese-held Rabaul 500 miles to the northeast, enemy airfields on New Guinea itself, and enemy shipping. Walker threw himself into the job with characteristic intensity. He proved himself a hands-on commander. Even before being named to lead V Bomber Command, he participated in three combat missions over New Guinea in an effort to familiarize himself with the difficulties facing air crews. In a letter to his sons about an attack on an enemy convoy, he wrote, "Fortunately there were no Zeros around, although I was foolishly disappointed for a while." The bomber came under antiaircraft fire. "Shell fragments sounded like hail on the wings, and we got one fair-sized hole in the right wing. It was my first time under fire, but I was so interested that I forgot to be concerned," he wrote.[7]

His enthusiasm earned him a Silver Star. The citation noted, "The large amount of firsthand information gained by General Walker has proved of inestimable value in the performance of his duties. His complete disregard for personal safety, above and beyond the call of duty, has proved highly stimulating to the morale of all Air Force personnel with whom he has come in contact."[8]

Despite his reputation as a strategic thinker, Walker also took a personal interest in the welfare of his men. He demanded that the food be improved in the enlisted men's mess and waited his own turn in the chow line along with everyone else, declining to exercise the privilege of rank. Maj. Bernhardt L. Mortenson, V Bomber Command's historical officer, recalled that Walker was waiting his turn for chow one day when an officious second lieutenant tried to cut in at the head of the line. "General Walker, standing at the end of the line, stepped up, took the upstart by the arm and led him to the rear of the line to wait his turn, demonstrating to the offender that it sometimes takes more than an act of Congress to make a gentleman," Mortenson observed approvingly.[9]

The general also continued to share the dangers experienced by his bomb crews, flying an average of a mission a week against the Japanese in an effort to better understand the combat situation, witness bombing tactics, and refine doctrine as he strove to improve results. It was ironic that Walker—the crusader for precision bombing of key industrial targets—should end up in the Southwest Pacific, where such targets were virtually nonexistent, but his men appreciated the gesture. "The boys in the north [of Australia] think the world of him," Walker's aide, Capt. Fred P. Dollenberg, told a reporter. "They figure things aren't so bad if a general's willing to go along and get shot at."[10]

Toting an oxygen bottle at high altitude, Walker would amble from station to station during the mission. "He climbs through the bomb bay and watches the rear gunner or the side gunners blast at Zeros and when we are over the target he watches the bombardier as he gets set to drop his bombs," Dollenberg recounted. "Wandering all over a plane like that isn't healthy, but the general figures he can't tell the boys how to go out and to get shot at unless he's willing to get shot at, too. . . . [He] figures he can't direct flights from the ground and tell the boys what they are doing wrong. So he goes along and directs a flight from the air. If a plane gets out of formation he shouts his orders over the radio to 'Get the hell back in line.'"[11]

Learning that Walker had participated in a bombing mission to Rabaul on which one of the accompanying B-17s was lost with its entire crew and the others suffered casualties, Kenney ordered the general to stay on the ground. He was too valuable to risk. "I can always hire a ten dollar-a-week man to sweep the floors," he remarked pointedly of personnel priorities. "No more combat missions."[12]

Walker ignored the directive. He continued to fly. He also stubbornly insisted on adhering to Bomber Mafia doctrine calling for high-level bombing attacks by masses of planes. In fact, the doctrine wasn't working. Lacking large numbers of aircraft and unimpressed with bombing accuracy from higher altitudes—especially against moving targets such as ships—Kenney suggested low-level attacks with bombs armed with instantaneous fuses. Walker objected. Kenney ordered him to try instantaneous fuses for a while in order to accumulate data on their effectiveness, but a few weeks later he found that Walker had failed to comply. Walker resisted until Kenney dragged him out to witness a low-level attack demonstration against a target ship. When the bombs with instantaneous fuses hit the water and detonated, the fragments riddled the side of the ship.

Walker reluctantly conceded that Kenney was right, though he was far from abandoning his advocacy for high-altitude strategic bombing. "Ken was okay," Kenney observed. "He was stubborn, over-sensitive, and a prima donna, but he worked like a dog all the time. His gang liked him a lot but he tended to get a staff of 'yes-men'. He did not like to delegate authority." Kenney did harbor reservations about Walker's "durability," as he put it. "[He] kept himself keyed up all the time and he just couldn't seem to relax a minute," he observed later.[13]

In December, learning that a B-17 with Walker aboard had lost three feet of wing when it clipped a tree during a nighttime reconnaissance mission, Kenney once again ordered him to stay on the ground. "I told him that from then on I wanted him to run his command from his headquarters. In the airplane he was just extra baggage. . . . In fact, in case of trouble, he was in the way," observed Kenney.[14]

There was also the danger that the general might fall into enemy hands during one of these unnecessary missions. Kenney explained,

One of the big reasons for keeping him home was that I would hate to have him taken prisoner by the Japs. They would have known that a general was bound to have access to a lot of information and there was no limit to the lengths they would go to extract that knowledge from him. We had plenty of evidence that the Nips had tortured their prisoners until they either died or talked. After the prisoners talked they were beheaded anyhow, but most of them had broken under the strain. I told Walker that frankly I didn't believe he could take it without telling everything he knew, so I was not going to let him go on any more combat missions.[15]

Meanwhile, it appeared the Japanese were gathering for a major operation. Photo reconnaissance on January 3 revealed large numbers of ships in Rabaul's expansive Simpson Harbor. Allied codebreaker intercepts indicated that the Japanese were assembling a convoy of reinforcements to bolster forces operating at Lae on the New Guinea mainland. Kenney directed Walker to launch an all-out bombing attack on Rabaul in an effort to destroy the convoy before it put to sea. The coordinated strike would consist of B-17s and B-24s flying from Port Moresby. They would be bolstered by B-24s flying from Australia for a total of more than twenty bombers, the largest force ever to raid Rabaul in daylight. Kenney told Walker to time the attack so that the raid arrived at dawn, when the Japanese at the heavily defended base would least expect it.

Walker balked at the timing. He told Kenney a dawn attack would force the bombers to launch in the dark, complicating the process of forming up. He recommended a noon attack. "He was worried about the bombers making their rendezvous if they left Port Moresby at night," recalled Kenney.[16] Walker's plan called for B-17s from the 11th Bomb Group and 403rd Squadron to hit the Japanese airfield at Lakunai at 11 a.m. He expected this initial strike to stun enemy fighter response. That, in turn, would allow the main assault at noon by B-17s from the 64th Squadron and B-24s from the 90th Bomb Group to ravage the Japanese convoy in Simpson Harbor with little interference.

Walker's argument had some merit. Poor weather and the difficulty of gathering aircraft from different fields and forming up for nighttime flights to Rabaul had been problematic in the past. Walker himself had experienced some of those difficulties firsthand in a presumably unauthorized personal reconnaissance mission in the predawn darkness on New Year's Day. But Kenney insisted. "I told him that I still wanted a dawn attack. The Nip fighters were never up at dawn but at noon they would not only shoot up our bombers but would ruin our bombing accuracy. I would rather have the bombers not in formation for a dawn attack than in formation for a show at noon which was certain to be intercepted."[17]

Kenney was also entertaining heightened concerns about Walker's physical condition. "Ken had not been sleeping well and was getting tired and jumpy," he wrote later. "The strain and the tropics were wearing him down. I decided that at the end of this month, if a couple of weeks' leave didn't put him back in shape, I'd have to send him home."[18]

Walker scheduled the attack on Rabaul for January 5. Then, dismissing Kenney's concerns, he ordered the strike to take off in daylight so that it would arrive over Rabaul at noon. When one of his squadron commanders objected, Walker, in an apparent fit of pique, cut those planes from the mission. In further defiance of Kenney, he arranged to go along as an observer on the lead B-17 bomber, the *San Antonio Rose*, from the 64th Bombardment Squadron, 43rd Bombardment Group. Accompanying him were Maj. Jack W. Bleasdale, executive officer of the bomb group, and Maj. Allen Lindberg, commanding the 64th Bombardment Squadron. The briefing officer, Maj. David Hassemer, questioned the wisdom of risking so many senior officers in the same plane, but his reservations were ignored.[19] A 64th Squadron pilot was more scathing, dismissing the presence of the "observers" as a ploy to obtain medals for officers who "had no reason to be on a combat mission and could only degrade crew performance."[20]

The mission began to go wrong from the start when, due to a last-minute command decision, the 11th Bomb Group B-17s became unavailable. Then nine B-24s from the 320th Bomb Squadron were unable to take off due to heavy rains. That left Walker with only six B-17s and six B-24s based at Port Moresby, but there was apparently no thought of canceling. *San Antonio Rose* lifted off at 8:48 a.m. with eleven men on board. Capt. Benton H. Daniel of Hollis, Oklahoma, the usual pilot, ceded that seat to Major Bleasdale of San Fernando, California, and took the copilot spot. Others on board included Major Lindberg (observer) of New York City; 2nd Lt. Robert L. Hand (bombardier) of Fields Store, Texas; 2nd Lt. John W. Hanson (navigator) of Missoula, Montana; T/Sgt. Dennis T. Craig (engineer) of New York City; Pvt. Quentin W. Blakely (radioman) of Washington, DC; Sgt. Leslie A. Stewart (gunner) of East Chicago, Illinois; Pvt. Leland W. Stone (gunner) of Oakland, California; PFC William G. Fraser Jr. (gunner) of San Antonio, Texas; and Brig. Gen. Kenneth N. Walker.

This would be the first daylight raid on Rabaul since October 5. Piloting a B-17 on *San Antonio Rose*'s wing, twenty-five-year-old Lt. Frederick Wesche worried that they were embarking on a "suicide mission"—and he wasn't the only one.[21] They had reason to be nervous. Rabaul was—or soon would be—the most heavily defended target in the South West Pacific Area. Located inside an enormous volcanic caldera, Blanche Bay provided one of the best natural harbors in the Southwest Pacific. Circled by hills that provided convenient antiaircraft positions, the bay was about 6 miles long and 2.5 miles wide and was divided into four inner harbors. The most developed of these was Simpson Harbor, which had space for at least 300,000 tons of shipping.

By late 1942, the Japanese had emplaced 367 antiaircraft weapons to defend Rabaul. The harbor area was further protected by an estimated forty-three coastal guns and twenty searchlights. There were 97,000 troops and five airfields either in operation or under construction.[22] "When it was announced that [this] was going to be done in broad daylight at noontime, as a matter-of-fact, at low altitude, something like 5,000 feet over the most heavily defended target in the Pacific almost . . . most of us went away shaking our heads," Wesche admitted. "Many of us believed that we wouldn't come back from it."[23]

By contrast, Walker was looking forward to the mission. He told Major Hassemer he hadn't had many opportunities to fly in combat. Scheduled to pilot one of the accompanying B-24 heavy bombers, Donald L. Sanxter overheard the general remark that he had a new camera and hoped to get some good photographs.[24]

Their luck seemed to take a turn for the better as they arrived over Rabaul at noon to find only scattered clouds over Simpson Harbor. Air crews spotted numerous ships in the inner and outer harbors. Despite General Kenney's fears, there were no fighters aloft, and enemy antiaircraft crews were slow to respond. Unfortunately, though the air crews could not know it, the whole point of the raid had already become largely moot: the congregation of shipping below did not include the transports Kenney hoped to smash. Those ships had already left the harbor and were anchored miles away off the nearby coastal village of Kokopo.

The bombers made their runs from about 8,500 feet, breaking formation to go after individual targets with a total of forty 500-pound and twenty-four 1,000-pound bombs. The B-24s claimed two hits. The B-17s claimed hits on nine vessels, including a destroyer and a cargo ship that broke in half. In fact, though half a dozen ships were damaged and some small fires broke out, only one—the 5,833-ton *Keifuku Maru*—was sunk, falling victim to a pair of bombs that straddled her. Somewhat miraculously, only one crewman was injured. Another ship suffered twenty casualties.

The B-24s followed the B-17s. Looking down through the Plexiglas nose of his Liberator, navigator William Whitacre saw "at least three ships hit in the harbor and left burning." Antiaircraft fire, light at first, seemed to be picking up, and he "could see the nearby airdrome with Zeros taking off to come up and get us" as the bombers began to withdraw and reform.[25] The airfields at Lakunai and Vunakanau were now a hornet's nest of activity as enemy fighter pilots rushed to get airborne.[26]

As his B-24 completed its run and turned away from the harbor, Donald Sanxter noticed a B-17 circling below. He assumed it was Walker, observing the effects of the mission and trying to get photos with his new camera.[27] The initial lack of opposition may have persuaded Walker that he could safely linger over the target area to observe and photograph results of the strike. Both Japanese and American witnesses indicated that one bomber—almost certainly *San Antonio Rose*—circled the harbor at lower altitude before heading off to catch up with the main formation.[28] It is also possible the aircraft had been damaged. As Wesche turned his B-17 away, his tail gunner reported a B-17 circling behind them at about 5,000 feet with its number-one engine out. When Wesche circled around to assist the damaged bomber, he was unable to find it.

He soon had more pressing concerns as an estimated fifteen Japanese fighters caught up with the strike force in a running fight to the south of Rabaul. "The results of the raid, I'm not sure what it was, whether it was successful or not, but it certainly was a most hair-raising experience you want to go through. I mean, suddenly, you look ahead of you and see about fifteen or twenty airplanes all shooting at you at the same time," observed Wesche. "I was shot up. Nobody was injured, fortunately, but the airplane was kind of banged up a little bit."

Wesche had no sooner dropped his bombs than his tail gunner radioed, "Hey, there's somebody in trouble behind us."

"So we made a turn and looked back and here was an airplane, one of our airplanes, going down, smoking and on fire, not necessarily fire, but smoke anyway, and headed down obviously for a cloud bank with a whole cloud of fighters on top of him," said Wesche. "There must have been fifteen or twenty fighters. Of course they gang up on a cripple, you know, polish that one off with no trouble, but he disappeared into a cloud bank and we never saw him again. It turns out it was the general. . . . He actually had a pilot, but he was the overall air commander for the operation. He was conducting it from the astrodome, just behind the pilot's seat, where he could look out with a microphone and directing what should be done and so on."[29]

As he went into his bomb run, Whitacre also saw the B-17 was "losing altitude and at least one engine was smoking."[30] Missing aircrew reports for *San Antonio Rose* later reported, "This B-17 was last seen over the target area, east of Vunakanau Airfield at 5,000 feet closely pursued by four (4) to five (5) Zeros [*sic*: Ki-43-I Oscars]. Last seen going into clouds, closely pursued by four to five Japanese fighters. The left outboard engine was observed to be smoking."[31]

The remainder of the bomber force finally managed to shake pursuit, though at least one B-24 reported undergoing fighter attacks for more than half an hour. Another B-17 made an emergency landing near Buna, and a damaged B-24 landed at Milne Bay. The Japanese lost two Zeros: one pilot was killed; the other took to his parachute and survived. A third pilot was badly wounded but managed to land his damaged fighter.[32]

Hours later, a livid General Kenney learned that Walker had accompanied the mission and was now missing. "Walker off late," he noted in his diary. "Disobeyed orders by going along as well as not starting his mission when I told him."[33]

It briefly appeared all would end well when a search plane on January 6 reported a downed crew stranded on a reef. "A report came in during the evening that Walker's airplane was down on a coral reef in the Trobriand Islands off the eastern end of New Guinea," recalled Kenney. "I told General [Douglas] MacArthur that as soon as Walker showed up I was going to give him a reprimand and send him to Australia for a couple weeks."

MacArthur responded, "All right, George, but if he doesn't come back, I'm going to send his name to Washington recommending him for a Congressional Medal of Honor."[34]

Kenney's relief was short-lived. The stranded airmen turned out to be from a B-17 that had taken off at dawn on the day of the Walker raid to attack Rabaul's Lakunai airdrome. The pilot paddled out to the flying boat sent to rescue them to find a cameraman looking at him.

"Where the general?" asked the cameraman.

"What general?" said the pilot.

"General Walker," said the cameraman.

"I don't know, but he sure isn't here," replied the pilot.[35]

"I ordered the search kept up, but I had no hope for Ken," admitted Kenney. "I was certain that his airplane had been shot down in flames and unless the crew bailed out they were gone. If they did bail out and the Japs had them, that was bad."[36] On January 11 Walker's eldest son Kenneth was notified by telegram that his father was missing in action.[37] The notification was followed by an official public announcement.

Kenney's fears that Walker could be taken prisoner were far from idle. Unknown at the time, at least two of the men aboard *San Antonio Rose*—Maj. Jack Bleasdale and Capt. Benton H. Daniel—had bailed out of the stricken bomber and were subsequently captured.

According to Japanese sources, one of the B-17's port engines had been knocked out by antiaircraft fire before it began its bomb run. The pilots regained control, and "[the] airplane flew off to the south, losing altitude as it went," observed the report. Japanese fighters followed the crippled bomber in a long-running battle. "In the neighborhood of the mountain peaks north of Wide Bay [Bleasdale] sensed his danger and parachuted to earth. After this he wandered in the mountains for twenty days, discovered a native dwelling and hid there to recuperate." Betrayed by natives, he was subsequently taken prisoner by members of a naval lookout post. "A captain [Daniel] taken prisoner at the same time as this man was sent under guard to Kavieng at request of the Navy," noted a Japanese report.[38]

Both officers apparently endured lengthy interrogations into February and March 1943. Daniel was questioned about the technical details of the B-17. The resulting information was compiled in a Japanese report titled "The B-17 and Its Armament." A Catholic priest being held at Rabaul later testified that Daniel had been brought into the camp but was later transferred to Kavieng. What happened to him afterward is unknown: neither he nor Bleasdale was ever heard from again.[39]

Some more clues surfaced after the war when 2nd Lt. Jose Holguin emerged from a Japanese prison camp on Rabaul. The bombardier on the B-17E *Naughty but Nice*, Holguin was shot down on a night mission to Rabaul on June 26, just over six months after Walker's disappearance. Severely wounded in the jaw and back, he bailed out of the stricken bomber and parachuted into the jungle, the sole survivor of the ten-man crew. He wandered in the jungle for weeks before some villagers handed him over to the Japanese on July 17.

The Japanese ignored Holguin's wounds, but they did take the time to interrogate him. "One of the first things they asked me was the name of the commander of the V Bomber Command," said Holguin. When Holguin balked, his interrogators presented him with a report containing some information on Major Bleasdale and General Walker. "They said it was no use trying to lie; that they knew General Walker was dead and Major Bleasdale captured; therefore they wished to know my new commander's name," recalled Holguin. "From what I could gather, General Walker was killed while still in the air, after his plane was hit by Jap Zero fighters. The plane caught fire and Major Bleasdale managed to get out somehow. General Walker being dead aboard the ship had to go down with it."[40] Despite lack of medical treatment, Holguin miraculously survived his wounds and brutal treatment in captivity. He was liberated by Australian troops in September 1945.

Meanwhile, MacArthur's recommendation that Walker be awarded the Medal of Honor went rapidly forward. Perhaps inevitably, the question arose as to whether it was "considered above and beyond the call of duty for the commanding officer of a bomber command to accompany it on bombing missions against enemy-held territory," though it seems unlikely any skeptics would prevail over MacArthur's wishes. Maj. Gen. George E. Stratemeyer, Gen. Hap Arnold's chief of staff, replied in writing, "It is the considered opinion of Headquarters Army Air Forces that the conspicuous leadership exemplified by Brig. Gen. Kenneth N. Walker on the specific mission as cited by General MacArthur does constitute action above and beyond the call of duty."[41]

Omitting any reference to his repeated disregard for orders, the subsequent citation recognized Walker for "conspicuous leadership ... involving personal valor and intrepidity at an extreme hazard to life" for repeatedly accompanying units on bombing missions, which allowed him to develop "a highly efficient technique for bombing when opposed by enemy fighter airplanes and antiaircraft fire." The citation also credited the January 5 attack with achieving "direct hits on nine enemy vessels" before his plane was "disabled and forced down by ... an overwhelming number of enemy fighters."[42]

On March 25, 1943, sixteen-year-old Kenneth N. Walker Jr. accepted his father's Medal of Honor from President Franklin D. Roosevelt in the Oval Office at the White House. General Kenney, who attended the ceremony, later praised the president for his sensitivity. "The kindly, fatherly way the President handled the situation, putting young Walker, who was about seventeen, at ease and sending him away with his eyes shining with pride over the nice things F.D.R. had said about his father, was something to watch and listen to," he observed.[43] Later that same year, ten-year-old Douglas Walker accepted his father's Legion of Merit, awarded for the general's efforts in the War Plans Division between July 1941 and March 1942.

After the war, the 604th Graves Registration Company investigated reports regarding the numerous missing aircraft in the Rabaul area. Many crash sites were found, but the wreckage of the *San Antonio Rose* was not among them. It was originally believed the plane had gone down at sea and was unrecoverable. However, a closer study of the evidence—including the capture of Bleasdale and Daniel—indicates a strong possibility that the bomber went down somewhere in Rabaul's rugged, mountainous interior. In 2017, Douglas Walker, then in his eighties, mounted a personal campaign to encourage the Defense POW/MIA Accounting Agency to pursue new leads in the case—even enlisting a U.S. senator in the cause—but with little result. The downed plane has yet to be found.

Fred Wesche survived the war. Years later he still harbored reservations about the Walker mission and subsequent events, including the Medal of Honor award. "The rest of us got the Air Medal [although] of course he did all the planning and whatnot, too, even though many of us thought it was foolhardy, to tell you the truth."[44]

Perhaps the greatest irony is that Walker was killed by the very instrument he had spent his career disparaging, the single-engine fighter—that, and his own stubborn insistence that bombers reigned supreme.

—◠◡—

While Army air units concentrated on Rabaul and Japanese enclaves on New Guinea, Marine fighter squadrons were beginning to expand their dominance of the skies over the Solomons, moving up the chain from Guadalcanal. Among those Marine pilots was a slow-talking twenty-one-year-old from Louisiana bayou country named Jefferson J. DeBlanc.

1st Lt. Jefferson J. DeBlanc
Solomon Islands
January 31, 1943

Jeff DeBlanc was not very far into his combat career before he realized there were two kinds of fighter pilots: aggressive and not so aggressive. There was no doubt which category he fell into—and on January 31, 1943, he proved it in no uncertain fashion.

By the time he arrived in the combat zone in October 1942, Jefferson Joseph DeBlanc had been in the service just over a year. A son of one of Louisiana's oldest families, he had been born in Lockport on February 15, 1921, the fourth child of Frank and Nollie DeBlanc, and was raised in St. Martinville. His father was a brakeman on the railroad. "We lived a slow pace here in Louisiana during the 1930s," remarked DeBlanc. "Since money was scarce, I worked at odd jobs on weekends and was fortunate to work in the sugar cane mills as a bench chemist during the grinding season in the Fall."[45]

The slow pace of DeBlanc's life quickened in the Summer of 1941 when he dropped out of Southwestern Louisiana Institute to enlist in the U.S. Navy's flight program. DeBlanc's fascination with aviation dated back to his boyhood when a pilot made a forced landing near his home and let the excited youngster climb into the cockpit. Right then and there Jeff DeBlanc "switched cowboys and Indians for Eddie Rickenbacker," as he put it.[46] He opted for the Marines after earning his wings at Corpus Christi in May 1942. His graduating class had been earmarked for reconnaissance aircraft; by transferring to the Marines he guaranteed he could stay in fighters. "I had no real knowledge of the Marine Corps except that they were always in the news," he admitted.[47] Less than six months later, with only about 250 flying hours under his belt, the voluble, brash Louisianan joined Marine Fighter Squadron 112 (VMF-112) as it embarked for the war zone.

The squadron arrived at Guadalcanal on November 10. The situation there remained unsettled. "We were fired on by Japanese troops as we landed," DeBlanc recalled. "We were always under fire on takeoffs and landings."[48] DeBlanc found himself flying F4F-4 Grumman Wildcats, though he had only ten hours of experience in the aircraft. "The Wildcat was a flying brick," he remarked. Due to its design, it was also the perfect gun platform. "It was idiot proof," DeBlanc observed.[49]

Flying out of the auxiliary airstrip known as "Fighter-2," DeBlanc downed two Betty bombers and got a probable during an enemy raid on U.S. ships in Ironbottom Sound on November 12. "The action was too fast and too fierce for fear to catch up with me," he said later. "I flew through the barrage from the fleet and locked onto the tail of a Betty and opened fire, killing the rear gunner and watching my tracers strike the engines. The plane burst into flames immediately, and I almost flew into the bomber due to target fixation."[50] DeBlanc recovered, locked onto the tail of another bomber, and flamed it with just a short burst.

Going after a third Betty in a head-on run, he started the left engine smoking and shattered the glass "greenhouse" pilot area. "As I flashed by the bomber and looked down into the cockpit, I clearly saw a third man, kneeling behind and between the two pilots, reach over and pull the pilot in the left seat (who was slumped over the controls) off the controls," he remembered. "The pilots looked like mannequins at the controls."[51] He could not confirm the plane as destroyed, so it went into the books as a probable.

On December 18, he downed a Mitsubishi F1M Pete float biplane, bringing his score to three. Spotting the Pete on the tail of a U.S. dive bomber, DeBlanc made a close head-on attack. The enemy pilot was so intent on the bomber, he didn't see the approaching Wildcat until it was too late. "I could see his frantic motion to move out of my line of fire when he did spot me." The Pete fell off the dive bomber's tail and plunged toward earth.[52] DeBlanc's adventures continued on January 29, 1943, when he had to make a predawn water landing in Ironbottom Sound after his aircraft suffered mechanical failure. Rescued by a destroyer, he was returned to his squadron, still in one piece but with a hearty distaste for night water landings.

On the afternoon of January 31, only two days after his water landing, DeBlanc and seven other pilots were on standby alert. They were playing acey-deucy when orders came down to escort a flight of twelve SBD Dauntless dive bombers in an attack on several Japanese ships about 250 miles from Guadalcanal. According to American intelligence, the ships were carrying troop reinforcements to Guadalcanal. In fact, they had been sent as part of an evacuation effort, not that it mattered to the pilots.

Takeoff time for the mission was 3 p.m. DeBlanc was assigned a Wildcat sporting a painted rendition of a scantily clad blonde on the cowling, accompanied by the optimistic title *Impatient Virgin*. Twenty minutes into the mission, one of the fighter pilots aborted due to a rough engine. A few minutes later, another pilot aborted after radioing that his fuel gauge was malfunctioning. DeBlanc was unimpressed. Few of the Wildcats were problem-free; he doubted more than a couple of the aircraft they were flying would have met stateside flight standards. It was just something the pilots had to put up with.[53]

The remaining pilots had been in the air for some time when DeBlanc noticed that *Impatient Virgin* seemed to be guzzling gas at an inordinately high rate. He tried using the hand pump to bring the fuel pressure back up. When the needle continued its downward sweep, he switched from the belly tank to the main internal gas tank. The needle rose back up to normal, and the engine smoothed out. DeBlanc doubted he could have used up the 50 gallons in the belly tank so quickly unless he had an especially gas-hungry aircraft or the tank itself was malfunctioning—a not-unusual occurrence as the belly tanks were still in the experimental stage. He did some quick figuring and decided he could continue the mission and still get back to the airstrip—barely—if he leaned out the gas to the engine as much as possible.[54]

But as the Wildcats passed by Kolombangara Island at 14,000 feet, the gas gauge needle began dropping again. "I was using gas like mad," he recalled.[55] He now knew for sure he had a gas-hungry plane or there was a leak somewhere. He leaned out the mix some more and radioed the others of his predicament but decided to stick with the flight. "I decided, 'Well hell, I can't make it back, but I'll go ahead and lead the mission,'" he recalled. "We've got to get as many guns as we can up there or the dive bombers would be in trouble. I knew I could get far enough out of enemy territory so when I bailed out it would be nighttime."[56]

They soon arrived over the enemy shipping, and the dive bombers began their attacks. From what DeBlanc could observe, it wasn't a very successful effort; all twelve dive bombers achieved some near misses, but there were no hits that he could see.[57] As the bombers turned away to form up for the flight home, DeBlanc's headphones crackled with a call for assistance. Peering through his canopy, he saw two Petes closing in on the SBDs, one behind the other. An all-metal biplane, the Pete typically carried three 7.7mm machine guns, two fixed forward and one manned by a backseat gunner. Never one to worry much, DeBlanc figured he could knock them both down in one run. He radioed twenty-two-year-old S/Sgt. Jim Feliton of Syracuse, New York, to cover his tail in case he overshot the rear Japanese. If he overshot, Feliton, one of the few noncommissioned pilots in the air group, could nail the rear plane, while DeBlanc took out the leader.

Arming four of his six .50-caliber machine guns, DeBlanc came in on the tail of the trailing Pete. The Japanese rear-seat gunner opened up on him. DeBlanc dropped below to the six o'clock position and squeezed the trigger. "The Pete flamed immediately and dropped off in a slow, grave-yard spiral, burning furiously," he noted. "The plane exploded as I flew over and settled on the tail of the second one, the leader."[58] Again settling in at six o'clock, he centered the gun sight on the cockpit and opened fire. Like DeBlanc's first victim, the fighter caught fire immediately. The pilot had just started a low climbing turn to the right when the doomed plane exploded in a brilliant flash.

DeBlanc was climbing for altitude with Feliton on his wing when a voice on the radio shouted, "Zeros!"[59] In fact, the planes were actually about ten Nakajima Ki-43 Oscars, an Army fighter Allied pilots often mistook for Zeros. Like the Zeros, the Oscars were highly maneuver-able and made difficult targets, though they tended to break apart quickly when hit. The typical versions at this point of the war were armed with two 7.7mm machine guns in the cowling.

Heading for the main formation of American fighters, the Japa-nese pilots failed to see DeBlanc and Feliton, who were about 500 feet below the others and still climbing after knocking down the two float-planes. DeBlanc climbed toward the Japanese leader, laid his gunsight onto the Oscar's flight path, and gave him a burst. "It was like shooting at a fixed target sleeve I had fired on during advanced cadet training," recalled DeBlanc. "There was no way I could miss." The Oscar rolled out of DeBlanc's sights with tremendous violence and tumbled away to the left. The burst had either killed the pilot and his last reflex was to yank the plane over, or "he was the fastest evader I had ever seen," remarked DeBlanc. "I never saw him again and could not claim him."[60]

The leader's wingman started upward in a slow leftward climb, trying to figure out what had happened. DeBlanc got onto his tail, followed the Oscar into a slow upward roll, and then fired. There was no doubt about this kill. The Oscar exploded in midair.

DeBlanc's kill sparked a melee as more Oscars piled in, the dog-fighting aircraft twisting and diving. "To this day I cannot say how many more [Oscars] came down on us," admitted DeBlanc. "Targets were everywhere."[61] Feliton and DeBlanc covered each other with a scissors weave; then Feliton went too wide, took a hit in the engine, and started down, trailing a plume of heavy black smoke.

Almost as quickly as the attack started, the sky was empty of fighters. DeBlanc saw the SBDs starting back to base. As he climbed to overtake them, he spotted two Oscars closing in from behind. He had taken a few hits in the dogfight melee but nothing serious. He was more shocked when he glanced at his fuel gauge and saw how little gas he had left. Now, as the Oscars approached, he had a choice: he could do the safe thing, join the bombers, and hope their combined firepower could hold off the Oscars, or he could tackle the Oscars himself and draw them off the bomber formation. One thing was beyond question: if he took on the Oscars and survived, he would be stranded far from home when he ran out of fuel.

DeBlanc switched on his other two .50s—giving him six—and turned toward the Oscars.

He took on the first fighter in a climbing head-on run. Diving, the Japanese pilot started shooting while still out of range, his tracers looking "like Roman candles on a pair of railroad tracks," recalled DeBlanc. "I put the pipper right above his cockpit."[62] They closed in an instant, and DeBlanc gave him a burst from his six .50s. The enemy plane caught fire immediately but continued straight at him in an apparent effort to ram. DeBlanc frantically held the trigger down, and the Oscar exploded in a ball of flame. Chunks of debris peppered the Wildcat as DeBlanc struggled to regain control, at the same time banking sharply in an effort to get on the tail of the second Oscar. The Japanese fighter had flashed by and turned and was now coming down on DeBlanc in a high-side run.

Too eager for the kill, the enemy pilot misjudged DeBlanc's speed. "When I saw him coming down, I simply dropped the throttle, dropped my flaps and skidded," said DeBlanc. "He fishtailed to stay on my tail, but he passed me up and we looked at each other." For a moment they were wingtip to wingtip. "I could recognize that man today. He knew he was a dead man," observed DeBlanc.[63] The Japanese pilot froze on the controls and flew straight ahead of DeBlanc's Wildcat. They were at 2,000 feet when DeBlanc sent him plummeting into the sea with one short burst. "He couldn't go above me; he couldn't go under me. He had to pull up," explained DeBlanc. "And when he did, I burned him."[64]

DeBlanc just had time to glance at his watch and see that it was nearing 6 p.m. when the watch suddenly flew off his wrist and the instrument panel exploded. A machine-gun bullet had torn off his watch, followed by a projectile (he thought it was a 20mm shell) that came over his left shoulder and smashed into the instrument panel. Another burst caught DeBlanc's Wildcat in the engine. As he struggled to evade, he saw an Oscar (he thought it was a Zero) banking for another pass. Then his shattered canopy blew away with a bang and disappeared.

As the airplane came apart, DeBlanc unbuckled his safety belt, stood up, and jumped for the trailing edge of the left wing. Seconds later he was falling through space, grateful for the sudden quiet. He pulled his ripcord and came up with a jerk as the parachute deployed, but as an Oscar headed back toward him, he realized he should have waited. He played dead, hanging limp in the straps, head down, as the Oscar circled. The enemy pilot went so far as to slide open his canopy as he eyeballed the helpless Marine, but finally the Oscar turned away.

As he swung down toward the glassy sea, DeBlanc tried to calculate his distance to the water. When he judged he was at about ten feet, he unbuckled his harness and fell free. The ten feet turned out to be more like forty, and he went deep under the water but managed to get to the surface with the help of his Mae West. Floating there, gasping for air, he noticed that the life vest was only half inflated—the other half had been shredded. He had also been wounded in the arms, legs, and side.[65]

DeBlanc knew he had come down in Vella Gulf between Kolombangara and Vella Lavella. Considering his options, he decided to swim to enemy-occupied Kolombangara, get ashore, and maybe try to steal a Zero from the Japanese airfield there. That was about the only way he could think of to get home unless he decided to hide in the jungle until the Solomons campaign ended.[66]

It took him several hours to reach land. Dragging himself off the beach and into the undergrowth, he promptly fell asleep. Come daylight he headed down the shoreline. The next night he slept in a tree, but on the second day he found an abandoned hut and moved in. "I heard the birds singing," he observed. "Now I was reared in the swamps [in Louisiana]. When the birds are singing, everything is okay." On the fourth morning, the birds went silent. "And then I knew I was in trouble," said DeBlanc. He looked out of the hut to see a short native with a bone through his nose. The man had a machete and was accompanied by six other natives. "In my mind they were head hunters because they look[ed] like it," said DeBlanc. "I could see myself in the pot." The natives poked at DeBlanc's sunburned skin, apparently amused at the way it turned white, then took him by canoe to a village where he was placed under guard. "They weren't friendly," observed DeBlanc. He was pretty sure they planned to trade him off to the Japanese.[67]

The next day another native, a "very forceful man," arrived in the village, recalled DeBlanc. "This guy came in and threw down a ten-pound bag of rice which he stole from the Japanese. He threw it down at their feet, and they picked it up and let me go. The way he took over and the way he handled those people, I knew I was in safe hands."[68]

Evading Japanese patrols, DeBlanc's rescuer took him through the bush. When they stopped in one village, a native demanded DeBlanc's belt buckle, which was embossed with the Marine Corps eagle, globe, and anchor. DeBlanc recalled a military instructor who advised pilots that if native captors took something from them, they should take something in return, so he promptly grabbed the man's spear. Apparently the trade was satisfactory, for the native departed without making a fuss.[69]

DeBlanc stayed briefly with a British missionary, before continuing on through a chain of friendly natives and Coastwatchers. Along the way, he reunited with Feliton, who had parachuted into the trees on Kolombangara Island and been found the next day by men loyal to the Coastwatchers. A PBY flying boat finally picked them up on February 12. It was twelve days after DeBlanc had been shot down and only three days before his twenty-second birthday. He came out wearing a Japanese uniform he had salvaged from a wrecked enemy cargo vessel.

Receiving a promotion to captain in June, DeBlanc flew with Marine Fighter Squadron 122 for just over a month before returning to the States. He returned to the shooting war in November but had no more aerial victories until May 28, 1945, when he shot down a Japanese dive bomber off Okinawa. The victory was his ninth and last.

DeBlanc's decision to attack the enemy Oscars and protect the SBD dive bombers, despite knowing he wouldn't have enough gas to get home—along with his tally of five kills on January 31—earned him the Navy Cross. That decoration was later upgraded to the Medal of Honor. The medal was presented on December 6, 1946, by President Harry S. Truman during a ceremony at the White House. DeBlanc remained humble. "My life changed when they traded me for a sack of rice," he remarked years later. "It changed all my sense of values."[70]

After the war, DeBlanc married his high school sweetheart and started a family. He and his wife, Louise, eventually had five children. The fighter ace went back to school, taking advantage of the GI Bill, and earned a BS, MS, MA, and PhD. He taught math and physics in St. Martin Parish, later becoming a school system supervisor. Well into his seventies, he was still teaching in the public school system part-time, serving as director of the local planetarium, and taking active part in the state Senior Olympics.

Jeff DeBlanc died on November 22, 2007, in Lafayette, Louisiana, from complications of pneumonia. He was 86. Predeceased in 2005 by wife, Louise, he left four sons, a daughter, seven grandchildren, and four great-grandchildren. He was buried at St. Michael Cemetery in St. Martinville, Louisiana.

Prior to his death, DeBlanc made arrangements to donate his Medal of Honor to the World War II Museum in New Orleans. As for his actions on January 31, 1943, he reiterated that it was his job to protect the dive bomber crews, and he wasn't going to bug out and have their deaths on his conscience. "Now I'm not a brave man, but I have to live with myself," he explained.[71] Some pilots are aggressive and some are not, he observed. As for him, well, he admitted, "I'm a born agitator."[72]

—⁂—

With Guadalcanal in hand, planning began for a move up the northern Solomon Islands. Next stop would be Bougainville, but intelligence on the anticipated landing area was limited. The planners needed photos. The quest for those photos would result in the most decorated single mission in Air Force history.

2nd Lt. Joseph R. Sarnoski
Capt. Jay Zeamer Jr.
Solomon Islands
June 16, 1943

As far as the 22nd Bomb Group was concerned, 1st Lt. Jay Zeamer was a bit of a screwball. The twenty-four-year-old New Jersey native was affable and competent enough on the ground, but once he climbed into the copilot's seat of his B-26 Marauder bomber, he seemed to just zone out. Called on the carpet for losing formation during a bombing attack, a pilot complained he had been trying to wake Zeamer up from a sound sleep—actually pounding on the copilot's chest before he finally awoke. Zeamer then performed his duties and dozed off again. The guy was a nut.

Zeamer's family might have told the frustrated pilot that his narcoleptic nemesis was not a nut exactly—he was just a little different. He was born on July 18, 1918, the first of four children of Jay and Marjorie Zeamer, with family roots extending back to the American Revolution. His father, who had a lucrative job as an international salesman and later vice president of a global leather export business, moved the family from Pennsylvania to Orange, New Jersey, when Jay was two years old. Reasonably well to do, they spent summers in Boothbay Harbor, Maine, where the youngster demonstrated a strong independent streak, exploring Penobscot Bay aboard a rickety rowboat he built out of scrap lumber. Also fascinated with flying, he filled his room with model airplanes, "impressive for their quality and complexity," recalled his brother.[73] If Jay was interested in a subject, his energy was boundless—he became an Eagle Scout at the age of fourteen—but those passions often came at the detriment of other, less stimulating obligations, such as his schoolwork.

Unimpressed with Zeamer's grades as a freshman at Orange High School, his father packed him off to Culver Military Academy in 1933 in hopes, as Zeamer later said, it would "knock some schooling into me."[74] Well liked by faculty and students, he earned laurels as a crack marksman and was dubbed the "pride and joy" of Company A, according to a school newspaper columnist, while still managing to graduate in the bottom of the Class of 1936. His counselors suggested he might be wise to pursue a trade. Instead, the unflappable youth applied to the Massachusetts Institute of Technology (MIT). When MIT turned him down, Zeamer drove to Cambridge and sought an audience with the dean of admissions. Through a combination of persistence and Zeamer charm, he finagled a deal that if he performed well during a year of junior college at Culver and attended summer school, MIT would reconsider. Applying himself to a rigorous curriculum, Zeamer satisfied those conditions and was admitted to MIT in the Fall of 1938.

It was at MIT that Zeamer's boyhood interest in aviation became a passion when a fellow student introduced him to the school's flying club. Going up for a ride in the club's lone aircraft, a forty-horsepower Piper Cub, Zeamer was hooked. Pursuing his new passion with typical single-mindedness, he earned his pilot's license within a year and even flew the club's Piper Cub home to New Jersey during school vacations. Following his sophomore year, he applied for Navy flight school but was turned down when he failed the eye test. Undeterred, he began a series of exercises in an effort to strengthen his eyesight.

As it turned out, the Navy's loss was the Army's gain. That September an Army Air Corps flight surgeon visited MIT offering to give physicals to students interested in applying for flight school. Twenty-seven students took the physical. Surprisingly, Zeamer, who stood six feet tall and was a veritable scarecrow at about 140 pounds, was one of only four to be accepted, even passing the eye test. Graduating from MIT in June 1940 with a degree in civil engineering, he reported for Army flight training. As was typically the case when his interest was engaged, he excelled. He was named captain of cadets of his training class, and his fitness for military service was deemed "superior."[75] He received his wings in March 1941 and was commissioned as a second lieutenant in the U.S. Army Air Corps. His only disappointment—and this one he would not be able to surmount—was that he was too tall to qualify for fighters.

The outbreak of war found Zeamer flying with the 22nd Bomb Group as copilot on the recently introduced B-26 Marauder. Ironically, while adept at the controls of a wide variety of other aircraft, the somewhat quirky Marauder, sometimes called the "Widowmaker" or "Flying Coffin," seemed to be beyond Zeamer's mastery. Powered by two powerful

Pratt & Whitney R-2800 eighteen-cylinder radial engines, the Marauder required unusually high takeoff and landing speeds. Despite intense tutoring, Zeamer's efforts to land the aircraft almost invariably resulted in near disaster. To his disgust, it appeared he would never be promoted from copilot to first pilot with a crew of his own.

After a stint flying antisubmarine patrols off the West Coast, Zeamer's bomb group was deployed to Australia in March 1942. Settling in at coastal Townsville, the group flew the first B-26 mission of the war—a night raid on Rabaul—on April 6. Over the next few months, the squadron conducted raids on Japanese bases on New Guinea and flew patrols against enemy shipping. Still flying as copilot—essentially a passenger with no prospect of being promoted to pilot—Zeamer apparently fell victim to his own boredom and stopped focusing on what was expected of him. When all air crews were ordered to wear their issue coveralls when flying, Zeamer blithely continued to show up in shorts. In the air he seemed oblivious, a detachment that reached a climax when he famously fell asleep during a bombing raid on Lae in late summer. As a result, when he requested a transfer to the 43rd Bombardment Group—a B-17 outfit he had served with briefly before ending up in the 22nd with its frustrating Marauders—he was promptly sent on his way with blessings.

He reported for duty with the 403rd Bombardment Squadron at Torrens Creek, Australia, on September 22. Lacking experience in B-17s, he became a self-described "errand boy" for the squadron but scrounged up flights where he could in whatever capacity was available, even flying as navigator if that was the only available opening.[76] His patience paid off on November 20 when he filled in for a pilot on a photo reconnaissance mission over Rabaul. No one asked if Zeamer had been officially checked out to fly as first pilot on a B-17—he hadn't—and Zeamer, anxious to fly, didn't feel compelled to elaborate.

Arriving over Rabaul's Simpson Harbor with cameramen from the 8th Photographic Reconnaissance Squadron, he found the target area obscured by heavy cloud cover. He had been ordered not to descend below 25,000 feet due to the threat of antiaircraft fire, but in typical Zeamer fashion, he blithely disregarded the directive. "I never took the pressure from the higher-ups very seriously," he said later. "It wasn't so much outright disobedience as it was just trying to do what we thought was the right thing."[77] Descending through the clouds to a mere 8,000 feet, he popped out over the harbor in skies that were, as he said later, "clear as a bell."[78] The harbor was choked with shipping—some 110 vessels, ranging from warships to cargo carriers, by the bombardier's count—and they immediately filled the skies with antiaircraft fire as Zeamer appeared overhead.

"Zeros above!" the waist gunner suddenly warned.[79] The turret gunner counted over a dozen Zeros heading after them as Zeamer wrenched the B-17 into a stomach-churning dive that blew the entry hatch off the belly turret. "We peeled the damn paint off the wings in the power dive," recalled lower ball gunner Jim Eaton. "We certainly didn't take any pictures because nobody was nuts enough to be hanging out of the window with the plane hurtling downward."[80]

Zeamer leveled off at 3,000 feet, skidding the big bomber from side to side as three of the Zeros pounced. The port waist gunner knocked down one of the enemy fighters. The starboard waist gunner blasted the tail off another as Zeamer skidded left. The third disintegrated in a hail of .50-caliber slugs from the top turret gunner. Zeamer ducked into the clouds and eventually managed to elude any further pursuit.

Unperturbed, Zeamer then decided to check out what he mistakenly believed to be a newly captured airstrip at Buna. "As we approached the airstrip at Buna I see nine Zeros flying right on the deck," recalled Jim Eaton.[81] The fighters immediately turned their attention to the lone bomber. Maneuvering the huge plane at treetop level—so close to the ground that dust clouds eddied up in their wake—Zeamer put the bomber into a violent series of evasive skids, at one point actually turning directly toward one enemy fighter, forcing the Japanese pilot into a game of chicken. The Zero soared upward and fell victim to Zeamer's turret gunner. His gunners claimed two more before the remaining attackers broke off and the bomber crew made their exit, the most serious damage being a flat tire.

Zeamer was recommended for the Silver Star for the harrowing mission—an award a shaken Jim Eaton felt was definitely misplaced. Eaton recalled that after they were finally safely on the ground, "I got out, went up to the pilot, asked his name, and told him I wasn't ever going to fly with him again."[82] But for Zeamer, the mission had a huge benefit: the Silver Star award finally allowed his permanent transition from copilot to first pilot.

At about this time, Zeamer reconnected with an old friend from his training days, Joseph Raymond Sarnoski, a twenty-eight-year-old sergeant from Pennsylvania coal country. The two had first met back in the States when Sarnoski, considered one of the two most outstanding bombardiers in the Air Force at the time, was teaching would-be pilots the rudiments of bombing. Completely indifferent to their disparity in rank, Zeamer asked Sarnoski to join him for a beer so that he could pick his brain. The two rapidly became good friends, though their backgrounds could not have been more dissimilar.

Three years older than Zeamer, Joe Sarnoski was one of sixteen children of Polish immigrants. His father had worked in the coal mines to scrape up enough money to buy a small farmstead, which allowed them to live pretty much hand-to-mouth. Joe, who shared a room with his six brothers, was the first in the family to finish high school. Though small in stature, he was a natural athlete, earning renown as a standout infielder on the school baseball team. He learned to play the accordion and became accomplished enough to pick up gigs at various parties and events. A devout Catholic, he regularly attended Mass and was never without his hand-carved wooden rosary beads stowed in a convenient pocket.

Sarnoski, like Jay Zeamer and so many others of their generation, became enthralled with aviation as a youth, building models and clipping pictures of aircraft from newspapers and magazines to adorn his bedroom walls. In 1936, having turned twenty-one and assured by his parents that his siblings would be able to carry his load at the farm, Sarnoski hopped on a bus to Baltimore and enlisted in the Air Corps. By the time Zeamer encountered him at Langley Air Force Base five years later, the kid from coal country was a highly respected staff sergeant, teaching a bombing and gunnery class.

Sarnoski had arrived in New Guinea as a squadron bombardier, but his squadron commander had recently been lost flying as an observer on another mission, and his crew was on the verge of being split up. Sarnoski was anxious to get his share of the shooting war. He wrote to his family that he'd like to sink at least five enemy ships, adding he would be ashamed to come home without having made a contribution to the war effort. So when Zeamer asked him to help form a crew of their own, he jumped at the chance.

A squadron commander who knew Zeamer later wrote that he recruited "a crew of renegades and screwballs."[83] While that comment subsequently became part of the Zeamer myth—a misfit accompanied by a crew of misfits—it is essentially nonsense. Zeamer may have had his quirks, but he was a highly competent pilot, and he valued competence in others. Though he would never shake the "screwball" label as the Zeamer myth evolved, his close friend, Walt Krell, recalled him as unhurried, steady, and methodical. He was "pensive, calm and collected ... never raised his voice, lost his temper, swore, criticized, or found fault with the situation."[84] Whatever ball turret gunner Jim Eaton might have thought, Zeamer simply knew what the B-17 was capable of and was willing to push the plane to limits that other pilots would not dare.

As it ultimately shaped up—and there would be changes along the way—Zeamer's volunteer crew members were also perfectly capable. Aside from tormenting the crew with Polish serenades over the aircraft interphone, Joe Sarnoski was certainly no screwball. Others that signed on with Zeamer—copilot Lt. Hank Dyminski, radio operator Sgt. Willie "Willy" Vaughan, gunner Sgt. Johnnie Able (such a talented mechanic that he had not been allowed to fly, much to his distress), waist gunner Sgt. George Kendrick, tail gunner Sgt. Herbert ("Pudge") Pugh (another devout Catholic who regularly attended Mass with fellow Pennsylvanian Joe Sarnoski), and flight engineer Sgt. Bud Thues—were most certainly not renegades and screwballs. What they did have in common was a keen desire to fly and a willingness to undertake challenging missions that gave other crews pause.

They got results: among their early victims was an 8,000-ton Japanese freighter, a coup that earned them all Air Medals. However, another mission was reportedly foiled by the highly religious Sarnoski—who, while anxious to get at the enemy, also paid heed to a higher moral authority. In February the crew was sent to bomb a Rabaul hotel where intelligence suspected high-ranking Japanese officers were billeted. Troubled that the attack would inevitably kill civilians, Sarnoski directed his bombs toward a fuel depot instead. Ordered out a second time with the same objective, Sarnoski again avoided the hotel and dropped the bomb load on an ammunition dump. They were not sent back again.[85]

The following month, Zeamer and his crew transferred into the 65th Bombardment Squadron, leaving their navigator, who decided to stay with his old unit. Zeamer was promoted to captain on April 9 and soon afterward was designated operations officer. The latter was a gift from the gods as it allowed Zeamer to volunteer for specific missions. And volunteer he did. "We'd fly anything that needed to be done," Zeamer recalled.[86] He and his assembled crew soon became known as the "Eager Beavers" for their enthusiasm.

Without an assigned B-17 of their own, Zeamer's crew could fly only as other planes became available. But one day waist gunner George Kendrick told Zeamer of a B-17E that might be available. The aircraft, #41-2666, had started with the 8th Photographic Reconnaissance Squadron, where it gained a reputation for being a "Hard-luck Hattie" as it seemed to get shot up on a regular basis. Jumped by three Japanese fighters on December 22, it had survived a damaged left wing and loss of an engine, which required lengthy repairs.

The 8th Photo Squadron had been glad to see the last of the plane when it went over to the 65th Squadron, where Kendrick spotted it. "Nobody will fly it anymore because every time it goes out it gets shot to hell," he observed.[87] Zeamer found the bomber had been set up for reconnaissance and still had its K-17 trimetrogon camera mounts. Seizing the unexpected opportunity, he obtained permission to revamp the unpopular B-17—soon to become known as *Old 666*.

As it turned out, "revamp" was an understatement; Zeamer's crew transformed *Old 666* into what may have been the most heavily armed B-17 in existence. To increase speed, they stripped out any "unnecessary weight"—2,000 pounds of it, everything from ammo chutes to piss pipes—and installed four new Wright Cyclone engines cannibalized from other junked planes. Then they added extra .50-caliber machine guns, including twin .50s in the radio hatch and at the waist. They cut a port in the bottom of the fuselage to add another .50-caliber and installed yet another on the nose deck forward of the cockpit, rigged so Zeamer could fire it from the pilot's seat. Zeamer dubbed this addition the "Snozzola gun." By the time they were done, *Old 666* sported no less than sixteen machine guns. "Everyone was talking about [Zeamer] and his renegades and their loaded .50-calibers," recalled another bomber pilot.[88]

Now with their own plane, Zeamer and his Eager Beavers quickly became the go-to crew when photos were needed. "You couldn't keep them on the ground," wrote flight commander Walt Krell. "It was the damnedest thing."[89] It was the perfect fit for Zeamer's individualistic personality. Flying alone, unescorted, he did not have to answer to anyone else and could exercise his own judgment. His crew believed in him implicitly. "As Captain Zeamer's crew, we thought so much of him and had such absolute trust in him and his ability, that frankly we didn't give a damn where we went, just so long as he wanted to go there," observed Able. "Anything okay by him was okay by us."[90]

Among their more memorable missions was a night bombing raid on Japanese-held Wewak Airfield on the north coast of New Guinea in May. Zeamer had been ordered to get in and get out—no strafing—but when he saw searchlights pinpointing the bombers coming in behind him, he ignored that directive and tore down the field shooting up the lights in a low-level strafing run. Initially threatened with disciplinary action for that bit of disobedience, he escaped punishment after the press got a hold of the story and praised his bold response. Instead of a reprimand, he received a second Silver Star.

Meanwhile, Zeamer had caught wind of plans for a photo reconnaissance mission to map the western coast of Bougainville near Empress Augusta Bay for a potential landing by U.S. Marines. The area looked promising, but little was known about the reefs and topography. The 8th Photographic Reconnaissance Squadron had attempted to obtain photos four times, but equipment failures and bad weather had foiled each effort. It was not a mission for the faint of heart. The unaccompanied aircraft making the 1,200-mile round-trip would have to fly a steady course for over twenty minutes at 25,000 feet along miles of coast well within reach of fighters from nearby enemy installations. In order to obtain proper photo coverage, the crew would be unable to take evasive action from ground fire or attacking enemy fighters during that run. Even a slight tilt of the wings—as little as a degree—could throw the accuracy off by as much as a mile, rendering the photos useless. Zeamer asked his crew if they wanted to go. All stepped forward.

Week after week, uncooperative weather and cloud cover over the target area repeatedly forced postponement of the photo flight. Finally, on June 15, the Eager Beavers got the call. "On June 15, they called me; they said tomorrow's the day," Zeamer remembered. "We're finally getting a day clear enough. So we worked like mad that whole day finally getting the airplane ready."[91]

Two of Zeamer's regular crew members—copilot Dyminski and flight engineer Bud Thues—had been hospitalized with malaria and were unable to make the mission. Dyminski was replaced by 2nd Lt. John T. Britton, a former University of California boxing standout. The squadron's armaments chief, Sgt. Forrest Dillman, who had graduated near the top of his class in gunnery school but never flown combat before, would man the belly turret. The usual belly turret gunner, Johnnie Able, would take Thues's position in the top turret. Also going along was 1st Lt. Ruby Johnston, a cool-headed bantam of a Floridian, who had come aboard after Zeamer's original navigator opted to stay with their former squadron. Joe Sarnoski would man the bombardier's spot in the glassed-in nose of *Old 666*, which Zeamer had newly renamed *Lucy* in honor of a girlfriend back in the States. Recently promoted from the ranks to second lieutenant at Zeamer's urging, Sarnoski was on the verge of returning to the States as an instructor. Though Zeamer didn't need a bombardier for this reconnaissance mission—the bomb bay itself housed two auxiliary fuel tanks to increase the aircraft's range—Sarnoski was not about to be left behind. He would man one of the nose machine guns.

At 10 p.m., as Zeamer tried with little success to catch some sleep before their 4 a.m. departure, he received a phone call from Fifth Bomber Group Operations Command. An officer, whose name Zeamer did not catch, told him there seemed to be an increase in activity at Buka, a small island with a Japanese-built airfield located across a narrow strait just north of Bougainville. The 8th Photographic Reconnaissance Squadron had sent a plane over Buka earlier in the day, but the effort went for naught when the specialized cameras malfunctioned. The officer ordered Zeamer to reconnoiter the Buka airfield before commencing the main photo mission.

Zeamer could scarcely believe his ears. The order was lunacy. Swinging over Buka would alert every enemy fighter in the region just before he spent the next twenty-some-odd minutes plodding along photographing the Bougainville coast. "Hell no!" he snapped. "I'm going up to do a mapping and that's it; nobody's going to interfere with that."[92] He hung up before the caller could respond. But the officer, whoever he was, wasn't done yet. Six hours later, as Zeamer taxied *Old 666* onto the runway, a Jeep raced up, and a courier handed over a written order to reconnoiter Buka before the main mission. The order was signed by a colonel who had promised Zeamer full autonomy to run the mission as he saw fit. Zeamer doubted the colonel had ever even seen the order, much less signed it, but he put it from his mind as they roared down the runway and lifted off into the darkness. It was Zeamer's forty-seventh mission.

Three hours later, as dawn creased the eastern horizon, the Bougainville coastline came into view thirty minutes ahead of schedule. "The air was just clear as a bell, but the sun wasn't high enough yet to do mapping," recalled Zeamer. "We had to kill half an hour." Earlier he had assured the crew he intended to ignore the order to reconnoiter Buka. But now, with time to kill, he reconsidered. "I called the crew on the interphone," he said. "I said we can fly out over the ocean for fifteen minutes and come back to this, our starting point here, or if we really wanted to, we could fly out to Buka passage and do the reconnaissance and come back here and do the mapping. And they came back to me and said, 'What the hell, let's do the damned reconnaissance.'"[93]

Once over Buka, Zeamer realized his decision had been a mistake. The airfield was crowded with planes—at least twenty Japanese fighters in the open with a dozen or more visible in revetments. Pilots were already scrambling to get aloft as the B-17 came into view. Seconds later, the fighters began lifting off by twos and threes. It was 8:30 a.m.

Zeamer briefly considered abandoning the Bougainville mission and running for home. "I should have just broke out for home and to hell with the mapping," he admitted later.[94] But he knew the success or failure of any amphibious landing on Bougainville could well hinge on the photos he was supposed to obtain. With luck, it would take the Zeros from Buka a half an hour to reach altitude and catch up with him. Against his better judgment, he turned south along the Bougainville coast, cameras clicking. Down below, still more Zeros were visible lifting off from Bougainville's Buin airdrome.

They almost made it. *Old 666* was 21 minutes and 15 seconds into the run when Zeros from Buka finally began to close. Kendrick, operating the cameras, radioed, "Give me forty-five more seconds."[95] Four Zeros and some type of twin-engine fighter—probably an Army Ki-45 Nick—were climbing toward them at a 45-degree angle. Zeamer was dismayed to see that the Zeros, sporting Navy gray paint jobs, were the newer, fast-climbing Model 22 A6M3s. "They were heading straight up at us," he recalled.[96]

Dillman in the bottom ball turret and Pugh at the rear gun let off bursts that momentarily deterred the approaching fighters. Then one of the Zeros came at them from the ten o'clock position. "Give 'em hell!" shouted Sarnoski over the interphone as he opened up with the .50-caliber in the nose.[97] Zeamer saw the tracers arching toward the attacking Zero. Flashes appeared along the wings and from the nose of the Zero as the pilot replied with his machine guns and two 20mm cannons. Zeamer thought Sarnoski had scored a hit, but as the Zero spun out of sight, the others executed a simultaneous frontal attack.

Zeamer opened up with his forward-firing "Snozzola gun." He thought he scored a kill, but as the Zero fell off, several 20mm shells tore into the nose and cockpit area. An explosion blew out the window next to Zeamer; another shell ripped a gaping hole in the fuselage between the cockpit and the navigator's compartment and sent shards of metal spraying all over.

Dazed, Zeamer wondered if he was dead. Cold air rushed through the hole in the cockpit. As he started to regain his senses, he saw Britton slumped in the copilot's seat, his eyes closed. The instrument panel had been shattered; the altimeter hung from a wire. One of the rudder pedals had been blown away; the other was bent at a 90-degree angle. The interphone was out, but he could hear machine-gun fire from the top turret manned by Johnnie Able. Then he became aware of the pain. His left leg had been shredded, broken both above and below the knee, pieces of bone gleaming whitely in the tatter of bloody flesh. His knee looked like a heap of raw hamburger. He had also been hit in the right leg and both arms. Blood squirted from his left wrist with every heartbeat, pooling in his lap.

Another 20mm shell had torn through *Old 666*'s Plexiglas nose and exploded in the compartment, hurling Sarnoski to the deck. Stationed just behind him, Ruby Johnston, bleeding from a wound to his head, crawled to the fallen bombardier and rolled him over on his back. The blood pouring from Sarnoski's neck and a gaping hole in his abdomen was already starting to turn to slush in the frigid air blasting through the shattered Plexiglas.

As Johnston poured sulfa powder in the horrific wounds, Sarnoski opened his eyes and looked up at him. "I'm all right," he managed, blood running from his mouth. "Don't worry about me."[98] The bombardier struggled to his hands and knees and crawled back to his machine gun, leaving a smear of gore in his wake. Crouching behind the gun, he resumed firing as the twin-engine Japanese fighter began a run on *Old 666*. Zeamer saw flashes at the enemy plane's wing roots as the aircraft broke off and disappeared.

Zeamer tried to get a damage report, but the interphone was dead. Johnston stuck his head through the hole blasted between his compartment and the cockpit. He had been hit in the head, back, and side and was covered with purple hydraulic fluid, but he was still functioning. The main hydraulic reservoir had been knocked out, he reported. The landing gear could be lowered manually, but no hydraulics meant no brakes if they ever got to the point of landing *Old 666*, which at the moment seemed highly unlikely.

Manning the top turret, Johnnie Able had been firing away with his twin .50s. A Zero, apparently trailing smoke, fell off, barely missing *Old 666*'s right wingtip just before the spray of metal shell fragments tearing through the cockpit hit Able in the legs and knocked out power to the turret. Tumbling to the deck, he saw that the oxygen bottles and hydraulic tubes behind the cockpit were burning and tried to beat out the flames with his bare hands. Ruby Johnston, who had emerged from the navigator's compartment to seek bandages for the gash to his head and his injured left forearm, pitched in, and they managed to extinguish the fire.

Meanwhile, Britton, who had slammed his head during the explosion, regained consciousness. "They were up there after us . . . and it was hell," he said later. "They shot out my window, but everything [came] in on Jay's side and he caught hell."[99] Britton had been lucky: leaning forward in his seat, he had narrowly escaped being hit by a spray of shrapnel that slammed into his head rest. But the cockpit was a mess. The only workable instruments in the shattered dash were the manifold pressure gauge and the magnetic compass. Climbing out of his seat as Zeamer continued to fly the plane, Britton went aft to check on the rest of the crew and assess any other damage. He returned with more bad news: a shell had destroyed the oxygen tanks behind the cockpit. They needed to get below 10,000 feet before what little oxygen they had left in their individual bottles ran out and they lost consciousness.

"The blood was running down from my hands and my hands were slippery on the wheel," remembered Zeamer. "I figured we had to get the hell out of there because there were seventeen more [Zeros] pulling up on the tail so I just pulled the airplane over on the right and pushed it into a steep dive. I figured one more time [Japanese attack] and we'd be done."[100]

Zeamer put *Old 666* into a screaming dive, finally wrenching the plane level at what he guessed to be about 10,000 feet, estimating their altitude by increases in the engines' manifold pressure. The rapid descent solved the oxygen problem but failed to shake the Japanese. "We straightened out at about 10,000 feet and the Zeros started to line up on both sides," he recalled. "I counted about seven or eight on one side and about the same number on the other side and I just rolled over and pulled back for all I was worth to make a side step. I must have done that maneuver about six or seven times, so I had to fly that thing like crazy. We didn't need any more hits."[101]

Zeamer headed southwest under continual attack by enemy fighters. The Japanese formed a loop, attacking one after the other, concentrating on the front of the battered bomber. The wire to Zeamer's "Snozzola gun" had been shot out, leaving the forward-firing machine gun inoperative. Up in the nose, Joe Sarnoski, who had been returning fire as best he could despite his grievous wounds, finally collapsed over his machine gun. Ruby Johnston returned to the navigator's compartment, where he manned the .50-caliber machine gun, though nearly blinded by a mask of blood from his head wound. Behind the cockpit, Willy Vaughan was bleeding from a wound to his neck, but Kendrick blasted away from the waist, scrambling from gun to gun, while Pugh defended the tail. The power line to Dillman's ball turret had been knocked out, leaving him stuck with his guns facing aft. Fortunately, *Old 666*'s engines remained undamaged.

Zeamer kept turning into the oncoming fighters, keeping just inside the trajectory of their fixed fire, throwing off their aim and allowing Kendrick to get a shot at the attackers as they flashed by. His flying boots filled with blood from his leg wounds. During a lull he pulled off his belt and made a futile effort to tie a tourniquet around his left thigh. He might have simply bled out entirely except that the cold wind rushing through the holes in the cockpit by his legs helped coagulate the blood seeping from his wounds. Britton pleaded with Zeamer to let him take over the controls. Zeamer stubbornly refused, convinced he was the only one capable of executing the violent maneuvers that were keeping them alive.

At long last, the Japanese began to break off. They had chased *Old 666* for forty minutes and over 100 miles. Now, low on fuel and believing the bomber was doomed, they finally turned for home. Though the bomber crew was later credited with shooting down five enemy fighters, Japanese records indicate that only one Zero had been forced to ditch; another pilot had broken off the attack and returned to base after his fuel tank was holed in the initial run on the B-17.

Zeamer, realizing his shot-up plane wouldn't make it back to base over New Guinea's towering Owen Stanley Mountains, decided to head for Dobodura Airfield, which was a hundred miles closer. Finally relinquishing the controls and in excruciating pain, he allowed Britton to stick him with a morphine syrette. With Britton, who had the most medical training, tending to the wounded, Johnnie Able temporarily took over in the copilot's seat. He knew the controls and systems almost as well as the pilots, and Zeamer helped with the finer points as he drifted in and out of consciousness.

Herbert Pugh came forward from the tail gun position and squirmed through the crawl space to the shattered nose of the aircraft in search of his friend Sarnoski. The compartment was covered in blood. He found Sarnoski slumped by the machine gun. Pugh pulled his friend's head onto his lap, cradling him as he retrieved the ever-present rosary from the bombardier's pocket and pressed it into his hand. A few minutes later, Sarnoski briefly opened his eyes. He lifted the rosary to his lips, then closed his eyes again. Johnston called into the compartment to ask how Sarnoski was doing. Distraught, all Pugh could bring himself to say was, "He's all right. He's all right."[102] But soon afterward, the gallant bombardier drew his last breath.

The sun was overhead as they approached the 7,000-foot grass strip at Dobodura. Britton took over the controls from Able. Lapsing in and out of consciousness, Zeamer saw the control tower flash by as Britton brought them in with no brakes or flaps. *Old 666* touched down and raced far too fast toward the end of the runway. Britton turned the wheel as hard as he could, intentionally throwing the plane into a ground loop. The big bomber skidded around in a shower of dirt and dust and finally came to a halt in what Britton recalled as the best landing of his life. It was 12:15 p.m. It had been more than eight hours since they had taken off from Port Moresby.

"All of a sudden I felt the wheels touch the ground," recalled Zeamer. "All I could see was gray. I was passing out off and on from loss of blood."[103] Slumped in the pilot's seat, he heard a voice from very far away say, "Get the pilot last. He's dead."[104] He didn't have the strength to protest. "I was too weak to respond to that," he remembered. "I wanted to lift my head and tell him he's full of shit. But a moment later I felt myself being pulled out the top of the airplane by my shoulders."[105] Then he blacked out.

By all rights, Jay Zeamer should have been dead. He had lost nearly half the blood in his body. The medics managed to keep him alive with infusions of plasma, and the following day he and his crew were flown in to Port Moresby, where Zeamer continued to hover near death. A call went out for type O blood. Airmen lined up to donate for transfusions that continued for the next two and a half days. Surgeons removed 120 chunks of metal—including pieces of the plane's rudder pedals and control cables—from Zeamer's legs, arms, and torso. They would have amputated his left leg but felt he had lost too much blood to survive the operation. Due to a premature report, his family back home in Orange, New Jersey, was notified that he had been killed in action—an error that wasn't cleared up until three days later as his relatives were making preparations for a memorial service.

Joe Sarnoski's family was not so blessed. "For two weeks in the hospital, I kept asking 'Where's Joe?'" recalled Zeamer. "Finally, they told me. He was dead."[106]

Old 666 sported 187 bullet holes and five cannon holes but had survived one of the longest continuous fighter pursuits in the history of the U.S. Air Force. The valuable photos of the Bougainville coast were sent on to the planners of the upcoming invasion. Zeamer was back in the States undergoing treatment at Walter Reed Army Hospital when he received a phone call from an officer at the Pentagon. The caller asked if Zeamer would prefer to receive his medal in Washington, DC, or in his own hometown. Perplexed, Zeamer replied that he already had all his medals, including two Silver Stars, two Distinguished Flying Crosses, two Air Medals, and the Purple Heart. No, said the officer, the medal he was referring to was the Medal of Honor. Zeamer dropped the phone.

Zeamer received the award from Army Air Forces chief Gen. Hap Arnold on January 16, 1944, at the Pentagon. Joe Sarnoski was also awarded the Medal of Honor. The posthumous award was presented to his widow, Mrs. Marie Maddox Sarnoski, the following January in her hometown of Richmond, Virginia. It was the only instance of the war wherein two members of the same air crew were awarded the medal for separate and independent acts of heroism in the same engagement. The remaining members of *Old 666*'s crew were each awarded the Distinguished Service Cross. Six of them also received the Purple Heart for wounds suffered in the action. The flight remains the most highly decorated single air mission in Air Force history.

Zeamer had hoped to continue flying, but though he made a valiant effort, the effects of his wounds were too great, and he was eventually discharged from the Air Force. He returned to MIT, obtained a master's degree in aeronautical engineering in 1946, and enjoyed a long career in the aerospace industry. He married in 1949. He and his wife, Barbara, had five daughters. Barbara Zeamer said he rarely talked about the medal. "I think he didn't feel he deserved it. He was so close to his bombardier and he felt terrible about his being killed," she said after Zeamer's death in 2007.[107] Zeamer admitted he felt guilty. "I kept kicking myself. I was a 'stupe' flying that recon mission," he confessed years after the war. "I feel Joe's death was my fault. I got him promoted [to lieutenant] and then I got him killed."[108]

Zeamer moved to Boothbay Harbor, Maine—the scene of so many childhood escapades—in 1968. When he died in a nursing home at the age of 88 on March 22, 2007, he was the last living Air Force Medal of Honor recipient from World War II. He was interred with appropriate honors at Arlington National Cemetery. His passing received considerable media coverage, but Zeamer may have left his own best epitaph in a conversation with a reporter in 1947 about those terrible hours during his final mission. Asked what life's experiences had taught him, he replied, "I learned that there is always a way—that you can do anything if you set your mind to it and work hard enough for it."[109]

6

Whistling Death

THE MAINSTAY U.S. FIGHTER DURING THE STRUGGLE FOR GUADALCA-
nal and the dark days of 1942 had been the F4F Wildcat. But as the year
ran out, a new fighter, the F4U Corsair, began to make its appearance.
Originally intended as a Navy carrier plane, the distinctive gull-winged
Vought F4U featured a powerful Pratt & Whitney R-2800-18W radial
engine generating 2,235 horsepower driving a four-bladed propeller.
The massive (for a fighter) plane had a maximum speed of about 450
mph, a climb rate of 4,360 feet per minute, and a maximum range of
between 900 and 1,000 miles; it was armed with six .50-caliber machine
guns.

When the Navy had difficulty adapting the Corsair to carrier use—
primarily due to visibility issues with the cockpit arrangement during deck
landings and takeoffs—the planes were passed on to the Marines, who
considered them a godsend. With Guadalcanal now in hand, the Marines
needed a fighter with more range than the Wildcat as they began escort
missions into the Northern Solomons. The fact that the big fighter had
proved troublesome for carrier service was not important as most of the
Marine flying was done from land bases.

The first F4Us arrived on Guadalcanal in February 1943. The Japanese would come to call their new nemesis "Whistling Death" (the
Marines called the Corsair the "Bent Wing Widow Maker"). By the
end of the war, Corsair pilots would claim 2,140 enemy aircraft for an
overall kill ratio of over 11:1. Eighty-six Marines and thirty-four naval
aviators would become Corsair aces. Three pilots, all Marines, would be
awarded the Medal of Honor. A fourth, Lt. Jim Swett, earned his medal

in a Wildcat, then went on to score 8.5 more aerial victories after transitioning to the Corsair.

1st Lt. James E. Swett
Solomon Islands
April 7, 1943

First Lieutenant Jim Swett spent the morning of April 7, 1943, cutting lazy circles through the skies over Guadalcanal with little expectation that he would see any excitement. He and Marine Fighter Squadron 221 (VMF-221) had arrived at Guadalcanal's Fighter-2 airstrip in late January, and he hadn't so much as seen an enemy plane until April 1, when the Japanese launched a rare raid on Guadalcanal. "I saw the fight way off in the distance and heard a lot of the action on the radio, but we didn't get into it at all," he recalled. "It was boring."[1]

Described as "quiet, cool and unassuming," James Elms Swett came from a life of some privilege.[2] His father owned a manufacturing company that produced marine pumps and turbines. The family's neighborhood in San Mateo, California, was populated with lawyers, businessmen, corporate executives, and their live-in servants—none of which was worth two cents in the skies over Guadalcanal. Swett had learned to fly with the Civilian Pilot Training Program while attending San Mateo Junior College. He intended to fly for the Coast Guard, but that entailed attending U.S. Navy flight school. He qualified in August 1941 and was training at Corpus Christi when a Marine officer, noting he was in the top 10 percent of his class, approached him about a commission in the Marine Corps. Swett signed on. He received his commission in April 1942 and shipped out to the Pacific in November.

The tall, gangling twenty-two-year-old, dubbed "Zeke" by his fellow pilots, arrived at Guadalcanal in late January. Since then, his squadron had been primarily engaged in escorting bomber strikes on Munda or Rekata Bay. By this time the Japanese had conceded possession of Guadalcanal to U.S. forces, and the pitched battles around Henderson Field were a thing of the past.

If Swett was feeling a bit disappointed by the lack of action, things were about to change in dramatic fashion. U.S. photo reconnaissance planes had spotted a large increase in the number of Japanese planes on fields in the Northern Solomons. A total of 114 were counted at the big Japanese airdrome on Kahili on southern Bougainville, as opposed to only forty the day before; there were another ninety-five at Ballale, where there had been none at all the day before.[3] The Japanese were clearly planning something big, and that threat had Jim Swett and a flight of seven other F4F-4 Wildcats from VMF-221 circling at 14,000 feet as the sun made its way higher in the sky on the morning of April 7.

Hours later, with no sign of trouble, the pilots returned to Fighter-2 for a hasty breakfast of powdered scrambled eggs. By 11:30 a.m. Swett was back in the air in his Grumman, whimsically named *Melvin Massacre*, but again there was no sign of the Japanese.[4] The patrols were headed homeward when their radios belatedly crackled with reports of enemy planes converging on Guadalcanal. They landed, hastily topped off their fuel, and roared back into the air shortly before 3 p.m. As Swett climbed into the cockpit, his armorer told him he had added an extra fifteen rounds to each magazine for his six .50-caliber machine guns, giving him just over 1,500 .50-caliber shells divided between tracer, armor piecing, and incendiary.

The Japanese air assault, first spotted by Coastwatchers who relayed the information to Henderson, was comprised of sixty-seven Aichi D3A Val dive bombers covered by 110 Zeros. They appeared to be heading for Tulagi, about 40 miles from Henderson Field, to attack U.S. shipping at the anchorage. The Guadalcanal command broadcast a warning to all ships and troops in the area: "Condition *very* red." A total of seventy-six Army, Navy, and Marine fighters rose to engage the intruders.[5] The weather was very clear.

Leading a division of four Wildcats, Swett was proceeding at full throttle toward Tulagi when he heard a pilot shout over the radio, "My God! There's millions of them!" Moments later Swett spotted the enemy air armada looking like a swarm of mosquitoes. "The sky was black with them. They were all over the place," he recalled. "The dive-bombers were already peeling off to go down into their dives."[6]

The Wildcats were strung out for over half a mile at an altitude of 15,000 to 20,000 feet with Swett in the lead. The pilots behind him got tangled up with the Japanese fighter escort, but Swett continued to bore in on the bombers. The Vals, easily identified by their fixed landing gear, were painted a brownish gray and looked new. "I was scared to death," he admitted later. "They were the first Jap planes I had ever seen, but there was no mistaking those big red meatballs on their sides."[7]

Swett had never fired his guns in combat. Now he got in behind two V formations consisting of half a dozen Vals and picked his victim. "I caught the first one just as he was pushing over and getting ready to dive," he recalled.[8] Roaring to within 50 yards of the Val, he opened fire, walking short bursts of only two or three rounds per gun forward along the fuselage. He killed the rear gunner and was trying for the pilot when the bomber suddenly burst into flame and nosed toward the water. "I just picked one and just gave him a squirt and he flamed like crazy," he said later.[9]

As antiaircraft fire from the ships below blossomed all around, Swett continued after the next Val, which was now about halfway down in its dive on the ships below. He flamed that one too, riddling the right wing and then the fuselage. He set a third on fire just as it neared the bottom of its dive over the American ships. "It surprised me that they burned so easily," he said. "Just one burst and they were gone." The enemy tail gunners, armed with a 7.7mm machine gun in the rear cockpit, tried to keep him off without success. "By the time the third one caught on fire, I was a lot less scared than I'd been when I first opened fire," he observed.[10]

Peering through his windscreen, Swett could see bombs sending up cascades of water around ships in the harbor below. Too low and moving too fast to pursue the dive bombers still in front of him, Swett pulled out of his dive at about 500 feet. An instant later the Wildcat shuddered as a 40mm antiaircraft round from one of the ships slammed through the port wing at the outboard machine gun. The shell left a hole about a foot in diameter in the wing, destroyed the landing flaps, and bent the outboard gun barrel straight up into the air.

Swett decided it was time to exit the battlefield. "I was: number one, scared; number two, frightened; number three, ready to bail out of that darn thing," he said later. "You couldn't believe how nervous I was."[11] Turning away to the east, he flew low through some heavy cloud cover, emerging on the other side of Florida Island to find a mob of Japanese dive bombers apparently trying to regroup. "They were scattered all over the sky!" he recalled. "There must have been at least a dozen of them."[12]

Only 500 or 600 feet over the water and traveling at about 150 mph, Swett made a slight left turn to get behind the nearest bomber and knocked it down with a short burst. Turning right, he flamed another Val as the rear gunner jumped for his life, then went after a third. By the time the enemy pilot realized what was happening, the slow-moving Val was on fire. "I was down below them so that the rear gunner couldn't shoot me when I fired my guns," he explained. "I'd just stick the nose up a little bit and give a quick blast. It was fantastic how they burned. Each one of them went down in turn as I was chasing them like this and shooting. It only took two or three rounds per gun and it ripped them up something awful and they'd flame just like that."[13]

Having never been in air combat before, he could scarcely grasp what was happening. "I was really sweating. I was soaking wet," he remembered. "Then I got overconfident after the sixth one went down." He shot down number seven before the pilot saw him coming, but as he closed on number eight, "the rear gunner stuck his gun practically in my face and let me have it. . . . I was only 25 to 30 feet behind him when the rear gunner knocked the living hell out of my windshield and oil cooler—and me." Recovering from the spray of flying glass, Swett used up his last few rounds, killing the rear gunner at close range. "I can still see his eyes right now, the terror in his eyes while he was shooting at me and when I fired back he fell down into the cockpit," he recalled. The bomber remained airborne but was smoking heavily. "He wasn't actually on fire, but he was smoking like the dickens," noted Swett.[14]

Hoping to get his shot-up Wildcat back to Guadalcanal, Swett turned away from the Val, but as he came back low over Tulagi Harbor, the engine seized, one of the propeller blades sticking straight up in front like a mocking finger. Adding to the indignity of the occasion, a U.S. machine gunner somewhere on shore began picking away at the doomed Wildcat. "I knew I was in deep trouble," he observed. "So I just eased it down. No flaps. My flaps were inoperable. The airplane hit and bounced and then dove for water. I went down maybe 20 feet or something like that. I was struggling to get out of the damn thing."[15]

As dark water closed in around him, Swett unfastened his seatbelt and shoulder straps, but when he tried to kick free, his parachute harness caught on the raft compartment release hook behind the cockpit. "It took a couple of good struggles to get free," he recalled, but he managed to break loose and kick to the surface, where he inflated his Mae West.[16]

He had broken his nose when his face whacked into the gunsight during the landing, and he had some cuts from the windshield glass the Japanese tail gunner had sent spraying into the cockpit, but he was alive and still undaunted. Spotting a picket boat off in the distance, he pulled out his .45, drained the water out of the barrel, and fired some tracer rounds into the air. Within fifteen minutes or so the boat drew up, crew members standing at the ready with rifles. "You an American?" one of them demanded.

"You're goddamn right I am!" retorted Swett.

"Okay," said the skipper. "It's one of them smart-assed Marines. Pick him up."[17]

Swett's report that he had shot down seven enemy bombers and a possible eighth raised eyebrows, but any skepticism was soon put to rest. After talking with ground troops, natives, and other witnesses, an intelligence officer looking into the claim was able to verify the seven kills. Some days later, the wreck of a Japanese bomber—widely thought to be the Val Swett had expended his last rounds on—was found on a small island, though ultimately he was not given credit for it.

On April 14, the squadron's war diary noted, "Scuttlebutt has it that Lieutenant Swett is up for the Congressional Medal of Honor. His seven victories have been confirmed and also the 8th one that he was not sure about."[18] Swett's incredible performance—seven kills in less than twenty minutes on a single combat flight—brought a new phrase to fighter pilot vocabulary: "doing a Jimmy Swett."

The doctors fixed Swett's nose, but he remained grounded. "I am in the hospital and feeling fine—I sure bagged 'em!" he wrote to his fiancée back in San Mateo.[19] The recommendation for the Medal of Honor brought a chance to return to the States, which Swett declined. He had just gotten into the war, and he wasn't going to walk away now. Early in May, the "Fighting Falcons" of VMF-221 were relieved and reequipped with the new Vought F4U Corsairs in place of their Wildcats. They were back in combat by late June, flying out of a fighter strip in the Russell Islands, 70 miles north of Henderson Field.

Swett, now a captain, was helping provide cover for the New Georgia landings on June 30 when twenty-seven Mitsubishi bombers escorted by thirty Zeros bored in on the U.S. amphibious force. Navy Wildcats scattered the Japanese fighters, while the Corsairs went after the torpedo-laden bombers. Swett hammered a bomber on his first pass, setting the engine aflame and sending the plane plummeting into the lagoon. Back at 6,000 feet he spotted a torpedo plane sneaking in low over the water as other planes were dogfighting above. Swett got behind him and pressed his gun button at 400 yards. Hunks of metal flew off the enemy plane. As Swett roared past, the pilot jettisoned his torpedo, but the plane smashed into the ocean an instant later. Swett later estimated that the plane was no more than 20 feet off the water when he fired the fatal burst. He finished the day by gunning down a Zero, sharing credit for the kill with a Wildcat pilot.

Swett's adventures continued on July 11 while he and wingman Lt. Harold E. Segal, an aggressive New Yorker known to his squadron mates as "Murderous Manny," were on patrol over Rendova.[20] At 26,000 feet, their radios alerted them that approximately seventy Japanese planes were headed in their direction. At 12:20 p.m., they spotted about a dozen twin-engine Mitsubishi bombers escorted by ten to fifteen Zeros. Though Segal was having problems with his supercharger, they went after the bombers with a high-side pass from astern. Trailing behind, Segal shot a Zero off Swett's tail as Swett concentrated on the bombers.

"I picked the last Betty in the starboard echelon, firing for his engines," reported Swett. "I could see that I was getting hits, but the bomber did not burn. I had to split S to roll out without hitting it." Emerging from a cloud, he spotted a smoking Corsair in the distance with three Zeros following behind. "I caught up to the last Zero and put a six or seven-second burst into him. He began to pull up and lost his starboard wing about halfway from the wing root. He fluttered into the water." The other two Zeroes fled.[21]

The damaged Corsair disappeared into a cloud. As Swett looked for him, he spotted a Betty bomber low on the water with a Zero just above.

"He was going like hell with the Zero about two thousand feet above him doing wing-overs and rolling all around," observed Swett. Waiting until the Zero was out of position, he descended on the Betty, gunning for the motors. "I was about 50 yards behind him when he nosed over and hit the water."[22]

Swett pulled up over the splash and headed for the clouds to avoid the Zero, only to find a second Zero making a pass at him. "He got my motor right away—I could see the holes appearing in the cowling." The engine sputtered and quit. Swett put down in the water about five miles off Lingutu Entrance toward the northern end of New Georgia Island. The plane stayed afloat, giving him plenty of time to get out—an exit hastened by two Zeros that began strafing him. As bullets churned up the water around the downed Corsair, Swett dove overboard. "The tail of the plane stuck out of the water for about ten minutes and I spent my time ducking around behind it every time the Zeros came by. They were coming in on opposite courses and I was quite active for a while."[23]

The Zeros finally departed, and Swett inflated his life jacket, retrieved his raft, and began paddling toward shore. He paddled all afternoon before finally coming ashore at Lingutu Entrance. He wrapped himself up in his parachute and went to sleep. "I spent a very restless night, waking up at every slightest noise," he admitted.[24] The next morning he breakfasted on a chocolate D-bar and a couple of green coconuts before clambering into his raft and paddling for Segi Point, 30 miles away on the southern end of the island. Swett knew that Marine Raiders had landed there several days before, and he hoped to find a friendly face.

Putting in at an abandoned native village, he found a melon and some papayas, which he stowed on his raft. He also chased some chickens, which proved to be more agile than Japanese bombers. He was paddling down the lagoon later that afternoon when he encountered two natives in a dugout canoe who put down their hatchets and took him aboard once he convinced them he was an American. They brought him to a village and then to a Coastwatcher who sent him on to the American airstrip at Segi. The next morning he reported back to his home field aboard a naval patrol craft after what he nonchalantly described in his report as "a very pleasant trip."[25] Back at the field, he found his wingman, Murderous

Manny. Segal had shot down three Zeros, then been downed himself. He floated around in his life raft all night before he was finally fished out of the drink by a passing destroyer.

Swett was flying again within a matter of days but saw no action. The squadron was sent to Australia for a rest, then back to Espiritu Santo. There, on October 9, 1943, Swett was decorated with the Medal of Honor for downing seven enemy planes on April 7 during his first combat. As of that time, no other U.S. fighter pilot had succeeded in shooting down seven enemy aircraft on a single mission. "They had the whole danged air group out there, flags flying all over the place. . . . I was shaking in my boots then," remarked Swett. The medal was presented by Gen. Ralph Mitchell, the commanding general of Marine aviation in the South Pacific. Swett recalled, "I remember him saying, 'Jim, this is the first time I've ever awarded one of these things.' I replied, 'Sir, this is the first time I've ever been awarded one.'"[26]

Swett's war was far from over. Nine days after his Medal of Honor ceremony, he downed a Zero over Kahili Airfield on Bougainville. Two weeks later, he knocked down two Vals over Empress Augusta Bay. A few days later, the Fighting Falcons were ordered back to the United States. The squadron had chalked up seventy-two claimed kills at the loss of two of their own. Interviewed on November 8, 1943, Swett downplayed his own 14.5 victories. His primary ambition, he said, was to get through the war in one piece, take a job in his father's business, and marry one Miss Lois Anderson of Oakland, California.

He accomplished the latter first, marrying Miss Anderson on January 22, 1944, before heading back overseas. His last aerial victory was on May 11, 1945, when he shot down an enemy kamikaze off Okinawa. The pilot seemed unskilled. "There was no evasion and I can imagine that the pilot was very frightened," recalled Swett. "He lost control and dove into the ocean. He had to be dead by then as I hit him many, many times."[27]

Swett returned to find his home carrier, USS *Bunker Hill*, had been devastated by two kamikaze hits. Almost four hundred men were killed, including over two dozen pilots. Swett and about twenty other homeless aircraft landed on USS *Enterprise*. Their planes were then pushed overboard due to lack of space.

Swett finished the war as the ninth-leading Marine Corps ace with 15.5 kills. "Some of them I didn't like," he admitted. Among them was the final kill, the enemy suicide pilot. "He looked up and we made eye contact and I can see him to this day," he said years later.[28] As for his feat of shooting down seven planes on one mission, only one American pilot, Navy Cmdr. Dave McCampbell, surpassed that score. McCampbell knocked down nine enemy planes on one mission off the Philippines in late 1944.

After the war, Swett commanded Marine Fighter Squadron 141, a Corsair squadron based at the naval air station in Alameda, California. He left active duty in 1950 and went to work at his father's manufacturing company. After his father's death in 1960, Swett took over the company and ran it for twenty-three years before passing it on to his son. As for the medal, he once remarked that notoriety could be "a damn nuisance," particularly when inquisitive police spotted his special license plate and pulled him over on the highway. On the other hand, he rarely got a traffic ticket, he admitted.[29] In retirement, he was a frequent speaker at schools, emphasizing the values of respect and responsibility.

Jim Swett died of congestive heart failure on January 18, 2009, in Redding, California. He was survived by his second wife, Verna, and two sons from his first marriage to Lois, who predeceased him in 1999. Swett was a modest man who did not consider himself a hero, friends recalled. He once said of his exploits, "We just did a job." He did have one small complaint, which he admitted during a newspaper interview in 1991. He said he was sure he had downed the last Japanese bomber that had sent him into the drink that April day in 1943. "Actually, I shot down eight of those Japanese dive bombers," he observed. "I'm still mad at the Marine Corps for confirming only seven."[30]

1st Lt. Kenneth A. Walsh
Solomon Islands
August 15 and 30, 1943

As part of an organization boasting more than its share of characters, Ken Walsh had one fairly unique claim to fame: he had earned his wings as a

Marine private. A lesser man might have been self-conscious about that fact. Walsh considered it a point of pride.[31]

Kenneth Ambrose Walsh was born poor and Brooklyn Irish in New York City on November 24, 1916. His father, who worked as an electrician, died when Ken was seven years old; four years later his mother moved the family—Ken and his younger sister—to Harrison, New Jersey. It was there that shy little Ken Walsh became fascinated with aviation, pedaling his bicycle to the local airport almost every evening to watch the mail plane take off.

Walsh attended parochial schools and was active in Boy Scouts. He was an outstanding track athlete at Jersey City's Dickinson High School. Graduating in 1933, he promptly enlisted in the Marines. He opted for aviation and spent two years as an aircraft mechanic and radioman. He must have made a very favorable impression for he was accepted for flight training while still a private. At that time a commission was not required to become a pilot. He earned his wings in April 1937.

Walsh worked his way through the ranks, making warrant officer in the Spring of 1942. He was commissioned as a second lieutenant a few months later during his third enlistment. By February 1943, he was in the Pacific with Marine Fighter Squadron 124 (VMF-124), the first squadron to fly the new Chance-Vought F4U Corsairs against the Japanese. The F4Us were faster than the Zero in level flight, could outdive it, and were more heavily armored. Walsh loved the Corsair. "Some of us came back with as many as seventy holes in our planes," he said later. "Hit a Jap once or twice and his ship falls apart."[32]

Ironically, a Corsair almost became Walsh's crypt before his combat career could even begin. On February 1, 1943, flying tactical maneuvers in the New Hebrides, he had to make a water landing when his engine quit. The plane went down like a brick. "I got hung up with my parachute and all that paraphernalia we had to wear," he recalled. "I couldn't get out. I don't know how deep it was, but when I finally struggled out, my last view of the plane was like it was one big gray whale vanishing." Drowning, Walsh had just enough strength to pull one of the toggles on his Mae West; the life vest inflated and brought him to the surface. He saved the expended CO_2 cartridges from that vest for the rest of his life, keeping them safely tucked away alongside his many medals and other awards. "I'll always keep these," he said years later. "This is what saved my life. This is what made all this other stuff possible."[33]

Walsh saw his first combat on April Fool's Day 1943 in a wild melee over the Russell Islands. "We jumped a flock of twenty-five Zeros and I shot down two in my first five minutes of fighting," he said.[34] He was credited with three of the four enemy planes his squadron downed in that chaotic action. "It was like a five-man boxing match," he recalled. "Everybody was trying to knock out everybody else."[35] Less than two weeks later, on April 13, Walsh gunned down three more Zeros, becoming the first Corsair ace. "It was about the same thing as in every fight," he said self-effacingly. "They try to sneak up on you and you try to sneak up on them and the best sneaker wins."[36]

His score mounted: April 1, two Zeros and one dive bomber; April 13, three Zeros; June 5, one Zero and one floatplane. But in August Walsh nearly became a statistic himself. On August 12, he led a flight protecting a B-24 Liberator bomber formation in a raid on the Japanese airdrome at Kahili. "The bombers certainly hit the target well," he observed. "I could see several huge columns of black smoke and one fire was so large I could see the flames when 20 miles past the target at 25,000 feet."[37]

Things began to go south when about thirty Zeros attacked the bombers. Much of the fighter protection became separated from the Liberators while passing through a heavy cloud formation, and Walsh found himself with only thirteen fighters—five Corsairs and eight P-40s. He and his wingman, Lt. Bill Johnston of Birmingham, Alabama, took up station about 5,000 feet above the center of the bomber formation, diving down on Zeros that ventured too close to the Liberators. "The first overhead pass I made was the best of any I have ever made, including target shooting on a sleeve," Walsh said. "The Jap never saw me. I opened up early and followed through with a long burst which lasted until I was so close I had to duck from colliding. While I was firing he rolled over on his back and white smoke seemed to be coming from his belly; looking down after I passed I observed him in flames."[38]

Walsh went back on station, then dove again. "This procedure worked beautifully for four or five passes, in which time I am certain I destroyed two Zeros of the Zeke type and probably a third."[39] But the Japanese eventually got wise to his tactic. As Walsh started down on yet another pass, he suddenly heard a racket "like rocks hitting a tin roof." A Zero had latched onto his tail and was pouring it into him. Johnston zoomed in to get a shot from the right, but the Zero was so close to Walsh's Corsair, he had to wait before shooting. As Walsh's rudder fin passed through his sight picture, he opened fire. The Zero followed right into the burst, rolled over, and disappeared beneath them. "I can't say how grateful I am for having a wingman like Johnston—another second later and I surely would of got it," said Walsh. "He not only shot him off my tail but shot him down as well."[40]

In that interval, Walsh's Corsair had been hit by seven 20mm cannon shells and over twenty 7.7mm machine-gun slugs. "As soon as I got hit my cockpit filled with smoke," said Walsh. "I immediately rolled over on my back and started to bail out."[41] However, when he opened the canopy, the smoke dissipated, and he decided to stay with the plane. Taking refuge under the bombers, Walsh made it to an emergency strip at Segi, New Georgia. With his hydraulics shot out, he was able to crank the wheels down manually but had no flaps or brakes. Touching down, he rolled about three-fourths of the way down the field before the plane went out of control and smashed into another Corsair on the line. Both planes were totally destroyed, but Walsh walked away from the wreck.

Three days later, Walsh was assigned to help provide cover for the U.S. landing on Vella Lavella only 90 miles from the big Japanese air base at Kahili. Jumped by five Zeros at 10,000 feet, he chased an enemy fighter and shot it down five miles north of Vella Lavella. He then turned alone into nine enemy Val bombers and dumped two of them. "I saw two of them drop in flames and about the time I anticipated another 'Capt. Swett Episode,' I was attacked from the rear by a Zero who certainly had me bore-sighted," he reported with some chagrin.[42] He managed to escape but took two 20mm holes in his right wing and another through the horizontal stabilizer; machine-gun fire had perforated a wing and his tail and shot out one of his tires. It was a tribute to the toughness of the Corsair that it stayed in the air. "The wing really should have come off," Walsh said. "I managed to land, but the plane was beyond repair. They scrapped it."[43]

He remained unfazed. The tobacco-chewing former "grease ball," who sported a pencil-thin moustache and wore an old mechanic's hat when not in the air, had the reputation of being an eager pilot who took every opportunity to get into combat. "Fairly short in stature, Walsh was a talkative man with a Brooklyn accent and more than a little intensity," recalled Ralph Eubanks, one of the ground ordnance men.[44]

That intensity paid off as the aerial war heated up around Vella Lavella. On August 21 Walsh and four other Marines tackled fifteen Zeros. Walsh knocked one of them down. Two days later Japanese fighters went after the U.S. patrols over Vella Lavella. Walsh, low on gas and oxygen, landed at Munda. "I've got to get back up!" he told the ground crew. "They're coming right in!"[45] The ground crew topped off his tanks, and Walsh went back up and shot down two Zekes: "One seemed to explode around the engine and went down with falling parts accompanying him—the other one caught fire in the left wing," he reported.[46]

VMF-124's mission on August 30 was to escort a flight of Liberators on a raid on Kahili airdrome. The Marines would fly out of Guadalcanal, receive a final briefing and top off their fuel tanks in the Russell Islands, then link up with the B-24s near Rendova Island. Enemy air opposition was expected to be heavy.

Walsh indulged in a breakfast of Spam, French toast, canned orange juice, and coffee before lifting off from Fighter-2 at 11:15 a.m. for the short hop to the Russells, 60 miles to the northwest. The Corsairs were back in the air by 1:30 p.m. and soon rendezvoused with the bombers. Walsh flew Corsair No. 13. He wasn't the least bit superstitious, but to his frustration No. 13's engine began to lose power as he climbed for altitude. The supercharger had failed. Walsh signaled to his wingman, waggling his wings to get his attention, then holding his nose and pointing to his engine. Having conveyed the problem, he dropped out of the formation and headed for the U.S. airfield at Munda as fast as he could push the aircraft. Far from conceding failure, he hoped to get to Munda, obtain another Corsair, and get back in the air in time to rejoin the attack on Kahili.

Setting down at Munda, Walsh jumped out of the balky Corsair and got permission to take one of the armed and fueled F4Us waiting on standby. Barely ten minutes later, he was in the air again, heading north-west with the throttle full out in an effort to catch up with his squadron. Climbing gradually to 28,000 feet, he searched the sky for the bomb-ers and Marine fighters but saw nothing. Finally, crossing the Shortland Islands and approaching the enemy airdrome at 30,000 feet, he caught sight of specks in the distance. There were forty or fifty of them, and they seemed too small to be bombers. They were Zeros! At almost the same time, he picked up the bombers off to the left and further ahead. The B-24s were completing their bombing run on Kahili, and the Japanese fighters were forming up to hit them as they left. Excited shouts sounded over Walsh's radio as the Liberators came under fire.[47]

"I reacted instinctively," he said years later. "I performed as I was trained."[48]

Alone and unnoticed by the Japanese, Walsh turned slightly and dove toward the Zeros, hoping surprise would compensate for the 50:1 odds. His guns were bore-sighted for 1,000 feet. He pulled in behind the Zero on the far right of the formation and opened up with his six .50-caliber machine guns. The Zero began to break up. As Walsh closed to within 300 feet, the enemy fighter fell out of formation, started down, and then exploded.

Walsh immediately closed on the next Zero, just ahead and slightly to the left. The plane was a dirty-brown color with big red meatballs on each wing tip. As the wingspan filled his sight ring, he pressed the firing button at point-blank range. The burst seemed to have no effect. Then the right wing dipped. Trailing a plume of thick black smoke, the Zero went into a vertical dive toward the ground.

The other Japanese belatedly noticed the wolf on their heels and moved to eradicate the threat. A flight of Zeros circled to Walsh's left in an effort to get on his tail. Another Zero roared in head-on, wings blink-ing with gunfire. Enemy fighters swarmed all around as Walsh jinked about, trying to elude them and join up with the other Corsairs now visible in the near distance. Diving away from the swarm of Zeros, he passed through the B-24 formation, then pulled up. Spotting a Zero to his left, he turned abruptly, rolled out, and hit the gun button. The Zero plunged away. Other Zeros began closing again. The American bombers were being hit; there were parachutes in the air, and he saw a B-24 going down in flames.

The sky seemed full of desperate fights. A bomber began trailing smoke. A Zero went down in flames. An American P-40 headed down with three Zeros after it. Kahili was now miles behind as the air battle moved east toward the American airfields. The Zeros continued to try and break through the fighter screen but with diminishing success.

As the pressure eased, Walsh heard other bomber crews on the radio calling for help from near Gizo, an island just south of Vella Lavella: "There are more bombers in trouble near Gizo—let's go!" he radioed before peeling off and heading south.[49] The other Corsair pilots, still intent on protecting the first group of bombers, failed to follow. Once again Walsh was on his own.

Pushing the Corsair at full throttle, Walsh soon caught sight of planes several thousand feet below. Several Corsairs and P-40s and a couple of P-39s were trying to defend a formation of B-24s. A least a dozen Zeros were attacking. Spotting a gaggle of Zeros forming for a run on the rear of the B-24s, Walsh bored in. There were five enemy fighters, big orange circles on their wings, and they had not seen him. Taking the rear Zero from about 7 o'clock, Walsh poured tracers into the wing roots. The enemy fighter staggered and seemed to hesitate in the air. The prop slowed, followed by a flash as the plane blew up, completely disintegrating before his eyes. Debris rained down toward the sea, trailing separate tendrils of black smoke.

Walsh spotted a brownish-green enemy fighter circling in an effort to get on his tail. A P-39 plunged toward the sea, leaving a plume of smoke in its wake. Bomber crews continued to call for help on the radio. Walsh picked up speed, turned inside the Zero, and hammered it with all six guns. The Zero hesitated, and the right wing dipped. Walsh kept firing. The Zero began trailing smoke and plunged toward the water. Walsh followed him down to be sure he was finished—9,000 feet, 8,000, 7,000, 6,000, 5,000, 4,000, 3,000, still no sign the enemy was bluffing and intended to pull up at the last moment. The Zero continued its plunge past 1,000 feet and smashed into the sea. There was no parachute.

Walsh had little time to savor the victory, his fourth of the day. Four Zeros had followed him down toward the water and were closing fast. Low on ammunition and lacking altitude, Walsh tried to run for it, but the Zeros caught up. One came at him from directly behind and opened fire, while the other two boxed him in on each side, limiting his maneuverability. He heard the thump of shells and bullets slamming into the Corsair. Holes suddenly appeared in both wings. "I heard an explosion from my engine. I guess a 20mm hit it," he said.[50] White smoke trailed from the engine, and he began to lose power. His oil and fuel pressure fell. He could see Vella Lavella in the near distance. There were friendly forces there, but as the Corsair shuddered under repeated hits, he had small chance of making it. Munda, 30 miles away, might as well have been on the other side of the moon.

Miraculously, a P-40 accompanied by Corsairs suddenly appeared off to his left. The P-40 pilot opened up from beyond range in an apparent attempt to distract the Zeros from Walsh's stricken Corsair, now barely above the wave tops. Suddenly there was silence. The Zeros had finally turned away, but Walsh knew his flight was over as the engine began to cough its last. He dropped his flaps to reduce speed, eased back on the stick, and rolled back the canopy. The riddled Corsair hit the water with a thump, bounced a few times as it skimmed along the surface, and then settled down.

Walsh clambered out as water poured into the cockpit. He inflated his Mae West and watched the Corsair disappear beneath the surface. It was 5 p.m. Incredibly, he was still alive and only about a mile from Barakoma Point on Vella Lavella. Exhausted, he was struggling feebly toward land when a Higgins boat manned by Navy Seabees approached. Working at Barakoma Point, they had seen the Corsair go down and organized a rescue party. Walsh spent the night in the hospital and the next morning boarded an LST for the trip back to Guadalcanal.[51]

Walsh was credited with four kills on the Kahili raid—bringing his total to 20 and making him the top Marine ace in the Pacific at that time. More importantly, his perseverance in sticking with the mission, his one-man attack on fifty enemy fighters, and his tenacity in air-to-air combat were credited with keeping American bomber losses that day from being even higher than they were. In recognition of his actions, he was recommended for the highest decoration the nation could bestow. On February 8, 1944, in a ceremony at the White House, Ken Walsh, accompanied by his wife, was presented with the Medal of Honor. "Scared, young man?" asked President Franklin D. Roosevelt as he made the award.

"Yessir!" was all the former Marine private could manage to say.

"Lieutenant Walsh, will you shake my hand?" asked President Roosevelt.

"Yessir!" replied Walsh.

"So, I meet the president of the United States and all I could say was 'yessir' twice," he recalled years later, sitting in his den amid squadron photographs, prints of World War II fighter planes, and pieces of a Japanese Zero. "I guess I was awed. Still am."[52]

Promoted to captain, Walsh spent some time training new pilots in combat tactics. He didn't sugarcoat it. The Japanese would have no mercy, he told the trainees; they "will shoot you when you are hanging in a parachute or have crash-landed in the water." U.S. pilots had to be equally hard, he told them. He told of one instance when a Japanese tried to bail out of his disabled plane. "I finished him off before he completed the job," he said bluntly.[53] It was war, and war was a tough business.

Stuck in the States, he lobbied to return overseas and get back into combat. "The happiest day will be when I shoot down a Jap plane over Hirohito's head," he remarked.[54] Walsh eventually did return to the shooting war, and during an enemy kamikaze attack on June 22, 1945, he shot down his first enemy plane since that hectic day in the Solomons in 1943. The victory, his last kill, brought his tally to 21. He finished the war as the fourth-leading Marine Corps ace. He remained modest about that accomplishment. "I wasn't the Red Baron going off into the wild blue yonder to do battle single-handedly," he said. "I knew the Zero. I knew how to attack it. Everything was a risk, but a calculated risk."[55] He also noted that in the course of his career, he had lost five Corsairs—four to combat damage and one to his near-fatal water landing—which some of his friends claimed qualified him as a Japanese ace, he chuckled. He also derived some amusement from the "deadstick landing" mentioned in his Medal of Honor citation, remarking, "It's just a fancy way of saying I crashed."[56]

Ken Walsh remained in the Marine Corps after the war, retiring in 1962 as a lieutenant colonel and settling in Santa Ana, California. In later years he suffered a rare eye disease—a deteriorating retina—losing almost all his forward vision while retaining only peripheral sight. On July 30, 1998, he suffered a fatal heart attack at his home. Survived by his wife of forty-eight years, Beulah, and a son, he was buried in Arlington National Cemetery on August 3, 1998, with full military honors.

A few years before his death, Ken Walsh talked a bit about his out-standing combat performance. "You train and train and train," observed the former Marine pilot. "When you're in mortal combat, you act instinc-tively, and the trained man survives. Courage is a split-second decision. And let's face it, you have to be lucky. I'm not going to say I had a charmed life. But what would you call it?"[57]

Maj. Gregory Boyington
Solomon Islands
September 12, 1943–January 3, 1944

Pappy Boyington once said, "Just name a hero and I'll prove he's a bum."[58] Sadly, that injudicious comment was more a reflection of his own trou-bled life than a sweeping indictment of heroes.

Gregory Boyington was born in Coeur d'Alene, Idaho, on Decem-ber 4, 1912. His father, Charles, was a successful dentist; his mother, Grace, a high-spirited pianist who had played in theaters prior to her marriage. Their union was brief, breaking up soon after Gregory's birth amid accusations of abuse and adultery—including Charles's assertion that he was not the boy's biological father.[59] Grace's response was to move in with Ellsworth J. Hallenbeck, a twenty-seven-year-old book-keeper with a drinking problem. Young Greg grew up thinking Grace's common-law husband was his natural father. As far as he knew, he was Greg Hallenbeck.

The family moved to Washington State when Greg was in junior high school. Despite a dysfunctional home life, he did well in school. "He can't be beat," observed his school yearbook of the boy's dogged persever-ance in all endeavors.[60] Enthralled with flying ever since going aloft with a visiting barnstormer as a youngster in Idaho, he went on to attend the University of Washington, where he earned a degree in aeronautical engineering, supporting himself with jobs at a parking garage and summer work in road construction. A member of the college wrestling team, his stocky build made him a formidable opponent on the mat, and he won the Pacific Northwest middleweight wrestling championship during his junior year. He was a captain in the Reserve Officers Training Corps and earned membership in the elite Scabbard and Blade Society.

Hallenbeck received a commission in the Coast Artillery Corps Reserve following graduation in 1934. He promptly married his girlfriend, Helen Clark of Seattle, who had graduated from high school only two months earlier, and took a job as a draftsman at Boeing Aircraft. But the new graduate was restless. He looked into entering the newly instituted air cadet program intended to expand the pool of military pilots, only to learn that married men were ineligible. Deciding to try anyway, he obtained a copy of his birth certificate and was stunned to find that his biological father was a total stranger by the name of Charles Boyington. It turned out to be a fortuitous discovery: suddenly the married Greg Hallenbeck was transformed—on paper at least—into bachelor Gregory Boyington, who immediately applied for flight training with the Marine Corps Reserve.

He received his wings in April 1937. It should have been the start of a promising career for the twenty-four-year-old, now the father of a young son. Unfortunately, while in flight training, Boyington—previously a nondrinker—became ensnared in the hard-partying culture of the high-spirited flying fraternity. Previously described as likable, hardworking, responsible, and reliable, he found himself unable to stay away from the booze and was soon well on his way to becoming a full-blown alcoholic. As a pilot, he earned a reputation as a gifted dogfighter during air-to-air combat exercises, while at the same time his life on the ground spiraled toward disaster. By 1941, he was deeply in debt, his marriage was failing, and his military career was in a shambles due to his incessant drinking.

Salvation appeared in the guise of the American Volunteer Group (AVG), the famed "Flying Tigers," which was signing up pilots to fight against the Japanese on behalf of China. The Tigers offered Boyington a way out of his immediate troubles, plus the then princely sum of $500 a month, with an additional $500 for each Japanese aircraft he shot down. Boyington signed up with the understanding that he would be reinstated in the Marines upon his return. Actually, the Marines were glad to be rid of him: a notation in his file recommended that he not be reappointed.[61]

Leaving the Marines and his now-failed marriage in his wake, Boyington spent nearly a year with the Flying Tigers. He flew over 300 combat hours in P-40 Warhawks and on February 6, 1942, was credited with shooting down two enemy Nakajima Ki-27 fighters (later code-named Nates by U.S. intelligence). The Ki-27 had first gone into action in China in March 1938 and was outclassed by the ruggedly built Warhawk, which had a higher dive speed and self-sealing fuel tanks. Boyington recalled he took the pilot of the first Nate by surprise and put a couple of bursts into the fuselage. "Seconds later, he burst into flames and went down." A couple of minutes later, he spotted another Ki-27. "I followed this guy along and put a steady burst into him at point-blank range. Pieces of aircraft started to fall off and hit my plane. He rolled over and headed for the ground on fire and twisting crazily."[62]

Unfortunately, on the ground Boyington was nothing but trouble as he continued his uncontrolled boozing. His lack of discipline was not well received by AVG commander Claire Chennault, who tried unsuccessfully to impose limits on his drinking. "He was also less than pleased by the fact that we all enjoyed the company of the local girls, and I was no angel," recalled Boyington unapologetically.[63] When Boyington finally quit the AVG in a fit of pique in April 1942, three months before his contract ended, Chennault retaliated by bestowing a "dishonorable discharge" on the troublesome pilot.

Returning to the United States, Boyington requested reinstatement in the Marine Corps, claiming he had scored six victories while flying with the AVG in China. Actually, four of those "kills" had been enemy planes destroyed during strafing attacks on Japanese ground installations, but the Marine Corps did not question the claim. In desperate need of pilots with combat experience, the Corps decided to overlook the bad boy's previous transgressions and take him back with the rank of major.

Boyington served a tour as executive officer and then as commanding officer (CO) of Marine Fighter Squadron 122 (VMF-122) on Guadalcanal in April 1943, but he did not see combat. Capt. Hunter Reinburg, the squadron operations officer, had known Boyington before the war and was familiar with his previous bouts with the bottle. "Greg had not changed because I never saw him sober as CO of VMF-122 and I was continually flabbergasted how he could fly so well. . . . Greg never missed a mission assigned to him thanks mostly to the fact that his plane captain literally 'poured' him into the Wildcat's cockpit."[64] About a month later, Boyington broke an ankle during a drunken brawl with one of his pilots. When he returned from the hospital, he was assigned to administrative work at Espiritu Santo.

Once again, fate—or maybe it was just circumstance—intervened. The Marines were in need of additional Corsair squadrons as more F4Us arrived in the theater. Someone got the idea of forming a squadron from the pool of replacement pilots waiting for assignment. Who to lead them? Greg Boyington. Despite his troubled past, he was a top-notch pilot, and he was available. Legend would subsequently claim Boyington enlisted a squadron of troublemakers and misfits and turned them into an elite unit; in fact, his ersatz squadron included a large number of experienced pilots and combat veterans. The only notable misfit—at least on the ground— proved to be Boyington himself.

Squadron intelligence officer Frank Walton recalled meeting Boyington for the first time. He was "a thick-necked, slope-shouldered, stocky individual dressed in a baseball cap, rumpled khaki shirt open halfway down his chest, wrinkled trousers, and house slippers," observed Walton of his new commanding officer.[65] Designated Marine Fighter Squadron 214 (VMF-214), the squadron dubbed itself "Boyington's Bastards," a title soon changed to the "Black Sheep" when a public relations officer ruled the original language too impolite for home front consumption. Due to Boyington's advanced age of thirty-one, the other pilots sometimes referred to him as "Gramps," though thanks to a reference in a nationwide news story, he would subsequently become legendary to the American public as "Pappy." Otherwise he was just "Greg." Informal in manner and a superb pilot, absolutely fearless in the air, he was popular with his men. If he drank too much—and he did—most of the others were far from teetotalers themselves and were willing to make allowances. Boyington also benefited greatly from his executive officer, Stan Bailey, a top-notch organization man whose administrative abilities allowed Boyington to exercise his greatest strength: leading the air missions.

Flying out of Banika in the Russell Islands, just 70 miles northwest of Guadalcanal's Henderson Field, the squadron's first two missions were uneventful, but the lull was not to last. Flying escort on September 16 for a bombing raid on a Japanese airfield at Ballale just west of Bougainville, the Black Sheep ran into thirty to forty Zeroes over the target. Boyington never saw them coming, but hearing the call "Tally ho!" on the radio, he instinctively broke hard left. His quick reaction saved him from a Zero that had lined him up for an easy kill. Instead, the Zero skidded past him and fell to the guns of Boyington's wingman.

His own chance at the enemy arrived in bizarre fashion. "The first thing I knew, there was a Japanese fighter plane, not more than 25 feet off my right wing tip," recalled Boyington. Not recognizing the Corsair as American, the enemy pilot waggled his wings for Boyington to join up, then pulled ahead. Incredibly, Boyington, the supposed hardened veteran, was completely unprepared. "Good God! It had all happened so suddenly I hadn't turned on my guns switches, electric gun sight, or, for that matter, even charged my machine guns," he admitted.[66] He remedied that oversight in a hurry and sent the Japanese fighter spiraling down in flames.

With his head abruptly back in the game, Boyington turned his attention to a Zero making a run on the U.S. bombers. Homing in on the enemy fighter, he directed a burst into the cockpit area, expecting the pilot to take evasive action. "But this Zero didn't do any of these things," he recalled. "It exploded. It exploded so close, right in front of my face, that I didn't know which way to turn to miss the pieces. So I flew right through the center of the explosion, throwing my arm in front of my face in a feeble attempt to ward off these pieces."[67] Chunks of debris banged into the Corsair. Luckily, the Zero's now derelict engine with its still-turning propeller hurtled off in another direction.

Turning back toward the American bomber formation, he saw an A6M Zero dive on two Hellcats flying escort. The Japanese pilot missed.

He started to pull up, obviously intending to loop over for another try. Boyington followed him up. As the Zero slowed near the top of the loop, Boyington poured .50-caliber slugs into it, holding the trigger down while continuing to pull back on the stick to follow the Zero's ascent. As it reached the top of the loop, the Zero suddenly burst into flame, arced over, and plunged toward earth trailing fire and smoke.

Climbing for altitude, Boyington had turned for home when he spotted another Zero flying low and slow over the water. He worked his way in behind the enemy pilot but remained suspicious. It all seemed too easy. Abruptly reversing course, he found a trailing Zero coming at him head-on. Guns blazing, they winged toward each other in a lethal game of chicken. Boyington was so close he could see his machine-gun slugs ripping pieces off the other plane's cowling. The Zero nosed down, started to smoke, and began a long glide toward the water below.

Casting around for the original "decoy" Zero, Boyington attracted the attention of two other enemy fighters apparently on their way back to Ballale Airfield. When they turned to attack, Boyington gunned his Corsair straight at them, taking on the leader in yet another game of aerial chicken. When the Japanese pilot lost his nerve and jerked his plane out of the way, Boyington raced right past and opened fire on the wingman. He thought he set the Zero smoking but did not see it go down as he broke off and again turned toward home.

Now seriously low on fuel, Boyington made for the airstrip at Munda, but his adventures were not quite over. As he neared the strip, he saw a crippled Corsair low over the water with two Zeros in hot pursuit. "I made my run from behind on the Zero closer to the Corsair," recalled Boyington. He opened fire. "This Zero pulled straight up—for they can really maneuver—almost straight up in the air. I was hauling back on the stick so hard that my plane lost speed and I began to fall into a spin. And as I started to spin, I saw the Zero break into flames."[68]

Boyington landed at Munda with bone-dry gas tanks and thirty rounds of ammunition. He had shot down five Zeroes and possibly damaged a sixth—achieving status as an ace in a day. He was only the third Marine to do so and the first to do it in a Corsair.[69] The Black Sheep indulged in an alcohol-soaked celebration that night—"one would have thought we'd won the war then and there," remarked Boyington, who "took aboard a load of issue brandy," courtesy of the squadron flight surgeon.[70]

Boyington chalked up nine more victories over the next thirty-five days. Three came on October 4 over Bougainville's Kahili Airfield when a line of Zeros came up gunning for an American bomber formation. Boyington swung in behind one. "It felt as though I had the Nip leader in my sights for at least an hour," he recalled. "When I reached the point where I could wait no longer I let go with the six .50-caliber machine guns, and their leader practically disintegrated in front of my eyes." Boyington's momentum carried him behind a second Zero. As he opened fire, the Japanese pilot hastily bailed out. He lined up on a third Zero, hitting it in the wing root, sending it down in flames. In a masterful piece of flying, he had knocked down three Zekes in less than a minute; all three victories were witnessed and confirmed by other pilots.[71] Thirteen days later, he shot down three more Zeros in a thirty-minute brawl with fifty-six enemy fighters over Kahili.

The Black Sheep were back the next day to find empty skies over Kahili. Knowing the Japanese had English-speakers monitoring American radio transmissions, Boyington keyed his throat mike and taunted them: "Come on up and fight you yellow bastards!" Whether it was Boyington's challenge or just a belated reaction, Zeros began lifting off from the field. The Corsairs dove into them, claiming fourteen. That number was drastically overblown, but Boyington did get one confirmed victory.[72]

Boyington's growing record—and the respect and loyalty he elicited from his pilots—came despite his continued heavy drinking. Historian Bruce Gamble adeptly sums up this dynamic in his outstanding biography about the troubled ace, *Black Sheep One*. "Nobody realized the extent to which he was under the influence," observed Gamble. "His bodacious drinking and occasional brawling were attributed to his charismatic personality, which made him seem all the more charming. He was outgoing, with a quick homespun wit, and was admired because of his legacy as a former Flying Tiger." His boldness in the air was contagious, inspiring the Black Sheep to a "sensational" record—twenty-three victories and eleven probables in just their first eleven days in combat, noted Gamble.

"The record grabbed far more attention than Boyington's character flaws, which everyone considered minor."[73]

In a pensive mood, Boyington wrote to his mother, "I was sidetracked for a while. . . . Now I'm as calm and happy as I've ever been in my life."[74] On the ground he continued his boisterous, hard-drinking ways, often engaging in drunken wrestling bouts and other foolishness. But in the air, he was the consummate professional. "One time I saw him stoned at 2:30 in the morning and then sober enough at 4:30 to take his mission," recalled a Black Sheep. "He was an amazing man."[75] Fellow pilots knew action was imminent when the chain-smoking Pappy cracked his canopy open to pitch out his cigarette before charging into the enemy fighters. "Personally he may not have been the greatest guy in the world, but when he got up in the air he had real aptitude," remarked a fellow pilot.[76]

By late October, the wheels were turning to nominate Boyington for the Medal of Honor. A commendation from Fighter Command on Guadalcanal praised his "brilliant combat record, readiness to undertake the most hazardous of missions, and superior type of flight leadership." The commanding general called him "one of the five outstanding fighter pilots that have operated in this theater since the beginning of operations."[77]

On a sweep over Rabaul two days before Christmas, Boyington shot down four more Japanese fighters. The first enemy pilot was apparently daydreaming. Boyington came in from dead astern and flamed the mottled-green Zeke with a single burst. The pilot took to his parachute. Climbing to 11,000 feet, Boyington spotted two A6Ms, one of them streaming smoke and apparently damaged, slightly below him and to his right. As he came in from behind, the cripple dove away, but Boyington stuck to him and fired from a range of about 100 feet. The Zero flamed, and the pilot took to his parachute.

The second Zero started a run on Boyington but broke off when Boyington dove away. Boyington climbed back to altitude to find the Zero circling protectively over his parachuting comrade. "I closed in on him from the sun side and nailed him about a hundred feet over the water," recalled Boyington. "His Zero made a half roll and plunked out of sight into the sea. No doubt his swimming comrade saw me coming but could only watch."[78] Twenty minutes later, circling Rabaul's harbor at 18,000 feet, he spotted nine Zeros in a classic V formation. With the sun at his back, he dropped in behind the rearmost enemy fighter, set it on fire, and then ran for home.

When combined with the supposed six kills he compiled as a Flying Tiger, the four victories brought his record to twenty-four, only two behind fellow Marine Joe Foss's record of twenty-six. Back at base, his report was greeted with jubilation as the pilots carried him around on their shoulders, shouting, "Just three more!"[79]

Their cry was quickly taken up by news correspondents, with unanticipated results. Reporters hounded Boyington. "They always wanted him to break the record for downing Japanese planes," recalled Black Sheep Fred Avey. "There were always four or five guys who wanted to interview him. I resented them because they should have let Boyington and us rest. They didn't think about what it was like for us. Boyington was tired and at times shouldn't have gone up, but he did."[80]

During a well-fueled Christmas Eve party, one of the pilots cautioned Boyington, "Listen, Gramps, we all want to see you break the record, but we don't want you to go up there and get killed doing it."

"Don't worry about me," Boyington replied. "They *can't* kill me. If you guys ever see me going down with thirty Zeros on my tail, don't give me up. Hell, I'll meet you in a San Diego bar six months after the war and we'll all have a drink for old times' sake."[81] Three days later, he knocked down a Zero over Rabaul for victory number 25.

The pressure intensified. Cornered in the mess hall on December 30 by a news correspondent pestering him about the record, Boyington finally exploded, slamming his fist down on the table and overturning a plate of food onto the correspondent's lap. "Goddamn it, why don't you guys leave me alone?" he demanded. "I don't know if I'm going to break it or not. Just leave me alone till I do or go down trying."[82]

On January 3, 1944, Boyington mounted up for a fighter mission over Rabaul. His wingman was twenty-four-year-old Capt. George M. Ashmun of Far Hills, New Jersey, a 1941 graduate of Hobart College with a degree in economics. Boyington had seemed unusually jittery over the past days. The record was clearly on his mind. "You go ahead and shoot all you want, Gramps," said Ashmun. "All I'll do is keep them off your tail."[83]

It was a magnanimous gesture: Ashmun, a former flying instructor, had been in theater since July but had yet to score an aerial victory.

Approaching Rabaul at 20,000 feet, Boyington started the formation in a wide turn over the mist-covered harbor when he spotted Zekes just 5,000 feet below. It was about 8 a.m. Pushing over, he fell in behind the tail end Charlie in what should have been a routine stern run. Instead, apparently overanxious, Boyington uncharacteristically opened fire from 1,200 feet—much too soon—but closed quickly to within 300 feet. As the bullet stream converged on him, the Japanese pilot bailed out an instant before the Zero burst into flames for Pappy's twenty-sixth victory.

But Boyington's luck was about to run out. With Ashmun still on his wing, he dropped down on another formation of Zeros 3,000 feet below. It was a trap. Twenty to thirty Zeros dove out of the sun onto the two Corsairs. Instead of trying to dive away, the two Americans violated Boyington's own tactical mantra and went into a defensive weave. According to Boyington, Ashmun shot down one of the enemy planes, and Pappy nailed another. Then Ashmun started down in a long glide, a dozen Zeroes following. Smoke streamed from the Corsair, followed by flames. Screaming futilely for Ashmun to dive or bail out, Boyington charged after the Zeros, but Ashmun—already dead or incapacitated—was doomed. As the stricken Corsair plunged into Saint George's Channel, Pappy sent one of the Zeros splashing in alongside for his twenty-eighth and last kill, or so he claimed.[84]

With a swarm of Zeros in pursuit, Boyington ran for home, only 100 feet over the water. "I could feel the impact of the enemy fire against my armor plate behind my back, like hail on a tin roof," he recalled. "I could see enemy shots progressing along my wing tips, making patterns." All of a sudden his main gas tank exploded. "The sensation was much the same as opening the door of a furnace and sticking one's head into the thing," he observed.[85]

Boyington later claimed he catapulted himself out of the doomed aircraft, simultaneously yanking on his ripcord. His parachute barely opened before he slammed into the water. Four Zeros then took turns strafing him. Boyington kept ducking under water until they left, then inflated his life raft and climbed aboard. "Pieces of my scalp, with hair on the pieces, was hanging down in front of my eyes," he recalled.[86] Bits of shrapnel peppered his arms and shoulders. His left ear was nearly shot off. A 20mm round had shattered his left ankle; his left calf had a hole in it, and a bullet had blown a fist-sized chunk out of his left thigh.

Much of this account was almost certainly exaggerated and perhaps even largely fabricated. Boyington once admitted he was a "psychopathic liar," and many of his claims—those that can be checked in some way—tend to support that confession.[87] A last radio message he appears to have sent out just before going down indicates he actually made a water landing. It does not appear that he suffered any burns—which he most certainly would have if the gas tank had exploded—nor had his left ankle been shattered, a fact confirmed by X-rays after the war. What is true is that he had been seriously wounded. A chunk of metal had torn through his left thigh, leaving a large hole. The left side of his face and head had been peppered with metal as if from a shotgun blast, possibly the result of fragments of the armor plate behind his seat breaking off under the pounding.

Whatever actually happened, it was a near miracle that he survived the shoot-down. There were more miracles to come. By all rights, Boyington should have died out there in the ocean. Instead, after floating around for several hours, he was plucked from the water by a passing Japanese submarine. The enemy sailors treated him well, but that changed when they handed him over to the garrison at Rabaul. The Japanese tortured him on and off over the next six weeks. He was blindfolded, beaten with ropes, kicked, and burned with lighted cigarettes. But again, Boyington beat the odds. For some reason, possibly his intelligence value as a squadron commander, he wasn't executed. His tormentors finally sent him to Japan, and he spent the rest of the war in a POW camp.

Carried as missing in action—and widely presumed to be dead (though documents captured on Saipan over six months later revealed he had initially been taken prisoner)—Boyington created a public sensation when he emerged from a prison camp at war's end. Nor had he changed much. According to one probably apocryphal but nevertheless illuminating story, Pappy bullied and cajoled his way onto a series of military aircraft to Washington, DC, burst into the office of the top Marine financial officer, and yelled, "I want my fucking back pay and I want it now! Even my uniform allowances! Including interest!" The finance officer supposedly put his head down on his desk and moaned, "Why me, God! Why me!"[88]

Boyington received the Medal of Honor from President Harry S. Truman in the Rose Garden on October 5, 1945. "A superb airman and determined fighter against overwhelming odds, Major Boyington personally destroyed [22] of the many Japanese planes shot down by his squadron and, by his forceful leadership, developed the combat readiness in his command which was a distinctive factor in the Allied aerial achievement in this vitally strategic area," noted the citation.

Boyington was promoted to colonel upon his retirement from the Corps in 1947—a departure hastened by his renewed drinking and erratic behavior—but the postwar years were not good to him. He suffered from alcoholism and experienced marital and income tax troubles. Married four times (including his first marriage as Greg Hallenbeck), he bounced from job to job. He worked briefly as a referee for professional wrestling, a beer salesman, a stock salesman, and a jewelry salesman. "Liquor was always present," observed an acquaintance.[89] A higher point was provided by his memoir, *Baa Baa Black Sheep*, published in 1958. "He wrote every word himself," recalled his son, Gregory Jr., one of three children by Pappy's first marriage.[90] The book is full of exaggerations and outright fabrications, but it's a great read and rapidly became a best seller.

At times he seemed to tire of talking about his wartime exploits. "That stuff is all gone and I'd just as soon let it go and forget it," he said in a 1972 interview. "I rarely ever talk about it unless someone brings it up. I don't want to bore anybody or give the impression of being a bore."[91] As for the Medal of Honor, he snapped, "They only gave me the Medal of Honor when they thought I was dead. . . . I keep it out in the garage along with the stuff we don't want in the house."[92] He was wrong about the timing of the medal—the awards process had begun before he was shot down—but Boyington remained unreasonably bitter. Nevertheless, he continued to appear at air shows and other events where he would promote his book and describe his exploits. An Army officer who encountered the war ace in Pensacola in 1975 remembered that "Boyington came roaring into the

O[fficer's] Club bar demanding triple shots of everything the bar stocked. His face was blood red and bloated. Out he roared, leaving a vapor trail of alcoholic fumes."[93]

In 1976 a television series based on his wartime exploits brought him new acclaim. Boyington served as technical advisor on the show, which starred Robert Conrad as the irascible Pappy. The show got mostly venomous reviews from veterans of the original squadron. Pilots were depicted as oddballs and misfits, constantly drunk and in trouble, flying while hungover and still managing to thrash their Japanese opponents. "The only thing accurate about the show was that we flew Corsairs," said a former Black Sheep in disgust. "That was it."[94] Called out by his former comrades, a chagrined Boyington confessed, "I only did it for the money."[95]

Boyington moved to Fresno, California, in the early 1970s with his fourth wife, Jo. He painted for relaxation, focusing mainly on desert and combat scenes. He also joined Alcoholics Anonymous, though he never completely licked his craving for booze. His addiction to alcohol, he admitted in a reflective moment, was "no doubt the most damning thing in my character." His poor health included an operation for lung cancer— and it was cancer and emphysema that finally downed the old warrior. Boyington died in Fresno on January 11, 1988, and was buried in Section 7-A of Arlington National Cemetery near the Memorial Amphitheater and the Tomb of the Unknowns. He was seventy-five years old.

Boyington's claim after release from captivity that he downed three Zeros before being shot down, combined with his supposed six victories as a Flying Tiger, would have made him the leading Marine Corps ace of World War II with twenty-eight victories—two more than Joe Foss. Those claims were subsequently reduced by six—four Flying Tiger victories and two of the Zeros he claimed on his final flight—to give him an official total of twenty-two. That number leaves him the third-ranking Marine Corps ace of the war behind Joe Foss and Bob Hanson.

As for his flamboyant and often outrageous behavior through the years, the closest Pappy ever came to an apology was when he remarked, "My skull is full of hunks of shrapnel and now and then, one works out of the bone, so if I'm a little nutty, I've got a legitimate reason."[96] But perhaps one of his Black Sheep summed him up best when he observed, "I know Greg had his problems, but he was a fine combat pilot and a good combat commander. A little rough for a peacetime Marine Corps—actually his own worst enemy."[97]

1st Lt. Robert M. Hanson
Bougainville/New Britain
November 1, 1943–January 24, 1944

Seventeen days. Six missions. Twenty victories. That, in brief, sums up the incredible record of Lt. Robert Murray Hanson of Marine Fighter Squadron 215 (VMF-215).

Some skeptics in Hanson's squadron thought it was a little too incredible.

Hanson had an unlikely start in life for one of the great fighter pilots of World War II. The second son of Methodist missionaries from Newtonville, Massachusetts, he was born in Lucknow, India, on February 4, 1920. He grew up in India and attended school there, with a couple of brief interludes. When he was four years old, he came to the States for a year when his father, who was professor of economics at Lucknow College, returned home on sabbatical. During a two-year stay during his early teens, he attended elementary school and then junior high school in Newtonville.

He demonstrated a headstrong, independent nature from an early age, wandering off on his own and defying authority. "Bob's boundless energy took him into everything. He had blond curls and blue eyes and pink cheeks and was always big," recalled his mother. His parents found it difficult to keep an *ayah* (nurse) employed to help with the boy as each new hire soon quit in exasperation with his hyperactive antics. "He was strong willed from babyhood," conceded his mother.[98]

Growing into a big, muscular, and well-coordinated youth, Hanson participated in the All-India Olympics, winning the light heavyweight and heavyweight wrestling championship of the United Provinces. By the spring of 1938, ready to return to the United States to enter his freshman year at Methodist Hamline University in Saint Paul,

Minnesota, he and a pal traveled home by way of Europe, bicycling across the Continent. The same terrific reflexes that would serve him so well in combat brought him acclaim in college sports. The beefy—he stood five feet, eleven inches and weighed 200 pounds—athlete became the conference light heavyweight wrestling champion and starred on the football and track teams. He paid his own way through college, first waiting tables as a freshman. "That was slick, Mom," he wrote. "I could finish all the pies." He subsequently put his size to good use, working as a bouncer in a Saint Paul nightclub, unfazed when some malcontent put a bullet through the windshield of his jalopy when he started back to college one night.[99]

War came while Hanson was a senior at Hamline. Just a month short of graduation, he dropped out of school in hopes of becoming a Marine Corps fighter pilot. He was accepted for flight school and earned his wings in the Spring of 1943. His parents were home in Newtonville on sabbatical when Bob showed up at the door on leave. It was Good Friday. Highlights of the visit included meeting his four-year-old sister Edith for the first time and working diligently on construction of a massive combat knife that reminded his mother of a Roman sword. Wiping dishes for his mother one evening, he asked, "Mom, did I ever give you any trouble when I was a kid?"

"Bob," she told him affectionately, "you took more thought and prayer than the other three put together. You were always in mischief." However, she later confessed she was encouraged by his enthusiasm for aviation. "In flying I felt when he was last home that he was completely happy," she observed. "For the first time he had found something that absorbed his tremendous vitality."[100]

Sent to the South Pacific as a replacement pilot, Hanson did his first tour flying Corsairs with VMF-214, the "Swashbucklers." Fellow pilots found him kind of an odd duck with an occasional belligerent streak. "He was a real husky boy and he was a different sort of guy," recalled Lt. Joe Curran. "We'd be walking through the camp area and he'd say, 'Do you see that guy over there? Do you like him?'

"'I don't know him.'

"'I don't like that SOB.'"[101]

Hanson took off on his first combat mission on August 4, 1943, flying wing for 1st Lt. Stanley ("Chief") Synar on a patrol over Munda where the Swashbucklers were jumped by Japanese fighters. A 20mm shell slammed into Hanson's Corsair, blowing an impressive hole in his right wing and knocking out the guns on that side. Another enemy fighter—an Army Ki-61 Tony—put a round into Synar's Corsair, wounding Synar in the leg.

The Ki-61, the only Japanese fighter with a liquid-cooled engine, was a relative newcomer to the theater. Its sleeker design sometimes caused Allied pilots to mistake it for a German or Italian fighter. Armed with two 12.7mm Ho-103 machine guns, it had a self-sealing fuel tank and armor to protect the pilot and could take more punishment than a Zero or an Oscar.

Fortunately for Synar, that added robustness didn't help in this case. Before the Tony pilot could finish off the Corsair, Hanson got behind him and "shot his ass off," as Synar gratefully put it, with just his left-wing guns, sending the enemy pilot to his death. Both he and Synar got away and returned safely to base.[102]

Hanson scored his second victory on August 26 while flying escort for a B-24 raid. Battling a cranky supercharger, he had fallen behind the other fighters when a lone Zero emerged from the layer of clouds overhead. The Zero, painted a dirty brown with bright red meatballs on the wings, settled in behind the other Corsairs just 150 yards in front of Hanson. "Just when I was beginning to wonder what possible good I could do, a Zero practically dropped in my lap," he remarked.[103] The Zero started a roll, and just as he came out, Hanson gave him a short burst. When nothing happened, he drew closer, brought the Zero into his sight, and gave him another burst. The Zero flamed at the port wing root, pulled up, then fell off in its final plunge, trailing fire like a comet.[104]

With a pair of victories under his belt, Hanson was reassigned to VMF-215 on Vella Lavella for his second tour in October. Flying a fighter sweep on November 1, 1943, in support of the amphibious landings at Empress Augusta Bay on Bougainville, Hanson motioned to the flight leader that he was having problems with his oxygen. The leader took the flight down from 20,000 to 13,000 feet. "There they saw 6 Zeros at about 10,000 feet coming from the northeast over Augusta Bay. Each member of the flight tailed in behind a Zero," noted the subsequent after-action report.[105]

"I picked one of this first flight that seemed to be diving for the beach at Augusta Bay," reported Hanson. "I tailed in behind him in his dive and gave him a burst. He seemed to try to pull away to the left, but I think he had too much speed to maneuver. I gave him another burst and he started smoking and burst into flames. He slowed down and, as I passed over him, pulled his nose up and snapped a few tracers at me but missed. Then he fell off and down, burning as he went."[106]

Banking right, then left, he got in behind another Zero. "When I was sure I had him in my sights, I gave him a long burst. He smoked slightly, then exploded." Pulling up to 8,000 feet in a steep climbing turn, he spotted a half dozen Nakajima B5N Kate torpedo bombers above and to his left. A single-engine carrier-based torpedo bomber, the Kate carried a three-man crew—pilot, navigator/bombardier, and radio operator/gunner—and had first seen combat in the Sino-Japanese War. Hanson had enough speed to make a low-side beam run on the Kate, but results were disappointing. "He peeled off to the right as I shot. I saw no smoke or damage to this one," Hanson reported.

Pulling through the run, he ended up above and to the left of the bombers. As he started a "fairly low, high-side run on the left plane of the formation," the Kates jettisoned their bombs and tried to turn away. Hanson gave his target a long burst. The Kate nosed over very slightly. "Then his dive became steeper and steeper," Hanson recalled. "He did not burn or smoke. I followed him down in his dive, weaving from side to side, picking at him with two to four guns working spasmodically." The Kate continued its descent and finally smashed into the water.

Hanson went to pull up, only to find he no longer had power. During one of his passes, he had apparently taken a hit in the engine, though he had seen no tracers from the Japanese rear-seat gunners. He headed toward the U.S. task force in the bay below and made a deadstick water landing about five miles from the ships. "I crawled out of my plane which sank in thirty seconds or less. I inflated my old, inferior life jacket, which deflated again almost at once. I then broke out my rubber boat, inflated it, and started paddling for the DDs [destroyers]. I paddled with considerable effort because I knew they were due to leave soon. I was also singing 'You'd Be So Nice To Come Home To.'" Four and a half hours later he was picked up by the USS *Sigourney* and made his way back to the airfield at Vella Lavella by November 5. "I had some very welcome meals, noting the conspicuous absence of Spam," he quipped of his journey home. "The eggs, steak and ice cream were a real treat."[107]

Upon his return to the squadron, he discovered that no one had seen him go down. He had been reported as missing in action. In an exuberant letter to his family, he reassured them that all was well. "Healthy, happy, not hurt and three more Japs under my belt. That makes five and one probable," he wrote.[108] He was an ace.

Up to this point, Hanson, for all of his quirks, had cooperated as part of the team, but that was about to end. VMF-215 began its third tour in January, flying out of Vella Lavella as escorts for bombing missions on Rabaul. Hanson had seen no air-to-air combat since being shot down on November 1. On January 14, he took off as part of an early-morning mission escorting a formation of torpedo bombers to Rabaul. As the torpedo planes crossed the coast of New Ireland, they were attacked by fifty to seventy Zeros. "They were looping, slow-rolling and making an occasional pass at our flight, continuing the fight and pressing harder and harder as it approached the target," observed the squadron war diary.[109] The fighting grew intense as the bombers completed their runs on shipping in Rabaul's Simpson Harbor and Blanche Bay and turned for home.

Hanson saw some bombers and a Corsair under attack by three Zekes. He and his wingman, 2nd Lt. Richard V. Bowman, ducked into a cloud and came out astern of two Zekes at 1,500 feet. They opened fire. "Mine flamed brightly immediately," reported Hanson. "Bowman's flamed a little and turned into a cloud." Flying around the cloud, Hanson lost track of Bowman but came up on two Zekes. The enemy pilots saw him and split up, one going into a cloud. "The cloud wasn't very thick: you could see about 200 yards in it," said Hanson. "I followed the one that went into the cloud and chased him down. We came out of the cloud at about 300 feet and opened fire. I saw my tracers going right into him and before I pulled away, I saw him explode."[110]

Playing hide-and-seek in and out of the clouds, he saw two Zeros about to cross his course. "I opened up on one when I had a 45-degree deflection shot and saw him burst immediately into flame. I pulled out well below and turned back into the cloud." At 2,500 feet he looked out of the clouds again and saw he was behind and a little below yet another Zero. "I ran right up to him and fired. My tracers went right into his belly and he burst immediately into flame." Looking toward the rally point, he could see no friendly planes, only a few Zekes "flying around apparently without any plan." He dove on one from about 3,000 feet and took a 25-degree deflection shot from astern and above. "He started to smoke right away at his wing roots then I saw tongues of flames from his wing roots and engine."[111]

Now sure the rest of the U.S. planes had left for home, he headed out over New Ireland. "Then I saw two Zeros on my tail. I ducked into the clouds and did a violent right turn and beat it for home." He arrived at Bougainville's Torokina airstrip about twenty minutes after the rest of his group. He had 20 gallons of gas and 400 rounds of ammunition left. The Corsairs claimed nineteen Zekes. Hanson led with five; another pilot claimed four.[112]

Six days later, on another mission to Rabaul, Hanson knocked a Zero off of a B-25 bomber. A Tony then got on his tail, but another Corsair picked it off. Two days afterward, on January 22, again on a bomber escort mission to Rabaul, he had another big day. After the bombers dropped their ordnance, Hanson noticed Zeros trying to sneak in from low altitude. He made passes at a couple but couldn't catch them. Finally he came down in a split S to 1,200 feet and managed a 25-degree deflection shot on one of the Zeros from above.

He tried to pull up but I kept firing at him. He rolled off to the right and went into the water flaming. Then I climbed back up and saw two more below me. I split-Sed down in the same manner. One of the Zeros turned back under me and the other crossed over me. I pulled up into him and started firing. As he pulled up harder and harder, I pulled up with him. He finally flamed and went down. Then I climbed back up and saw a Tony diving in on my right. I pulled to the left and

*split-Sed down behind him and got in a very long burst at him. He
didn't pull up as fast as the other so I kept firing into him. He finally
did a wingover to the right and pulled through. I saw him go right
into the water.*[113]

By now it was clear to his fellow pilots that Hanson had gone rogue.
He thought nothing of breaking formation to chase after enemy aircraft.
He paid no heed to his wingman, abandoning him at any opportunity in
order to go off on his own.

Unimpressed with Hanson's antics, VMF-215 commander Maj. Bob
Owens tried to instill some caution in him, but the youngster refused to
listen. "I came out here to kill Japs. If they were going to get me I'd be
dead now," he retorted. "They have had plenty of chances."[114]

His wingman, Lt. Sam Sampler, gave up in exasperation. No one
could stick with him, he said of Hanson. "He flies at top speed every
moment, executing every known maneuver and then some. Sooner or
later [he's] off by himself tackling huge formations of Zeros."[115] Apparently the headstrong little boy who gave nurses fits in India had grown
into an equally headstrong young man intent on doing as he pleased.

In the air Hanson was "a demon," observed Sampler. His features
seemed to freeze into a mask, and he would chain smoke incessantly in
the cockpit, though he rarely smoked on the ground. His drive to kill
the enemy seemed relentless, almost abnormal. No risk seemed too great.
Major Owens seemed surprised his lone wolf had lived as long as he had.
"For every Hanson, there are at least ten dead Marine pilots who tried to
do only once what Hanson does every day," he observed.[116]

Hanson's mounting number of claimed kills was moving him ever
nearer to the top aces in the theater. But with his third tour rapidly
drawing to a close, he was also running out of time. After rotation and a
thirty-day leave, he would almost certainly be returned to the States as an
instructor. Some pilots might have welcomed that respite. Not Hanson.
He had set his sights on the record now held by Joe Foss.

On January 24, Hanson's squadron flew cover for a torpedo-bomber
raid on enemy shipping at Karavia Bay at the southern end of Rabaul. As
the Corsairs circled protectively overhead, thirty to fifty Zeros and Tonys

rose to contest control of the air. Circling at 26,000 feet, Hanson "was straggling a little as [his] ship was not functioning properly at high altitude," he reported later. A few Corsairs dove on some Zeros about 4,000 feet below. The Zeros zoomed upward and looped over on their backs as if to make a retaliatory attack, but they hadn't reckoned with Hanson. They reached the top of their loop just below him, presenting a 30-degree deflection.

"I lowered my nose and opened fire at them, firing right into the belly of the one nearest me," Hanson reported. "When I saw flames coming from him around his wing roots and engine, I went after the second one and caught him about half [a] mile to the south, still on his back. I ran right up his tail in a no-deflection shot while he was still in an inverted position. I saw him flame immediately and fall into sort of an inverted spin."[117]

Now "pretty much by myself," he headed for Japanese-held Tobera Airfield to the south of Rabaul and ducked into a large cumulus cloud in hopes of remaining undetected. Enemy planes were landing and taking off from the airfield. Spotting a lone Tony down at 12,000 feet, he dove after him and opened fire. "He smoked and went into a turn and dive, trailing streamers of smoke that extended for a couple of hundred feet." Hanson did not see the plane crash and claimed it only as a probable.

Ducking back into the cloud, he waited for the U.S. bombers to come back along the channel. A pair of Zeros appeared first. Hanson pulled in behind, and when one broke to the right, he followed and got in a good long burst from dead astern. "He flamed up almost immediately and I ducked into the clouds, knowing that the other one would probably be looking for me." He caught sight of two other Zeros but was unable to close. By now the bombers were coming back down the channel engaged in a heated aerial battle with enemy fighters. Hanson saw two planes go into the water "just out from Rapopo" and three others go in by Duke of York Island—one after making a head-on run at another. As he started toward the bombers, he noticed five or six Zeros also heading toward the air battle. Hanson zoomed down and caught them at about 12,000 feet. "I ran up on the last one and saw him burst into flame immediately and went after the next one, but saw no results. Then I came on back with the bombers."[118]

With his score rapidly increasing, Hanson was beginning to get some public attention. Someone started calling him the "Flying Missionary" in recognition of his parents' long service in India, but he was to become more familiarly known as "Butcher Bob."[119] The aerial butchery continued on January 26 during yet another strike on Rabaul with Hanson claiming three Zeros. "I started down with the last of the TBFs [torpedo bombers] in their dive, when I saw four Zeros coming in from the west toward the bombers," he reported. "I was out a little to the left of the formation and when the Zeros crossed in front of me, I pulled in behind the last one and gave him a long burst from dead astern. He flamed immediately. . . . Then I tailed on after the other three which were flying right down along the course of the bombers. I dove in below these and pulled up under the last one at 4,000 feet. I shot him in the belly and his whole belly exploded." He finished the morning by knocking down yet another Zero that was chasing a Corsair at 4,500 feet, reporting, "He burned almost as soon as I opened up on him."[120] His official total was now twenty-one.

Twenty-three-year-old Lt. George Brewer, who had joined the squadron just before its current tour and had yet to score a single aerial victory, approached Hanson to ask him his secret. Zeros were becoming scarcer and scarcer, and yet Hanson seemed to have no difficulty racking up multiple scores. Hanson told Brewer that instead of heading for the rally point after the bombers made their runs, he would proceed to the enemy airfields south of Rabaul. Using the clouds for cover, he would dart out and shoot down Zeros as they returned to home base. "It seemed like a good idea to me," admitted Brewer.[121]

Hanson did not fly on January 27, remaining behind, despite his objections, to take his regular turn as duty officer. Scheduled for an afternoon mission on January 30, he ate his usual light lunch of salad and canned fruit—he habitually ate light before a mission, believing that a more substantial meal made him sit too heavily and impaired his agility. The late-afternoon raid saw the Marine Corsairs tangling with a strong force of Zekes while U.S. torpedo planes dropped down after the shipping in Rabaul's harbor. Two Corsairs and one Avenger torpedo plane were shot down, but the Americans claimed twenty-one Zekes. Hanson got credit for four of them.

The first was a Zero he caught on a Corsair's tail. Coming in from astern, he knocked pieces off the plane, then finished it with a 15-degree deflection shot. Swinging into a cloud, he emerged behind a pair of Nakajima Ki-44 late-model Tojos. Again racing in from astern, he sent one of the Japanese drifting down in a right spiral, white flame billowing from the underside of the aircraft. Hanson lost sight of the second Tojo in the clouds, then picked him up again. The two pilots played hide-and-seek for a few minutes, before Hanson caught the enemy pilot from behind. A burst from his six .50-calibers brought a flash of flame at the enemy's wing root, and the Tojo fell off to the right. Returning to the rally point, Hanson found a wild melee in progress. Quick passes at the darting Zeros scored no hits until one of the enemy pilots dove at him head-on. As they closed, Hanson fired. The Zero whooshed by, burst into flames, and tumbled earthward.

In just seventeen days, Hanson had scored an astonishing twenty victories. With his score now at twenty-five, he was only one victory behind leading Marine ace Joe Foss. Bets began to accumulate on how long it would take him to surpass Foss as his amazing streak continued.

But there were also some nagging doubts about Hanson. It was hard not to notice that he always returned from missions to claim multiple victories, most of which no one else was able to verify. Since no gun cameras were in use at the time, claims were vetted by the squadron intelligence officer, who relied on his own judgment and the honor system. As a result, claims were generally rubber-stamped, whether they could be confirmed by others or not.

At least one pilot was apparently suspicious of Hanson—or perhaps just tired of having him disappear on his own instead of cooperating with the team. Prior to their next mission to Rabaul—escorting bombers in an attack on Tobera airdrome on February 3—George Brewer's flight leader took him aside. He was assigning him as Hanson's wingman, he told Brewer. He wanted him to stick with Hanson from takeoff to landing "so [he] could observe and confirm whatever happened."[122] As far as Brewer was concerned, the implications were obvious.

Hanson maintained formation until the bomb run was complete, then headed for the thick clouds south of Tobera airdrome. Anticipating action, Brewer stuck close to the other Corsair, knowing visibility would be extremely limited once in the clouds. He was "totally unprepared for what happened next," he said later.[123] Hanson suddenly began a series of violent acrobatic maneuvers—at one point nearly colliding with Brewer—in a blatant effort to shake him off. Brewer doggedly stuck with him, growing angrier by the moment, until Hanson finally gave it up. He emerged from the cloud and headed back toward Bougainville with the stubborn Brewer still on his wing.

Minutes later, Brewer spotted a Zero below him and to his right heading toward the cloud he and Hanson had just vacated. Two Corsairs were in pursuit but clearly were not going to catch the enemy pilot before he ducked into the cloud. For his part, Hanson seemed oblivious—whether he didn't see the Zero or was in a snit, no one would ever find out. As Brewer considered breaking away for a run on the Zero, tracers flashed by his canopy. Another Zero had approached unseen and latched onto his tail. Brewer dove away and lost him, but his engine had been hit. Fire washed back toward him. He jettisoned the canopy as he prepared to bail out, but when he retarded the throttle, the flames went out, and he decided to stay with the plane. Trailing smoke, he headed toward home. Hanson, to Brewer's immense anger and disgust, was nowhere to be seen. He had just flown off and left him.[124]

Brewer made it back to Vella Lavella accompanied by two other Corsairs who had seen his predicament. Safely on the ground, he headed toward the operations tent to offer an earful on the squadron's wayward ace. There was no need. Hanson was dead.

After leaving Brewer, Hanson had joined up with the other VMF-215 pilots heading back to base. But as the formation approached the southern tip of New Ireland, he suddenly broke away to strafe a lighthouse located on Cape St. George. The lighthouse, used by the Japanese as an antiaircraft position, formed part of an early-warning system and had resisted repeated efforts to knock it out. Hanson himself had strafed it on the way back from Rabaul four days earlier, referring to it as "a large house."[125]

Guns blazing, he made a pass over the structure. He turned sharply and was making a second run when his Corsair was struck by enemy antiaircraft fire. The hit blew off part of the wing. Watching from above, the other pilots saw him struggle to gain control. He had leveled out just over the surface of the water and was about to set down when a wing caught in the rough sea. "The plane's right wing struck the water," reported Lt. Creighton Chandler of West Point, Mississippi, not knowing at the time that it was Hanson. "The gasoline tank burst into flames and the plane somersaulted into the water. I dropped down, but could see nothing except pieces of debris."[126] It was one day before Hanson's twenty-fourth birthday.

Hanson's parents learned he was missing in action on the evening of February 5, the news coming only twenty minutes before a *Boston Globe* reporter was scheduled to arrive at their home in Newtonville to do a feature story on their son. Since Bob had turned up once before after being listed as missing in action, the Hansons remained hopeful. "Mrs. Hanson and myself feel confident Bob will turn up," his father declared.[127] Mrs. Hanson added hopefully, "He was always wonderful at figuring things out.... That's why we know that if he had any chance at all he was able to save himself when he crashed." Following his November 1 crash landing, Bob had written to his mother, "Don't give up hope if I'm reported missing. I could be forced down on any one of thousands of islands hereabouts, and it might take me weeks to reach one of our bases."[128]

Ironically, only two days after the Hansons received the dreaded telegram, a letter arrived from their son. Dated January 22, the letter remarked, "It's the rainy season here, and you know what that is like. Clouds and all. It is really bad and dangerous for flying. But I guess the war must go on.... I ought to be home fairly soon now," he added. "At least it seems soon. Four months more or less ought to make it. However, nothing is certain."[129]

Despite their hopes, it soon became clear that Hanson could not have survived the crash of his Corsair. He would not be found on some remote island; nor would he miraculously emerge from a Japanese POW camp after the war. The lone-wolf pilot who had defied violent death so many times in the air had been downed by some anonymous Japanese ground gunner while strafing a lousy lighthouse.

On August 19, 1944, Lt. Robert Murray Hanson was posthumously awarded the Medal of Honor in recognition of "his great personal valor and invincible fighting spirit in keeping with the highest traditions of the United States Marine Corps." The medal was presented to his mother, Jean, in a ceremony on the Boston Common, his father having returned to India to serve as president of Lucknow University. "Mrs. Hanson's eyes were bright with unshed tears," observed a reporter. Among those in attendance was Massachusetts governor Leverett Saltonstall, who had learned only a few hours before that his own son, Marine Sgt. Peter Saltonstall, had been killed in action during the fighting on Guam.[130]

Bob Hanson's astonishing record had been compiled so quickly that he remained virtually unknown outside the combat area until after his death. If some were skeptical of his claims, no one challenged them. He did not catch Joe Foss, but with twenty-five victories, he is recognized as the highest-scoring Marine Corsair ace of the war. He was the third and last Corsair pilot to receive the Medal of Honor in World War II.

"He was a magnificent flyer and fighter," said squadron leader Bob Owens. "But he would have been better if he had known a little fear—I don't think he realized what chances he took. He seldom was hit and he had a 'record complex' he was desperately anxious to break."[131]

7

Fatal Skies

DESPITE THE GROWING DOMINANCE OF AMERICAN FIGHTER PLANES IN the Pacific war, the aerial struggle was far from one-sided. U.S. aircraft conducting low-level attacks on Japanese bases such as Wewak in New Guinea and heavily defended Rabaul suffered heavy casualties during the Summer of 1943. Air missions up through the Northern Solomons also took their toll.

Lt. Cmdr. Bruce A. Van Voorhis
Hare Island
July 6, 1943

In late 1945, a U.S. Army quartermaster party searching for the remains of an air crew that disappeared more than two years before in the vicinity of Kapingamarangi Atoll, the southernmost of the eastern Caroline Islands, heard a remarkable story from the natives on tiny Hare Island. Their story led to one of the more unusual Medal of Honor awards of World War II. At the center of the tale was a thirty-five-year-old naval officer, Lt. Cmdr. Bruce Avery Van Voorhis, and the ten men aboard a PB4Y-1 Liberator patrol bomber that disappeared on July 6, 1943.

Born in Aberdeen, Washington, on January 9, 1908, Bruce Avery Van Voorhis was the older of Lillie and Walter Van Voorhis's two sons. Of Dutch lineage, the Van Voorhis line's American roots extended back to colonial times. At the time of Bruce's birth, Walter was the Indian agent at the Quinault Reservation in Taholah, Washington. The following year he brought the family to Nevada to take a job as superintendent of the Indian school at the Stillwater Paiute Reservation. Bruce's younger brother, Wayne, was born that December. Walter served as superintendent of the Indian school until 1917, when he went to work as a salesman for a lumberyard. Two years later, at the age of forty, he died of pneumonia, leaving Lillie with two young boys.

Lillie, a former teacher at the Indian school before her marriage, was apparently made of stern stuff. After Walter's death she worked as a bookkeeper, then as a secretary. In 1921 she married rancher Leo Pinger. Seven years later she ran as a Republican against two male candidates and won a seat in the Nevada State Assembly, where—as the first woman to hold that office—she became an outspoken advocate for children's rights.

The Van Voorhis boys attended Churchill County High School. Bruce was known to classmates as "Clint," and his class yearbook predicted he would become a "pugilist." Despite the apparent allusion to fisticuffs, he originally aspired to a career as an agriculturalist. However, an appointment to the U.S. Naval Academy after his graduation from high school in 1924 changed his destiny from man of the soil to man of the sea.

Known to his Annapolis classmates variously as "Van," "Chicken," or "Brute," Van Voorhis seems to have been an off-and-on student, not particularly enthusiastic about "boning," as intensive studying was referred to among his classmates. His yearbook observed,

> Plebe summer he spent most of his time teaching the city slickers from the East the correct pronunciation of 'Nevada.' Boning, for him, seems to be an unnecessary evil. About once a year he gets ambitious, does a little serious boning, and pulls star grades for the month. He then secures for the year, thinking he has done his duty by Uncle Sam and earned his $780. Every spring he gets restless, makes out his resignation, and plans big things; but he never gets around to turning it in. We shall find him in the Navy until he gets too old and decrepit to be of any further use.[1]

Meanwhile, on the romantic front, "Chicken does not fall in love, but in three cruises and four years in blue serge and brass buttons has left a trail of broken hearts extending the full lengths of both coasts and radiating for miles around Crabtown," revealed his 1929 yearbook entry.[2]

Despite the jibe about his study habits, Van Voorhis finished 86th in a graduating class of 241. Following graduation, he took basic flight training at the naval base in San Diego. Rated as showing "average flying ability," he was authorized to undergo training as a naval aviator at the naval air station in Pensacola "when his class [was] eligible for such detail."[3] He reported to Pensacola in November 1930 following a tour aboard the battleship USS *Mississippi*. He received his wings on September 3, 1931, and was assigned to the USS *Maryland* as a catapult pilot with Observation Squadron 4B, where he earned high marks over the next thirty-two months, taking on additional duties at his own request.

There followed a variety of billets, including service with bombing squadrons on the aircraft carriers *Ranger* and *Saratoga*, flying patrol planes in the Panama Canal Zone, and commanding the aviation detail aboard the light cruiser USS *Honolulu*. Along the way, he met Kathryn Warden of Beaufort, South Carolina. The daughter of a Navy commander, Kathryn had married a British Army Royal Artillery major at the age of eighteen and had lived in India for a few years before her husband's untimely death in 1937. She then returned to the United States with her young son. She and Van Voorhis were married on February 19, 1938. Their first son, named after his father, was born on June 17, 1939, in California; another son, John, followed two years later.

Meanwhile, Van Voorhis's naval career continued to advance. "This officer is considered outstanding," wrote one commanding officer in 1939 of Van Voorhis's efficiency as an acting squadron commander. "I would especially desire to have him in time of war.... He has, while acting Commanding Officer, not only maintained but actually materially increased the efficiency of his squadron and demonstrated marked ability as a leader. He has proven himself a Naval Officer and Naval Aviator of marked ability."[4] While he was senior aviator commanding the aviation detachment aboard the light cruiser *Honolulu*, his unit earned first prize for overall excellence in all gunnery practices throughout 1939 and 1940. In July 1941, he reported for duty at the naval air station in Anacostia, California.

The outbreak of war four months later had personal significance to Van Voorhis beyond his profession as a naval aviator. His younger brother, Wayne, a graduate of the University of Nevada, had been called to active duty as a second lieutenant in the U.S. Army Air Forces in August 1941. He was immediately ordered to the Philippine Islands. As the Japanese tide surged through the Philippines and Corregidor finally surrendered in May 1942, Lt. Wayne Van Voorhis was listed as missing in action. The news greatly affected his older brother. "He was assigned to the Atlantic, but wanted to go to the Pacific after hearing about Wayne," Kathryn recalled many years later.[5]

Promoted to lieutenant commander in December 1942, Van Voorhis assumed command of Patrol Squadron 14 equipped with the big Catalina flying boats. Soon afterward, he and most of the personnel were transferred to Bombing Squadron 102 (VB-102) to fly the PB4Y-1 Liberator, which was the Navy version of the Army's B-24 four-engine heavy bomber. He last saw Kathryn and the two boys—John, now two, and Bruce, four—in January on his final leave in Coronado, California. On May 2, under his command, VB-102 arrived at Guadalcanal's Carney Airfield.

Carrying a ten-man crew with a maximum speed of 290 mph and a range of 2,100 miles, the PB4Y-1 was armed with ten machine guns and could carry a 5,000-pound bomb load. The squadron's primary mission was to fly long-range patrols to monitor enemy activity and to intercept hostile shipping. As Adm. Marc Mitscher, then serving in the capacity of commander aircraft, Solomon Islands, was to note later,

[VB-102] was assigned the important and difficult task of search in the areas to the north of the Solomons and bombing of targets found therein. The required search covered the Greenwich Islands, about 700 miles north of the Solomons. The search had to be made daily. This sector was most important for the Japanese were known to have large concentrations of fleet units in Truk. The United States Forces were driving the Japanese slowly but certainly north, out of the Solomons with comparatively small forces. The Japanese would sooner or

later attempt to ease this relentless pressure on their ground forces by an attack with their Fleet Units. If the Japanese could make such an attack by surprise their chances of success were good. . . . It was vital that the search to the north be made daily and that no area through which the Japanese Fleet might pass be left uncovered.[6]

Daily search sectors of 800 miles were conducted in conjunction with Bombing Squadron 101 (VB-101), which had arrived at Carney Airfield about a month before. Lt. James Claire Nolan, a pilot with VB-101, noted that the field was mobbed with aircraft "all jammed together wingtip to wingtip and nose to tail, making it extremely difficult to get out. Altogether, there are about 60 B-24s on the field (14 of VB-101's, 15 of VB102's, and the rest Army) and two squadrons of B-25s (Army)," he wrote in a diary, which he kept against regulations.

The place did have amenities, however. "VB-102 has built itself a damn nice Officers Club in the camp," observed Nolan. "Three beers per day per officer are allowed. Also cokes, crackers, and peanuts. The walls are decorated with some very excellently drawn nudes, around which everyone stands with an evil gleam in their eye, commenting on the various fine points of feminine anatomy."

Nolan, a veteran of the failed effort to defend Java the year before, was less impressed with Van Voorhis. The newly arrived squadron commander once marked by his high school classmates as a future "pugilist" was aggressive to the point of recklessness in Nolan's opinion. Writing in his diary on July 3, he observed,

This horses [sic] ass of a skipper of VB-102 [Van Voorhis] cooked up a night strike for six planes (3 of 101's and 3 of 102's) last night in stinking weather. They left here at dusk to attack one CL [cruiser] and three DDs [destroyers] near Treasury Island on their way south to bombard Rendova. The ceiling was 500 feet with heavy rain. Within an hour most of them were lost. No one ever saw the target and it was only by the grace of God that they all managed to find their way back to the field on radar.

The bad weather continued all the next day, but Van Voorhis was undeterred. "This evening that bastard Van Voorhis cooked up another strike but the Japs didn't materialize," observed Nolan. "I was scheduled for it, but fully intended refusing to take off. I came down here to get killed by the Japs, not to ram a mountain on instruments; I could've done that in the States in comfort!"[7]

On July 3, the same date James Nolan registered his disapproval of Van Voorhis, a search plane in the Greenwich Island sector reported the presence of a Japanese radio and weather station on Hare Island. Only about a mile long and 300 yards wide, the island was located just southeast of Kapingamarangi Atoll. A bombing attack inflicted some damage to a barracks and other installations. The following day, another search plane, arriving at about the same time, was attacked by six seaplane Zeros (A6M2-N Rufes) stationed off the western side of Hare Island. "These Zeros were operating from the lagoon of Greenwich," observed Mitscher. "Apparently the Japanese were determined to stop the search. The Japanese reinforcement of Greenwich with fighter type seaplanes was significant and made the continuation of our searches in that area extremely hazardous and might portend a move of Japanese Fleet Units."[8]

Receiving reports of the activity at Hare Island, Van Voorhis sought permission to vary the time of the search pattern so that one of his VB-102 bombers would arrive at dawn and hopefully catch the Japanese floatplanes on the water where they could be destroyed. "At the same time," Mitscher observed, "he stated that he desired to pilot the flight to insure that the task would be satisfactorily accomplished." As Mitscher wrote later, "The proposed flight was fraught with danger and it was with reluctance that I acquiesced to this arrangement but the necessity to destroy the seaplanes which were a menace to our essential search was paramount."[9]

At 2 a.m. on July 7, PB4Y-1 Liberator (Bureau No. 31992) lifted off from Carney Airfield with Van Voorhis at the controls and began the 700-mile trek to Hare Island. In addition to Van Voorhis, the crew included copilot Lt. (j.g.) Herschel A. Oehlert Jr. of Woodburn, Iowa; navigator Lt. (j.g.) Jack Orville Traub of Pekin, Illinois; AOCM Charles D. Linzmeyer of Long Beach, California; ACRM Johnny A. Renner of Kansas City, Missouri; AMM1c George Charles Stephens of San Diego, California; AOM2c Donald B. Clogston of Temecula, California; AMM2c Charles A. Martinelli of Dunkirk, New York; AMM2c Henry Ford Watson of Upland, California; AMM3c Frederick C. Barker Jr. of Winters, California; and ARM3c Richard W. Roscoe of Brainerd, Minnesota.

After takeoff, there was no further radio contact with Van Voorhis. As the hours ticked by long after the plane's estimated time of return, it became clear that the plane had gone down. James Nolan noted in his diary, "The skipper of VB-102, Van Voorhis, failed to return from patrol this evening. His intention to attack Kapingamarangi may have backfired on him. A damn fool and senseless stunt which cost the lives (apparently) of 10 good men. Nobody much gave a damn about Van Voorhis himself, though."[10]

The latter individuals presumably did not include Van Voorhis's mother or his wife, who received word two weeks later that he was missing in action. Sadly, some months later, Lillie, who had been widowed a second time when Leo Pinger died only seven days after the attack on Pearl Harbor, learned via a War Department telegram that her younger son, Wayne, first listed as missing in action after the fall of the Philippines, had died of malaria on July 10, 1942, in a Japanese prison camp. As for the fate of her other son, there was little to go on. Photographs taken by a search plane over Hare Island the day after the plane's disappearance revealed that the radio station had been destroyed, but there was no sign of the missing bomber. "After analyzing the situation, we decided that the plane would have given us some warning had it run into trouble with the Zeros, since we were guarding his frequency most carefully," observed Mitscher. "It was also possible that the plane had run into the mountains of Malaita Island, for the Northern Islands of the Solomons Group were constantly backed by heavy squalls on the windward side making navigation difficult due to intense and varying winds and low visibility."[11] Back on Guadalcanal, Nolan, in a final postscript to the disappearance of the Kapingamarangi mission, observed, "No trace of Van Voorhis, so he may be considered lost in action. It was VB-102's first loss and was a bit of a shock to some of them."[12] Fellow officers packed up the skipper's personal effects—ranging from photographs and tobacco pipes to pajamas and bath clogs—and sent them off for return to his wife.

And so things remained until nearly two months after the end of hostilities when a Graves Registration team discovered a mass burial on Hare Island. On July 31, 1945, Lillie Pinger had written a poignant letter to the Navy Department, asking if there was any further information regarding her son. "My two sons, my only children, have both been reported missing in action," she wrote. At least some of her questions were now about to be answered.[13]

In a summary dated October 8, 1945, a Maj. J. A. Witherspoon reported that the grave was marked "Nameless American Airmen, War Dead: July 6, 1943." Local natives told the search team that the dead men were crew members of a bomber that had made six separate runs on an antiaircraft position on the island. The repeated attacks destroyed the position. The plane had also shot down a Zero when it came under attack by three Japanese fighters. According to Witherspoon's report, the bomber "was fired at by AA guns on Hare and also three (3) Japanese fighters which were forcing it lower and lower." Natives told Witherspoon, "It tried to rise often, but it couldn't." It appeared to the eyewitnesses that the low-flying PB4Y-1 was caught in its own bomb blast on its final run and crashed into the lagoon.[14] That account was contradicted by an enemy report found after the war. That report claimed the bomber was shot down by one of the floatplanes. Whatever the case, there were no survivors.

The natives said they arrived on the scene at about the same time as Japanese troops and helped to collect bodies and parts of bodies that had washed ashore; "the native informants further stated that the bodies were mutilated beyond recognition," noted the Witherspoon report. The bodies were buried in a common grave about four feet deep under the supervision of an Ensign Takinaka, the only Japanese officer on the island. Another "mutilated body" floated up on the nearby island of Torongohai about a week later and was buried there. "The natives assumed that the grave on Hare Island held five (5) bodies, but the badly mutilated remains contained in the grave there makes it impossible to regard any present estimate as final," noted Witherspoon.

The team recovered a variety of items from the natives that indicated the dead men were members of the Van Voorhis crew. Items included an identification tag for Richard William Roscoe, a gold ring engraved with the initials GCS (George Charles Stephens), a .45-caliber Mark 1911 A-1 automatic pistol, a Smith & Wesson .38-caliber automatic pistol, a .38-caliber revolver with the serial number filed off, and a marked bombsight plate. A further search of Hare, Tounou, and Urru Islands turned up a pair of size-seven shoes, a single shoe marked "RENNER" in ink on the inside, and a scrap piece of plane marked "B-24-P No. 1231 Engine No. 2—L.H." In December 1948, another team returned to Hare Island, and divers recovered partial human remains from the wreckage of the bomber itself, which was located in the lagoon in 20 to 30 feet of water.[15]

Based on the testimony of native eyewitnesses and the circumstances of the mission, Adm. Marc Mitscher recommended Lieutenant Commander Van Voorhis for the Medal of Honor. The award was approved, and the medal was presented to his widow by Secretary of the Navy James Forrestal in Washington, DC, on July 31, 1946. Copilot Herschel A. Oehlert Jr. was awarded a posthumous Navy Cross. The remaining crew members were awarded posthumous Distinguished Flying Crosses.

The remains of the crew were eventually sent to Hawaii for examination by an identification unit of Graves Registration Services. A comparison of the dental and physical characteristics of the remains with the dental records and physical descriptions of the members of the crew allowed identification of five men: Traub, Stephens, Clogston, Watson, and Roscoe. The unit was unable to individually identify Van Voorhis, Barker, Linzmeyer, Martinelli, Oehlert, or Renner. Remains presumed to be theirs were interred on March 15, 1950, in a group burial in Section 79, Graves 279–281, at Jefferson Barracks National Cemetery in Saint Louis, Missouri.

Lillie Van Voorhis Pinger's only other son—thirty-two-year-old Wayne—was buried in the cemetery at Fort William McKinley in Manila, Philippines. Lillie outlived both her sons by more than fifteen years, passing away on December 27, 1959, while on a holiday visit to California. She is buried in Churchill County Cemetery in Fallon, Nevada.

Widowed twice in six years, Kathryn Van Voorhis never remarried. In 1956, then living in Greenville, South Carolina, she traveled to Camden, New Jersey, to christen the destroyer escort USS *Van Voorhis* during launching ceremonies. Contacted by a Nevada newspaper reporter in 1977 for an article about how her husband—the only Nevadan to be awarded the Medal of Honor—had been largely forgotten in his home state, she had little to say. "It's been so long. I've forcibly pushed a lot of things out of my mind," she confessed.[16] She died in 1995 at the age of 84 and is buried in Beaufort, South Carolina.

Six weeks after the disappearance of Lt. Cmdr. Bruce Van Voorhis and 720 nautical miles away from Kapingamarangi Atoll, an Army major earned a Medal of Honor for his actions during a bombing raid on the Japanese airdrome at Wewak on New Guinea's northern coast.

Maj. Ralph Cheli
Wewak, New Guinea
August 18, 1943

March 21, 1950, was a Tuesday with a hint of spring in the air in Saint Louis, Missouri. Earlier in the month, Silly Putty, soon to become an indispensable staple of American childhood, had gone on sale in the country. On March 9, legendary bank robber Willie Sutton had hit Manufacturers Bank in New York City for $64,000 and was now the subject of an intensive search by the Federal Bureau of Investigation.

But bank robbers and Silly Putty were surely far from the thoughts of those gathered that day at the Jefferson Barracks National Cemetery in Saint Louis. The mood was subdued as the remains of twenty-one American servicemen from the U.S. Army Air Force, the U.S. Navy, and the Marines were interred in a common grave in Section 78, Grave Lots 930–934. Consigned to the earth with little public notice, they included the intermingled remains of a private first class, eight sergeants, nine lieutenants, a captain, and two majors. The youngest had been nineteen years old when he died; the oldest was twenty-nine.

Retrieved from a murder scene nearly 8,000 miles away from the expansive cemetery's neatly ordered graves, the remains are presumed to include those of twenty-four-year-old Army bomber pilot and Medal of Honor recipient Ralph Cheli (pronounced "Kelly"). Born on October 19, 1919, in San Francisco, Ralph was the only offspring of the short-lived marriage of Albert and Julia Cheli.[17] Albert, who had arrived in the United States from Italy with his family as an infant, was a musician and accordion player of some renown on the San Francisco club scene. At the time of Ralph's birth, he was leader of a jazz ensemble at the legendary Caesar's Grill. Julia, the daughter of Italian immigrants, had her own connections; her brother, Frank Martinelli, became well-known in the city as owner of Bal Tabarin, another prominent night club.

Whatever Albert and Julia might have had in common, it was not enough to sustain their marriage. The two divorced when Ralph was still a boy. Julia remarried in 1935 and settled in New York City, though she and her new husband, who was apparently an entrepreneur of sorts, divided their time between New York and San Francisco. They were prosperous enough to send Ralph to The Taft School, a tony preparatory school in Connecticut. Graduating in 1937, he enrolled in the Class of 1941 at Lehigh University in Bethlehem, Pennsylvania, to study engineering.

A blond, blue-eyed, heavyset youngster, Cheli joined the Physics Society as a sophomore but otherwise doesn't seem to have been particularly involved in campus activities. Perhaps he preferred to spend his spare time pursuing twenty-three-year-old Geraldine Reilly, a local girl whose father was a yardmaster with the railroad. The oldest of three sisters, she lived at home and worked as a clerk. In any case, young Cheli was not to finish his engineering degree. In February 1940, some five months into his junior year at Lehigh, he dropped out of school and joined the Army Air Corps. "He enlisted promptly after a recruiter came to the university," recalled Geraldine.[18] He and Geraldine tied the knot that same year.

After primary flying training at Tulsa, Oklahoma, basic flight training at Randolph Field, Texas, and multi-engine advanced training at Kelly Field, Texas, Cheli was commissioned in November 1940 and assigned to B-17s. Several months after Pearl Harbor, now a captain, he moved from B-17s to twin-engine B-25 Mitchell medium bombers, serving as operations officer for the 405th Bombardment Squadron (the "Green Dragons") of the 38th Bomb Group. Twenty-three-year-old Garrett Middlebrook, a former Texas law student turned pilot, was greatly impressed by Cheli. "[He] elicited respect without demanding it and gained admiration because he earned it," observed Middlebrook. "I never met a calmer, more confident pilot."[19]

The squadron was soon ordered overseas. In August, Captain Cheli led a flight of B-25s to Brisbane, Australia—the first overwater flight of B-25s to the Southwest Pacific war zone—to join the Fifth Air Force. He flew his first combat mission—a strike against Japanese installations at Buna—on September 15, 1942.

While originally developed as a medium bomber, the five-man B-25 proved more useful as a ground-attack aircraft in the Pacific environment. Fitted with additional forward-firing machine guns and a 20mm gun, the Mitchell was deadly as a low-level strafer. Mast-level skip-bombing attacks on enemy shipping took a devastating toll, while parafrags—small bombs attached to parachutes to slow the descent of the bomb so that the B-25 wouldn't be caught in the explosion—proved deadly as the bombers raced in just over the treetops to attack enemy airfields and ground facilities.

Middlebrook described an attack he, Cheli, and four other B-25s made on some enemy barges the Japanese had tried to conceal in the undergrowth by a river island. "Blowing all the limbs off the barge on my first pass, I saw a boatload of the enemy . . . at least twenty huddled inside," he recalled. "I came back to annihilate them all or a better word might be 'mutilate' for their bodies were torn to bits and blown out of the boat into the water while the boat itself was shattered into splinters. . . . We strafed the island time and time again, blowing human beings out of barges, boats, camouflaged dens and even out of trees. . . . Rubber boats and wooden boats and rafts went floating down the river and finally I noticed the murky water had a reddish tint as it lazily drifted toward the sea." Completing the massacre, the Mitchells proceeded to fight off four Zeros and returned safely to the airfield where an exuberant Cheli approached Middlebrook, grinning widely. "Middie," he enthused, "I'd say that we are doing a fairly good job of holding off half the damn Jap navy considering that we are only a six-plane air force."[20]

"I could not help but share his humor," recalled Middlebrook, "but at the same time I was amazed, as I had been previously, to realize that Cheli actually liked combat. He loved the challenge of combatting the enemy." Middlebrook admitted this revelation left him somewhat apprehensive, both for himself and for Cheli, whom he found to be "a very competitive person"—perhaps too much so in this case.[21]

In January, Cheli took over the 405th Bombardment Squadron after its previous commander was killed in a crash. He was promoted to major, and on March 3, during the Battle of the Bismarck Sea, he led his squadron in the first daylight masthead-level skip-bombing attack (previous attacks had been conducted at night). The target was an enemy convoy attempting to bring troop reinforcements from Rabaul to the Japanese base at Lae. Racing in at low level, the B-25s released their bombs so that they skipped off the water into the sides of the vessels, then followed with strafing attacks.

Middlebrook was appalled by the slaughter they wreaked. Noticing piles of debris on the deck of one of the transports, he belatedly realized the "debris" was bodies—seemingly hundreds of dead enemy soldiers killed by aerial strafing attacks. Another ship was on fire from stem to stern. Others were sinking. The water was full of survivors struggling for their lives. Gunners in the planes opened fire on them. It was less a battle than an execution, but every soldier killed on the water was one less that had to be dug out and killed on land. Shaken by his close-up view of the carnage, Middlebrook later expressed his horror to Cheli, who proved less sensitive—or perhaps more practical. War was a cruel business and one that left little room for idealism, he advised Middlebrook.[22]

By summer, Gen. Douglas MacArthur's advance along the northern coast of New Guinea had set the stage for the seizure of the enemy stronghold at Lae. Preliminaries for the ground assault, planned for September, required the neutralization of Japanese airpower concentrated around Wewak, located about 300 miles west of Lae. A province capital, Wewak was home to the largest Japanese air base on mainland New Guinea. Based at four fields—Wewak, But, Boram, and Dagua—air units there appeared to be receiving reinforcements. Intelligence indicated there were more than a hundred bombers and as many as ninety fighters based at the airfields.

A series of raids against the enemy buildup were scheduled for August 17 to 21. The first took place the night of August 16–17 when fifty B-17s and B-24s hit all four airfields. Cheli did not participate but was determined to go along on the August 18 mission despite efforts by some of his officers to dissuade him. No one doubted the popular squadron commander's guts—if things got tough "we could be sure Cheli would be out there with us," one observed—but there was a feeling he had already pushed his luck to the limit with thirty-eight missions and 135 hours of combat flying hours to his credit.[23] Now serving as deputy group commander, he was more valuable in his ground role than as a pilot. They also knew full well from photos and stories Cheli had shared that he had a wife and a one-and-a-half-year-old son, Ralph Jr.—referred to by the pilots as "Butch"—back home in Pennsylvania. "[We] did not want to lose Cheli," observed Middlebrook of the efforts to talk the major out of leading the attack; "we actually pleaded with him to stay on the ground. We even told him we thought his leadership was more important on the ground than in the air, especially since we had many new pilots and two new squadrons which were to join us shortly."[24]

But Cheli was not to be dissuaded. He refused to stay behind while his men risked their lives on a particularly dicey mission. He exuded confidence. A couple of days before, already marked as one of the youngest and fastest-rising commanders in the Army Air Forces, Cheli remarked that he expected to be a colonel before he was twenty-five years old. "I remember thinking it was dangerous talk," recalled pilot Walter Krell, who tended to take a more cautious view of their mortality.[25]

Flying out of Durand airdrome just north of Port Moresby, Cheli would lead two squadrons of the 38th Bomb Group—thirty bombers in all—to the target area. He would then execute the attack on Dagua Airfield eighteen miles west of Wewak with one of his squadrons. The other squadron would continue on and attack But airstrip, about eight miles further up the coast. Concluding the pilots' briefing, Cheli admonished, "Be careful and get out fast, boys, and I'll see you back here at noon." The mantra "see you back here at noon" was the standard closer—part encouragement, part prayer that all would return safely. Out on the airfield, Middlebrook had just fired up his second engine when Cheli taxied by in the lead plane. Irrepressible as always, Cheli waved and flashed "his famous grin," Middlebrook recalled.[26]

Despite Cheli's show of optimism, the raid got off to an inauspicious start when a severe weather front moved in. Sixty-two B-25s took off from Durand and Schwimmer airdromes starting at 6:30 a.m. Nine aborted, including one from each of Cheli's two squadrons. The remainder rendezvoused with the P-38 fighter escorts and headed toward Wewak, 500 miles away. Emerging from heavy cloud cover some two hours later, Cheli's formation of B-25s dropped low over the hills surrounding Dagua as they began to line up for their run.

Cheli's copilot on this mission was Flight Officer Don M. Yancy, a twenty-four-year-old Texan who had been married only the previous Christmas Eve. Other crewmembers were navigator 1st Lt. Vincent A. Raney of Struthers, Ohio; radioman/gunner Sgt. Raymond C. Warren, a twenty-three-year-old former factory worker from Logan, West Virginia; and turret gunner S/Sgt. Clinton H. Murphree, a former high school track star from Caddo, Oklahoma. Cheli also had a passenger aboard, an Australian liaison officer, John Massie, who had come along to help guide the lead aircraft through the hilly terrain to the target.

As he followed along at about 240 mph, Middlebrook was mentally urging Cheli to increase speed when a panicked voice broke in on his radio: "Zeros, high eleven o'clock!" The speaker was clearly terrified, his voice so shrill that Middlebrook could scarcely understand him. They were still two miles from the target area when ten to fifteen Ki-43 Oscars emerged from the cloud cover about 500 feet above and slashed into the bomber formation. They attacked with "reckless savagery," observed Middlebrook, almost as if they were prepared to ram the approaching bombers if all else failed.

An Oscar opened up on the B-25 piloted by 1st Lt. William F. Pittman on Cheli's left wing. Middlebrook could plainly see tracer rounds punching through the fuselage, entering through one side and exiting out the other. Cheli's plane was also taking damage; Middlebrook could see hits around the right wing and engine inflicted by an Oscar that had closed from just below. "Maneuver, Cheli, maneuver!" he urged. His copilot turned to look at him, and Middlebrook realized he had been shouting.

Two other fighters followed with a head-on pass at Cheli's plane. Heavy black smoke erupted from the bomber's right engine. Horrified, Middlebrook saw flames licking from the trailing edge of the nacelle. Cheli doggedly maintained formation and flew on, cresting a ridge through a storm of antiaircraft fire as they approached the target area.[27]

The engine fire was spreading. Flying alongside, Pittman's copilot, 2nd Lt. Edward J. Maurer Jr., saw flames in the fuselage. "The entire right wing and right engine of Major Cheli's ship were on fire, but he continued on his bombing run and continued to lead the squadron," said Maurer.[28] A crewman Maurer identified as John Massie was visible; the back of his clothing appeared to be on fire.[29]

With flames streaming from his stricken bomber, Cheli led the formation slightly past the enemy airdrome before wheeling to the right and starting down the airstrip, opening up with all forward-firing guns. Parafrags blossomed from the bomb bay and floated down onto the runway and parked enemy aircraft. The 38th Bomb Group's history reported, "Thirty Dinahs or Helens were destroyed by the bombing and strafing, and the parafrag explosions caused further explosions and fires in the revetments and around planes on the runway. Large columns of black smoke rose to 2,000 feet while fires continued to spread through the dispersed planes."[30]

"We knew that we had caught them by surprise," said Maurer. "Jap personnel was running around the airdrome. It was obvious that they were organizing an attack. Props were still turning. We were only 100 feet above them and could see everything clearly. And at that time we started our strafing and bombing attack. We ran down rows and rows of planes which caught on fire, and strafed the crews that were around the planes."[31]

Completing his run, Cheli calmly radioed his wingman, "Take the formation home, Pittman," and began a shallow descent over the beach at the end of the airstrip.[32] Still under control, he brought the burning bomber—the right landing wheel hanging from the engine nacelle with the tire on fire—down in a spray of saltwater out beyond the surf line about a half mile offshore. It was now about 9:15 a.m.

Under continued attack by enemy fighters, the remainder of the flight passed overhead and made for home. In addition to Cheli's bomber, a second B-25 was shot down over Boram. A P-38 was also lost. Other bombers suffered damage and wounded crewmen but managed to extricate themselves and get back to base. There all the talk was about Ralph Cheli, shot down on his thirty-ninth mission—a flight he never had to make. Dozens of airmen had watched in awe and horror as the deputy group commander refused to break off the attack to save himself, maintaining his stricken bomber in the lead position until the mission was fulfilled. A fellow pilot said of Cheli's doggedness, "I believe this action of continuing on the run, while fully realizing his critical condition, constituted one of the bravest deeds I have ever seen."[33]

Paradoxically, considering the vividness of that scene, witnesses differed on the fate of Cheli's aircraft. Some said it had exploded and crashed into the water or in the jungle; others maintained he had successfully ditched offshore. Middlebrook's copilot had the most encouraging report. He said he had seen the plane afloat with the fire out and that crew members were exiting through the pilot's escape hatch. Two of them were already out on the wing when he last saw the plane.[34]

The only indisputable fact, beyond Cheli's startling act of heroism, was that he and the other five men aboard were missing in action. With Maj. Gen. George C. Kenney's approval, Brig. Gen. Ennis C. Whitehead, deputy commander of the Fifth Air Force, began compiling affidavits with an eye toward recommending Major Cheli for the Medal of Honor.

Geraldine Cheli, who was staying with her parents in Bethlehem, received the bad news within days. On August 26, a headline in the *San Francisco Examiner* reported, "Major Cheli Killed in Raid / Famed Flyer Casualty of Wewak Assault." Citing an August 25 dispatch from New Guinea, the *Examiner* reported that Cheli's plane had been hit by anti-aircraft fire. "Brother pilots saw his plane explode and burn upon striking the ground," the report added. Cheli's mother, Julia, who had received a letter from him only the week before, was so distraught she had to be placed under a doctor's care.[35]

Meanwhile, the push to recognize the major's heroism moved rapidly forward. Congress approved a posthumous award, which was formally announced on November 25. The medal was to be presented to Geraldine, who continued to hold out hope that her husband had survived.

Those hopes gained a major boost just nine weeks later when a broadcast from Germany reported that Cheli was a Japanese prisoner of war. This was followed by an English-language broadcast from Tokyo, picked up in Australia, that Cheli and two crewmembers had been captured after crashing in the ocean. In Bethlehem, Geraldine, described as "overjoyed," said she "had never lost confidence for I knew he had made a perfect landing—pilots in his bomber squadron told me so."[36] This was apparently a reference to a visit she had received four weeks earlier from Col. Bryan O'Neill of Yonkers, New York, who, according to a news report, "told Mrs. Cheli that her husband's plane had not crashed into the sea but that the major had made a perfect landing on the water and undoubtedly had gotten out of the plane safely."[37]

Julia Cheli was more restrained, saying she hoped the report was true. However, the Japanese broadcast, consisting of a purported letter from Cheli that was read on air, was persuasive in its detail. It referred to Geraldine as "Gerry," which was Cheli's nickname for her. The letter said,

Darling Gerry: At last I have the opportunity of writing you. I have been very anxious to let you know that I am alive and a prisoner of war of the Japanese. It has been a long time since I was shot down and I know that you have been wondering all this time whether I was alive.

It may take a long time for this letter to be delivered but I know it will make you happy. Please write my mother as soon as you receive it so she, too, will be relieved of her worry over me.

I think of you and the baby always. I pray daily that we shall be rejoined soon for I miss you very much. I am constantly making plans in my dreams for our life after the war.

Take care of baby because he is so important to both of us. I hope you will spend my finances in the bank and that you have sufficient income to live comfortably. Give the baby all he needs.[38]

In fact, it was true. Cheli had survived. A Japanese fishing boat recovered the major and two enlisted crewmen—Clinton Murphree and Ray Warren—and brought them to shore. Yancy, Raney, and Massie had apparently died in the air or the subsequent water landing. A Japanese officer in the *51st Airfield Battalion* observed that Cheli was shirtless but could walk without assistance. Murphree and Warren were in worse shape. Murphree had been shot in the abdomen and one thigh. Warren had broken ribs and an eye injury. The three prisoners were taken to *59th Flying Regiment* headquarters and then to *9th Flying Brigade* headquarters. At some point in this process, Murphree either died of his wounds or was murdered.

Warren apparently didn't live much longer. "There are first-hand accounts of Warren surviving the plane crash with two broken ribs and an eye injury," said his niece, Linda Warren Giles. "From another POW report, the last known sighting of Raymond was that he was tied to a post at the Japanese POW camp in Wewak."[39] It is likely he was executed when the Japanese learned he was an enlisted man and had little intelligence value.

Presumably left alive because of his rank and as a potential source of information, Cheli was initially held at Wewak but was transferred to Rabaul in early October. Also imprisoned at Rabaul, 2nd Lt. Jose Holguin shared a cell with Cheli for about three weeks and was later able to shed some light on what had transpired at Dagua. Cheli was in bad shape and was "slapped and beaten in a most disgraceful manner" by the Japanese guards, said Holguin.[40] "He did not know how he got out of the cockpit," Holguin recalled, "but remembered having to swim to the surface as the airplane was sinking to the bottom. He tried to help his copilot, but could not. One or two of his other crewmembers were, supposedly, also captured, but once interrogations at Wewak were finished, around the end of September, he lost track of his men, and as far as anyone knows, they never arrived at Rabaul."[41]

According to Holguin and two fellow POWs, Lt. James McMurria and Lt. Alphonse Quinones, "Cheli was the ranking officer at our camp at that time and the Japs really made life hell for him. They held question and answer sessions with him ten times a day and beat him when he stubbornly refused to answer anything beyond his name, rank and serial number. He always was given the worst kind of work detail." Pale and thin, Cheli was depressed at the turn of events, observed Holguin.[42]

Despite Holguin's first impression, Cheli seems to have recovered his equilibrium. The former POWs told an interviewer after the war that the major "was always cheerful and optimistic, despite his atrocious treatment."[43] That may have been the truth—it is certainly more reflective of Cheli's personality—or it may have been an effort to put a kinder face on a horrific situation for the sake of Cheli's family. Certainly there was little to be upbeat about. McMurria, captured after the B-24 he was piloting was shot down over Wewak on January 20, recalled, "The food consisted exclusively of rice and water. The daily amount of rice consisted of about six (6) ounces. On infrequent occasions a piece of dried fish, the size of your little finger, might garnish the rice. There was no such thing as sanitation. Living conditions are best exemplified by the fact that we had about a 10% survival rate. There was no medical treatment."[44]

Still, there were indications the noose was closing on Rabaul. The Allies had decided to bypass the fortress but were intent on neutralizing it by air and by sea. On the morning of March 2, 1944, a carpet-bombing attack left the town on fire and in ruins. Probably more for security reasons than any concern for their safety, the Japanese decided to move the approximately sixty POWs in their custody away from the town/harbor area. Blindfolded and handcuffed in pairs, the prisoners were strung together with electrical wire in groups of ten or twelve and crammed onto three open-bed trucks. Handcuffed to Major Cheli, Jose Holguin slipped his blindfold enough to see "toppled buildings and fires everywhere, smoke covering the entire area, and men cursing and shouting as they tried to control the flames."[45]

Their destination was Tunnel Hill, a deep road cut through a ridge about a mile away. Unloaded from the trucks, the POWs were led to a cave dug into the side of a gully. The excavation had originally served as a storage area for gasoline drums. "The Tunnel Hill Prison camp in reality was not a tunnel," said McMurria. "It was a cave approximately 5 feet wide and 25 feet long, dug back into the mountain. We were hand-cuffed at all times while in the cave. There was not sufficient room for all of us to sit down. After we were sent into the cave, about half our number had to stand."[46] Once the prisoners were crammed inside, the Japanese barricaded the entrance with coconut logs, leaving a narrow opening that was covered with a blanket. A wooden bucket provided toilet facilities for the entire group. The bucket was soon filled.

The bombing of the harbor area continued on March 3 while the POWs spent their hours in the dark hole. The next morning several guards appeared at the entrance and began calling off names, reading from a written list. As a prisoner's name was called, he would struggle to the mouth of the cave still cuffed to his partner. Once outside, the guards would uncuff the man whose name had been called.

Ralph Cheli's name was called. He and Jose Holguin shuffled out of the cave and were uncuffed. By now Cheli had weakened to the point that he was "visibly sick," Holguin observed.[47] Holguin was cuffed to another POW and sent back into the cave. Cheli remained outside. Eventually, he and about fifteen other prisoners were marched away. The next morning, the guards returned, and another group of prisoners was escorted away. The other POWs never saw any of them again, and their questions were met with evasion. The prisoners had been taken "to a safer place," they were told. Still later, the remaining POWs were informed that the missing men had been killed in an Allied bombing attack.[48]

A few months later a report appeared in a San Francisco newspaper that Major Cheli had been killed when a Japanese prison ship transporting POWs from Rabaul to Tokyo was bombed and sunk by American planes. The war drew to a close with no further word of his fate. "For a while I didn't know what to believe," recalled Geraldine Cheli. "I kept hoping the report was erroneous but as time went on, I began to realize it must be true. The war ended and American occupation forces moved into Japan but there was never any more word."[49]

Confronted by the victors, the Japanese all told the same story. The prisoners had been removed in an effort to relieve overcrowding at Tunnel Hill. While being held at a temporary shelter at Talili Bay on March 5, they had been hit by a bomb. Twenty-six of the thirty-one prisoners were killed outright; the other five were brought back to the Kempeitai camp but died of their wounds. A similar story maintained the POWs had died in a bombing attack on their prison ship.

It was all a lie.

Interrogators learned that the victims of the supposed bombing attack had subsequently been cremated. Why? Hundreds of POWs and thousands of laborers had been killed or died of abuse on New Britain. None had been cremated. Why these particular casualties? There was no reasonable answer. Furthermore, though interrogators appear to have overlooked it, there had been no Allied air attacks in that particular area on March 5. The prisoners had clearly been executed—the incident is now widely known as the "Tunnel Hill Massacre"—but as long as the Japanese stuck to their story, there was no way to prove it or assign culpability. And there the matter rested.

Eventually, the ashes of the victims—which included a number of Australian military personnel in addition to Americans—were recovered. The remains were divided, with three-quarters going to the United States and one-quarter to Australia based on the ratio of nationalities. The remains of the twenty-one Americans were interred on March 21, 1950, at group burial Section 78, Grave Lots 930–934. Their names were listed together on a plaque. There was no fanfare and no national newspaper coverage.

Geraldine Cheli eventually remarried. She had a son with her new husband, but the marriage did not work out. The couple had been separated for about seven years when, on April 21, 1971, Geraldine died in a fire at her apartment in Bethlehem. Fire investigators believed she had fallen asleep while smoking. She was fifty-five years old. Her obituary noted that she was the widow of Maj. Ralph Cheli.[50]

⚊⚊

Like Ralph Cheli, Ray Wilkins was an Army bomber pilot. His day of reckoning came during a raid on heavily defended Rabaul two and a half months after Cheli was shot down over Wewak.

Maj. Raymond H. Wilkins
Rabaul
November 2, 1943

Ray Wilkins thought he enjoyed some indefinable protection—he called it "magic"—that would keep him alive.

That confidence may have had its beginning in his miraculous escape from death on July 29, 1942. Flying A-24 dive bombers out of Port Moresby with the 8th Squadron of the 3rd Bomb Group, he and six other pilots bored in on an enemy convoy running reinforcements into Buna on New Guinea. The A-24 Banshee was the U.S. Army's version of the Navy's SBD dive bombers. Carrying a two-man crew, they were slow and lightly armed with two forward-firing .50-caliber machine guns and a .30-caliber machine gun operated by the backseat gunner. While it was a superb dive bomber, crews had long since learned it was no match for Japanese fighters in aerial combat. As a consequence, a fighter escort of P-39s had been assigned to fly cover for the mission.

However, when Wilkins and the others located the enemy convoy—six troop transports accompanied by two destroyers—about 50 miles from Buna, the fighter escort was nowhere to be seen. Squadron commander Capt. Floyd ("Buck") Rogers decided to attack without them. He waggled his wings, and in they went. Rogers was an excellent and much-respected officer, but his decision to attack without fighter cover was a fatal error. The slow-flying dive bombers were quickly swarmed by two dozen Zeros protecting the convoy.

The first casualty was Rogers himself. Riddled, his Dauntless abruptly rolled over and plunged into the water. Flying on Rogers's wing, twenty-four-year-old 2nd Lt. Ray Wilkins pressed the attack, somehow eluding the Zeros and scoring a direct hit with a 500-pound bomb on one of the transports. As he turned toward the coast and some looming rain clouds in a desperate effort to escape, the doomed crews of three other A-24s were already plunging toward the sea in flames. Another, piloted by twenty-five-year-old Lt. John Hill, dove on an enemy ship, but the bombs missed. Bullets tore through the aircraft and wounded Hill's gunner, twenty-six-year-old Sgt. Ralph Sam, a Paiute Indian from Nevada, nearly tearing his right hand off and breaking his right leg. Hill followed Wilkins back toward the coast as Zeros crowded in on him. Ralph Sam struggled back up behind his machine gun and fired at their attackers until he ran out of ammunition, then pulled his .45-caliber pistol and emptied that as well. Behind Hill, the third surviving A-24, piloted by Lt. Joseph Parker, also turned for home after dropping wide but was quickly gunned out of the sky. Only Wilkins and Hill escaped. Wilkins made it back to base; Hill was forced to land his shot-up plane on an emergency airstrip. Sam was still alive when they got down but succumbed to his wounds three days later.

Wilkins seemed unaffected by his near brush with death. He was not a big talker, but after a few beers one night, he confessed that he thought there was some "magic" that would keep him alive.[51] Truth be told, so far in life Ray Wilkins's magic had been mostly of his own making. Born on September 18, 1917, in Norfolk, Virginia, Raymond Harrell Wilkins was the second son of Florida Harrell and William Samuel Wilkins. His father worked for the New York, Philadelphia and Norfolk Railroad. The marriage was not a success, and Florida eventually packed the two boys off to her hometown of Columbia, North Carolina. "Wilkie" or "Ray," as he was known to friends, was considered "amiable and reserved in nature" but also seen as a high achiever.[52] He entered the University of North Carolina, Chapel Hill after graduating from Columbia High School in 1934 and studied chemistry and pharmacy until December 1935, when he left school. Seven months later he enlisted for a four-year hitch in the Army Signal Corps.

As an enlisted man, Wilkins attended Air Corps Technical School and became a radio instructor before eventually applying for flight training. He began flight training in March 1941, receiving his pilot's wings and a commission as a second lieutenant on October 31. Contemporary photographs show a somewhat long-faced man with wavy brown hair and a serious, almost intense gaze. One of his good friends, twenty-two-year-old Bill Webster, a former Cornell College football player, recalled Wilkins as being a little older than the rest of the men. "He was older not only in age but older in experience and older in outlook," observed Webster. "I never did remember seeing him fooling around or play[ing] ball on the baseball team or [such]. . . . He was pretty much, pretty serious."[53]

Wilkins was on his way to the Philippines when the war began. Diverted to Australia, he began flying missions with the 8th Bombardment Squadron (Light) in early April 1942, piloting the A-24 Banshee. Over the next few months, participating in raids on Lae and other New Guinea bases, he was credited with destroying a number of Japanese planes on the ground and knocking a Zero out of the air. He was awarded the Silver Star for missions against Japanese airdromes and shipping from April through July 1942. For his actions during the July 29 convoy debacle, he was recommended for the Distinguished Service Cross.

The July 29 disaster gutted the 8th Squadron. The vulnerable A-24 was removed from combat, and Wilkins and the few surviving pilots were temporarily assigned to the 89th Squadron, which was receiving A-20A Douglas Havoc twin-engine bombers. Wilkins served as communications officer and soon received his first lieutenant's bars. He was already beginning to stand out. The official history of the 8th Squadron would later praise him as "a cool, yet determined and eager pilot and forceful combat leader. . . . He was at times hard but always fair. He earned and held the respect of all his enlisted men and officers in a manner rare in the Air Corps."[54]

Command was not far off. In May the 8th Bombardment Squadron began to receive B-25s. Wilkins, now a captain, was sent back to the squadron as operations officer. Over the next months, the squadron flew a variety of missions ranging from barge hunting to attacks on enemy airdromes. On August 17 he led twelve Mitchells in a strafing/parafrag attack against Boram airdrome outside Wewak, claiming destruction of twenty-five enemy fighters and bombers on the ground. On August 25 he led a low-level attack on enemy shipping in Hansa Bay southeast of Wewak. He was credited with hitting two enemy ships, sinking one, while the remainder of the squadron claimed five more. Three days later, during a follow-up raid on Hansa Bay, he scored direct hits on two more ships, earning a second oak leaf cluster for his Distinguished Flying Cross.

In September Wilkins, recently promoted to major, was named squadron commander. Friend and fellow pilot Bill Webster observed that Wilkins brought "a unique business-like personality" that differed from the "happy-go-lucky styles" of some other squadron leaders. "He moved away from the other pilots, because, as he told me, 'You can't be both a good friend and a good combat squadron commander at the same time and I am choosing the latter,'" recalled Webster. "He seldom laughed or joked with the pilots at meetings. He addressed everyone by his rank, and he ran a tight ship both in Squadron Headquarters and on the flight line. He seemed to know what was going on all the time in every section."[55]

Pilot Andy Weigel met Wilkins when he arrived at Dobodura toward the end of August 1943. A West Point graduate and first lieutenant with seniority but no combat experience, Weigel found himself in an awkward position. Three other squadrons had already invented reasons to pass him along before he landed with the 8th. "When I went to the 8th, Major Wilkins invited me to his sack for a little chat," recalled Weigel. By now Wilkins had scores of missions to his credit and had turned down the chance to rotate home in order to remain in combat. "I think you will agree it might not be appropriate to make you a flight leader immediately with flight officers and second lieutenants with thirty-five or forty missions as your wingmen," he observed to the new arrival.

Weigel was not about to disagree. Wilkins assured him, "I will do my best to have you get the necessary experience as soon as possible so that you can take your proper place in the squadron." To that end, he told Weigel he could fly with him as his copilot. The green lieutenant soon learned that flying as Wilkins's copilot might be considered a mixed blessing. "When that situation became known, most of the older boys thought that was hilarious as everyone knew that Wilkins always led the hairiest missions," he recalled.

But Weigel saw yet another side of Wilkins when he flew his first Rabaul mission with the squadron commander. As they droned over the water, the crew spotted a small sailboat. "Wilkins tried to get onto it by making a steep side slip toward it," remembered Weigel. "It seemed to me we couldn't make that without hitting the water. Without thinking, I grabbed the control column and pulled it out. Major Wilkins later told me that was probably a good idea and didn't complain at all."[56]

On September 27, Wilkins earned a third oak leaf cluster for his Distinguished Flying Cross when he was credited with destroying a 4,000-ton vessel during a mission against enemy shipping off Wewak.

This was followed in early October by an attack on Rabaul's Rapopo Airfield. Accompanying the raid, war correspondent Lee Van Atta observed that this was Wilkins's "86th combat mission in twenty-two months of combat duty, unequalled by any man in the Fifth Air Force." Van Atta reported that Wilkins was offered yet another oak leaf cluster for his Distinguished Flying Cross for his leadership on the mission but preferred that it be awarded to his second in command.[57]

In late October, as planning began for a massive raid on Japanese shipping in Rabaul's Simpson Harbor, Wilkins was on a much-deserved leave in Australia. On an earlier leave in March, he had met twenty-six-year-old Phyllis Byrne, the daughter of a prominent family in Rockland, Queensland. The two hit it off, and upon his return Wilkins had her nickname, "Fifi," painted on his plane. Now, some seven months later, he and Phyllis were engaged to be married.

With Wilkins absent, 8th Squadron operations officer Bill Webster attended the initial briefing for the Rabaul raid on October 30 at Group Headquarters. As he later recalled, the battle plan involved about a hundred P-38 fighters and seventy-five B-25s. The P-38 fighters would go in first to hit the Japanese airfields "to hopefully keep the Jap fighters on the ground." Six squadrons of B-25 strafers would then go after the numerous antiaircraft batteries emplaced around the harbor, even dropping phosphorus bombs as a smoke screen to mask the attacking aircraft. More P-38s would strafe shipping in the harbor to "minimize or at least disperse the shipborne anti-aircraft firepower capability."[58]

Finally, the 3rd Bomb Group's three squadrons—the 90th, the 13th, and Wilkins's 8th—would go after the concentration of warships, troopships, and freighters in the harbor. Led by the 90th, they would approach in a line of squadrons approximately a minute apart. In recognition of the lethal Japanese antiaircraft capability against low-flying bombers, they would slip through the gap between two volcanoes—Mother Peak and the North Daughter—on the east side of the deep caldera containing the harbor. It was imperative that they use this approach and maintain the proper 225-degree heading as it offered cover, the best angle on the targeted shipping—which, due to the tide, would be broadside to the attack—and the quickest and most effective route through the heavily defended harbor area.

The mission was scheduled for Sunday, October 31. All planes were fueled and armed, and flight crews climbed aboard to await the signal to start engines. The signal never came. Three hours later they were told to stand down. A reconnaissance flight over Rabaul had found the weather too marginal to proceed. That same afternoon, Bill Webster, who had been scheduled to fly the mission, was informed he was being reassigned to Group Operations for about a week prior to being rotated back to the States. "I was speechless—snatched right out of the fire just in the nick of time," he recalled. "I was going home to see my wife and meet my six-month-old son!!!" He started packing immediately.

Later that night, Webster got word to report to Wilkins's tent. "He had cut short his leave to Australia and come back to participate in the upcoming Rabaul raid," recalled Webster. "He told me he was happy for my good news and that he had three bits of good news also. First, the 8th Squadron was due to receive new A-20 Havoc twin-engine attack bombers shortly; next, he was scheduled to move up to Group Head-quarters; and third he and his fiancée had set a wedding date for late December."

Then Wilkins asked Webster the impossible. "Will you delay your departure long enough to fly one more mission for the 8th Squadron?" he asked. "I need you as a flight leader and deputy commander on this upcoming Rabaul mission."

Webster hesitated. "My immediate thought was an emphatic nega-tive," he admitted, "but I remembered his twenty-two-month stint of combat flying, particularly the first six months in the A-24s and all of the times he had put his personal war effort above possible personal prefer-ences. Equally important to me was his commitment to keep on fighting the enemy as long as he was able."

Against his better judgment, Webster agreed to fly. At the briefing that night, the mission plan was reaffirmed. "We were still assigned to attack the shipping in the harbor and follow the same plan to come in low off St. George's Channel between the two volcanoes at a 225 angle to catch the anchored ships broadside," observed Webster. "Sounded simple enough, but the effectiveness of the 3rd Group role would depend on close timing and the approach plan as briefed."[59]

But the waiting wasn't over. The next day, Monday, November 1, the mission was again aborted due to bad weather over the target area. The crews stood down but were up again at 4 a.m. to grab a quick breakfast before trying again. "At the Operations tent, we had another pre-flight mission briefing ... with an even more ominous forecast of heavy flak, and a review of the attack plan by Major Wilkins," recalled Webster.[60] The bomb load consisted of two 1,000-pounders armed with eight- to ten-second delay fuses for skip-bombing attacks on the ships, along with approximately 500 rounds of .50-caliber machine-gun ammunition for each of the eight forward guns, belted sequentially, two explosive, two incendiary, and one tracer.

Wilkins was enthusiastic about the 8th Squadron's role in the mission, recalled Webster, but his optimism was not universally shared. Flying with the 13th Squadron, Lt. Richard L. "Dick" Walker recalled the briefing as being "a very somber affair." Reconnaissance indicated heavy aerial reinforcement of Rabaul and many more ships in the harbor than originally anticipated. The latter meant more targets, but it also meant more antiaircraft fire directed at the low-flying bombers. "Hearing the latest word on the extent of the Japanese defenses was pretty much a prediction that all of us would not be coming home," he remembered. "The twelve crews that were assigned to fly the mission sat grey-faced and quiet during the briefing."[61]

"We were all in our planes by 6:30 A.M. and again the waiting began," recalled Webster. "By now all of us were getting pretty skittish, staring into the early light waiting for the start engine signal."[62] The sky was overcast, and there were some scattered rain showers to the east. Piloting *Fifi*, Wilkins would lead nine 8th Squadron B-25s. Andy Weigel, who normally would have flown as his copilot, had been assigned to fly with Webster when it was assumed Wilkins would be on leave in Australia. Rather than break up that arrangement now, Wilkins took 2nd Lt. Bob Murphy as his copilot.

Murphy, a twenty-two-year-old from Orlando, Florida, was a new arrival to the squadron with only five missions under his belt. He had been anxious to get overseas, but combat had already provided a chilling reality check. Writing home less than a week earlier, clearly troubled, he observed, "Mother, it's hard to see why some boys that lead such clean Christian lives must die in this war, but I've seen one of the finest and cleanest living boys I've ever known shot down. His ship blew up when it hit the ground. And yet God saw fit to save me."[63] The remainder of Wilkins's crew consisted of his navigator, twenty-three-year-old Howard R. Bunce of New Britain, Connecticut, and his gunners, twenty-four-year-old George H. Chamberlain of Cattaraugus, New York, and twenty-two-year-old Miles L. Rowe of American Falls, Idaho. Bunce was an extra addition to the typical crew, but Wilkins wanted a navigator along in case he had to lead the squadron back "over the top" of bad weather, explained Webster.[64]

After two hours of sweltering in 90-degree heat on the runway, the crews finally got the start-engine signal. The raid was on. Engines roared as the bomb-laden B-25s began to lift off from the 6,000-foot dirt airstrip and head out toward Rabaul, 500 miles away. About twenty minutes after takeoff, one of Wilkins's nine B-25s developed some sort of mechanical problem and turned back to base. "I am sure Wilkins was furious, but he would not break radio silence to reprimand," remarked Webster. "The other eight bombers continued on, last in the long string of B-25s heading northeast at about 3,000 feet. The cloud level above was scattered to broken, but lots of rain squalls," observed Webster.

As they neared the coast of New Britain, Wilkins signaled the squadron's bombers to spread out and test all guns. The B-25s then resumed formation. "We put on our steel helmets and hunkered down in our seats with the armor-plated backing," said Webster. "By now the fighter cover was running into Jap fighters, and the radio chatter on our common frequency became quite frenzied."[65]

The pilots in Wilkins's eight-plane formation could barely make out the 90th Squadron bombers four or five miles ahead as that formation began to turn toward the slot between the two volcanoes—Mother Peak and the North Daughter—which would provide passage through the high ground rimming the harbor. Anticipating this approach, enemy shore batteries threw up a tremendous amount of antiaircraft fire across the opening.

At this point, the carefully crafted plan of attack "literally went down the tubes," as Webster later put it.[66] Following behind the 90th Squadron, the leader of the 13th Squadron was a last-minute substitute for the original flight leader who had fallen ill that morning. The replacement officer had apparently not attended the mission briefings and failed to understand the importance of sticking to the designated route. Deterred by the amount of antiaircraft fire visible in the gap, he opted not to thread the needle. Instead, he continued on by, intending to loop around the far side of the North Daughter volcano.

Wilkins kept waiting for the formation in front of him to make the turn. "Hey, you're past the attack angle," he exclaimed, finally breaking radio silence as the gap slid by on the left. By then it was too late. The 13th Squadron bombers made the wide turn around the North Daughter, now completely out of position to attack through the harbor. They would accomplish nothing.[67]

Now committed to following the 13th around the North Daughter, Wilkins was about a mile behind but slightly inside the other squadron's path. As the formation turned directly over the town of Rabaul—so low at 200 feet that the smoke from buildings set afire by previous strikes made it difficult to breathe—he spotted the ship concentration in the harbor and yanked his plane violently over in an effort to get back on a viable attack path. "If he gave a radio signal or a wing dip to indicate his intentions, I wasn't aware of it," said Webster, following behind. "First thing I knew he had racked his plane into a vertical right bank to get lined up on a destroyer. I don't know how his wing man avoided hitting him."[68]

Chaos reigned as each pilot was forced into a similar violent maneuver to avoid the plane on his left, all the while hoping the pilot on his right was alert enough to do likewise. The squadron roared over the water at 240 mph, but the time spent going around the volcano instead of through the slot had cost them whatever remained of the element of surprise. "The defenders definitely were waiting for us," said Webster.[69] A storm of antiaircraft fire rose toward them from shore batteries and ships.

"The radio was a constant rattle of fighters calling to each other, and strafers calling out targets to each other," recalled Webster. "I don't recall hearing anything on the radio identifiable from our group other than

Wilkins yelling at the 13th Squadron leader. I can still hear the continuous warnings going out over the radio to somebody: 'Bogies at five o'clock high,' 'three bogies astern,' 'there's one over to your left,' 'get that guy off my tail,' etc. etc."[70]

Wilkins ended up roughly over the center line of the harbor. Under the original plan, his eight B-25s would have come through the slot and attacked abreast down the harbor, but the detour left the other seven planes more or less in echelon to his right with about 50 yards between each plane, increasing their vulnerability. Webster was fourth in line. "The noise from the wide-open engines and the eight machine guns made conversation impossible, even between pilots 24 inches apart," he said. "The smoke from our eight machine guns filled the cockpit and made vision difficult."[71]

On the extreme left, Wilkins bored in on what later reports described as a destroyer but may have been a minesweeper with a destroyer-like profile. He dropped his first bomb, reportedly scoring a hit, but did not escape unscathed as antiaircraft fire punched into *Fifi*'s right wing. Wilkins continued on, bombing and strafing a merchant vessel. Directly ahead were two destroyers and the heavy cruiser *Haguro*.

With the B-25 piloted by Lt. William C. Mackey on his right wing and the bomber piloted by Flight Officer Woody H. Keyes in the number-three position, Wilkins went straight at *Haguro*. The cruiser threw up a curtain of fire at the approaching Mitchells. As Wilkins and Mackey began strafing the warship, *Fifi* took another hit, this one to the vertical left stabilizer. Wilkins continued to bore in, machine guns hammering. A hail of return fire blew off his left stabilizer.

Cognizant of the other B-25s trailing to his right, Wilkins "threw his plane into a turn to the left in order to avoid cutting us off or forcing us to make a violent turn right over the cruiser," reported Keyes. "This caused his belly and full wing surfaces to be exposed to the direct fire of the cruiser and, as a result, antiaircraft fire caught his left wing, causing one third of it to fold up. The plane then rolled over on its back and split-Sed into the water."[72] Mackey's plane was also hit in the torrent of fire and plunged into the harbor. Keyes's bomber was hit numerous times—one crewman was killed and another wounded—but managed to stay aloft and make its way out of the harbor area.

In the number-four position, Webster was about halfway across the harbor when he suddenly realized there were no B-25s to his left. Wilkins, Mackey, and Keyes had been right there just a few moments earlier. Now they were gone. Flying at 50 feet or less off the water, he and the remaining five B-25s roared across the harbor, bombing and strafing whatever shipping happened to be in their path. "By now all fifty to sixty ships in the harbor were scrambling for open water—some were smoking from the bomb damage of the 90th's attack, and the others were laying smoke screen to add to the confusion," he observed. "It was sheer chaos—Dante's Inferno couldn't be worse. . . . Columns of water shot up in our path as the Japs depressed their guns to purposely cause an added hazard. . . . From high above all sorts of spent bullets, shell casings and belt linkage showered down on the water. It looked like it was raining 'spent metal!'"[73]

Webster finally exited the harbor caldera area and made for open water. "The flight back to New Guinea was like a trance," he remembered. "We took off our helmets, but felt no elation at still being alive. My only conversation was to keep asking the turret gunner if he could see any B-25s trying to catch up, like Wilkins, Mackey or Trout."[74] There was no sign of them.

Back at base, two days passed, and hopes that Wilkins and Mackey had somehow survived to be plucked from the water by a Navy PT boat or PBY faded. "The realization that Ray Wilkins, the one pilot who had outlasted all others in the Southwest Pacific and for twenty-three months had dodged that bullet bearing his name, was lost in action finally set in," observed Webster of his friend.[75] There would be no December wedding to Fifi Byrne in Australia.

"Several of the pilots and the gunners in the squadron saw the crash and there were no survivors due to the violence of the impact and the fact that the plane landed on its back, thus barring the use of escape hatches," a squadron officer wrote to Bob Murphy's mother. "It may seem rather heartless of me to present the facts so baldly but it is my sincere belief that the knowledge that he is dead is to be preferred over the suspense of wondering hopefully if Robert will ever come back."[76]

The Fifth Air Force claimed fifty-two Japanese aircraft and one stores ship destroyed, as well as damage to two heavy cruisers, a destroyer, a minesweeper, and another stores ship, and hailed the November 2 raid a great victory. The participants were less sanguine. It was, said one member of the 8th Squadron, "a debacle."[77] Eight B-25s and nine P-38s were shot down, and several others were heavily damaged. Forty-five airmen were lost. Significantly, the mission went down in history as "Bloody Tuesday," an unlikely title for what was being billed in some quarters as a resounding victory.

Some officers blamed the leader of the 13th Squadron aircraft and his failure to stay on the prescribed course for disrupting the plan and causing at least some of those losses. There was talk of court-martialing the officer, but nothing ever came of it. Bill Webster suggested that the wolves were silenced with a promise from the higher-ups to recognize Ray Wilkins for his display of heroism during the attack.[78]

That recognition came on March 24, 1944, with the posthumous award of the Medal of Honor. By committing virtual suicide by breaking left over the *Haguro* in his damaged B-25, he had given his fellow pilots a chance to survive. His remains and those of his crew were never recovered. Ray Wilkins, Howard Bunce, George H. Chamberlain, Robert E. Murphy, and Miles L. Rowe are commemorated on the Tablets of the Missing at the American Cemetery and Memorial in Manila, Philippines. Major Wilkins is further remembered with a memorial stone at Olive Branch Cemetery in Portsmouth, Virginia; Lieutenant Murphy, with a stone at Greenwood Cemetery in Orlando, Florida; Lieutenant Bunce, with a stone at South Burying Ground in Kensington, Connecticut; and Sergeant Rowe, with a marker at Falls View Cemetery in American Falls, Idaho.

—◦—

While Ray Wilkins and his crew did not survive the catastrophic low-level crash of their aircraft, those airmen who did survive a water landing, while obviously facing a serious predicament, were not without hope. Not all the brave men flying against the Japanese were killers—some were saviors. On February 15, 1944, fifteen airmen shot down in a raid on the Japanese base at Kavieng on the northern tip of New Ireland would survive thanks to the pilot and crew of a PBY Catalina flying boat who refused to give up on them.

Lt. (j.g.) Nathan G. Gordon
Bismarck Sea
February 15, 1944

Chaos reigned in the skies as Lt. William J. ("Smitty") Smith's B-25D medium bomber—irreverently titled *Pissonit*—swept in over Kavieng Harbor the morning of February 15, 1944. Copilot Smith, the twenty-one-year-old son of a doctor from Ashland, Kentucky, had survived twenty-four missions, but now, flying a mere 100 feet off the ground into a storm of antiaircraft fire, he could be forgiven for wondering if he would live through the twenty-fifth.

Everyone had known this wasn't going to be easy. Located on the northern tip of New Ireland, Kavieng, with its harbor facilities, seaplane base, and two airfields, was a key supply depot and staging area supporting Japanese installations in New Guinea and the Bismarck Archipelago. Its neutralization was considered key to the Allied effort to strangle and bypass the Japanese stronghold of Rabaul on nearby New Britain, but previous high-altitude air attacks on Kavieng had been disappointing. The February 15 operation represented a significant change in tactics. Over a hundred A-20 Havocs and B-25Ds—specially adapted for low-level bombing and strafing attacks—would go in and smash the enemy facility at point-blank range. Four squadrons of Havocs, forty-eight planes in all, would go first. They would be followed by seven squadrons of B-25s from the 38th and 345th Bomb Groups, a total of seventy-two aircraft, escorted by sixty-one P-38s from the 475th Fighter Group.

In briefings, pilots had been told Kavieng was a "target-rich" environment.[79] At the moment, the "richest" targets seemed to be the bombers themselves. Approaching with the second wave at 270 mph, 100 feet off the ground, Smith flew into a maelstrom of dense black smoke and ground fire comprised of everything from small arms to five-inch shells. The low-level attack gave Japanese antiaircraft gunners point-blank targets, and they exacted their toll from the opening bell. An A-20 from the 13th Bombardment Squadron piloted by 1st Lt. William T. Pearson turned away with its right engine on fire after being caught in the explosion of a bomb dropped by the plane ahead of him. Pearson managed to horse the crippled bomber out to sea, but when he attempted a water landing, the aircraft cartwheeled, broke into three pieces, and sank. Hit by antiaircraft fire, another A-20 went straight down from about 200 feet with the left engine and wing on fire. The aircraft exploded when it hit the water, leaving nothing but about six feet of wing on the surface. A B-25 crashed and exploded on the beach to the west of Kavieng's Chinatown, killing all five crewmen.

Then it was *Pissonit's* turn. As the pilot, 1st Lt. Frank E. Benson, brought the bomber over the target, Smith heard "a sharp clap" as they were hit by antiaircraft fire. The plane lurched as the left engine burst into flames. A second shell hit the fuselage, rupturing the hydraulics and igniting the 200-gallon auxiliary fuel tank. Streaming fire, *Pissonit* turned out to sea. The crew braced for a water landing. Smith saw tail gunner Sgt. Harold J. Gross, who had been terribly burned, crawling toward him. Unbeknownst to Smith, the plane's radioman, T/Sgt. James C. Healan, in a desperate effort to escape the flames, had already bailed out at about 75 feet with no chance for his parachute to open.[80] Before Smith could do anything for Gross, the bomber slammed into the water. Gross disappeared, apparently thrown through the open entry hatch on the floor behind the cockpit. The three survivors—Smith, Benson, and navigator Hollie Rushing—scrambled out the hatch over the copilot's seat. Wearing their life vests and clinging to Smith's parachute pack, they watched as *Pissonit* slowly sank below the surface.

One hundred miles away, a big PBY-5 Catalina flying boat named *Arkansas Traveler* lumbered through the air toward Kavieng. Commanded by twenty-four-year-old Lt. (j.g.) Nathan Green Gordon, the slow, ungainly aircraft carried a crew of ten. Nearly 64 feet long and powered by two 1,200-horsepower Pratt & Whitney "Twin Wasp" 14-cylinder, air-cooled radial piston engines, the flying boat was capable of a cruise speed of 125 mph and had a range of over 2,500 miles. Originally designed as a patrol bomber, the PBY, with its long range and ability to land and take off from the water, also turned out to be the ideal aircraft to locate and rescue downed aviators. And it was downed aviators that Gordon was coming for now.

The second son of an attorney, Gordon was born in Morrilton, Arkansas, about 50 miles west of Little Rock. He attended Columbia Military Academy in Tennessee before earning a law degree in 1939 from the University of Arkansas and briefly returning to Morrilton to practice law. Realizing he would soon be swept up in the draft, he joined the Navy in May 1941, opting for the V-5 air cadet program to train as a naval aviator. He had never so much as set foot in an aircraft before, but there was a logic to his decision to take to the skies. "I didn't want to be a foot soldier," he recalled. "I had been in military school, and we were marching every day, so I decided I didn't want to be walking around all the time."[81]

Gordon graduated from flight school in February 1942 just two months after the Japanese attack on Pearl Harbor and was assigned to Patrol Squadron 34 (VP-34), the "Black Cats," flying the big Catalina PBYs. After a stint fruitlessly searching for German U-boats in the Caribbean, VP-34 was sent in June 1943 to the Pacific, where crews began flying everything from nighttime bombing raids, to scouting and patrols, to search and rescue. Most recently, the Black Cats had been flying support for the Fifth Air Force from an advanced seaplane base located on Samarai, a speck of an island about three miles off the southeastern tip of New Guinea.

Now, as Gordon and the crew of *Arkansas Traveler* headed for Kavieng an hour before noon, it looked as if they were in for a busy day. Distant billows of smoke marked their objective. Radio traffic indicated numbers of crashed aircraft and downed crews. The first call for "Gardenia Six," Gordon's call sign, came almost immediately: a report of an A-20 that had ditched offshore. This was Lieutenant Pearson's aircraft, which had gone down an hour before.

Accompanied by four P-47 fighters, Gordon headed for the location southwest of Kavieng. "I flew over it and the plane had already sunk, it wasn't there," he remembered.[82] An oil slick, dye from the dye markers aviators carried to mark their position in the water, a couple of life jackets, and a half-inflated raft were visible on the surface. "I couldn't see anybody, but the sea was very rough with swells of 15 to 20 feet," observed Gordon. "There could have been somebody in those life jackets."[83] Sometimes too, downed aviators would hide under life jackets or a raft if they thought enemy planes were overhead. Despite the dangerous swells, Gordon decided to put down, just to be sure.

"When you land in swells, you've really got to be careful," he explained later. "You've got to be sure and keep your nose up out of the water, don't let it get in first because if you do, you're going to flip over and kill everybody."[84] Adding to his difficulties, the windshield kept fogging up. "The plane didn't have a defogger, so I couldn't see worth a damn."[85]

After dropping two smoke bombs in an effort to judge the wind and line up properly, Gordon brought the plane down. "I made a good landing by power stalling the plane. This meant bring it in really slow and cutting the power so the plane drops out of the sky straight down to land in the shortest distance."[86] Despite his best efforts, the PBY hit the water with a jolt that popped rivets in the bottom pontoon. They motored slowly through the debris field, but there were no survivors. "So we took off, which was as bad as landing. The breakers could throw you 35 or 40 feet in the air," said Gordon.[87]

The PBY had scarcely struggled back into the air when a spotter plane reported a downed B-25 in Kavieng Harbor. This turned out to be *Gremlin's Holiday* from the 345th Bomb Group. Piloted by 1st Lt. Edgar R. Cavin, *Gremlin's Holiday*—carrying a five-man crew and one unauthorized joy rider—had been strafing Japanese sailors on the deck of a submarine in the harbor when an antiaircraft round punched through the bottom of the fuselage and set the auxiliary gas tank on fire. The explosion blew out the top turret dome and badly burned the gunner, S/Sgt. David B. McCready. As the fire intensified, Cavin prepared to ditch.

The plane stalled as they came in. The nose plunged under the water but bobbed back up. The six crew members scrambled out, some through hatches and at least two underwater through a hole ripped in the bottom of the fuselage, and clambered into two rafts. Three had suffered serious injuries. Their unauthorized passenger, Capt. Robert Huff, who had come along for the ride, suffered three broken bones in his lumbar vertebrae and a bloody gash to his leg; the radioman had a broken shoulder and a torn cheek that exposed teeth and the bare bone; and McCready was in agony from burns to his arms and hands, a compound fracture of the ankle, and a slashed-open hip.[88]

Guided to the crash by a B-25 flying cover over the downed crew, Gordon saw he would be forced to land well within range of Japanese shore positions, but he didn't hesitate. He set *Arkansas Traveler* down in the swells—making a somewhat smoother landing this time—and taxied toward the two rafts, which the survivors had lashed together. "Gunfire from shore was hitting around us," recalled Gordon. "Machine guns, small arms and some larger shells. Luckily, none hit us, and I think the swells helped us here, as the plane would have disappeared behind a swell to anyone trying to shoot at us from the shore."[89]

The PBY crew threw a line to the rafts, but with the props still turning, the forward momentum of the PBY was too great for the rafts to catch up or be pulled in. Gordon radioed to the back of the aircraft to see what was wrong. "We can't pull 'em in," replied Ens. Jack Kelly. "Can you cut your engines?"[90]

The last thing Gordon wanted to do was cut his engines. Not only would this make the Catalina a stationary target for shore batteries, but there was no guarantee the engines would restart. He asked flight engineer Ens. Walter L. Patrick, "Wally, if I cut these engines, am I going to get them started again?"

"I think so," said Patrick.[91]

Despite that less than reassuring response, Gordon cut the engines. The two rafts were hauled up to the PBY and the occupants dragged inside through the blister window. Huff and McCready were in agony from their injuries. The last aboard was pilot Cavin. The rafts were cast off. Up front, the pilots pushed the starter buttons. The engines roared to life, and *Arkansas Traveler* wallowed back into the air.

By now, Lieutenant Smith, Benson, and Rushing had been in the water for over two hours. Smith's moustache and eyebrows had been burned off in a secondary explosion after the plane went down, and the saltwater stung his face, but otherwise the three men were in reasonably good shape. They clung to Smith's parachute pack as they rode the swells, high on the crest one moment, deep in the trough the next, only about a half mile from shore. The yellow-orange dye markers from their Mae Wests had quickly dissipated. Every shadow below brought fears of sharks.

Suddenly they heard planes overhead. They were P-47 Thunderbolt fighters. The three airmen used the mirrors on their life vests to signal them. The fighters came lower and began to circle. Soon *Arkansas Traveler* lumbered into view. As Gordon maneuvered for yet another landing, a stream of tracers floated toward the PBY from shore. The big plane set down among the waves, and again Gordon cut the engines as his second mechanic, Joe Germeau, widely acknowledged to be the strongest man in the crew, guided a line toward the men in the water, then dragged them in. Settling down in the crowded interior, Smith could not help but consider his prospects for survival greatly improved.

Airborne once again, Gordon turned *Arkansas Traveler*, now loaded down with nineteen men—and with pencils shoved into popped rivet holes and then broken off in an effort to plug leaks—toward home. "I would say we got about 20 miles away from Kavieng when again, our radio went off," he recalled.[92]

It was the same B-25 spotter as before. He had another downed crew, this one very close to shore—only about 600 yards out. Gordon's P-47 escort, low on gas, had already left. The PBY was heavily loaded with the rescued airmen. He had also been told there were Japanese floatplanes in the area, and he was worried about running into one of them without fighter cover. "Are you going to stay with me?" he asked the B-25 pilot. The pilot said he would.

In the back of the aircraft, Lieutenant Smith felt the big PBY executing a long turn back toward Kavieng. "Of course, the decision was mine," observed Gordon. "I wasn't going to leave it up to the crew to make the decision." He knew he was taking a terrible risk on a day that had already been full of them. "But I just couldn't leave them back there. I knew I had to go back and try." Everyone aboard knew what was likely to happen to the downed airmen if the Japanese got ahold of them. "I did not consult with the crew, there was no time for making decisions. I just did it, and nobody complained," recalled Gordon. "That is what had to be done, there was no time to discuss things."[93]

The B-25 shot down in the harbor had been piloted by Capt. William J. Cavoli, operations officer for the 500th Bombardment Squadron. Making their bombing run through the dense pall of smoke rising over the target area, he and copilot 2nd Lt. George H. Braun had been forced to rely on instruments. Racing through the blackness, their B-25 shuddered as it took a direct hit to the right engine. The engine exploded in flames, which spread over the wing and along the starboard side of the fuselage. "The plane was losing altitude all the time and the fire had already melted away half the right engine nacelle, the right flap and the whole right side of the fuselage," recalled Cavoli.[94]

Dodging palm trees as they lost altitude, they limped out over the beach. Cavoli knew the bomber was probably within seconds of exploding, and he wasted no time putting her down. The plane bounced lightly on a wave, then slammed down in a torrent of spray. The impact tore the B-25's nose open. By some miracle, all six crew members survived, though it was a close run. The top turret gunner had to swim out from under water. Radio operator T/Sgt. Thomas B. Freeman broke his right arm in the crash and was caught near the rear escape hatch unable to get out of his parachute. Hearing his cries for help, Cavoli and his engineer, Sgt. Weldon Isler, paddled up to the side window, got Freeman's chute off, and managed to pull him out the opening and into their raft.

The crew paddled desperately away in two life rafts as Japanese on shore fired on them. "We were up to our bellybuttons in water," recalled Cavoli. "We figured we'd be good as dead if the Japanese captured us. They supposedly were beheading American bomber crews who fell into their hands."[95] The Japanese launched a small boat in an apparent effort to capture the stranded airmen, but Maj. Chester Coltharp, riding herd on the rescue effort in *Princess Pat*, roared down and opened up with the B-25's .50s, chopping the boat to bits in a cascade of water.

As Gordon approached in the heavily laden Catalina, he saw he was going to have to make a low-level approach over land in order to set down by the two life rafts. "We had to make our approach over the town, where later I was told some of the heaviest AA fire was coming from," he recalled.[96] He came over the enemy shore positions at a mere 300 feet and set *Arkansas Traveler* down in what was his best landing of the day. Cutting the engines, the crew hastily began hauling Cavoli's people aboard as shells from shore batteries landed all around. "I don't know how they missed us—maybe because the waves were so large," observed Gordon. "Shells and bullets were popping all around."[97]

The downed airmen grabbed the line to their raft. "When we got pulled aboard the Catalina, we said, 'Thank God, we're going to make it home,'" recalled Cavoli.[98] But they weren't home yet. With Cavoli and his crew aboard, Ens. Wally Patrick hit the starter button to restart the engines. The starboard engine fired right up, but the portside engine refused to catch. As the plane started to run in a circle with Japanese shells falling ever closer, Gordon realized the balky engine was flooded, and he pushed Patrick's hand away from the starter button. They waited a couple of moments—a near eternity, it seemed—and then Patrick tried again. This time the engine coughed and came to life. Gordon pushed the throttles forward, and *Arkansas Traveler* lumbered into the air and finally headed for home. The series of rescues had lasted an hour and a half.

Gordon flew to Finschhafen in northern New Guinea, where a U.S. seaplane tender had a doctor aboard. "That was the last time I saw any of them," said Gordon of his passengers. "We simply refueled and returned to Samarai. Total flying time was 7.4 hours to Finschhafen and another 2.6 hours more back to our base at Samarai."[99] Coltharp, who had stayed overhead during the final rescue, made an emergency landing at Cape Gloucester with only ten gallons of fuel left in his tanks. He was subsequently awarded the Distinguished Service Cross for his actions that day.

The low-level bombing attack on Kavieng was considered a resounding success. Harbor facilities burned for days. That success came at a cost: five B-25s and three A-20s were lost and twenty-five crewmen killed. The number of dead would have been much higher had it not been for the men of the *Arkansas Traveler*.

Back at Samarai, Gordon and his crew continued to fly patrols over the next few months. Eventually word trickled down that Gordon had been recommended for the Medal of Honor. "And I thought well, if I get it maybe I'll get to go back to Washington and see the president," he recalled years later.[100] Instead, he and his crew were told to fly to Melbourne, Australia. There, on July 31 he was awarded the Medal of Honor by Vice Adm. Thomas C. Kincaid, commander of the Seventh Fleet. The rest of the crew received Silver Star medals. "We flew back the next day,

700 miles back to where we were," remarked Gordon. "I thought at least they'd give a little relaxation there but we didn't even get that."[101]

Sent back to the States in August to serve as an instructor, Gordon never returned to combat. Leaving the Navy in 1945, he returned to practice law in his hometown of Morrilton. In 1946, he was elected to a two-year term as lieutenant governor of Arkansas. He was reelected nine more times, finally leaving office in 1967. Gordon died of pneumonia "and other ailments" on September 8, 2008, only four days after his ninety-second birthday. His wife of fifty-one years predeceased him in 1999. They had no children.

In an interview after the war, Gordon addressed the subject of heroism. "It's not whether you're a hero or not," he replied. "You've just got a job to do and you try to do it the best way you can."[102] At a celebration shortly after the war, someone else, perhaps struggling for some common ground, asked him, "What did you like best about receiving the Medal of Honor?"

Gordon looked at him and replied, "That it was not presented posthumously."[103]

1st Lt. James Swett
(U.S. Navy).

F4U Corsair on board the carrier USS *Bunker Hill*. Due to visibility problems during deck landings, early Corsairs were turned over to the Marines, who used them extensively in the Bougainville campaign (U.S. Navy).

1st Lt. Ken Walsh (USMC).

1st Lt. Ken Walsh receives the Medal of Honor from President Franklin D. Roosevelt on February 8, 1944 (USMC).

Maj. Gregory ("Pappy") Boyington (USMC).

Maj. Gregory Boyington with a Vought-Sikorsky F4U-1 Corsair at Torokina airstrip, Bougainville, in 1943 (U.S. Navy).

1st Lt. Robert Hanson (USMC).

Lt. Cmdr. Bruce A. Van Voorhis (U.S. Navy).

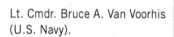

Maj. Ralph Cheli (U.S. Air Force).

B-25s drop parafrags on Dagua field New Guinea during a raid in February 1943. The parachutes delayed the descent of the bombs, allowing the low-flying aircraft to avoid the subsequent blasts (U.S. Air Force).

Maj. Raymond H. Wilkins (U.S. Air Force).

B-25D Mitchell bomber of the 13th Bomb Squadron pulls out of its bomb run and exits Rabaul's Simpson Harbor during the Bloody Tuesday raid on November 2, 1943 (U.S. Air Force).

Columns of smoke rise over Simpson Harbor as a B-25 medium bomber streaks above a Japanese ship during the Bloody Tuesday raid on Rabaul (U.S. Air Force).

Lt. (j.g.) Nathan G. Gordon
(U.S. Navy).

A PBY-5 Catalina lumbers into the air in this photo taken in an unknown location
in 1943 (U.S. Navy).

The crew of a PBY-5A Catalina practice the recovery of downed airmen. Lt. Nathan Gordon contended with less accommodating seas during his rescue of downed pilots at Kavieng (U.S. Navy).

A PBY-5 from Lt. Nathan Gordon's Patrol Squadron 34 moored at Samarai Island, New Guinea, around the time of Gordon's rescue mission to Kavieng in mid-February 1944 (U.S. Navy).

Col. Neel Kearby with his P-47 sporting flags indicating fifteen aerial victories. He scored his twenty-second on the day he was lost near Wewak (U.S. Air Force).

P-47Ds of the 348th Fighter Group in flight over New Guinea. Col. Neel Kearby proved that the heavily armed "Jug" was a killer when used with the proper tactics (Australian War Memorial).

Maj. Thomas B. McGuire
(U.S. Air Force).

Maj. Richard Bong and Maj. Thomas McGuire, the two leading players in the so-called Ace Race on November 15, 1944, in the Philippines (U.S. Air Force).

Armed with four .50-caliber machine guns and a 20mm cannon in the nose, the twin-boom, twin-engine Lockheed P-38 Lightning was flown by top aces Maj. Richard Bong and Maj. Thomas McGuire (U.S. Air Force).

Maj. Richard I. Bong
(U.S. Air Force).

Cmdr. David McCampbell
(U.S. Navy).

Grumman F6F Hellcats crowd the deck of USS *Hornet*. Cmdr. David McCampbell twice achieved "ace in a day" status flying the rugged carrier fighter, which decimated Japanese air units at the Battle of the Philippine Sea (U.S. Navy).

Maj. Horace S. Carswell
(U.S. Air Force).

Maj. William A. Shomo
(U.S. Air Force).

S/Sgt. Henry E. ("Red") Erwin
(U.S. Air Force).

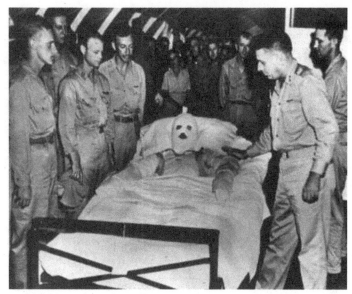

Swathed in bandages and not expected to live, Red Erwin receives the Medal of Honor from Maj. Gen. Willis Hale (right) at the hospital on Guam. Aircraft commander Capt. George Simeral (left, with hat) and other crew members look on (U.S. Air Force).

The crew of the B-29 bomber *Snatch Blatch* or, alternatively, *The City of Los Angeles*. S/Sgt. Henry Erwin is second from the right in the front row (U.S. Air Force).

An Aichi D3A Type 99 Val carrier bomber starts to burn. Jim Swett downed seven Vals in less than twenty minutes off Guadalcanal on April 7, 1943 (U.S. Navy).

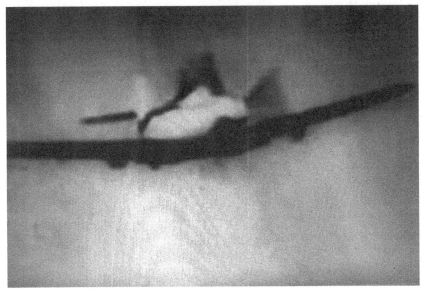

Gun camera footage captures the demise of a Japanese aircraft in air-to-air combat. U.S. fighter pilots learned to aim for the wing roots of enemy aircraft in order to explode the vulnerable fuel tanks (U.S. Navy).

Mitsubishi Zero A6M3 Model 22 from the 251st Kōkūtai over the Solomon Islands in May 1943. Based at Rabaul, the 251st was involved in heavy combat with Marine pilots flying out of Henderson Field (National Archives).

Gen. George C. Kenney (U.S. Air Force).

8

The Ace Race

Over a period of several months in late 1943 and into 1944, three U.S. Army fighter pilots vied for the coveted title of American Ace of Aces. Marine Joe Foss had been the first to break Eddie Rickenbacker's World War I record of twenty-six aerial victories; once the Guadalcanal campaign drew to a close, he would score no more. Now the race was on to see who would emerge from the war as the new Ace of Aces. Fueled by fevered press coverage, the leading candidates included an obsessively driven Texan, a wise-cracking fighter pilot from New Jersey who loved the limelight and hoped to go into the history books, and a former Wisconsin farm boy whose "aw shucks" reticence tended to mask his own ambition to own the title. None would survive the war.

Lt. Col. Neel E. Kearby
Wewak, New Guinea
October 11, 1943

Lt. Col. Neel Kearby made a favorable impression on Fifth Air Force commander Gen. George C. Kenney when he reported for duty in the latter part of June 1943. Kenney described the newly arrived commander of the 348th Fighter Group as "a short, slight, keen-eyed, black-haired Texan, about thirty-two," exuding a fighter pilot's elan. "About two minutes after he had introduced himself he wanted to know who had the highest scores for shooting down Jap aircraft," observed Kenney. "You felt that he just wanted to know who he had to beat."[1]

The youngest son of a dentist, Neel Earnest Kearby was born on June 5, 1911, in Wichita, Texas. By 1924, after a stop in Mineral Springs, the senior Kearby had moved the family to Arlington, just outside Dallas. Graduating from Arlington High School in 1928, Neel worked a few odd jobs before enrolling in 1930 at North Texas Agricultural College (now the University of Texas at Arlington), where he majored in business administration. Between part-time jobs, including a stint as a salesman at a Western Auto store, and various other interruptions, he did not receive his degree until 1937. He would never use it—at least not in the business world.

Kearby had taken flying lessons while in college and apparently found piloting planes more beguiling than doing business. Immediately after receiving his degree in March 1937, he joined the Army Air Corps, earning his wings seven months later. Stationed for a time at Randolph Field in San Antonio, he met a local girl, Virginia Cochran, a 1937 graduate of St. Mary's University whose charms had led to her selection as a "duchess" in the city's famous Battle of Flowers Parade of that year.[2] The two were married the following May.

Considered an outstanding pilot, Kearby progressed quickly in his chosen career. In October 1942 he was named to command the newly formed 348th Fighter Group. By the standards of the day, Kearby was a little long in the tooth for aerial combat—the average age of a fighter pilot during the war was about twenty or twenty-one. Twenty-five was considered "mature"; thirty was almost ancient. By the time Kearby arrived in General Kenney's office several months later, he was over thirty years old and the father of three young sons ranging in age from seven months to three and a half years. But Kearby clearly had the fire. Kenney, who liked go-getters, decided almost at first look that this intense, drawling Texan was "money in the bank."[3]

One major hurdle facing Kearby as he arrived in the Southwest Pacific was a widespread skepticism about the capabilities of his fighter group's P-47 Thunderbolts. The group's P-47s, nicknamed "Jugs" by virtue of their blocky appearance, were the first to arrive in the Southwest Pacific. Weighing in at more than 10,000 pounds empty, the big, heavily armored P-47 was a flying tank. One presumably apocryphal story told of a Jug that crashed through a brick factory, losing its wings on the way through but depositing its pilot, uninjured, on the far side of the building.

The plane was clumsy at lower altitudes and climbed like a proverbial brick, but it packed a punch. Armed with eight M2 Browning .50-caliber machine guns in the wings, it could deal out serious injury in an air-to-air or ground-support role. The Thunderbolt's biggest drawback was its limited range—just over 800 miles. The reigning Army fighter in the Southwest Pacific at the time of Kearby's arrival, the twin-engine, fork-tailed P-38 Lightning, had a range of just over 1,300 miles, an important advantage considering the vast distances facing pilots in the theater.

P-38 Lightning pilots scoffed at the new arrivals, joking that a "Thunderbolt" was the empty noise that follows "Lightning." But Kearby recognized that the P-47 could be a killer if employed with the proper tactics. It handled beautifully at higher altitudes, and it could drop like a stone and quickly zoom back up due to the power of its dive inertia. That advantage allowed a pilot to pounce on an enemy aircraft below, cut loose with the Thunderbolt's devastating armament, and quickly pull out and back to altitude. As for the plane's limited legs, work was already under-way in theater to develop an adequate auxiliary fuel tank to extend the Thunderbolt's range.

At about the time those fuel tanks became available in early August, Kearby got a chance to show off the Thunderbolt's capabilities—as well as his own skills—in a mock dogfight with P-38 fighter ace Dick Bong. Some witnesses thought Bong narrowly outperformed Kearby during the thirty-five-minute duel; others considered the match a tie. Either way, Kearby's performance earned a modicum of respect for the previously ridiculed Jugs.

The group spent its first weeks flying local patrols out of Jackson Drome about seven miles from Port Moresby but didn't score its first kills until August 16, when a 340th Squadron pilot shot down an Oscar near Huon Gulf. A 341st Squadron pilot claimed a second Oscar later that same day but never got a chance to celebrate as he was himself shot down and killed. The Thunderbolt pilots began to see more action as an Allied invasion fleet moved toward Japanese-held Lae in early September. Late in the afternoon on September 4—the day before the amphibious landing at Lae—Kearby, flying his personal P-47, *Fiery Ginger*, named in honor of his wife, led a flight of twenty Thunderbolts toward the battle area. Flying at 25,000 feet just east of Lae, Kearby spotted what he identified as a Japanese Betty bomber.[4] The bomber, painted in mottled gray camouflage, was cruising just above the waves, attended by a fighter off each wing.

Rolling into a dive, Kearby initially hoped to bag the bomber and one of the fighters in a single run but finally settled solely on the Betty. The concentrated fire of his eight .50-calibers tore hunks of metal off the unarmored bomber, which burst into flames as he flashed by. He glanced back to see the burning aircraft crash into the sea. One of the accompanying Oscars sped away; the other was nowhere to be seen. One of the Thunderbolt pilots reported that the missing Oscar dove into the water when Kearby first opened fire; whether the plane had been hit or the pilot simply panicked would never be known. Either way, Neel Kearby, who had arrived in theater brashly asking about the top scorer, had his first two aerial victories.[5]

Kearby added to his score ten days later while leading a flight to Nadzab Airfield—which had been seized by an Allied airborne attack on September 5—about 20 miles from Lae. Approaching at 20,000 feet, he spotted a Mitsubishi Ki-46 twin-engine reconnaissance plane—code-named Dinah by Allies—somewhat higher and to his right. As the Dinah fled toward the clouds, Kearby radioed his flight not to drop their belly tanks, which were in short supply. He then proceeded to drop his own tank and took off after the fleeing Dinah. Closing from behind and slightly to the left, he gave the enemy plane a three-second burst from about 300 yards. Trailing flames, the Dinah glided toward the sea for victory number three.[6]

The action picked up in earnest in October as V Fighter Command stepped up operations against Japanese bases around Wewak. Kearby took full advantage of his status as air group commander to add to his personal score. On October 11, he rounded up three pilots—Capt. John Moore, operations officer for the 341st Squadron; Maj. Raymond Gallagher, commanding the 342nd Squadron; and twenty-three-year-old Capt. Bill Dunham of Tacoma, Washington—for a four-plane mission to Wewak. Taking off from 5 Mile Drome outside Port Moresby, they refueled at

Tsili Tsili about 40 miles from Lae before taking off at 9:30 a.m. for the 300-mile jump to Wewak. "The weather was excellent with a few scattered clouds between two thousand and eight thousand feet," observed Kearby.[7]

Unbeknownst to Kearby, they were picked up by enemy radar about 50 miles from their destination. Lt. Col. Tamiya Teranishi, commander of the 14th Fighter/Bomber Group in the Wewak area, ordered an intercept, climbing into his own fighter to lead the charge. The Americans dropped their belly tanks as they orbited overhead at about 28,000 feet. At first there seemed to be no Japanese reaction. "We saw a number of aircraft parked on Boram strip and one aircraft taxiing on the runway," reported Kearby. "He did not take off."[8]

That soon changed. A few minutes later, Kearby spotted an Oscar (he misidentified it as a Zeke) about 8,000 feet below him. He immediately rolled into the attack. "I came in on him from seven o'clock above and opened fire at 1500 feet," he reported. "He took no evasive action, caught fire and dived into the sea."[9]

Gallagher went chasing off after another fighter, while Kearby, Moore, and Dunham climbed back to 26,000 feet. Now they spotted what Kearby described as a mixed formation of about thirty-six Zekes, Hamps,[10] and Tonys at 10,000 to 15,000 feet. Approaching from the east, these were presumably Lt. Col. Tamiya Teranishi's reaction force. Below that formation, flying at about 5,000 feet, were twelve bombers, "type unidentified," according to Kearby's report.[11]

The P-47s maneuvered around to the rear of the enemy formation, then rolled into the attack from about 8,000 feet above, screaming in at 425 mph. Kearby picked out the lead Oscar (also misidentified as a Hamp), opened up from 300 yards, and knocked it down in flames. Sliding to the right, he fired on another Oscar (again misidentified as a Hamp), which also promptly burst into flames. A Tony came after Kearby, but Dunham, watching Kearby's tail, alertly chopped it down.

"I looked up and another Hamp [presumably an Oscar] was turning slightly above and from about eight o'clock," reported Kearby. He pressed the gun button, and the plane "burst into flames after [it] had passed beyond my sights in the turn." With the element of surprise expended,

Kearby pulled up sharply to about 20,000 feet and headed for home.[12] Lingering, Dunham counted seven circles on the water below where planes had gone in. A pillar of black smoke rising from the jungle marked the grave of a Tony claimed by Moore.

Having lost track of his fellow Thunderbolts, Moore turned for home. He'd gone about 20 miles when he spotted a lone P-47 dueling with half a dozen Tonys. It was Kearby. As Moore dove to assist, Kearby sent one of the Japanese fighters down billowing smoke. Moore went after a flight of three Tonys. His first burst drew smoke from the trailing plane. He hit it again with mixed incendiary and armor piercing slugs. The plane flamed and fell off to the left in an uncontrolled spin. As the remaining two Tonys turned to get behind him, Moore dove away at full power. To his chagrin, the Tonys stayed with him, but now Kearby intervened. He later reported,

> *I turned and came in at 400mph on the tail of the rear Tony, opening fire at 1500 feet. He took no evasive action and burst into flame. I closed for another Tony but he must have seen me as he turned and dove down in front of me. I opened fire from about 2000 feet closing in and saw tracers going into him and pieces of his wing and fuselage flying off. I did not see him catch fire nor did I see him crash. Tonys were all over the sky. I made another pass at a Tony from about ten o'clock but deflection was wrong. I looked and saw a Tony closing in on my tail so I dived for the nearby clouds. When coming out of the clouds I could no longer see the Tony.[13]*

In the space of thirty minutes, Kearby had shot down six enemy fighters, a record for the most aerial kills by one U.S. Army pilot on a single mission in the Pacific up to that time. Moore was credited with two Tonys and Dunham with another for a grand total of nine enemy planes. Among their victims was the combative Colonel Teranishi.

Back at the airfield, Kearby's ground crew saw *Fiery Ginger* roar overhead executing roll after victory roll. Finally setting down, Kearby held up five fingers. "That's pretty good—five down for a flight of four P-47s," observed one of the ground crew. They soon learned it was actually six for

Kearby alone. Later Kearby confessed he had only claimed five because he thought he'd be ridiculed as a tale-teller if he claimed six. General Kenney later asserted that the six kills were all duly recorded on Kearby's gun camera—and felt the hotshot Texan would have been able to claim seven if the camera hadn't run out of film.[14]

Kenney happened to be meeting with Gen. Douglas MacArthur in Port Moresby when Kearby returned from his mission. "Kearby came over to my headquarters soon after he landed and told us the story of the fight," Kenney wrote. Always looking for opportunities to bring attention to his Fifth Air Force, Kenney observed that a Navy pilot had been awarded the Medal of Honor for scoring five victories in a single mission (apparently a reference to Butch O'Hare). "I added that as soon as I could get witnesses statements from the other three pilots and see the combat camera-gun pictures, if the evidence proved that Kearby had gotten five or more Nips, I wanted to recommend him for the same decoration." MacArthur weighed in to say he would approve the award and send it immediately to Washington with his personal recommendation if that turned out to be the case.[15]

It appeared that Kearby and the once-scorned P-47 had proved themselves to their many skeptics. In a preamble to the combat report on the mission, the 342nd Squadron intelligence officer gleefully observed that downing nine enemy aircraft "without a scratch on a single Thunderbolt demonstrates that this type of plane has come into its own in this theater, and that its terrific speed both in the dive and straightaway, its flashing aileron roll, and murderous firepower will henceforth strike terror into the hearts of the little yellow airmen."[16] Kearby, meanwhile, continued his streak. On October 16, he nailed another Oscar near Wewak. As flames poured from the Oscar's engine cowling, the pilot took to his parachute. Three days later, he shot down two Mitsubishi F1M Pete floatplanes off Wewak, bringing his score to twelve, only five behind Dick Bong, the leading Army ace in the Southwest Pacific.

Kearby's subordinates did not share his spectacular success. By month's end he remained the only ace in the 348th Fighter Group. His closest competitor was Bill Dunham with four victories; a couple of other pilots had racked up three. But if the others thought Kearby was hogging the best opportunities, there was no obvious indication of resentment. The colonel was known, perhaps not always affectionately, as the "Boss" and had a reputation as a stern disciplinarian, but he seems to have maintained a cadre of loyalists among his pilots.

Anecdotal evidence suggests he was less popular with his ground crews. On one occasion, immediately after landing, he brusquely ordered a line chief to get *Fiery Ginger* checked out and ready to go without delay. Already swamped with work, the chief replied, "We'll do the best we can, sir." Kearby spun on his heel and snapped impatiently, "You'll do it or I'll have you busted." The incident caused talk throughout the squadron and was apparently not the only brush Kearby had with the enlisted men charged with keeping the Thunderbolts flying. There were those who claimed Kearby's demanding exterior concealed a keen sense of humor; if so, that side of the new ace seems to have been reserved for a favored few.[17]

General Kenney, meanwhile, was becoming concerned that Kearby's unconcealed obsession with becoming the new Ace of Aces was likely to end in disaster. On the one hand, he liked the attention aces like Kearby brought to his command; on the other, he was all too aware of the negative effect on unit and home-front morale when some highly publicized hero got himself killed. In an effort to rein Kearby in, Kenney transferred him in early November to a desk job at V Fighter Command Headquarters and restricted him to combat flying just two times a week "or less."[18]

In letters home to his wife, Kearby expressed frustration at being tied to a desk. Nevertheless, he continued to squeeze in freelance flying time, dropping in on his former command to arrange personal four-plane fighter sweeps, always anointing himself as lead gun.[19] He also enjoyed the attention of news correspondents as they cranked out stories about the so-called Ace Race. "Kearby loves to call two or three veteran flyers from their desks and propose a little hunting trip," observed a widely published laudatory interview in early December. "'It isn't that I like to kill anybody, but I do like to hunt,' he explained as he leaned against his plane, 'Fiery Ginger,' named after his wife, who lives in San Antonio, Tex." The article appeared only ten days after Kearby knocked down three Oscars on a sweep over Wewak to bring his score to fifteen.[20]

Despite General Kenney's edict, Kearby continued flying, claiming a probable on December 17. Five days later he came across an Oscar at Wewak, pulled up from behind, and hosed it down from 300 yards. The Oscar promptly caught fire, and the pilot bailed out. Kearby chased after another, but seven of his eight .50-calibers quit on him, and he had to run for home. Undaunted, he led yet another flight to Wewak the next day. The Thunderbolts hadn't been on station at 27,000 feet for more than five minutes when they spotted two Tonys at 10,000 feet. "We dropped belly tanks and dived to the attack," reported Kearby.

Due to broken clouds I lost sight of the two enemy planes but sighted a bomber approaching Dagua [Airfield] for a landing. At this time a Tony appeared at 8,000 feet, so attacked him from 7 o'clock getting a 4 second burst in from 1500 to 500 feet closing rapidly at 350 mph. I saw strikes at the wing roots and fuselage. As I pulled up I lost him but saw another Tony at 200 feet heading for Dagua. I attacked him from dead astern at 250 mph opening fire at 1500 feet for a 10 second burst. He lazily banked to the left and crashed burning in the trees at the end of Dagua strip. No evasive action was taken by either Tony.[21]

The kill, Kearby's seventeenth, put him only four behind Dick Bong, who was temporarily out of combat, having returned to the States on leave. General Kenney again cautioned Kearby not to get greedy and take unnecessary chances. He offered to send him home for a month. Kearby declined, declaring that he wanted to beat Dick Bong and rack up at least fifty enemy kills. "If you send me home now, I'll never catch up," he told Kenney. "Let me get fifty first."[22]

On the morning of January 3, he shot down a Ki-21 Sally twin-engine heavy bomber as it took off from Wewak airstrip, then returned in the afternoon in search of more victims. At 2:45 p.m. he sighted what he described as a Zero, which was probably an Oscar, at 4,000 feet.

I opened fire at 1,000 feet from dead astern. . . . I saw strikes on the fuselage and after a three-second [burst] the Zeke burst into flames. As I passed him I turned slightly to see that he definitely went down.

Instead, the fire went out and the Zeke continued on its course. I made a 360 degree turn and came in from dead astern once more. No evasive action was taken by the enemy airplane. I gave him a six-second burst and he again caught on fire, but after I went by him the fire went out again. We were down to 1,000 feet now and when I turned to come in again; the enemy plane crashed into the sea.[23]

Six days later, he led three other Thunderbolts into a formation of about eighteen Tonys and shot down two of the enemy fighters, bringing his score to twenty-one to tie Dick Bong's record, with only five to go to be the first Army pilot to tie Eddie Rickenbacker's World War I record. On the heels of this accomplishment came news that his Medal of Honor had been approved. "Neel happened to be in my office in Brisbane when it came in," recalled Kenney. "I immediately rushed him up to General MacArthur and had the ceremony done by the Old Man himself."[24]

The recognition and accompanying news coverage did nothing to temper Kearby's obsessive quest to be top ace. If anything, his sense of urgency was growing. Bong would return from leave in February and presumably continue adding to his score. Meanwhile, Kearby's own window would soon be closing. As the Allies neutralized Wewak—his favored hunting ground—the shorter-range P-47s would almost certainly be diverted to more ground-support missions, and there would be less opportunity for air-to-air combat.

In yet another effort to rein in his ambitious hero before he got himself killed, Kenney reassigned Kearby to 308th Bomb Wing Headquarters, where he was charged with coordinating operations between fighters and bombers. Over the next few weeks, Kearby's quest to become Ace of Aces bogged down in a morass of paperwork and administrative duties. Meanwhile, as Kearby had feared, Bong returned to the theater and was adding to his string of victories. In his history of the 348th Fighter Group, John Stanaway weighs the effect on the ambitious Texan. "Time was pressing on Neel Kearby and he cut every corner of his safety margin to beat all comers in the ace race," notes Stanaway. "No matter how he may have tried to deny it, the magic number twenty-six was driving him as surely as if it were a hypnotic spell."[25]

On March 5, once again trailing Bong, Kearby showed up at his old air group, now flying out of Saidor, 100 miles northwest of Finschhafen. Though no longer associated with the 348th Fighter Group, he enlisted Capt. Bill ("Dinghy") Dunham and Capt. Sam Blair, and the three of them took off at 4 p.m., bound for Japanese-held Wewak. Ten minutes after arriving, they saw a Tony approaching the Dagua strip, but it was clear the plane would land before they could get to it, so they continued to circle at 22,000 feet. Their patience was rewarded five minutes later when three Japanese bombers in a V formation approached from the sea only about 500 feet off the deck. The Thunderbolt jockeys identified the green-painted ships as G3M Nells, but they were probably Ki-48 Lilys, a light twin-engine bomber introduced in 1940. No matter. As the bright red rondels on the wings attested, they were enemy. The Americans dropped auxiliary tanks and rocketed down with Kearby out front as usual.

The lead bomber was no more than 200 feet off the ground when Kearby took it under fire. The subsequent train of events is not completely clear. According to Dunham, "Colonel Kearby fired on the leading bomber and set it on fire. He then fired at the right wingman but did not knock him down. I made a run on the left wingman knocking him down in flames and then made a pass at the same one Colonel Kearby had fired at, but did not get him. I immediately made a sharp turn to the left. Captain Blair attacked the third bomber at this time and sent him down in flames."[26]

Blair had a slightly different take, reporting, "Colonel Kearby, leading our flight, fired on the lead bomber and it pulled up flaming and then dived into the ground. Captain Dunham fired at the one on the left and I saw it crash in flames. I closed to 200 yards and fired a two-second five-degree deflection burst at the third Nell and saw the fuselage burst into flames. The Nell fell off on the left wing and blew up on striking the ground."[27]

As Dunham turned, he saw Kearby's P-47 climbing directly toward him with an Oscar on his tail. There was no possible way the slow-moving Jug was going to outrun or shake off the speedy fighter. Dunham intervened, lowering his nose to make a head-on run at the Oscar. "My first burst struck the engine and fuselage," he reported. "The Oscar broke off the attack and turned into me. I held my fire on him and set him on fire. As I passed him the canopy flew off and the ship crashed in the same area the bombers went in."[28]

The air chase had taken them to the Boram Airfield. Turning away, Dunham saw a P-47 pass him "headed for the hills" and hastened to join up with the other fighter. It was Blair. There was no sign of Kearby. They tried to raise the colonel on the radio but got no response. "As we left the area I saw where a plane had crashed on the opposite end of the strip from the place the two bombers and one Oscar had hit," reported Dunham.[29]

Returning to Saidor and finding that Kearby had not shown up, Dunham had to be physically restrained from going back alone to look for him. It was assumed that the crash scene Dunham saw as he was leaving Boram was probably Kearby's plane. A missing aircraft report subsequently observed, "It is unknown whether pilot survived or not."[30] The bomber Kearby shot down on the day of his disappearance brought his score to twenty-two—two short of Dick Bong's twenty-four and four short of the record set by Eddie Rickenbacker in 1918.

Virginia Kearby was notified on March 14 that her husband was missing in action. Reporters descended on her San Antonio home to find her caring for her three little boys, who "romped and tumbled about the living room," unaware of the tragedy that had befallen the family. Through tears, Ginger maintained a brave front. "Until he is reported dead, I am not going to give up hope," she told reporters. "Anybody as ingenious as he is will find his way back, if there is a way. . . . For our children's sake, more than for my own, I hope he returns."[31]

A week later, she received a letter from General Kenney praising her husband but cautioning her not to hold out much hope that he had survived. He indicated that the "Zero" subsequently shot down by Dunham had apparently fatally damaged Kearby's P-47. Kenney noted, "Neel was seen to crash near Dagua," adding, "I do not think it fair to hold out much hope that he survived the crash, but that is not impossible."[32]

Kearby was officially declared dead in January 1946, but it would be years before any light was shed on what actually happened. Whatever crashed plane Dunham and Blair saw at the end of the Boram airstrip, it was not Kearby's Thunderbolt. In May 1946, an Australian graves registration team searching for downed aircraft found the wreckage of a P-47 Thunderbolt, #42-22668—the plane Kearby had been flying when he went down—near the village of Pibu about 100 miles from the presumed crash site at Wewak. Japanese records indicate that the Thunderbolt, probably already damaged during the encounter at Wewak, was sighted and pursued by a "Sgt-Maj Kumagaya of 3 Squadron," who "definitely shot it down with one burst" near Pibu.[33]

Natives from the area said the plane had been on fire when it crashed. Their stories were confusing, but it appeared the pilot had parachuted out at low level and become tangled in the trees about 100 yards from the village. He was dead when they found him; whether he was killed on striking the trees or died of wounds suffered in the air was unclear. The natives handed over a skull and some bones wrapped in bark, saying they were all that remained of the pilot. The remains were turned over to the American Graves Registration Service Mausoleum in Manila but were not formally identified as Kearby until January 1949, when his family was notified.[34]

Brought back to the United States aboard the U.S. Army transport *Private John R. Towie*, the remains were accompanied to Texas by Kearby's friend and fellow fighter pilot Bill Dunham. He was buried on July 23, 1949, at Hillcrest Memorial Park next to his older brother, Army Maj. John Gallatin Kearby III, who died in an airplane crash stateside on August 2, 1943.[35] Described by *TIME* magazine as "one of the great U.S. fighter pilots of World War II,"[36] Neel Kearby was honored by the U.S. Air Force in 1959 with the dedication of Neel Kearby Hall, a missile training facility at Sheppard Air Force Base in Wichita Falls, Texas. An exhibit at the National Museum of the United States Air Force in Dayton, Ohio, features a display of his medals and a full-sized replica of his legendary Thunderbolt. The tail section of the original Thunderbolt is also on display. Salvaged from the crash site on New Guinea in 2001, it still bears much of its original paint and U.S. Army serial number, as well as bullet holes suffered during Kearby's fatal last mission.

Virginia Kearby remarried, but further sorrows awaited. On Memorial Day 1974, two of her three sons, Kenneth, thirty-one, and Robert, thirty-six, were killed when the single-engine plane Kenneth was piloting struck power lines across the Arkansas River below the Keystone Dam in northeastern Oklahoma. Three years later her middle son, John Michael, died of heart failure at the age of thirty-six. Virginia passed away in San Antonio, Texas, in 1989, three days before her seventieth birthday. She lies at rest in the Cochran family plot in Mission Burial Park South in San Antonio.

Maj. Thomas B. McGuire Jr.
Luzon
December 25–26, 1944

In early January 1945, newspaper reporters crowded into the office of T. B. McGuire's Packard Motor Car Sales dealership in Ridgewood, New Jersey. The focus of their interest was owner Tom McGuire, father of Army Air Forces fighter pilot Thomas B. ("Tommy") McGuire. Tommy, then flying P-38s out of the Philippines, appeared to be on the verge of breaking Dick Bong's forty-victory record to become America's new Ace of Aces.

Following the gathering in New Jersey, the wire services sent out a photograph of Mr. McGuire holding a picture of his son. The caption read, "Thomas B. McGuire Sr. holds a picture sent to him by his son from the Southwest Pacific, where he has just become the number one Ace of WWII by outgunning Richard I. Bong." The caption contained a caveat: "Hold for future release."[37]

Tommy McGuire was born in Ridgewood, New Jersey, on August 1, 1920, less than two months before the arrival of his future comrade in arms and competitor, Dick Bong, in rural Wisconsin. His mother, Pauline ("Polly") Watson was the daughter of well-to-do industrialist Alfred B. Watson. Alfred owned Watson Machine Company in Paterson, New Jersey, specializing in cordage machinery. At the somewhat advanced age of twenty-eight, to her parents' dismay, Polly eloped with twenty-four-year-old Thomas Buchanan McGuire, a glib, fast-living car salesman, who had the added black mark in Watson eyes of being Roman Catholic. They were married in New York City on November 24, 1918, thirteen days after the end of World War I.

As Polly's parents had feared, the marriage was troubled. In 1927, after much turmoil, the couple finally split up for good. Polly and

seven-year-old Tommy moved in with her parents, now living in an affluent summer community in Sebring, Florida. Thin and long-faced with an
outsized nose that always seemed to be running due to his allergies—an
affliction that earned him the nicknames "Snooty" and "Honker" among
his adolescent peers—Tommy was also sometimes teased as a spoiled
mamma's boy. Doted on by both his affluent grandparents and his mother,
he stood out as the best-dressed kid at school, the kid with all the best
toys, the kid with his own sailing canoe on the nearby lake, and eventually
the kid with his very own car, who gained a reputation for driving reck-
lessly around town at high speeds. Despite it all, Tommy proved to be a
likable, outgoing youth, more than capable of holding his own thanks to a
quick wit and caustic tongue, and he did not lack for friends.

He developed a strong and early interest in aviation—an enthusiasm
fanned by his uncle Charles Watson. "Tommy always had a special interest in aviation," recalled one of his boyhood friends. "His Uncle Charles
had been a World War I fighter pilot and they talked about flying at every
chance. Tommy always wanted to be a pilot."[38] He spent hours building
model airplanes and read everything he could find about aviation.

After high school, where he played clarinet in the award-winning
Sebring marching band when not racing around town in his car, McGuire
headed off to the Georgia Institute of Technology to study aeronautical
engineering. With plenty of money at his disposal, he signed up for flying lessons at an airport near Atlanta. He also joined the Reserve Officers Training Corps, where he earned a reputation as "an eager beaver."
Despite his enthusiasm, he was not exactly a poster child for military
recruitment: his schoolmates took to calling him "T. B.," not because they
were his initials, they joked, but because he was so skinny, he looked like
he had tuberculosis.[39]

In February 1941, after reading about a call for American volunteers
to fly with the Eagle Squadron in England against the Germans, he filled
out an application but was turned down. The recruiters were looking for
military pilots with experience. Months later, at the end of his junior year,
McGuire joined the Army as a flying cadet. He was stationed at San
Antonio's Randolph Field, well on his way through the training program,
when the Japanese attacked Pearl Harbor on December 7.

That month brought another life-changing event when he met seventeen-year-old Marilynn Giesler, a freshman at Incarnate Word College, a private Catholic school in San Antonio. Giesler's nickname was "Pudgy," which was somebody's idea of a joke because the vivacious college student was anything but pudgy. McGuire—now sporting a pencil thin, Clark Gable–style moustache—was smitten. By the time he received his wings and commission as a second lieutenant on February 6, 1942, he and Pudgy were an item.

McGuire spent the next few months flying P-39 Airacobras in Alaska. Upon his return, he and Pudgy tied the knot on December 11, 1942. As with so many wartime marriages, their days of wedded bliss were brief: in April McGuire reported for duty with the 9th Fighter Squadron flying out of Dobodura Airfield in New Guinea. A few weeks later he was reassigned to the 431st Fighter Squadron, 475th Fighter Group, which was equipped with the long-range Lockheed P-38 Lightning. Armed with four .50-caliber machine guns and a 20mm cannon in the nose, the distinctive twin-engine, twin-boom fighter was capable of literally blowing the more lightly built Japanese aircraft to pieces. While it could not out turn the Japanese Zero, the Lightning had the advantages of superior speed and a good rate of climb. By war's end, the P-38 was credited with destroying more Japanese aircraft than any other U.S. Army Air Forces fighter.

McGuire's colleagues considered the new arrival a good pilot but a bit too cocky with a smart mouth. On August 17, now flying from Twelve Mile Strip outside Port Moresby, McGuire participated in his first "raid"—an attack on the Japanese airdrome at Wewak. The next day, as the P-38s escorted bombers in a return to Wewak, he had his first crack at air-to-air combat. Leading the last element of three planes, he spotted a Zero at two o'clock and turned for a head-on attack. As the Zero flashed by, McGuire horsed his Lightning around and got off two quick bursts. The Zero burst into flames and headed down.

An instant later, one of his fellow pilots shouted a warning as a Zero latched onto McGuire's tail. Kicking into a hard turn to the left, McGuire shook off his pursuer, then turned the tables and chased him toward the airfield below, firing burst after burst into the cockpit area. The Zero finally caught fire and fell off toward the ground. McGuire followed up with a head-on attack on yet another Zero. A midair collision seemed imminent as neither pilot would give way, and neither could score a fatal hit. They passed so close that they scraped wingtips before parting company, neither able to claim a victory.

But McGuire's day wasn't quite over. As the Lightning escort headed for home with the bombers, a Japanese Ki-61 Tony painted in a green, yellow, and brown camouflage pattern went after one of the departing B-25s. McGuire got onto the Tony and gave it three bursts. The Tony broke off, trailing smoke. McGuire lost track of his victim as he pulled away, but the bomber crew saw it crash into the jungle below and verified the kill.

Back on the ground, McGuire claimed four kills, but one of these was also claimed by another pilot. As was the custom in many Army air units, the two flipped a coin for it. The other pilot won the toss, leaving McGuire with three confirmed victories. Meanwhile, awed mechanics were examining a paint smear on the P-38's left wing—a memento of McGuire's game of chicken with the enemy Zero. It was the start of McGuire's reputation for being a hotshot pilot with the luck of a cat.

Three days later McGuire was back over Wewak, again flying high cover for bombers in his P-38, nicknamed *Pudgy* in honor of his young wife. Over a dozen Zeros came up. McGuire gunned down two of them in short order to become an ace—one of three pilots to reach the benchmark that day, as the squadron claimed a remarkable forty enemy aircraft destroyed in only ten days of combat. Sadly, the outside world intervened in tragic fashion on August 26 when McGuire received a letter and telegram from Marilynn advising him that his mother had passed away. Fifty-three-year-old Polly, who had long suffered from alcoholism, had been found dead on the floor of her room in the Sebring Hotel, where she lived. The news had taken a month to arrive—she had been found on July 22 after failing to appear for several days.[40]

Three days later, McGuire narrowly escaped death himself in another flight over Wewak. Latching onto a Zero that had just cut through the bomber formation, he fired several quick bursts. The Zero flamed up and spun out of control. Spotting an Oscar diving on the bombers, McGuire raced at it head-on, firing as he went. He scored hits, but the Oscar wouldn't go down. McGuire made a hard turn and stayed with it, targeting deflection shots into the wings and fuselage until the plane spewed smoke and fell out of control. Fixated on the Oscar, he had no idea he was about to become a target himself until a voice suddenly broke in on his radio: "Mac, break! There are three Zeros on your tail!"

A stream of tracers floated past as he broke into a hard turn just a little too late. Hit by a 20mm shell, his left engine burst into flame. McGuire considered bailing out, but the Zeros were still with him. He feverishly feathered the left prop and cut fuel to the engine, but the fire continued to burn. As a last resort, he put the Lightning into a dive. It worked. The fire blew out, and he lost the pursuing Zeros. Checking his map, McGuire set course for the nearest airfield, this being a rudimentary field at Marilinan 250 miles away, where he managed to put down without further excitement.[41]

By September, the 431st Fighter Squadron was flying out of Dobodura, providing air cover for the U.S. amphibious landings at Finschhafen. As the hottest pilot in the squadron, McGuire, now flying *Pudgy II* following his earlier escape, knocked down two more Zekes over Wewak on September 28 but took hits in his left engine from another Zero that latched onto his tail. His luck held as he was able to nurse the damaged P-38 250 miles to a landing at the airfield at Tsili Tsili. Writing to Marilynn, he reported, "We got into a little fight recently and I got 2 more nips which makes nine now."[42] On October 15, he scored number ten.

Two days later, pilots were scrambled to intercept a large formation of Japanese bombers and fighters heading for American shipping in Oro Bay 15 miles southeast of Buna. With *Pudgy II* being serviced and unavailable, McGuire brashly helped himself to squadron commander Franklin Nichols's P-38. Nichols was away for the day and had left standing orders that no one was to use his plane. McGuire, self-servingly categorizing the present situation as an exceptional emergency, took it anyway, brushing off the objections of Nichols's crew chief.

The Lightning drivers were at 23,000 feet when they spotted an enemy formation of fifteen planes slightly above them. Dropping auxiliary fuel tanks, they climbed to intercept. McGuire fired on a Zero on the right side of the formation, got it smoking, and followed it down to 18,000 feet before deciding it was done. Verification came from his wingman. Unable to drop one of his auxiliary fuel tanks, the wingman was forced to pull out much lower—at 4,000 feet—and saw the stricken Zero explode.

Twice finding Zeros on his tail, McGuire managed to dive away but did not escape unscathed. The second time, he was forced to put the P-38 into a near-vertical dive toward the sea from 18,000 feet as slugs from pursuing Zeros hammered his plane. Eluding his pursuers, he climbed back up to 12,000 feet to see seven Zeros closing in on a damaged P-38. With no time to set up, he made a desperate, low-percentage 90-degree deflection shot on the Zero moving in for the kill and was gratified to see the enemy plane break off and explode. He came in on another from the right rear, closing to within 100 feet before pressing the gun button. Pieces of the enemy aircraft tore off. The Zero erupted in flames, fell off to the left, and went down, the pilot apparently dead at the controls.

Then it was his turn. As he vainly tried to evade, another Zero raced in to within a few hundred feet, guns winking. A burst tore up his left engine, which began to spew black smoke. Then a 20mm cannon shell exploded in the radio compartment just behind him. Fortunately, his head was shielded by armor plate, but metal fragments sprayed through the cockpit, hitting him in the arms and hips. A machine-gun bullet cut a furrow across his wrist and smashed into the instrument panel. "I felt my whole plane start shaking—the left engine blew up—the right engine was fading and the controls were shot up," he recalled.[43]

In an effort to escape, he nosed over in a steep dive and pulled back on the controls. There was no response. The Lightning was finished. McGuire cut the throttle and pulled the emergency release to send the canopy hurtling away in the slipstream. Releasing his seatbelt and shoulder harness, he clambered onto the seat and jumped, only to slam into the side of the now burning aircraft as his parachute harness snagged on something in the cockpit. After banging against the fuselage for what seemed like an eternity, he managed to break free and pulled the ripcord on his parachute. Nothing happened. Shrapnel had severed the ripcord—all he had in his hand was the D-ring and a small length of cord. Desperately reaching around behind his shoulder, he found the other end of the cord, wrapped it around his wrist, and gave it a yank. The silk spilled out and deployed overhead, and he oscillated down toward the open water now only 800 feet below.

He retained the presence of mind to release the parachute when he hit the water, then found that his one-man survival raft was riddled with holes and wouldn't inflate. He pulled the tab on his yellow Mae West life jacket. Only one side inflated—the other had also been holed—but it was enough to keep his head above water. He kicked off his flying boots and dumped his side arm and shoulder holster before opening a yellow-green dye packet to mark his position, should anyone be looking for him. After about half an hour, dazed and in pain from his shrapnel wounds and the battering he took while hanging outside the P-38, he thought he heard an engine. It was a PT boat. The crew had seen his parachute and motored over to see if he had survived.[44]

McGuire spent three weeks recovering from his wounds, broken ribs, and an impressive assortment of bumps and bruises. He also managed to survive Major Nichols's ire at finding that his personal P-38 was now at the bottom of the ocean. Nichols grudgingly let it pass after seeing how badly McGuire had been beaten up. There were those who thought McGuire's combat career was probably over, but they underestimated his determination. Even so, he was sidelined until early December.

Back in the saddle, McGuire downed three Val bombers at Cape Gloucester on December 26 to bring his score to sixteen. Three days later he was named squadron operations officer and promoted to captain. Wearing his trademark "50 mission crushed hat," the new operations officer proved to be as energetic on the ground as he was in the air. His introductory flights for new pilots were legendary, gut-wrenching affairs that strained men and aircraft to the limit. His own plane, *Pudgy II*, had been subjected to so many violent aerial maneuvers under his hand that the wings had bent and rivets popped.

The next few months were frustrating for McGuire as there was little action, but he put the time to good use, focusing on his duties as operations officer and putting together a manual of combat tactics. His insightful tactical assessment was subsequently forwarded to Fighter Command for possible publication. Recognition of his administrative and leadership abilities led to his selection in late April to command the 431st Fighter Squadron. He made an immediate impact. "He had a lot of energy and he couldn't stand his people being sloppy," recalled a pilot. "Our flying improved. He insisted on it."[45]

Things were looking up as well from a combat standpoint as the squadron relocated to Hollandia. On May 16, McGuire broke his five-month drought when he flamed an Oscar while flying escort for a bombing raid on Noemfoer Island. Two days later he knocked down a Tojo for number eighteen. On June 16, after surviving a bout of dengue fever—also called "breakbone" fever for its debilitating symptoms—McGuire, now a major, shot down two Oscars over Jefman Airfield near the far western end of New Guinea.

Squadron command did not temper his nonchalant daring in the air. Famed aviator Charles Lindbergh, on an observation tour in the Pacific theater, happened to be at the squadron airfield one day when a P-38 with twenty Japanese flags painted on the nose, zoomed in. The pilot put the Lightning through a spectacular series of rolls and loops just off the ground before finally touching down. "The last time I saw anything like that was in an air show!" Lindbergh exclaimed. "Who's that?"

"That's Major McGuire, our leading ace," replied a pilot.

"He'll never live to be an old pilot doing that," remarked Lindbergh.

Unlikely as it seemed, Lindbergh and McGuire became good friends. Lindbergh flew as "an observer" with the squadron for a while, lived in the same tent as McGuire, and learned that the young commander might be a showoff, but he was not reckless—he was just thoroughly familiar with the capabilities of his aircraft. Unlike most other pilots, he routinely pushed those capabilities to the limit.[46]

In July the squadron moved to Biak, and on July 25 McGuire burned an Oscar for kill number twenty-one. As his mounting number of aerial victories began to attract media attention, he became increasingly obsessed with surpassing current Ace of Aces Dick Bong, whose score then stood at twenty-seven. McGuire's fixation on the top score was partly due to his highly competitive nature, but he was also intelligent enough to understand the ramifications of becoming the American Ace of Aces. He had seen the fame Eddie Rickenbacker enjoyed in the years following his heroic return from World War I and how Lindbergh had become a national icon following his transatlantic flight. This was his chance to join that elite pair. "He was certain he would emerge from combat with a higher score than Dick [Bong], and understood fully what that could mean in civilian life—Ace of Aces!" observed CBS News correspondent William J. Dunn.[47]

In letters home to Marilynn, he denied any obsession with breaking the record. In one, he wrote, "I'm just doing my job, if I should happen to break it that's swell, but I'm not out for a record." This was nonsense, no doubt intended to reassure a worried wife. He was disappointed when Bong became the first Army pilot to break Rickenbacker's World War I record of twenty-six victories. Intent on adding to his score, he repeatedly turned down opportunities to return to the States, but no matter how many planes he shot down, he always seemed to lag at least eight victories behind Bong. "I guess after the war I'll be known as 'Eight Behind McGuire,'" he complained to General Kenney in disgust.[48]

Despite his frustration, the outgoing ace was getting considerable attention in the press back home. "McGuire is a fast-talking, joking pilot like those in the movies," wrote a newsman.[49] Unlike the more reticent Bong, he enjoyed the limelight and was happy to provide a play-by-play about his victories for anyone willing to listen—to the point that some pilots, while conceding his abilities in the air, pegged him for a showboat. But McGuire's hopes of catching up to Bong faded further as the aerial war seemed to enter a drought. In early October, with his own squadron not assigned to fly, he attached himself to the 9th Fighter Squadron for a 7.5-hour escort mission to Balikpapan, Borneo, hoping for some action. He got it. The bomber mission was intercepted by fifty enemy fighters. McGuire gunned down three Oscars, bringing his score to twenty-four— within six of Dick Bong's latest total, but he also ended up in hot water. Learning of the unauthorized flight, the commander of the 475th Air Group advised McGuire he would be grounded if he went off on another such jaunt without permission.[50]

Things picked up in November when the squadron began flying out of Tacloban on Leyte in the Philippines. McGuire's arrival at the field seemed auspicious: alerted that an enemy plane was in the area as the squadron began to set down, he remained in the air and shot down a Tojo in full view of the airstrip. Back on the ground, he exulted, "This is my kind of place! You have to shoot down Japs to land on your own field!"

"How many rings did you lead him, Major?" asked a pilot.

"I don't know," replied McGuire. "I didn't have time to turn on the gunsight!"[51]

Flying out of Tacloban, with the Japanese contesting the Philippine airspace, McGuire now began a spectacular run at the record. Three days after arriving, he took a bullet crease across the buttocks from ground fire while strafing a Japanese convoy but refused to seek medical attention for fear he would be grounded. A few days later he knocked down an Oscar near Tacloban. As the enemy aircraft exploded, sending debris in all directions, a chunk of metal smashed through McGuire's canopy and gashed his head. He nursed the damaged P-38 back to the airfield and once again made light of his injury, swearing his ground crew to secrecy.[52] With twenty-six official kills, he had now tied Eddie Rickenbacker's World War I record. That same day, Dick Bong scored number thirty-four.

Two days later McGuire flamed two Mitsubishi J2M single-engine fighters (code-named Jacks); on December 7 he scored two more victories over Ormac Bay covering a landing by the U.S. 77th Infantry Division; a few days later he nailed another over Cebu. In a wild Christmas Day melee over Manila, he shot down three Zeros before his guns quit. Instead of fleeing, he spent the next thirty minutes diving on enemy planes and forcing them to take evasive action in an effort to keep them away from the bombers he had been assigned to protect.

The next day, he shot down three more Zeros to bring his score to thirty-eight. "[We] saw five Nips coming down out of the clouds," he recalled.

One was just about 50 yards off the last bomber's tail and I took a long shot—about 400 yards—which hit him about the cockpit and he

*burst into flames. I caught another coming in from the left by a deflec-
tion shot and saw him blow up, turned sharply and took a shot at one
of four coming in from the right, but he dove underneath me and I
couldn't see what happened to him. Then I dove down at some Zekes
coming up and hit one around the cockpit. He rolled over and went
down to crash in a dry river bed. I made my fifth attack at about 1,500
feet and hit him in the wing gas tank, and he burst into flames. All of
this happened in three or four minutes, and I don't mind telling you I
was pretty excited.*[53]

Flying with McGuire, newcomer Capt. Edwin R. Weaver couldn't
believe what he had just seen. "I'd never seen McGuire shoot before and
I couldn't believe it when his first burst, from 400 yards, hit the Zeke in
the cockpit. Minutes later he pulled the tightest turn I've ever seen a P-38
make. I tried to go with him but I blacked out and fell off!"[54]

On December 17 Dick Bong scored his fortieth victory and was
sent home on leave. McGuire was elated. He was only two behind Bong,
and it now seemed inevitable that he would easily surpass that total to
become the all-time American Ace of Aces. Back in New Jersey, wire
service reporters secured the photograph of Thomas McGuire Sr. holding
his son's picture in anticipation of that day.

General Kenney called McGuire in and told him to stop flying until
Bong arrived home and received his accolades as current Ace of Aces.
McGuire agreed but secretly continued to fly anyway. By now he had
flown 240 combat missions, and the long months overseas and hundreds
of hours in the air appeared to be taking their toll on him physically. Thin
to begin with, he looked weary and was thirty pounds underweight. The
bullet wound to his buttocks bothered him, and he suffered from the
usual assortment of tropical rashes. There was some talk about taking him
out of combat, but nothing was done.

Looking to boost his score, McGuire organized a four-plane flight
on January 7 to Japanese-held Fabrica airdrome on Negros Island. He
flew a borrowed P-38, theorizing that it was less apt to scare off enemy
pilots than his kill-flag-bedecked *Pudgy V*. Lest there be any misunderstanding, he told his three companions—Capt. Edwin Weaver, Maj. Jack

Rittmayer, and 2nd Lt. Douglas Thropp—that the objective was to "help him get three more kills" on this sortie. He had already been informed that he would be rotated back to the States at the end of January no matter what his score happened to be. It was getting to be do-or-die time if he was to break Bong's 40-plane record.[55]

Arriving at Fabrica at 7 a.m., they remained unchallenged. As they proceeded toward another airfield about 10 miles away in hopes of better hunting, Weaver radioed that he'd spotted an enemy fighter—it turned out to be a late-model K-43 Oscar—flying in the opposite direction about 500 feet below. As McGuire's three companions prepared to drop belly tanks in order to engage—standard procedure before air combat—McGuire, apparently thinking the Oscar would run for it and they should save their gas, radioed to hang on to the tanks. This time, the would-be Ace of Aces was wrong. The Oscar was piloted by WO Akiro Sugimoto, a former air combat instructor with the *54th Sentai* (Fighter Regiment), and he wasn't fleeing anywhere.

Instead, Sugimoto turned into them and got on Thropp's tail. Rittmayer gave the Oscar a burst, and it broke away but didn't go far. Pulling up steeply, Sugimoto made a tight turn to the left, which put him directly behind McGuire and Weaver. At an altitude of only about 500 feet, the late-model Oscar was much more maneuverable than the heavy P-38s. "He's on me now!" radioed Weaver as Sugimoto closed in.[56]

Still carrying the heavy external fuel tanks, McGuire threw his borrowed P-38 into a hard turn at full power in an apparent attempt to help Weaver. The plane shuddered as it started to stall, but McGuire stayed in the turn. But this time he had asked too much of his aircraft. The P-38 snap-rolled to the left only a few hundred feet off the deck. It hung briefly inverted with the nose down 30 degrees, then slammed into the ground in a massive explosion. McGuire had no chance to get out.

Weaver fired on Sugimoto's Oscar before the Japanese pilot disappeared into cloud cover at about 2,000 feet. He wasn't sure if he'd scored a fatal hit, but long after the war it was learned that Sugimoto was forced to make a wheels-up landing in the jungle. The veteran warrant officer survived the landing but was killed by Filipino guerrillas when he refused to surrender.[57]

Meanwhile, a Nakajima K-84A Type 4 Hayate (code-named Frank by the Allies) arrived on the scene and put a burst into Rittmayer's cockpit, probably killing him outright. The P-38 plunged into the ground and exploded in a huge fireball. Weaver and Thropp dueled briefly with the Frank, a very capable, heavily armed single-seat fighter introduced in late 1944. Weaver hit the other plane, and though it didn't go down, the pilot broke off, and the two Americans turned for home.

Marilynn McGuire got the bad news on January 17 via a condolence letter from General Kenney that somehow preceded the official telegram. A month later, as she continued to reconcile herself to her husband's death, a letter arrived in his familiar handwriting. Mailed on December 31, it observed, "This is a hard letter to write. I had been expecting to send you a cable telling you to expect me home but my plans fell through. I went up and saw the General and got his promise that if my going home got balled up again, he promised to send me home the last of February."[58] During a year and a half of marriage, he and Marilynn had spent a total of only nine weeks together.

On May 8, 1946, in a ceremony at city hall in Paterson, New Jersey—chosen out of deference to her father-in-law—Marilynn accepted her husband's posthumous Medal of Honor. The award cited McGuire's actions on December 25 and 26, 1944, and his supreme effort to save Captain Weaver on January 7, 1944. General Kenney made the presentation speech. Among those in attendance was Charles Lindbergh. Not quite two years after the presentation of the medal, Fort Dix Field in New Jersey was renamed in McGuire's honor.

McGuire's remains were removed from the crash site by local Filipinos, one of whom took a gold and black onyx ring from the finger of his severed left hand. The body parts were placed in a wooden box and buried on the grounds of a nearby hacienda. Rittmayer's body was buried next to his plane. A Graves Registration team recovered both sets of remains in late 1947. Dental records subsequently confirmed McGuire's identity. He was interred at Arlington National Cemetery. Rittmayer, who had four aerial victories at the time of his death at age twenty-five, was buried at Forest Lawn Memorial Park in Glendale, California.

A combat evaluation report written thirteen days after McGuire's loss by the 431st Squadron's operations officer, Capt. Fredric F. Champlin, a friend of the missing pilot, was highly critical of what the writer viewed as McGuire's lack of judgment in the actions that led up to his death. Champlin pointed to "two very serious combat errors" that led to the loss of the two pilots. "In the first place, they were turning with an enemy fighter and secondly their speed was less than 200 miles per hour not to mention being below 1,000 feet. In trying to get a shot at the enemy, the flight leader had tried to outturn him, and as a result had committed the flight into a Lufbery at low speed which gave the enemy distinct advantage."[59] These were all rookie mistakes that a pilot of McGuire's experience should never have made.

Years later, Thropp, one of the two survivors of the ill-fated flight, was asked why McGuire would violate his own mantra and order everyone to retain their external fuel tanks. Dropping tanks would have cut their mission short, he replied. "That wasn't what McGuire wanted. He wanted to get three more victories so he could go home as our number one ace."[60]

Maj. Richard I. Bong
Borneo and Leyte
October 10–November 15, 1944

The afternoon of Monday, August 6, 1945, was sunny and clear in North Hollywood, California, with temperatures ranging into the upper eighties. Twenty-eight-year-old Mrs. George H. Zane Jr. had gone out into her backyard on Satsuma Street when she heard the whine of an engine above.

Living only about a mile and a half from the Lockheed Air Terminal test area, she was accustomed to the sound of planes passing low overhead. Lately, the familiar drone of piston engines had been alternating more and more with the high-pitched whine of experimental jets. But the whine this time seemed to be punctuated by an unusual popping sound. Looking skyward, she saw a gray-colored jet low in the sky. It appeared to be in trouble. The wings wobbled, and the aircraft was rapidly losing altitude. As she watched, the pilot suddenly emerged from the cockpit, hands above his head. The figure jumped clear but abruptly disappeared from view as the jet smashed into the ground in a pillar of smoke, flame, and flying debris.[61]

As Mrs. Zane would soon learn, the pilot bailing out of the stricken jet was no ordinary airman: he was Maj. Richard Ira Bong, the highest scoring U.S. Air Force ace of the war with forty victories in the Pacific theater.

Bong's journey to a vacant lot in Mrs. Zane's North Hollywood neighborhood began on an eighty-acre family farm in tiny Poplar, Wisconsin, population less than five hundred souls. "Dick," as his family called him, was born on September 24, 1920, the first of Carl and Dora Bong's nine children in what became, as one younger brother was to recall, "a big bustling household."[62] Born in Sweden, Carl had arrived in the United States as a six-year-old, his family joining the large Swedish immigrant population in Wisconsin. Dora was native born. In addition to farming, Carl, an Army veteran of the Great War, operated a road-construction business.

Short but solidly built, with curly blond hair, blue eyes, and a pug nose, Dick played hockey and baseball as a youngster and took up the clarinet—the latter to mixed reviews. Like all the Bong menfolk, he was an avid deer hunter. He caught the aviation bug in 1928 thanks, at least indirectly, to President Calvin Coolidge, who was vacationing in the area. Each day the president's mail was flown into the city of Superior, and the flight path took the plane over Poplar. Years later, Bong recalled, that the plane "flew right over our house and I knew then that I wanted to be a pilot."[63] His sister Nelda remembered, "He would become almost mesmerized when he saw an airplane in the sky. . . . [H]e'd be in sort of a day dream until the plane went out of his sight."[64]

A good student, after graduating from Central High School in Superior, Bong enrolled at Superior State Teachers College, where he juggled his studies with his responsibilities on the family farm. He had no intention of actually going into teaching. He had set his sights on becoming an Army Air Corps pilot but needed two years of college to be eligible for flight school. In early 1941, having put in the requisite college time, he applied to the U.S. Army's Aviation Cadet Pilot Training Program. By June he was undergoing primary training at Tulare Aeronautical Academy in Tulare, California. In a letter to his family, he reported, "I got in 50 minutes of flying and I got a little bit air sick but not much." The coordinator of training at Rankin Field recalled that the soft-spoken, boyish-looking farm boy was an enthusiastic student and eager to learn but didn't particularly stand out among the sixty or so students in the class. "He was one of the herd," remarked the coordinator. "Nobody would select him as a hotshot or hot pilot."[65]

Bong had moved on to advanced training at Luke Field in Arizona by December 7, 1941, when the Japanese attack on Pearl Harbor brought the United States into the war. "Well, it seems from the radio this afternoon that we are having a little trouble with Japan," he wryly observed in a letter home. He was presently engaged in skeet shooting, the standard preliminary to air gunnery. "I'm still awful bad at skeet shooting," he wrote. "Every time I shoot at those clay pigeons I get worse."[66]

In the air, however, he was proving to be an apt pupil, no longer dismissed as just "one of the herd." A check pilot running Bong through aerial evasive tactics described him as the finest natural pilot he had ever encountered. Even flying the slower AT-6 trainer against the instructor's P-38 Lightning, Bong was able to keep on the instructor's tail, he observed. By May 1942 Bong himself was in the pilot's seat of the twin-engine Lightning, the aircraft he would eventually fly in combat. "Wooey! What an airplane," Bong wrote home, later observing, "It's the fastest plane I have ever flown."[67]

His enthusiasm for the P-38 landed him in hot water in July after a series of incidents involving hot-dogging fighter pilots, which included roaring along San Francisco's Market Street at window level to wave at secretaries in office buildings. Bong ended up in front of Gen. George C. Kenney, then commanding the Fourth Air Force on the West Coast. Legend has it that Bong was called on the carpet for "looping the loop" around the center span of the Golden Gate Bridge, but it appears he had actually been buzzing local neighborhoods, much to the annoyance of residents.

Kenney later described their first meeting in his office. "In walked one of the nicest-looking cherubs you ever saw in your life. I suspected that he was not over twenty and maybe even younger. I doubted if he was old enough to shave. He was just a little blond-haired Swedish boy about five feet six, with a round, pink baby face and the bluest, most innocent eyes—now opened wide and a bit scared."[68] Kenney grounded the young daredevil and supposedly ordered him to do chores for a woman whose laundry had blown off the line during his low-level antics.

Kenney could have imposed much harsher disciplinary action on Bong, but privately he admired the youngster's spirit.[69] Soon after this awkward introduction, General Kenney was named to command the Fifth Air Force in the Southwest Pacific, where American forces were being hard pressed both on the ground and in the air. Kenney managed to obtain a commitment for fifty P-38s and his choice of pilots. One of the first to be chosen was the recently reprimanded bad boy, 2nd Lt. Dick Bong, who was temporarily assigned to the 39th Fighter Squadron operating out of Schwimmer airdrome outside Port Moresby on New Guinea's southeastern coast.

Bong flew his first combat patrol on November 22 over Buna on the other side of New Guinea's Owen Stanley Mountains but saw no action for over a month except a minor scrape on Christmas Day when a bullet from ground fire punched a hole in his Lightning. But two days later, his war began in earnest. Flying a P-38F nicknamed *Thumper*, Bong was part of a four-ship patrol that encountered a mixed enemy force of about twenty-five Zeroes, Val dive bombers, and some Oscars north of Buna. The four Lightning pilots dove into them from 18,000 feet. "I'm not sure they definitely knew what we were. . . . [T]hey hadn't seen our P-38s in combat yet," observed Bong.[70]

Bong fired on several Zeros without noticeable effect. He realized later that he was overanalyzing his actions instead of just trusting his instincts, but he was about to get a gift. Diving to shake a Zero that had latched onto his tail, he pulled out at treetop level to find one of the slow-moving Vals directly in front of him. "I gave him a short burst and he blew higher than a kite."[71]

As he pulled up, a second Zero flew directly into his line of fire. Bong cut loose with everything he had, and the Zero "just rolled over on his back and went straight down." He tangled with another Zero and then another Val without result before running out of ammunition. As the

Lightnings returned to Schwimmer, Bong put *Thumper* through two slow rolls over the field to mark his first victories. In their first fight, the P-38s claimed eight Zeros, two Vals, and two Oscars without losing a plane. "Well, I've done it at last," he wrote home. "Saw the Nips at close range and shot down two airplanes on December 27th. If you watch the newspapers and Life and Time [magazines] you might read about it."[72]

On December 31, in a scrap over Lae, Bong knocked some pieces off a Zero. When last seen, it was heading down in a shallow dive, but he could only claim "a probable." Seven days later, flying cover for a bombing mission over Huon Gulf near Lae, he knocked down an Oscar in a head-to-head confrontation, instinctively ducking flying debris from the doomed enemy aircraft when it exploded just overhead. Two hours later, he encountered a second Oscar and sent it into the water in flames with a long burst at a distance of only 40 or 60 yards. In the air again the next day, covering a B-17 strike on a Japanese convoy in Lae Harbor, he went after an Oscar that had latched onto another Lightning's tail. On his second pass, the Oscar fell off and smashed into the sea. In less than two weeks he had downed five enemy planes to become an ace.

Soon after, Bong joined his permanent outfit, the 9th Fighter Squadron ("Flying Knights"), which had finally been fully outfitted. His new commanding officer considered him "a very quiet, modest young man. . . . [H]e simply was not a very colorful character. . . . [He was] just a good pilot who loved to fly and did his job very well."[73]

February was a dry month for the newly minted ace, but on March 3 he knocked down an Oscar in Huon Gulf. Soon afterward, the Flying Knights moved to a dirt strip at Dobodura on New Guinea's north coast, and the hunting improved. On March 11, a couple dozen Japanese Bettys, accompanied by the same number of Zeros, raided the American airfield. Bong's flight of three P-38s caught them as they turned for home. He got in a burst on a trailing bomber before a mob of enemy fighters jumped him. He later reported,

Nine Zeros dove on me and I had to dive to 475 mph indicated to get away. I tried to go back for another pass at the bombers but was intercepted by Zeros and chased down to water level. . . . I flew straight

until I could see only one Zero behind me. I made a 180-degree turn and put a long burst into the Zero head-on. Instead of only one Zero, there were nine or more and I turned five degrees left and put a short burst into another Zero head-on. Both these had their belly tanks on. Turned ten degrees right and put a long burst into another Zero from 20-degree deflection.

Turning away, he saw that the first two Zeros were burning around the cockpit and the third was trailing a long column of smoke. Before he could congratulate himself, three other Zeros tore into him and shot up his left engine and wing. Bong wisely ran for home. He feathered the damaged engine and landed safely, claiming two kills and one probable.

Undeterred by his narrow escape, he wrapped up the month on March 29 with a lone twin-engine Dinah bomber that was apparently on a reconnaissance mission. "On my fourth pass from the right I stayed on his tail until he blew up in mid-air," he reported.[74]

His string of victories continued on April 14 when the Japanese mounted an aerial attack—more than eighty aircraft, including at least three waves of G4M Betty medium bombers—on Dobodura. Bong and his wingman, twenty-four-year-old Lt. Carl Planck, tore into them at 26,000 feet. Bong set one of the bombers alight on his first attack, scored hits on a second, and drew smoke from a third before a Zero put a cannon shell through his elevator. Once again, he made it safely home, now a double ace with ten victories.[75]

Ironically, considering his success, Bong, by his own admission, was not a particularly good shot. He compensated by using his superb piloting skills to get as close as possible before shooting: "Get in so close ya can't miss, shove the guns up their butt and pull the trigger," he explained of his technique. He also seemed to have the devil's own luck in finding the enemy. Whereas many pilots could fly for weeks or even months without encountering an enemy plane, Bong seemed to make contact on almost every mission; he admitted he was "lucky in getting the breaks of frequent contact with the Nip."[76]

May was a quiet month for Bong and the Flying Knights, but the Japanese were reinforcing the theater, and activity was about to pick up.

Bong had a close call on June 12. He was flying cover with five other P-38s for a dozen C-47 cargo planes when eight Oscars bored in on them. Bong knocked one down but took cannon holes in his wings. On July 26, making a sweep over Lae and Salamaua, the Flying Knights got into a melee with at least thirty-five enemy fighters, including a number of the new Kawasaki Ki-61 "inline" jobs, code-named Tonys by the Allies. Outnumbered three or four to one, the Lightnings dropped fuel tanks and went at it.

Bong went after the nearest Tony without discernible result, pulled out, and took a head-on shot at a Zero. The Zero was heading down in flames when Bong spotted a Tony just below and ahead of him. He "knocked pieces off his fuselage," putting it out of an action, quickly set another Tony on fire, and then finished up by blasting the canopy off a Zero, killing the pilot instantly, for a total of four victories. He later observed modestly there were so many planes in the air he "couldn't help but hit something." Two days later, escorting a B-25 bomber mission in the Cape Gloucester area, he knocked down an Oscar for his sixteenth victory, which made him the top-scoring ace in the Southwest Pacific theater. General Kenney awarded him a Distinguished Service Cross and promoted him to captain.[77]

While outwardly modest, Bong was well aware of his burgeoning score and growing notoriety. "I suppose I hit the headlines with both feet," he wrote home after his sixteenth victory. "Got five more in the last three days, make 16 now. Got a few more bullet holes but not bad." When his mother asked about his decorations, he replied he had received everything but the Purple Heart and the Medal of Honor. "You have to get wounded to get the one and really do something to get the other so I don't want the one and probably wouldn't do anything to deserve the other."[78]

Meeting the rising ace in a chance encounter, Lt. Garrett Middlebrook discovered that Bong was not what he might have expected. "He did not articulate well nor as fast as some of the others; consequently, he seemed ill at ease in describing his experience when the little group of pilots was all present," observed Middlebrook. "He admitted that he was not a good shot, not nearly as good as some of his comrades; he, therefore, simply held his fire until he was so close to his enemy that he could not miss. Philosophically speaking, he felt boldness was the best safety factor a pilot could have in a dogfight, while timidity was the greatest danger."[79]

A CBS Radio reporter, perpetuating Bong's reputation as an "aw shucks" country boy who had somehow found himself involved in the Ace Race, observed, "Given a chance, Bong probably would have gone back to Wisconsin and sharpened his plow."[80] Middlebrook saw more deeply into Bong and recognized the intense competitiveness under the placid, sometimes inarticulate exterior. "I learned quickly from him that he had an obsession," observed Middlebrook. "He wanted to be the top American ace of all time. That obsession subdued his fears."[81]

On October 29, Bong shot down two Zeros while accompanying a bomber raid on Rabaul; seven days later, he shot down two more Zeros, raising his score to twenty-one. The victories were not without cost. Bong's wingman, twenty-three-year-old 2nd Lt. George Haniotis of Okmulgee, Oklahoma, was shot down. Haniotis was seen in his life raft, but when air-sea rescue finally arrived, he was nowhere to be found. Two days later, Bong lost another wingman, 2nd Lt. Stanley W. Johnson, as they went to the aid of a Lightning under attack by Zeros. The loss of two wingmen in quick succession did not go unnoticed—some pilots wondered if Bong might be more intent on scoring kills than looking out for his teammates—though it does not appear he was in any way at fault.[82]

With his most recent victories, Bong became the highest-scoring ace in the Army Air Forces. In the course of a year, he had flown 158 missions and downed twenty-one enemy aircraft: eight Oscars, seven Zeros, two Tonys, two Ki-46 Dinah twin-engine reconnaissance aircraft, a Betty, and a Val. His own aircraft had been hit by enemy fire seven times. His decorations included the Distinguished Service Cross, the Distinguished Flying Cross, the Silver Star, and a pocketful of Air Medals.

Always quick to capitalize on positive publicity for his command, Kenney shrewdly sent his top ace home on a thirty-day leave. Bong arrived in the United States to find he was a celebrity. He and his family were mobbed by reporters. Invited to Washington, DC, he received a standing ovation from the floor of the House of Representatives; he met famed crooner Bing Crosby and was feted at the Hollywood Bowl. Superior, Wisconsin, named January 7 "Dick Bong Day."

Bong spent the next two months selling war bonds, but self-promotion was not in his nature. A *Collier's Magazine* article observed, "It would be hard to find a man who looked and acted less like a hot pilot. . . . Bong is a blond, chunky fellow of twenty-three, with a turned-up nose and rosy cheeks that puff out in a cherubic sort of way. . . . Looking at him in the setting of his home town, it is impossible to think of him as a fighter pilot or a killer of Japanese."[83] He grew to detest the media attention and disliked speaking before crowds at bond rallies. He was happier during the weeks he was able to spend at home deer hunting and socializing with old friends. He also met a local girl, Marjorie ("Marge") Vattendahl, a student at Superior State Teachers College. The two hit it off, and the relationship quickly turned serious. Back in the Pacific in early February, Bong inscribed Marge's portrait and name on the side of his new P-38 and headed back into combat.[84]

He chalked up victory 22 on February 15 when he gunned down a Tony at a range of about 75 yards during a flight over northern New Britain. The Tony exploded "so close that I had to fly right through a ball of fire which was all that was left of him," recalled Bong. "I couldn't have been in the flames one-hundredth of a second, yet my cockpit was so hot then and for some minutes afterward that I nearly burned up myself."[85]

Upon his return to the theater, Bong was attached to Fighter Command Headquarters per order of General Kenney. He feared this reassignment to an administrative unit would keep him on the ground, but General Kenney had other ideas. He teamed up Bong with twenty-seven-year-old Maj. Tommy Lynch, a precise, combat-savvy Pennsylvanian with sixteen victories to his credit. He and Bong already knew each other well and were close friends. Now, with Kenney's blessing, they would act as a sort of roving hunter-killer team, authorized to fly wherever the action was. Flying new, unpainted P-38s, they became known in some quarters as the "Flying Circus."[86]

On February 27, Bong and Lynch hurriedly took off and set out for Wewak after intelligence picked up a Japanese radio message that a transport aircraft carrying a group of staff officers was scheduled to land at the airdrome there. Though it was late in the day, they arrived to find the just-landed transport taxiing down the runway. Bong gave the transport plane a burst; it flamed and promptly exploded. He and Lynch then proceeded to machine-gun what was apparently a welcoming party waiting on the runway. According to subsequent radio intercepts, the victims included a major general and a number of staff officers.[87]

It says something about Bong that he stubbornly demurred when Kenney tried to give him credit for destruction of the transport. Bong pointed out that the aircraft had not been airborne and didn't qualify as a "kill." Kenney tried to open the door a bit. "Couldn't it have been just an inch or so above the runway?" he asked suggestively. "Maybe the plane's wheels had touched and it had bounced back into the air temporarily?"

As Kenney recalled it, "Dick listened seriously, as if it were a problem in mathematics, and then looked up and said simply, earnestly, adding without a trace of disappointment, 'General, he was on the ground all right. He had even stopped rolling.'"[88]

Flying with Lynch, Bong scored two Sally bombers on March 3 (kills 23 and 24), followed by an Oscar on March 5 (number 25). But disaster struck on March 8—ironically, not in air-to-air combat with enemy planes but while the two were strafing half a dozen coastal supply vessels they had run across at Aitape Harbor west of Wewak. Racing in just off the deck, Lynch was hit by return fire from one of the luggers. As smoke poured from his right engine, he pulled up to about 2,500 feet and radioed Bong, asking if he could see his plane. Bong shouted to bail out—the right engine was on fire. He saw Lynch trying to get out as the P-38 fell. The plane was only about 100 feet off the ground when the canopy finally flew off and Lynch jumped. The parachute streamed, but Lynch disappeared as the plane blew up just beneath him. Bong circled but could see no sign of the parachute in the trees. Lynch, who had recently been promoted to lieutenant colonel, had twenty victories at the time of his death.[89]

Knowing that Bong had been very close to Lynch, Kenney sent him on leave to Australia to recoup, but the quiet youngster seemed to take his friend's death in stride. Back in the air on April 3, he gunned down an Oscar. "Guess you know that I have twenty-five confirmed Nips now," he wrote to his mother that night. "They tell me that if I get twenty-seven confirmed they will send me home so fast I won't know what hit me. Good idea, I think."[90] He added that he was getting mail almost every day from Marge. "I think I'm going to ask that girl to marry me, what do you think of that?" he wrote, again adding, "Good idea, I think."[91]

Nine days later he shot down two more Oscars (kills 26 and 27). He claimed a third, but the gun camera failed, and he only had witnesses to the first two. (After U.S. forces took the area, Kenney sent a diver to take a look in the shallow waters where Bong saw the plane go in, and it was verified as number 28). Nevertheless, the two victories broke the record set by ace Eddie Rickenbacker during World War I. Kenney recognized the occasion by promoting Bong to major and grounding him from further combat.[92]

Rickenbacker sent Bong a congratulatory telegram and, in a radio exchange with the Army's new Ace of Aces, promised to send him a case of Scotch—a gesture that immediately brought condemnation from various temperance organizations. Bong wasn't much of a drinker anyway— he preferred Coca-Cola—but he had intended to give the Scotch to his buddies. "Dick had said that if he broke the record, I would get a bottle of Scotch," recalled one squadron mate. "Instead, I had to settle for a bottle of Coke!"[93] Happily, the Scotch followed later, after the moralistic furor had dissipated.

Writing home on April 19, Bong observed, "I broke the record and by so doing procured for myself a lot of trouble, and besides that they have grounded me from combat flying. I suppose that doesn't make you mad, but it certainly doesn't make me happy."[94]

With the higher-ups growing increasingly nervous about the effect on morale should their new Ace of Aces be killed, Kenney sent Bong back to the States in May for—ironically—gunnery instruction. The idea was that he would then come back and teach gunnery and tactics to pilots in theater, but Bong wasn't pleased about being pulled out of combat. Arriving stateside, he was asked why Kenney had sent him home. "Because he didn't want me to get killed," he observed wryly.[95]

After a furlough in his hometown of Poplar, where he and Marge made their engagement official, Bong headed to Texas for gunnery training. By September he was back in the Southwest Pacific where Kenney assigned him to pass his knowledge on to other pilots, adding (possibly with a wink) that he could accompany combat patrols but was to fire only "in self-defense." Bong, who once confessed he would "go nuts if [he] couldn't keep on flying in combat," wrote home on September 18, "I don't know about the combat flying, but if I do any it will be very little and very safe."[96]

Whether he or anyone else actually believed that, on October 10 the new "gunnery instructor" shot down a twin-engine Nakajima J1N Irving typically used for reconnaissance, following up soon after by gunning an Oscar off the tail of another P-38 for victories 29 and 30. When Kenney called him to task, Bong told him he had chased after the first plane for fear it would alert the others.

"That doesn't sound much like self-defense to me," said Kenney. "How about the second one?"

"Oh, that really was self-defense. Honest, when I climbed back to join the rest of our fighters, the fight was on and this bird tried to make a pass at me. I had to shoot him down or he might have gotten me," Bong protested.[97]

It was widely believed that Kenney's order sending Bong around as a gunnery instructor was mostly a device to let him freelance. But the gunnery course was paying benefits, particularly in ammunition management. Bong had knocked down each of the last two enemy aircraft with just one burst. "Each time I pushed the gun barrels into the Nip's cockpit and pulled the trigger," he said. "I only fired two bursts, one for each Jap." He remarked that had he known in late 1942 what he subsequently learned during his recent stint at gunnery school: his score would now be seventy-five rather than thirty.[98]

Turned loose again, Bong shot down three enemy planes on October 27, an Oscar on November 10, and two Zeros on November 11, bringing his total to thirty-six. General Kenney approached Gen. Douglas MacArthur to suggest that Bong's record merited award of the Medal of Honor. MacArthur agreed. On December 12, under a light rain on the airstrip at Tacloban in the Philippines, MacArthur presented the medal to the nervous hero before an honor guard of pilots and a decorative semicircle of P-38s. As Kenney recalled it, MacArthur dispensed with the speech that had already been provided to the press by his publicists. In an apparently spontaneous gesture, he put his hands on Bong's shoulders and declared, "Major Richard Ira Bong, who has ruled the air from New Guinea to the Philippines, I now induct you into the society of the bravest of the brave, the wearers of the Congressional Medal of Honor of the United States."[99]

Kenney meanwhile was developing a serious case of cold feet about allowing Bong to continue to risk his life in the air. He later confessed that everyone from his own sergeant to General MacArthur repeatedly cautioned, "Why don't you send him home before he gets knocked off?" Bong, who had thirty-eight kills by the time of the Medal of Honor award, said he wanted to go for fifty victories. Kenney put the kibosh on that idea. "No," he said, "at forty you go home."[100]

As if to validate Kenney's decision, during a Japanese air raid on Tacloban on November 28, Capt. John Davis, assistant operations officer for the 49th Fighter Group, scrambled into the nearest P-38, which happened to be Bong's plane. As he tried to gain altitude, one engine burst into flames, and Davis crashed to his death. Kenney knew full well that the dead man could just as easily have been his Ace of Aces.[101]

On December 15, Bong knocked down an Oscar during a patrol over Negros. Two days later, he chased an Oscar that tried to outrun him down to 9,000 feet and gave him a burst. In his after-action report, he noted that the Oscar "disintegrated and caught fire and dived straight down and crashed about 20 miles north of San Jose."[102] It was kill number 40.

Looking at "a nice round number," as he put it, General Kenney decided it was time to stop gambling with Bong's life. He pulled the plug and grounded his pet pilot, and this time he meant it. "He was going home," recalled Kenney. "There would be no more combat, and that was that, so I didn't want any more arguments."[103]

Bong didn't fight it. He may have come to the same conclusion himself. Writing home to his mother on December 17, he mentioned having knocked down number 39 and added, "One or two Nips doesn't make any difference anymore."[104]

Bong arrived in Superior, Wisconsin, in time for Marge's graduation from Superior State College on January 26. On February 10, 1945, they were married at the Concordia Lutheran Church in Superior. As a national hero, Bong could pretty much choose his next billet. He chose jets.

Lockheed was then testing the P-80 Shooting Star, which was intended to counter the German Me 262, the world's first operational jet-powered fighter plane. Bong had become acquainted with the project on one of his bond tours and was intrigued. Kenney had already put in a word for him with Gen. Hap Arnold, pointing out that the ace's combat experience would be invaluable in the development of new jet age tactics. "Bong is a cool, level-headed thinker," he wrote. "From talking to him you get the idea that his thinking apparatus operates a little slowly but it has the tremendous virtue of being right most of the time."[105]

On July 14, the newlyweds moved into a cramped apartment in Hollywood, California, outside the Lockheed Air Terminal, where testing of the Shooting Star was being conducted. Marge spruced up the place with prints and decorated the bathroom mirror with a floral border, all of which her pilot husband seemed completely oblivious to, much to her amusement. Bong had already made his first flight in a P-80A Shooting Star on July 7, writing to his family, "It is quite an airplane all right."[106]

The Shooting Star was not just "quite an airplane"; it was unforgiving. On August 2 one of the jets exploded in midair, killing the pilot. It was the fifth fatality since the previous October. Bong shrugged off concerns, remarking that he "never worried about these things."[107] By August 6, he had made eleven flights in Shooting Stars and was about to make his twelfth. It was a routine flight. He had originally been scheduled for another plane but traded with another pilot in order to keep an afternoon golf date with popular crooner Bing Crosby. He had to break the date when he forgot his golf shoes, but by the time he got to the airfield, the other pilot had taken the first plane and was gone.

Bong completed his preflight check, closed the canopy, and taxied out onto the runway, where he was cleared to take off at about 2:30 p.m. Hurtling down the 6,000-foot runway at 120 mph, the Shooting Star lifted off the tarmac. Bong turned the jet to the right, passing over the Valhalla Memorial Park Cemetery as he climbed to about 200 feet. Among those watching was Dick Gray, an old pilot friend Bong had invited to come out to see the jets that afternoon. Gray saw the jet's right wing dip suddenly. The tailpipe belched puffs of black smoke. "It looked like something was haywire to me," Gray recalled. "He got into the air maybe 3,000 or 4,000 feet but the thing still was not operating right. All of a sudden he started to get out of it, then got back in and turned it. He started to get out again and the plane rolled on him. That was the last I saw of him."[108]

From her yard, Mrs. George H. Zane Jr. saw the pilot scrambling to leap from the cockpit. "He jumped on the side of the plane that faced me," she said. "I could plainly see him trying to free himself from the plane. Then the smoke swept over him."[109] The jet slammed into a vacant lot in a ball of fire. A woman standing in her backyard about 150 feet away suffered burns to her legs. Another woman, Mrs. E. Young, said the suction from the speeding, out-of-control plane nearly knocked her to the floor as it passed over her home five blocks from the crash site. "A column of smoke went into the air for about 400 feet," recalled a Lockheed mechanic watching from the airfield. "It was a terrible sight."[110]

Mrs. Zane and other witnesses ran to the vacant lot, now littered with crash debris. Bong's body lay about 100 feet from the flaming turbine. Someone threw a gray blanket over the body, but one hand protruded, the wrist still encircled with Bong's Army ID bracelet. His partly opened parachute had never had a chance to deploy at such a low altitude—whether he had pulled the ripcord in desperation or whether it had caught on something and popped open could not be established. Only an hour before the crash, he had phoned Marge to tell her he'd been able to buy the clothespins she'd been trying to obtain all week. "He said he was going to take me to a movie when he got home," she said forlornly.[111] An investigation was unable to pinpoint the cause of the crash, though it probably had something to do with the jet's trouble-plagued fuel system.

Bong's death made front pages around the country—sharing top billing with news of the atomic bomb dropped on Hiroshima that same day. Dick Bong, victor in forty air-to-air combats, had returned home safely only to die in an accident days before the end of the war. His body was flown back to Wisconsin aboard a C-54 transport plane, accompanied by his stunned widow. The plane touched down at Duluth Airport the morning of August 8, and the flag-draped casket was brought to Concordia

Lutheran Church in Superior, where he and Marge had been married only six months earlier.

Dick Bong was buried in Poplar Cemetery with full military honors on the afternoon of August 8. Thousands of onlookers lined the roads as the funeral procession passed by. Eighteen P-47 Thunderbolts roared overhead, dipping their wings in salute to the fallen ace. His record of forty victories remains unmatched to this day and is unlikely to ever be surpassed.

The War Goes On

By late 1944, the tide of war had turned inexorably against Japan. Japanese airpower had been, if not eradicated, fatally crippled at the Battle of the Philippine Sea in June. The veteran Japanese pilots of the early war years were dead. Japanese pilots and their planes, once among the best in the world, were now outclassed by U.S. flyers and equipment. But still, the war continued. On October 24, 1944, a Navy air group commander and his wingman piled into forty enemy planes—alone. Two days later, an Army bomber pilot remained with his stricken aircraft as his crew bailed out over the Chinese countryside. Not quite three months later, a Mustang pilot and his wingman encountered thirteen Japanese aircraft and shot down eleven of them. Each of these three separate actions resulted in an award of the Medal of Honor.

Cmdr. David McCampbell
Philippine Sea
June 19, 1944

The Hellcat pilots of Fighter Squadron 15 (VF-15) gathered in the ready room of their carrier, USS *Essex*, well before dawn on May 19, 1944. Despite their bold nickname—they had dubbed themselves "Satan's Playmates"—they were greenhorns, new to aerial combat. The upcoming mission, a sweep over Japanese-held Marcus Island less than 800 nautical miles from Wake, would be the first for most of them, and nerves were wound tight. "You could cut the tension in the ready room with a knife that morning," recalled Ens. Clarence ("Spike") Borley, a stocky nineteen-year-old from Yakima, Washington.

Air group commander Dave McCampbell stood up. A good-natured thirty-four-year-old Naval Academy graduate, he looked out over the apprehensive faces of his pilots and proceeded to launch into "the bluest joke I had ever heard in my life up to that time," said Borley. "It was dirty as could be and funny as hell, and just broke everyone up with laughter." The tension evaporated, and McCampbell got down to business.[1]

While no one in the cramped ready room could have known it, over the next several months they would become one of the most famed air groups in the U.S. Navy. Celebrated as the "Fabled Fifteen," they would destroy more enemy aircraft (312 in the air and 348 on the ground) and sink more enemy tonnage—including the gargantuan Japanese battleship *Musashi*, three carriers, and a heavy cruiser—than any other air group in the Pacific theater. A key element of their success would be the amiable jokester now standing before them.

Born January 17, 1910, in Bessemer, Alabama, David Perry McCampbell (Perry was his mother's maiden name) subsequently moved with his family to West Palm Beach, Florida, where his businessman father operated McCampbell Furniture Stores, offering "high class furnishings for the home," including everything from living room furniture to washing machines.[2] Young David graduated from Staunton Military Academy in Virginia and attended Georgia Tech for a year before entering the U.S. Naval Academy in 1929. He had intended to major in civil engineering at Georgia Tech, but his father's business ran into trouble as the Great Depression descended on the country. The Naval Academy provided a free education, relieving his family of that financial burden.[3]

While he earned renown as a champion diver at the academy, McCampbell's scholastic performance was less than stellar. "In academics Mac hasn't always had the wind abaft the beam, so to speak," observed his class entry in the 1933 *Lucky Bag* yearbook. Classmates did give a nod to McCampbell's outgoing personality, observing, "Mac will always find life enjoyable because he has an amiable disposition, because he is a gentleman, and because he is an optimist."[4]

McCampbell graduated in 1933 with a degree in marine engineering but was not immediately commissioned due to a tight Navy budget that year. Those graduating in the lower half of the class—of whom he was one—had to wait until June 1934 to receive their gold bars. After his obligatory sea service, he reported to Naval Air Station Pensacola in 1937 for flight training, receiving his wings a year later. On September 15, 1942, he was serving as assistant landing signal officer aboard the USS *Wasp* in support of the Guadalcanal operation when the carrier was struck by three torpedoes fired by the Japanese submarine *I-19*.

"[I] was crossing the flight deck as the first one hit, and I thought it was a bombing attack," he recalled. Then the second or third torpedo hit and the number-two elevator was blown about ten feet into the air. "[I] remember the ship was vibrating. The vibrations ran to the bow and then back to the stern, and it went back and forth. During one of these vibrations, it knocked me to the flight deck."[5] The abandon-ship order was given at 3:20 p.m. "We never heard the order to abandon ship, but we saw guys going over the side," he recalled. After making sure his people made it off, McCampbell prepared to make his own exit, shedding his shirt, shoes, and pants. As a champion diver, he had often boasted he would abandon any sinking ship with flair—maybe "a lay-out one-and-a-half with a twist"—but now, looking down at the bobbing heads and debris in the water, caution prevailed. Holding his nose with one hand and shielding the "family jewels" with the other, he jumped feet first "like a kid off a diving board."[6]

Picked up by a whaleboat from the destroyer *Farenholt*, McCampbell eventually ended up back in the States, where he was promoted to lieutenant commander and sent to instruct landing signal officers in Florida. This was not his idea of how to spend a war. He made such a nuisance of himself agitating for combat duty that he was finally named to lead VF-15, a Hellcat squadron that would ultimately end up on the USS *Essex*.

Ironically, the newly minted squadron commander now found that his air gunnery skills had accumulated considerable rust. After scoring a mere 8 percent hits on a towed target sleeve, he scheduled incessant gunnery training for all hands, himself in particular. "I practiced until I couldn't get any better," he observed. On the last hop before the squadron deployed, he actually shot the sleeve in half. "I can't do any better than that," he told his wingman before flying off, leaving the other pilots to practice on half a sleeve. As a result of the constant practice, observed one of his pilots, the whole squadron became "very good at shooting."[7]

In February 1944 McCampbell was elevated to command Air Group 15. VF-15's Hellcats were part of the group, but he would now also be responsible for the dive bomber (VB-15) and torpedo (VT-15) squadrons that would serve together aboard *Essex*, assigned to Task Force 58.3. The air group entered combat on May 19, 1944, with the raid on Marcus Island, a smidge of land—just about large enough for an enemy airfield—lying between Wake and the Japanese home islands. McCampbell personally led the fighter sweep, piloting an F6F-3 named *Monsoon Maiden*. The unappreciative residents of Marcus Island greeted the air strikes with a hail of well-aimed antiaircraft fire. A number of bombers and torpedo bombers were damaged, and a dive bomber was shot down during the second strike.

McCampbell himself narrowly avoided being shot down during a third strike on Japanese installations that afternoon. As he descended on a strafing run with wingman Ens. Wesley T. Burnam at about 2:45 p.m., antiaircraft fire shredded the lower rear section of *Monsoon Maiden*'s fuselage and severed the rudder controls. Burnam's Hellcat was also hit and went down in flames offshore. There was no parachute. Pilot Bert Morris saw smoke streaming from McCampbell's Hellcat. "Dave, your belly tank's on fire," he radioed.[8]

McCampbell dropped his auxiliary tank, which solved his most immediate problem. Wrestling with the controls, he headed back toward the *Essex*. Forced to lower his wheels and tail hook with the manual backup system, he waited for two accompanying Hellcats to land before making his approach, lest he crash and foul the deck. "I had one of the flaps shot up pretty badly," he recalled in what was apparently something of an understatement.[9] Bringing the crippled Hellcat around, he managed to stay level and snag the number-three wire. Deck crews looked over the damage, salvaged the Hamilton standard clock out of the plane, and pushed *Monsoon Maiden* overboard.

Three weeks later, on June 11, *Essex* provided support for the pending U.S. landings on Saipan. Flying a replacement F6F that he named *Minsi* in honor of a girlfriend back home, McCampbell was observing the airstrikes in accordance with his duties as group commander. He had yet to engage in aerial combat. "I was kind of eager to test out my ability," he admitted, "but when it came at me, it came all of a sudden. It was a surprise when the first guy came at me—practically head on. . . . We were making the first strikes of my group on Saipan . . . and this guy came out of nowhere at me, as I say, almost head on."[10]

It was a Zero. The pilot "came down from above our fighters and pulled up in a high wingover on my port beam," said McCampbell. "I turned into him and fired a short burst from close up, not more than 250 yards. The Zeke turned over on its left wing. I followed and got in another short burst, then got on his tail and gave him another burst. The pilot made another wingover, but he was already going down." McCampbell watched as the plane, camouflaged in a mottled green and brown pattern, fell off on its right wing and spiraled into the sea. It hit without burning and quickly sank. "No pilot appeared," he observed. It was his first air-to-air victory. "I knew I could shoot him down and I did," he remarked nonchalantly. "That's all there was to it."[11]

Two days later, with the Saipan landings less than forty-eight hours away, McCampbell led sixteen Hellcats, thirteen dive bombers, and eight torpedo planes in an attack on enemy cargo ships. Returning to *Essex*, they spotted a twin-engine Nakajima Ki-49 Helen. "He turned right, poured on coal and I chased him," McCampbell reported. "I caught up in about two minutes. My entire division engaged him. I made a run and then pulled up to kill speed, then made two runs before losing enough speed to get on him the third time and sit there til he blew up 50 feet above the water. There were no survivors. The airplane looked brand new with very bright paint, possibly being ferried south."[12]

McCampbell tangled with a Zero over Iwo Jima on June 15 as *Essex* was sent to interdict Japanese air reinforcements to Saipan. The enemy pilot eluded him, but there was plenty of action to come as the carrier rejoined the fleet off Saipan. Unwilling to concede control of Saipan, the Japanese *First Mobile Fleet*, with nine carriers and 450 aircraft, was now steaming toward the American task force with extreme prejudice. On June 19 U.S. flattops launched fighters as swarms of Japanese aircraft approached.

McCampbell led eleven fighters off *Essex*'s deck to assist Hellcats engaged with the first wave of the enemy air attack. By the time he got his people organized, the fighter controller reported another wave of about fifty enemy aircraft approaching from the east about 120 miles out. "I was to intercept and stop them," observed McCampbell.[13] Climbing to 25,000 feet, they soon picked up the enemy formation, now about 60 miles out. It consisted mostly of Aichi D4Y2 Judy dive bombers at about 18,000 feet, along with some Jill torpedo planes and Zeros. "We simply tore into them," said McCampbell. The six Hellcat .50-caliber machine guns were loaded alternately with incendiary, ball, and tracer—each third round being a tracer—400 rounds per gun total. "It had tremendous fire-power," observed McCampbell. As for the Japanese aircraft, "We learned real early that if you hit 'em anywhere near the wing roots where the fuel was they'd explode right in your face."[14]

McCampbell picked out a single-engine dive bomber. "My first target was a Judy on the left flank and approximately halfway back in the formation," he reported. He planned to make a run on the Judy, pass under it and beneath the formation, then hit another plane on the right flank with a low-side attack. "These plans became upset when the first plane I fired at blew up practically in my face," he reported. Pulling up to avoid the debris, McCampbell was forced to pass over the top of the entire formation. "I remember being unable to get to the other side fast enough, feeling as though every rear gunner had his fire directed at me."[15]

Surviving this initial mishap, McCampbell went after a Judy on the right flank, giving it "a rather long burst" from behind and above. "It caught fire and fell away out of control as I dove below and zoomed ahead. My efforts were directed at keeping as much speed as possible and working myself ahead into position for an attack on the leader." Setting a third Judy smoking, he went after the leader, but when his burst of gunfire had no visible effect, he shifted his attention to the port side wingman. As he came under attack, the Japanese pilot "commenced violent fishtailing," which only slowed him down, remarked McCampbell. Coming at his victim from seven o'clock high, he gave the Judy a burst. The dive bomber promptly exploded in "an envelope of flame." Now he turned his attention back to the formation leader. "Breaking away down and to the left placed me in position for a below rear run on the leader from 5 o'clock, after which I worked on to his tail and continued to fire until he burned furiously and spiraled downward out of control," he reported.[16]

Plagued with gun stoppages during his final attack on the formation leader, McCampbell charged both port and starboard guns in an attempt to clear them. By now the original enemy formation had been decimated and the attack effectively broken up, but McCampbell spotted a solitary Judy below him. He nosed down in a modified high-side run on the bomber. "Only my starboard guns fired on this run, which threw me into a violent skid and an early pullout was made after a short burst," he reported. "Guns were charged twice again and since my target had pushed over and gained high speeds, a stern chase ensued. Bursts of my starboard guns alone, before all guns ceased to fire, caused him to burn and pull up into a high wing-over before plummeting into the sea. Neither the pilot nor rear-seat man bailed out before the plane struck the water and disintegrated." Believing he had run out of ammunition (in fact, he had burned out his guns by prolonged firing), McCampbell headed back to *Essex*. "One very vivid picture stands out," he observed, "that of many fires and oil slicks closely strung in nearly a direct line along the track of the enemy raid for a distance of 10–12 miles on the water."[17]

McCampbell's score of five Judys and a probable made him the Fabled Fifteen's first "ace in a day," but he wasn't done yet. That same afternoon, leading twelve Hellcats in a sweep over Guam, he found over three dozen enemy planes in small formations circling Orote Field, "some with wheels down preparatory to landing on the field."[18] McCampbell and his wingman, Ens. Royce L. Nall, went after a pair of Zeros that sported light gray paint jobs with large red meatballs on the wings. McCampbell's victim burst into flames and exploded on his second pass. Nall drew smoke from the other.

Pulling out in the direction of two other Zekes, McCampbell and Nall lacked the speed to break away and were forced to turn into them. Nall's elevator was shot away, and McCampbell received six 7.7mm bullet holes in his tail and wing. They poured on the coal to get away, but Nall's damaged plane was unable to keep up. As he dropped slightly astern, the two Zekes began to close on him. McCampbell scissored across and fired on the closest Zeke, which burned and crashed after the one pass. The other Zeke fled. McCampbell gave chase. "The Japanese pilot then executed the most beautiful slow roll I had ever seen," he recalled.[19] McCampbell opened fire, but the Zero managed to evade him and escape.

Arriving as a replacement pilot after the Battle of the Philippine Sea, Ens. Jack Taylor found that McCampbell "already had a considerable reputation" and was greatly admired. "He was highly respected by those in the squadron and was regarded as a hell of a pilot—a particularly good gunner/marksman. To put it plainly, he had a tendency to hit things he aimed at. But he was also obviously very thoughtful and meticulous in planning his air-combat missions."[20]

The view from the bridge was less enthusiastic. Arriving to take over the task force (now redesignated 38.3) on August 1, Rear Adm. Frederick C. Sherman summoned McCampbell for a chat. After congratulating him on his numerous aerial victories—the most recent being a Zero shot down over Guam's Orote Field on June 23 and a shared credit for another—Sherman coolly pointed out that an air group commander wasn't supposed to be running around shooting up Japanese planes like some twenty-year-old fighter jockey. "The admiral called me up and specifically told me after June 19th, that he didn't want me taking part in any more scrambles or purely fighter-type missions," recalled McCampbell. "He wanted me to lead the deck loads of fighters, bombers, and torpedo planes on missions."[21] The air group leader was responsible for operations and target coordination and shouldn't be dashing off at every opportunity to shoot down some Japanese mother's son. Obviously, he could protect himself if attacked, but there was to be no more "Zero fever."[22]

As *Essex* entered the campaign to regain the Philippines, McCampbell heeded at least part of the admiral's directive: he diligently protected himself. On September 12, 1944, he shot down two Zekes, a Dinah, and one Jack single-seat interceptor. A day later, he shot down two obsolete Ki-27 Nate fighters and an Oscar and claimed another Nate as a probable. On September 22, while shepherding a rocket attack on Japanese shipping, he spotted a twin-engine Frances bomber at 18,000 feet. He chased after it and, in his enthusiasm, fired two rockets intended for ground targets. One of the rockets knocked off part of the bomber's vertical stabilizer. Though the rocket failed to explode, one of the bomber's seven-man crew leaped out and took to his parachute. McCampbell followed up with his .50s, concentrating on the right engine and wing root. The bomber caught fire, lost its right wing, and plunged into Manila Bay.[23] On September 24, McCampbell got a half credit for contributing to the destruction of an F1M Pete floatplane. On October 21 he shot down a Ki-46 Dinah reconnaissance plane and a Nate.

By now, despite his having been forbidden to fly offensive fighter missions, McCampbell's Hellcat, *Minsi III*, sported twenty-one rayed Japanese flags just below the cockpit, each representing an aerial victory. Some in higher command—as Admiral Sherman had already made clear—were inclined to view that impressive display as graphic proof that the air group leader was neglecting his command duties in his enthusiasm for adding to his score. In yet another effort to rein him in, McCampbell was directed to remain aboard ship on October 24 when the bulk of his air group left for a dawn strike against the Japanese fleet, which had been located in the Sibuyan Sea. Only seven fighters remained as the air group disappeared over the horizon in the opening moments of what would come to be known as the Battle of Leyte Gulf.

McCampbell was obediently slogging through paperwork at 9:50 a.m. when the carrier's radar picked up an incoming enemy air strike. Word came to scramble fighters. "All except the air commander," added the disembodied voice on the ship's intercom. "He is not, repeat not, to go." But with only six Hellcats available—*Minsi III* would be number seven—the powers-that-be experienced a belated reality check. After a moment, the ship's speaker came back to life with, "Now hear this! Air group commander is to fly. Affirmative. Air group commander is to fly!"[24]

Assuming the air officer had checked with Admiral Sherman, McCampbell grabbed his gear and headed topside. *Minsi III* was still on deck being fueled when he climbed into the cockpit. He recalled, "Pretty soon the word came down, *If the group commander's plane is not ready to go, send him below.* So with that I waved away the fueling detail. I looked at

my gauges and saw that my main tanks were only half full."[25] Followed by
his wingman, twenty-two-year-old Lt. (j.g.) Roy Rushing of McGehee,
Arkansas, he sped down the deck, lifted off, and climbed into the building clouds, the remaining five Hellcats following behind. The Japanese air
formation was now only 21 miles away.

As the Japanese came into sight, McCampbell picked up his binocu-
lars and counted three Vs of aircraft with what appeared to be approximately forty fighters—a mix of Zeros and Oscars—at 21,000 feet, flying
cover for about twenty dive bombers some 3,000 feet below them. "I'll
take the fighters," he radioed. Though it was not his intent, the five Hellcats that had been trailing behind took him literally. All five broke away to
go after the bombers, leaving McCampbell and Rushing to deal with the
swarm of fighters. It belatedly occurred to McCampbell that two Hellcats against forty enemy fighters did not offer very good odds. Opening
his radio channel, he called, "This is Nine Nine Rebel. I have only seven
planes. Please send help." *Essex*'s fighter control replied, "There is none."[26]

The following sequence of events bordered on the bizarre. Followed
by Rushing, McCampbell banked into a dive from 30,000 feet, locked
in on one of the Japanese fighters, and shot it out of the sky. Rushing
got another. Regaining altitude, they made a second overhead pass, and
McCampbell knocked down a Hamp. As they climbed to prepare for
a third pass, McCampbell was astonished to see the swarm of fighters
forming up in a defensive Lufbery Circle, which would allow each plane
to protect the others. Considering the 37:2 odds, it seemed a peculiar tactical decision, but after two unsuccessful head-on attacks on the Lufbery
Circle, the two Americans pulled up to contemplate the situation. "So
we had a cigarette apiece and in about, I don't know, ten to fifteen minutes—it's kind hard to judge time, but it was enough for me to smoke one
cigarette, so at least eight to ten minutes—and then they broke out of this
circle and then headed for Manila," McCampbell remembered.[27]

As the Japanese fighters headed away, strung out in a long line,
McCampbell dove, knocking down his third victim at a range of about
900 feet, while Rushing got his second. The Japanese, possibly low on
gas, continued doggedly on course. Each plane carried either a bomb or a
belly tank, McCampbell wasn't sure which. Unmolested, he and Rushing

began a series of passes, knocking enemy fighters out of the sky like clay pigeons. McCampbell recalled,

We zoomed down, would shoot a plane or two. Roy and I each would take one, and I'd tell him which one I was going to take, if it was to the right or to the left, which one it was. By telling him this, that allowed him to know which way I was going to dive. . . . This worked very successfully. . . . And I'd pick out my plane, then he'd pick out his. We'd make an attack, pull up, keep our altitude advantage, speed, and go down again. We repeated this over and over. We made about 20 coordinated attacks.

One of the Hellcats that had originally gone after the enemy bomber formation also put in an appearance and knocked down a couple of Japanese before running out of ammunition and heading back to the carrier.

Finally Rushing radioed, "Skipper, I'm out of ammunition."

"Well, Roy, I've got a little left," McCampbell radioed back. "Do you want to go down with me for a couple more runs, or do you want to sit up here and watch the show?"

Rushing said he'd go along. "So he followed me down for a couple more attacks, and then I looked at my gas gauges, and I saw I'd emptied one main tank. I was about on the second one and I was beginning to get low," recalled McCampbell. "By then I was out of ammunition, too."[28]

Their pursuit of the enemy formation toward Manila had taken them about 100 miles from their task group. Over the course of approximately ninety-five minutes, McCampbell had shot down five Zekes, two Hamps, and two Oscars destroyed, as well as two Zeke probables. Roy Rushing claimed another six enemy aircraft. "The only damage I had was from the debris hitting the leading edges of my wings," remarked McCampbell. "And I had quite a few little dents in both wings."[29]

Nearly out of gas, McCampbell arrived over *Essex* to find the flight deck crowded with planes. "I knew that to launch all those planes would take a good twenty minutes, and I didn't have that much gas left," he observed.[30] USS *Langley* came to his rescue, clearing her deck for the Hellcat. He had scarcely set down when the engine sputtered and quit.

Mechanics later told McCampbell he had exactly six rounds left in the outboard gun on his starboard wing—and he only had those because the gun had jammed.

Soon after McCampbell's arrival, *Langley's* air group commander returned from a flight. He was all excited, recalled McCampbell. "Dave, I just got five planes!" he exclaimed. "How many did you get today?" Describing himself as "almost embarrassed," McCampbell replied, "Well, I think I got eleven with a couple of probables thrown in there."[31]

Ironically, McCampbell was subsequently called to the flag bridge on the *Essex*, where Admiral Sherman "ate me out" for taking part in the scramble. As the tongue lashing concluded, the admiral's chief of staff piped up, "Well, Admiral, we were sent out here to kill Japs, and that's exactly what Commander McCampbell did."[32] Whether or not this gave Sherman pause, McCampbell never knew, but months later he found he had been recommended for the Medal of Honor.

McCampbell's war wasn't over. He added five aerial victories in November to bring his score to thirty-four and ensure his position as the top U.S. Navy ace of the war. Those thirty-four victories were also the greatest number of planes shot down by a pilot during a single tour, and he is the only American aviator to twice achieve "ace in a day" status. Overall, he ranks as the nation's fourth-leading ace of all time, behind Maj. Dick Bong (40), Maj. Tommy McGuire (38), and Col. Francis S. Gabreski, who scored 34.5 victories in the European theater.

During its seven months in combat, Air Group 15 destroyed more enemy planes (312 in air combat and 348 on the ground) and sank more enemy shipping (296,500 tons sunk and another 500,000 tons damaged or probably sunk) than any other air group in the Pacific war. Under McCampbell's command, the air group's victims included the battleship *Musashi*, three carriers, and a heavy cruiser sunk and three battleships, a carrier, five heavy cruisers, four light cruisers, and nineteen destroyers damaged. Years after the war, one of his pilots remarked, "What I remember clearly about David Campbell was his intensity. At times he was remote, but he was also aggressive, impressive and one hell of a good air group commander."[33]

On January 10, 1945, President Franklin D. Roosevelt awarded McCampbell the Medal of Honor to add to his previous decorations, which included the Navy Cross and Silver Star. McCampbell's mother did the honors as his sister looked proudly on. The citation noted his actions during the "Great Marianas Turkey Shoot" and his feat in shooting down nine planes, which was credited with turning back the enemy attack on his task group. "I guess they figured that I saved lives by interrupting this air raid to the point that no planes actually got in to bomb the ship," he remarked.[34]

Promoted to captain, McCampbell stayed in the Navy after the war. He served as U.S. naval attaché to Buenos Aires and later as captain of the carrier *Bon Homme Richard* and finally as head of plans for the chief of naval operations before retiring in 1964. While several of his peers made admiral, McCampbell suspected he was passed over at least in part because of his "considerable marital problems," which led to four divorces. "I blame the Navy itself, at least my duties, for two of the divorces—the first and second—and the third one just didn't work out," he remarked. "It lasted less than a year. The fourth one lasted about nine years."[35] When he died in Florida after a lengthy illness on June 30, 1996, he was survived by his fifth wife, Buffy; a daughter, Frances by his first wife; and two sons, David and John, by his second wife. He was buried in Arlington National Cemetery.

In his retirement, McCampbell wasn't much of a self-promoter and seldom gave interviews. However, in a lengthy interview in 1987 with Paul Stillwell of the U.S. Naval Institute, he emphasized a major point of personal pride. "I'm quite proud of the fact that I was never shot down by the enemy in air-to-air combat or by antiaircraft," he remarked. When Stillwell suggested this was attributable to his skill, McCampbell demurred. "No," he said self-deprecatingly, "I would rather describe it as luck."[36]

Maj. Horace S. Carswell Jr.
China
October 26, 1944

Growing up, Horace Carswell was considered the daredevil among his group of friends in Fort Worth, Texas. He was the kid who would launch himself into the swimming hole from the loftiest spot, the one who couldn't wait to ride the roller coaster or the Ferris wheel. A compact five feet, nine inches tall and 160 pounds—his classmates called him "Stump"—he was a standout quarterback on the North Side High School football team, gaining fame for scoring the winning touchdown in the 1933 Armistice Day matchup against Wichita. Only ten years later he would make the ultimate sacrifice in the skies over China for another team—this one the crew of his B-24 Liberator.

Born on July 18, 1916, in Fort Worth, Horace Seaver Carswell Jr. grew up in a middle-class neighborhood on the city's north side. His father was a longtime employee at Swift and Company, a meatpacking plant near the city stockyards. A well-rounded youngster, Horace played football and baseball in high school, sang in the Boys Glee Club, and was advertising manager for the school yearbook. As a member of the National Thespian Club, he won first place for individual acting in a citywide contest in 1934. In the summers he worked at the Swift and Company plant.

Graduating from North Side High School in 1934, Carswell was accepted at Texas A&M University, where he hoped to play football. To his disappointment, he was too small to make the team, and he decided to transfer to Texas Christian University (TCU) at the end of his freshman year. The move may have been encouraged by the fact that four of his uncles were Methodist ministers—or, more probably, the opportunity to play sports. At TCU he played varsity baseball for three years and as a senior played guard on the 1938 undefeated Horned Frogs football team that went 11–0. He helped pay his way through school by working in the shipping department of a local department store, graduating in 1939 with a degree in physical education and a minor in history.

Carswell initially went to work for an area insurance agency, but that was too tame to last long. In March 1940, he enlisted in the Army as a flying cadet. He completed the final phase of pilot training at Kelly Field in San Antonio and was commissioned as a second lieutenant in November 1940. One of his flying school classmates recalled him as "a very determined individual," and "though of a quiet nature," he was "reservedly friendly" and had a sense of humor, once joking that he was especially popular among "little old ladies and dogs."[37]

While training at Goodfellow Field in San Angelo, Texas, Carswell renewed a previous acquaintance with twenty-four-year-old Virginia Ede, whom he had first met on a double date while a student at TCU. Virginia had graduated from TCU a year before him with a degree in home economics. Her father was owner of a local Studebaker dealership in addition to serving as the mayor of nearby San Angelo. "He was happy-go-lucky and always a dare-devil, up to kid pranks," Virginia observed of the young pilot. One of those pranks involved buzzing the girls when they were swimming at her father's camp on the Concho River—"he'd wait until they were all in swimming, then zoom a plane low to scare them," she remembered.[38] She and Carswell were married in October 1941. Their son, Robert Ede Carswell, was born in September 1943 while Horace was stationed at Clovis Army Air Field in New Mexico.

Carswell attended the Army Air Forces Combat Crew School at Hendricks Field, Florida, and subsequently served as an instructor and flight commander with a variety of stateside bomb squadrons. Promoted to major on April 23, 1944, he was assigned to the 374th Bombardment Squadron, 308th Bomb Group, which had been flying B-24s with Maj. Gen. Claire L. Chennault's Fourteenth Air Force in China since early 1943. The 308th supported Chinese forces, attacking Japanese airfields, docks, and rail yards, as well as interdicting enemy shipping in the South China Sea. During the last nine months of 1943, the group had lost twenty-four officers and thirty-one enlisted men killed in action; twenty-three officers and thirty-seven enlisted men missing in action; and twenty-four men in non-battle-related deaths. Upon arrival at Fourteenth Air Force headquarters at Kunming—a primitive but important air hub at the terminus of the Burma Road in southern China—Carswell was assigned to group headquarters staff and soon afterward was appointed operations officer for the 374th Bombardment Squadron.

As operations officer, he flew with various crews to judge their proficiency. Copilot Lt. Charles F. Thompson was impressed by Carswell's ability and attention to detail. "The man could fly!" he exclaimed.[39] In July, hitting heavy weather, unable to locate their airfield, and running out of gas, Carswell and a crew were forced to bail out of their Liberator. All survived the jump. Assisted by Chinese guerrillas, they managed to make their way back to base eight days later, just in time for Carswell to stop a message to his wife that he was missing in action.[40]

By October, Carswell had moved on to command a detachment of radar-equipped B-24J bombers drawn from the group. Stationed at Liuchow, 400 miles from Kunming, the detachment's primary mission was to seek out and destroy enemy shipping in the South China Sea. The B-24J's radar made it especially useful for locating enemy vessels at night, stripping away the protection of darkness and leaving them vulnerable to low-level bombing attacks. The sweeps and attacks were routinely flown by single planes.

On October 15, Carswell was flying as copilot to Capt. Donald M. ("Smiling Jack") Armstrong on a night sweep when they detected a six-ship convoy about 150 miles east of Hong Kong. Taking over the controls, Carswell brought the B-24 down to 400 feet in a stern-to-bow attack on one of the ships. "As we passed over the vessel, I saw it was a destroyer," observed Lt. Carlos J. Ricketson, who normally flew as copilot but had been displaced by Carswell on this trip. "The first bomb hit aft of amidships on the starboard side and right alongside the vessel. The second bomb hit directly amidships and the third forward of amidships and right alongside the vessel on the port side."[41]

The destroyer lost forward momentum, and Carswell came around and made a second run on her. The destroyer's guns remained silent, but a tremendous amount of fire was directed their way by another ship that appeared to be an enemy cruiser. It was too heavy to be merely machine-gun fire, noted Ricketson. "Machine gun tracer fire is red. This stuff was white and green and not as rapid. It was probably 20 or 40mm stuff and maybe some heavier."[42] Carswell continued to bore in. Watching from the bomb bay, Ricketson thought the second run scored one hit on or near the destroyer's bow.

Once again Carswell swung around, but this time he was gunning for what the crew subsequently identified as a three-stack Nagara-class light cruiser. Carswell took the B-24 on a stern-to-bow approach through intense antiaircraft fire. "From bow to stern it was lit up by the gun flashes," recalled Ricketson of the ship's return fire. "I couldn't start to count the number of gun positions firing at us."[43] Racing low overhead, they loosed three bombs.

"We were right on her," Carswell said. At least one of their bombs apparently hit the cruiser in the magazine. Ricketson saw a brilliant flash as they pulled away. The whole center of the ship exploded, the bow and stern folding up like a jackknife. The explosion was accompanied by such a blast of heat that for an instant Ricketson thought his face had been burned. The big bomber lurched in the wake of the concussion and seemed to go momentarily out of control.

"There was a big explosion and we were right over it," said Carswell. The plane lurched nose down. "I thought we had our tails blown off," recalled Armstrong. "We pulled back as hard as we could. The plane leveled out and started climbing." The tail gunner exclaimed over the intercom, "The cruiser's blown up all over the sky!"[44]

Ricketson thought they had more than done their duty by this point, but Carswell came around yet again and made a run on a destroyer with their last three bombs. The bombs fell short, and they finally turned for home. The Navy subsequently credited the crew with sinking a light cruiser and a destroyer, though postwar Japanese records report only the loss of the *Hato*, an Otori-class torpedo boat. At 290 feet long with a 129-man crew, the vessel could easily be confused with a destroyer, though not a three-stack light cruiser. The auxiliary vessel *Santos Maru* was reportedly damaged. Carswell was awarded the Distinguished Service Cross for this action.

Only eleven days later, Carswell prepared to head out on a night mission from Chengkung Airfield to intercept a convoy that had been spotted southwest of Hong Kong. Word was there might be an enemy carrier. Associated Press correspondent Clyde A. Farnsworth found Carswell pulling on his shoes as he got his gear together. This time he would pilot the B-24 normally flown by twenty-two-year-old 2nd Lt. James H.

Rinker of Eureka, Illinois. Rinker would fly as Carswell's copilot. The regular copilot, 2nd Lt. James L. O'Neal of Proviso, Illinois, would go along as a passenger/observer. Other crew members included 2nd Lt. Charles A. Ulery of Marion, Ohio, navigator; 2nd Lt. Walter W. Hillier of Chicago, Illinois, bombardier; T/Sgt. Charles H. Maddox of Roanoke, Virginia, engineer/gunner; T/Sgt. Ernest Watras of Lebanon, Connecticut, radio operator; S/Sgt. Carlton H. Schnepf of Hicksville, New York, nose gunner; S/Sgt. Kaemper W. Steinman of Bellflower, California, armorer/gunner; S/Sgt. Norman Nunes of Harwich, Massachusetts, tail gunner; and T/Sgt. Adam J. Hudek of North Vandergrift, Pennsylvania, radar observer. The addition of Carswell expanded the bomber crew to eleven men. "I wouldn't send these boys after anything I wouldn't go after myself," Carswell told Farnsworth as he laced his shoes.

"I remember Hillier sitting on the edge of the porch, turning to me as I left Carswell's room," Farnsworth wrote later. "The bombardier grinned and called out, 'What kind of medal do you get when you sink an aircraft carrier?' The crew members were grimly jolly as they waited for Carswell and the weapons carrier that would take them to their plane," added Farnsworth. "In a little while they were gone."[45]

It was dark by the time the bomber crossed the coast and headed out to sea. At about 8:15 p.m., radar picked up a convoy of twelve enemy ships, which turned out to be two destroyers and what was probably an assortment of cargo ships and gunboats. There was no sign of an aircraft carrier. As Carswell raced in over one of the destroyers at 600 feet, Hillier toggled the bombs. "We didn't know we were aiming at a destroyer until the bombs were dropped," recalled Ulery. "We dropped six bombs. All fell short. There was no firing yet from the convoy."[46]

Watching from the tail gun position, Nunes observed that while there had been no direct hits, one of the bombs had exploded only 15 or 20 feet from the ship and appeared to have damaged it. For the moment, they waited. "We flew around for another half hour after our first run, studying its effects," Ulery reported later.[47] That was routine procedure, observed Watras. It allowed crews to plan another run or abandon the target, depending on the situation. From what Hudek was reporting on the convoy's very competent defensive maneuvers, it seemed to Watras they should break off the attack. The enemy was clearly now ready and waiting for a return visit. At low level, alone, and without the element of surprise, the B-24 would be like the target in a shooting gallery.

To Watras's dismay, the Liberator began to descend as Carswell brought them in for a run on what appeared to be a straggler. "We took the bait," Watras said later. Hillier was just toggling three more bombs when the whole convoy opened up on them from directly below. Flying at only 600 feet in the bright moonlight, the Liberator was hard to miss. Fire tore through the wings and fuselage.

"I don't know how many times we were hit," Ulery said. "But it was plenty. . . . One shell burst inside the bomb bay. It lit up everything. The radio operator and I were thrown against the armor plate behind the pilot and co-pilot. O'Neal, who had been standing just below the flight deck, was knocked back underneath towards the nose. Engineer Maddox, whose hand had been hanging over the open bomb bay, was thrown back into the plane."[48] Other fragments sprayed through the forward compartment, severely wounding copilot Rinker in the right hand. The number-one and number-three engines were knocked out, and the number-two engine and the hydraulic system were damaged.

Only Carswell's flying skills kept them in the air as the crippled bomber nosed toward the sea only 150 feet below. He finally managed to level out just above the water. The crew scrambled to jettison anything they could to lighten the load. Toolboxes and flak vests were tossed out. The remaining three bombs were jettisoned. Maddox and the gunners unbolted some of the aircraft's .50-caliber machine guns and threw them out, along with most of the ammunition.

The damage assessment was grim. Engines one and three were inoperative; the damaged number-two engine was still running but at reduced power; one gasoline tank had been punctured, and the hydraulic system was not functioning. The bomb bay doors had been damaged and would not close, which pretty much ruled out any attempt at a water landing. Their best chance was to try and make landfall where they could parachute out or, given some miracle, possibly nurse the stricken bomber over the mountains to make a crash landing on one of the Fourteenth Air Force fields in eastern China.

Twenty minutes into the return flight, O'Neal belatedly noticed that copilot Rinker was covered with blood and going into shock. A piece of shrapnel had punched through the back of his right hand, exiting through the palm, but he had remained in his seat without saying anything, doing his best to assist Carswell. They lifted him from his seat and laid him on the flight deck, tying a tourniquet around the arm between the elbow and shoulder in an effort to stop the bleeding and administering a syrette of morphine for the pain. O'Neal took over in the copilot's seat.

Carswell told Watras to send a message that they were heading back with two engines out. The B-24 porpoised as the pilots struggled to stay in the air. They "would put the plane into a climb until it almost stalled out, then point the nose down in order to pick up speed to go into a climb again," according to Ulery. "At no time could more than 125 to 130 mph be maintained and with two engines feathered and another damaged, it was with great difficulty the plane was held on course."[49]

Constantly battling for altitude, Carswell made it to the coast. "Carswell managed to get the ship up to 1,500 feet," said Ulery. "When we passed over the coast he had it up to 3,500. He asked me the course. I told him we had to get to 4,000 feet to cross the mountains to an alternate base. Nobody thought it possible to get one of those planes from sea level on two engines. But Carswell did it. Then No. 2 engine began to sputter and we lost 1,000 feet. This happened three times."[50]

The crew had expected to bail out once they made landfall, but the order didn't come. The reason was a monumental piece of bad luck in a night already full of ill fortune: the shell that hit the nose area had damaged Hillier's parachute, which had been lying on an ammunition box. There were no spares, and Hillier refused to trust the chute. If they jumped, they would have to leave Hillier behind or force him to rely on his shot-up parachute.

The number-two engine faltered, and they immediately plunged 1,000 feet. As the engine picked up again, Carswell and O'Neal were able to horse the bomber back up to 4,000 feet but could not keep her there. Wobbling from side to side, the plane rapidly lost altitude. By now they were into the mountains separating them from the friendly air bases in the interior, but they were much too low.

As Carswell and O'Neal struggled with the stricken plane, Hillier stood by them clutching his damaged chute. The other eight crew members gathered along the catwalk by the open bomb bay, ready to jump at a moment's notice. The interphone had gone out, but all were now aware of Hillier's damaged parachute and unanimous in the belief that Carswell and O'Neal only continued the struggle to stay airborne because they refused to abandon the bombardier. But it was a losing battle. "There was not enough power in the two engines to pull the B-24 up over the mountains," recalled Ulery.[51] "When we were squarely over the mountains No. 2 sputtered again. I looked out and saw mountain peaks right at our level."[52]

The end came quickly. At 11:15 p.m., an hour after crossing the coast, Carswell finally lost control among the looming peaks. An intelligence summary later estimated their altitude at about 2,000 feet, but that failed to account for the mountain peaks Carswell had been trying to dodge. Ulery later estimated their altitude at a mere 300 feet. Standing on the flight deck, Hillier motioned for the others to jump. "Let's get out of here," exclaimed Rinker. "The ship started into a spin and we bailed out," said Ulery.[53]

Rinker, who had somewhat recovered his senses, went first, followed by Ulery, Maddox, Watras, Hudek, Nunes, and Steinman. The last man to bail out, nose gunner Carlton H. Schnepf, saw Hillier kneeling with his ruined chute on the flight deck floor between Carswell and O'Neal. "The major and O'Neal were just sitting there, looking straight ahead," Schnepf said. "They knew the others were bailing out, but they made no move to stop them. They knew about Hillier's 'chute. I could see their faces. They were still trying to ride her in. Then the No. 2 engine sputtered and I jumped."

Schnepf's parachute had been soaked with fluid from the damaged hydraulic system. "I went out through the open bomb bay and pulled the rip cord," he said. "Nothing happened. I clawed at the pack with my hands and got the chute out. I landed on the mountain side. The plane crashed about 500 yards away. There was a big explosion and fire. The flames lit up the mountainside. I stayed at the spot until daylight. I couldn't go near the fire. There were continuous little explosions as the ammunition—what we hadn't jettisoned over the sea—kept going off. The three men must have been killed instantly."[54]

Schnepf was lucky to have survived the malfunctioning parachute during the low-level bailout. Rinker and Steinman were less fortunate. Their bodies were recovered three days after the crash along the flight path of the doomed Liberator. Rinker's parachute had never opened. Whether he was unable to pull the rip cord with his wounded hand, was too groggy from morphine, or had passed out from loss of blood will never be known. Steinman had pulled his rip cord but slammed into the mountainside before his parachute fully deployed.

The six survivors were soon located by friendly Chinese forces. "We who were on the crew feel quite sure that Carswell, O'Neal and Hillier never left the aircraft," Ulery reported later. "It exploded and burned violently several hours after the crash. There were practically no remains except a few bones. These were placed in three coffins and buried along with the other bodies at a Catholic Mission near Tungchen, China."[55]

Escorted by friendly Chinese, the survivors began the long trek home on October 31. "The terrain was mountainous and covered with bushes and vines," recalled Ulery. "The Chinese guerrillas were responsible for our getting out safely. We walked 15 to 20 miles a day and just made Nanning before the Japs took it."[56] All six made it safely back to the 374th Squadron at Chengkung and were returned to duty on November 9.

The story of Stump Carswell's sacrifice on behalf of a fellow crew member was recognized with the Medal of Honor, awarded on February 27, 1946, in ceremonies at Goodfellow Field in San Angelo, California. Maj. Gen. Albert Hegenberger, former executive officer of the Fourteenth Air Force in China, knelt to drape the medal around the neck of two-year-old Robert Ede Carswell as Horace's mother and his widow looked on.

The remains of Carswell, O'Neal, Hillier, Rinker, and Steinman were brought back from China in 1948. James Rinker was interred on January 25, 1949, in the National Memorial Cemetery of the Pacific—the Punchbowl—in Honolulu, Hawaii. James O'Neal, who had once flown as Rinker's copilot, was also interred at the Punchbowl. Though he had made the same sacrifice as Carswell, his highest decoration was a Silver Star. U.S. Air Force policy in these situations was to award the highest honor to the senior officer aboard the aircraft. Chicago resident Walter Hillier was buried at the National Cemetery at Springfield, Illinois. Kaemper Steinman was interred at Calvary Cemetery in Los Angeles.

The six crewmates who successfully bailed out into the darkness that October night in China all survived the war. Time eventually took what the war had spared. Charles Maddox died in 1977 in Virginia; Carlton Schnepf in 1980 in New York; Adam Hudek in 1981 in West Virginia; Charles Ulery in 2001 in Arizona; Ernest Watras in December 2015 in Connecticut; and, the last, Norman Nunes, in 2017 in Massachusetts at the advanced age of ninety-six.

Virginia Carswell remarried five months after Horace's remains were returned. Her husband, F. Wayland Myers, was an Air Force veteran who had piloted B-25 and B-26 bombers during the war. They had two sons together. Virginia passed away in 1986 in San Angelo, Texas.

An only child, Horace ("Stump") Carswell was initially buried on February 26, 1948, in Fort Worth's Rose Hill Cemetery. In 1986, at the request of his family, he was reinterred at Carswell Air Force Base in Fort Worth. The ceremony was attended by Robert Carswell, then forty-three years old, who observed of his father, "Flying was his entire life. He belongs here."[57]

But this resting place was not to last. When the Air Force base was scheduled for closure in late 1993, Major Carswell's remains were moved yet again and interred beside his parents at Oakwood Cemetery in Fort Worth near where he grew up. Flanked by walkways, the burial plot, known as Carswell Memorial Park, overlooks the Trinity River. A commemorative stone bears a rendition of the Medal of Honor, his name and dates of birth and death, and the inscription "A Native of Fort Worth, Killed in Action, Medal of Honor Recipient."

Capt. William A. Shomo
Luzon
January 11, 1945

The pilot of *Snooks 5th* raced in low over the airfield on the Philippine island of Mindoro and executed a slow victory roll. As ground crews cheered, the sleek P-51 Mustang pulled around and came in for a second roll, then a third.

A crowd began to gather, but the cheering grew ragged as the flying comedian continued to execute roll after roll to the rising annoyance of witnesses below, who disapproved of any mockery of the traditional fighter pilot's victory celebration. Finally, after seven rolls, the pilot, Capt. William A. Shomo, put down on the field, accompanied by his wingman, Lt. Paul M. ("Lippy") Lipscomb. The rolls were no mockery, they assured skeptical onlookers. Cocky, blond Bill Shomo, the son of a Pennsylvania grocery store clerk, had just gunned down seven enemy aircraft over Luzon. Liscomb, a slow-talking Texan, had downed three more.

In a service full of former college boys, twenty-six-year-old Bill Shomo boasted a somewhat unusual personal history: He was probably the only flying mortician in the Pacific theater. He had attended the Pittsburgh School of Embalming between 1937 and 1940 and then worked as an embalmer at Earle Miller Funeral Home in his hometown of Jeannette, Pennsylvania, before enlisting in the U.S. Army's Aviation Cadet Pilot Training Program on August 18, 1941. He was commissioned as a second lieutenant and awarded his pilot's wings on March 7, 1942.

Shomo served stateside at airfields in Louisiana, Georgia, and Texas before being sent in mid-1944 to the South West Pacific Area, where he was assigned to the 82nd Tactical Reconnaissance Squadron. Equipped with older P-39 Airacobras and Curtiss P-40s, the squadron specialized in photo reconnaissance and ground-attack missions, hopping from airstrip to airstrip along the coast of New Guinea as Gen. Douglas MacArthur's ground forces advanced toward the Philippines. Due to the Airacobra's short range, encounters with enemy aircraft were rare, but the ground-support missions were dangerous enough. Pilots were routinely lost both to antiaircraft fire and to operational accidents as they flew low enough to brush treetops in strafing runs on enemy airfields, truck convoys, and troop positions.

Shomo had a close call on March 12 when the cooling system on his P-39 failed. Black smoke filled the cockpit, and a small fire flared up in the engine. He considered bailing out but in the end stayed with the plane, though he had to kick the Airacobra's automobile-type doors off and lean out of the cockpit in order to see where he was going. As he came in to land, he went to pull the landing gear switch but hit the wrong toggle and came down with his wheels still up, skidding down the metal mat runway on a belly tank still three-quarters full of gas. By some miracle, the smashed-up tank didn't catch fire, and Shomo walked away from the crash.[58]

That might have been enough to give even a flying mortician pause, but it would take more than near incineration to deter happy-go-lucky Shomo. While his squadron was stationed on Biak—newly captured after hard infantry fighting among the island's multitude of caves— one of his tent mates noticed that Shomo's accumulation of souvenirs seemed to be taking up an inordinate amount of precious floor space. Most of the mementoes were stored in bulky boxes with Japanese writing on them. When the other pilots suggested he get rid of some of his junk, Shomo told them not to worry, it was "just dynamite" he had retrieved from the Japanese caves. "I'm going to use it for fishing down at the beach," he explained. "[We] almost lost our minds," recalled one of his tentmates.[59]

Shomo was promoted to captain in September 1944. In December the squadron was finally able to get rid of its obsolete aircraft when it was reequipped with F-6Ds—long-range P-51 Mustangs designed for armed photo reconnaissance. Equipped with cameras, the aircraft also carried the normal complement of six .50-caliber machine guns. The day before Christmas, Shomo was placed in command of the squadron, which was moved up to an airfield on Mindoro off the southwest coast of Luzon to support operations in the Philippines. He led his first combat mission in the P-51—a low-level recon to ascertain Japanese air strength on northern Luzon—during the Lingayen Gulf landings on January 10.

"We were flying in the Philippines and getting ready to make the landing at Lingayen Gulf above Clark Field," he recalled. "So they wanted to know how many Japanese aircraft in Northern Luzon could oppose this landing. My wingman and I were sent out with specially equipped photographic P-51s with guns on to determine photographically and visually what they could oppose the landing with."[60]

Flying *Snooks V*, named in honor of his crew chief's wife, whose pet nickname was "Snooks 5th," they were approaching the Japanese airfield at Tuguegarao when Shomo spotted an Aichi D3A Val bomber coming in to land. Racing in behind the slow-moving bomber, he hit the gun trigger and sent the Val crashing into the ground. It was not only Shomo's first air victory but the first enemy victim of a Mustang in the Philippines.

His luck was about to get even better. The following day, he and wingman Lieutenant Lipscomb were to conduct an armed photo reconnaissance around Japanese-held Tuguegarao, Atarri, and Laoag airstrips on Luzon. A tall, redheaded twenty-three-year-old from Fort Worth, Texas, Lipscomb was well respected in the squadron. He had badly burned his hands and face during a crash landing in August. Refusing to be sent home, he had spent weeks practically helpless with both hands heavily bandaged before he recovered enough to be able to fly again.[61]

Cover for their January 11 low-level recon mission was supposed to be provided by a six-ship flight from the Air Commandos, also equipped with Mustangs, but at the last minute the Air Commandos were called away. Shomo decided to go anyway. "Now the mission should have been aborted as the possibility of enemy intercept was not improbable," observed fellow pilot Warren L. Sparks. "Such was not to be. If you knew Bill you would know that he would just consider that the Air Commandos had just missed an opportunity and proceeded to Tuguegarao as planned. I'm sure Lippy may have had second thoughts. I would have, but that's what makes heroes."[62]

The 500-mile flight to Tuguegarao took them two hours. "We were right on the deck, just off the trees, which was our normal method of operation," recalled Shomo. "I looked up and saw through the breaks in the clouds, at about 3,500 feet above us, three airplanes going in the opposite direction, just above the clouds. Just a momentary glimpse of them and they were gone."

They had previously been briefed that some Navy Corsairs would be operating in the area. "Did you see that, Lippy?" Shomo radioed.

"Yeah," replied Lipscomb. "Those sons-of-bitches are Corsairs."

"I'm not so damned sure about that," said Shomo. "Let's go up and take a look."[63]

"We made a high-speed climb through the hole and found a whole formation of twelve fighters escorting one Betty bomber," recalled Shomo.[64] There were eleven Ki-61 Tonys and a solitary Nakajima Ki-44 Tojo, all painted in mottled green camouflage, heading toward the Japanese-held airfields. "They were flying in a V with the bomber at the point and six fighters on either side," observed Shomo.[65] They had big red-orange discs painted on the wings and fuselage. "There was no doubt what they were," remarked Shomo.[66]

"For Christ's sake, did you ever see so many meatballs?" exclaimed Lipscomb.

Though outnumbered more than six to one, Shomo didn't hesitate. "I had been over in the war for almost sixteen months at that time," he explained. "With one exception the day before, I had never had the opportunity to get a crack at an airplane in the air—that is a Jap airplane while I was flying. I'd seen them while they were bombing our bases but never while I was airborne. So the opportunity was the time of a lifetime and at that point I made up my mind I wasn't going to miss. I'd waited too long for the opportunity."[67]

The Japanese took no evasive action as the two Mustangs rocketed toward them. Some of the planes reportedly waggled their wings, possibly thinking the new arrivals were about to join the formation. It would have been an understandable mistake—the P-51s had only arrived in the theater recently and had a similar profile to the Japanese inline Tonys. But if so, it was a fatal error.

Shomo and Lipscomb tore into the left side of the formation. "I hit the tail-end Charlie and he blew up," recalled Shomo. "I hit the element leader, and about that time, the wingman of the second section or third element down threw open his canopy." Possibly thinking he was under friendly fire, the pilot looked back at Shomo and gestured violently with his arms in an apparent effort to wave him off. Shomo pressed his gun button. "I pinned him right to the damn cockpit, the dashboard, and he burst into a big ball of orange flame."[68]

Lipscomb knocked down another Tony. Only then did the stunned Japanese begin to break formation.

"The second element of two Tonys on the right side of the formation turned to the left and started after my wingman who was moving down on the remaining element of two Tonys on the left side," reported Shomo. "As this element crossed over, they passed directly in front of me, and I fired a burst into the wingman and he exploded in flames." Shomo continued down through the formation, and "this guy comes whistling down, right by me and I nailed him. So that was four."[69]

Lipscomb downed another Tony and followed up with a pass on the bomber, but with no apparent effect. Shomo then took a turn at the bomber. As he closed on the tail from the right quarter, the rear gunner opened fire. "I could see those flashes coming out of it, blinking right at me," he recalled. "So I just squashed the nose down and then horsed back on the stick and came up under the damned bomber at point blank range and started raking it across. I fired one burst right across the wing root. . . . Just as I hit the wing root and started out, it burst into a big ball of flame."[70]

Lipscomb reported, "I turned back sharply and saw Shomo shoot the bomber down in a mass of fire. Then I saw a Tony coming straight at me. I ducked under him or he would have rammed me for sure."[71]

Shomo saw the near collision between the two planes. "They were firing continuously," he said. "You could see the damn tracers and everything, both lines looked like they were going into the prop hub of the other. The Jap started smoking from the right side of the engine. A big black ball of smoke started rolling out. . . . Just about the time it looked like they were gonna absolutely collide prop hub to prop hub, [Lipscomb] popped the stick down and went underneath him. There were two inches on the top of his tail bent in, apparently from the belly cowling of that airplane when he ducked underneath him like that."[72]

The Tony began to burn as it rolled into a vertical dive from about 600 feet. Meanwhile, the pilot of the stricken bomber, now "blazing like a roman candle" from the right wing, had leveled out over what appeared to be some sort of grain field in an effort to crash-land. The plane had just touched down when it went up in a ball of flame. "It just disintegrated, pieces going everywhere," said Shomo.

But now he had his own problems as the lone Tojo got on his tail. Designed as an interceptor, the heavily armed Ki-44 Tojo had a high rate of climb and overall speed. Shomo put the Mustang into a twisting, spiraling climb, but the Tojo stayed with him, firing all the way. Every time the enemy pilot fired, Shomo tightened his spiral, which prevented the Japanese from getting a proper lead on him. "We made about three turns after that, going up, and I knew that he was gonna stall out because I had more power than he did. We were still vertical and he was still trying to get enough lead, when he stalled out and whipped over . . . and I dropped down behind him. Just as I was about to nail him, boom, he was in one of those damn big clouds, right beside where we were sitting. So he disappeared."

Shomo then picked out two Tonys in element formation, just beyond where the bomber crashed. They were so low over the field they were almost right on the grain or tall grass. As he went after them, the wingman broke off. Shomo stayed with the leader. "So I just sorta hit a short burst into the leader and he went tumbling end over end and burst into flames." Making a ninety-degree turn, he caught up with the fleeing wingman. "I nailed him about 150 yards out across the grain and he blew up."[73]

Suddenly the skies were empty. Shomo had shot down seven planes; Lipscomb got three. "He knew Shomo was crazy so . . . he's just trying to protect his ass to get home," remarked Lt. Charles Borders, a flight leader in the squadron who knew them both well.[74] The two turned and used their reconnaissance cameras to photograph the downed planes. "Everywhere you looked it seemed like there was a damn big old burning wreck," said Shomo. "The grass, or grain, was all burning."[75]

Shomo finally paused to look at his watch. "The whole thing happened in fifteen minutes and no Jap plane required more than one burst to down it," he recalled.[76]

Upon returning to their own airfield, Shomo celebrated with the long series of victory rolls that were first greeted with annoyance and then jubilation when it turned out he wasn't just horsing around. "One Mustang flew in circles about 5,000 feet, while the other made several passes down the runway doing seven victory rolls" recalled pilot Robert Klingensmith.

"Then, it was over our tent area about two miles away, seven more victory rolls—the last one at very low altitude almost hit the trees."

The pilot's identity was no mystery. "We knew it was Shomo and also knew he had been in the Pacific two years and 200+ missions and we figured he was the top candidate for a Section 8 [psycho] transfer to the States," said Klingensmith. "No one in their wildest imagination would think that anyone would shoot down seven enemy aircraft in a single sortie." Finally Shomo landed, followed by Lipscomb, who had watched Shomo's performance from above. "We asked the wingman [Lipscomb] why he did not do three victory rolls and he said combat flying was dangerous enough and he was not going to bust his ass doing victory rolls," remarked Klingensmith.[77]

Then and later there was speculation as to why a lone Japanese bomber had been escorted by so many fighters. Shomo and Lipscomb thought the bomber was probably transporting a high-ranking officer. However, there seems to be no record of any important Japanese officer being lost in that area on that particular date. It is more likely that the bomber was serving as a navigational guide for the twelve fighters, which were probably flown by green pilots with rudimentary navigational skills. The likelihood that the pilots were unskilled would also explain their apparent confusion and lack of a coordinated response when taken under attack by only two P-51s. Lending support to this theory, a flight from Shomo's squadron encountered another bomber escorted by a dozen fighters at roughly the same time in the same general area. They managed to set the bomber smoking but were unable to press their attack as they were low on fuel and had already expended most of their ammunition on ground targets.[78]

Maj. Gen. George C. Kenney promoted Shomo to major and put him in for the Medal of Honor. Lipscomb was promoted to first lieutenant and recommended for the Distinguished Service Cross. Both awards were approved. Shomo received his medal in a ceremony at Lingayen Field on April 3 but soon learned the award had a downside when he was grounded, forbidden to fly combat. Instead, he was assigned to the chief of staff of the Fifth Air Force, helping to plot missions. After another pilot destroyed *Snooks 5th* in an accident, the public relations people had a new P-51 emblazoned with the name *The Flying Undertaker* in a play on Shomo's previous occupation as a mortician. To his disgust, *The Flying Undertaker* was mostly just a prop for photo shoots. "It's pretty damned discouraging to sit by and watch the boys go up on combat missions," he admitted to a news correspondent.[79] Years later he told his son that the Medal of Honor was "like a millstone hanging around his neck" because they wouldn't let him fly.[80]

Nevertheless, Shomo refused to go home to his wife, the former Helen Ruth McCullough, a Jeannette girl he had married in 1941, and their two children. He said he planned to stay "until this damn thing is over."[81] He may also have managed to sneak in more combat flying. According to his son Jimmy, "There were times that he was able to weasel his way back into squadrons or fighter units. . . . That's what he lived for. That's what he enjoyed doing. But whenever they would find him in a fighter unit they would jerk him out and reassign him."[82]

Shomo stayed in the Air Force after the war, serving in a variety of command positions, before finally retiring in 1968 as a lieutenant colonel. In 1979 he became an administrator with the Pennsylvania Department of Transportation, a job he held for the next ten years. From 1982 to the time of his death, he worked as a special deputy in the Allegheny County Sheriff's Department. He and wife Helen had six children.

"Naturally, I miss the flying," he admitted in a 1983 interview. "I loved being a pilot, but there is quite a contrast between civilian and military life. In the military you all work together, whereas everybody in civilian life is headed in their own individual directions. You have to readjust your whole way of living."[83]

Son Jimmy said his father was an engaging person who didn't talk much about the day he earned the medal. "Most people never knew he won the Medal of Honor," he said. "He was not looking for any accolades. He was doing what he was trained to do." His one major weakness was for cigars, added Jimmy. It was a habit he'd picked up during the war. "Growing up, I don't care if my dad got up at 3 in the morning to take a leak, he had a lit cigar. . . . You never saw him without a cigar."[84]

The cigars ultimately did what the Japanese could not. Bill Shomo died of pulmonary fibrosis on June 25, 1990, in his home state of Pennsylvania at the age of 72. He was survived by his wife, four sons, two daughters, and eight grandchildren. He was laid to rest in St. Clair Cemetery in Greensburg, Pennsylvania.

A few years before his death, Bill Shomo ruminated about war during a rare interview. "It made me a lot more practical in my viewpoint towards things that were important and what wasn't important in life," he observed. "Life becomes awfully simple in war. You simply concern yourself with how you're going to live, how long, whether you're going to survive any length of time, what's your best methods of survival. That's all you think about. Life's real simple in war."[85]

Red Erwin and the B-29s

BY DECEMBER 1944, THE SEIZURE OF THE MARIANA ISLANDS WAS BEAR-ing fruit for U.S. strategists. Two and a half years after the daring hit-and-run attack by the Doolittle Raiders, the Japanese home islands began to come under continuous air attack by B-29 Superfortresses flying from bases on Guam, Saipan, and Tinian. Early high-altitude bombing efforts were disappointing, but a change to low-level attacks with incendiaries devastated Japanese cities. During the March 9 attack on Tokyo alone, an estimated 84,000 people died, 40,000 were injured, and 16 square miles of the city were razed. Attrition among B-29 crews was also high during the bombing campaign as Superfortresses were shot down over targets, lost in operational accidents, or lost or forced down at sea during the 3,000-mile, twelve-hour over-water flight to Japan and back. Thirty-eight were lost in March 1945 alone. On April 12, 1945, a Superfortress named *Snatch Blatch* nearly joined them. That it didn't was due to the actions of a twenty-three-year-old radioman from Alabama who earned the only Medal of Honor awarded to a B-29 crewman during World War II.

S/Sgt. Henry Erwin
Japan
April 12, 1945

It was obvious to everyone that Red Erwin was going to die. The twenty-three-year-old B-29 radio operator lay in his hospital bed, swathed in a mummy-wrap of bandages over horrific burns, his agonies dulled by blessed morphine. Thanks to Erwin, eleven fellow crew members were still among the living, but it appeared the price of their survival was to be Red Erwin's own life.

Red Erwin's road to a hospital bed on Guam began in Alabama coal country a few miles north of Birmingham. Born Henry Eugene Erwin on May 8, 1921, in Docena, "Gene" or "Eugene," as his family called him, was the oldest of seven children. His father, Walter, was employed in the coal mines, but the family fell on hard times when Walter died in 1931.

As the oldest, Gene helped out where he could, stocking shelves in the coal company commissary, earning fifty cents to a dollar a night. As the Great Depression deepened, he dropped out of high school after two years and in July 1938 joined the Civilian Conservation Corps. The seventeen-year-old spent his hitch planting kudzu in northern Alabama as part of an effort to prevent soil erosion, making a princely $45 a month. He was later transferred to California, where he worked in forestry, clearing dead timber and fighting fires. A year later, back in Alabama, he went to work for the Fairfield Steel Works located just outside Birmingham, hooking hot bars of steel as they rolled off the line. The money he earned went to help support his mother and siblings.

Meanwhile the war was breathing down his neck. Registering for the draft in February 1942, Erwin's paperwork noted he was five feet, ten inches tall and weighed 165 pounds with brown eyes and red hair. He went into the Army the following January. Despite his limited education, Erwin scored well on screening tests and qualified for the Air Force. "I had these Buck Rogers dreams that I was going to be a pilot," he recalled. "I was going to shoot down all these Japs or these Germans and I was going to win the Medal of Honor, believe it or not."[1]

Becoming a pilot was not to be. Instead, Erwin's aptitude for technical subjects landed him in an advanced radio course at Truax Field in Wisconsin. He impressed his instructors and was offered the chance to go to Yale University for more study with the chance of earning a commission as a communications officer. It was a rare opportunity for a young man of his underprivileged background, but Erwin turned it down. As "a kid then," he was afraid the war might end before he could get into it, he recalled with some chagrin.[2]

Finishing radio training, he spent a brief stint on B-17s before assignment as a B-29 radio operator with the 52nd Bombardment Squadron, 29th Bomb Group, part of the Twentieth Air Force's XXI Bomber Command, in Dalhart, Texas. The B-29 Superfortress was a marvel of technology. Powered by four 2,200-horsepower Wright R-3350 Duplex Cyclone 18 radial engines, the bomber had a wingspan of just over 141 feet, was equipped with remotely operated machine guns, and carried a crew of eleven men—pilot, copilot, bombardier, flight engineer, navigator, radio operator, radar observer, right gunner, left gunner, central fire control, and tail gunner—in its pressurized interior. It could carry 5,000 pounds of bombs over 1,600 miles at high altitude and 12,000 pounds at medium altitude.

"It was big, heavy, and fast," observed Erwin of the B-29. The aircraft was divided into two halves connected by a crawl tunnel. Five crewmen were located in the back, aft of the bomb bays, and the other six manned the forward section. "As the radio operator, I sat with my back to the bulkhead in the rear of the front half, looking forward at the flight engineer, the two pilots and, in the very front, the bombardier, who had the best view in the house," recalled Erwin.[3]

Home on furlough in December, Erwin tied the knot with Martha Elizabeth ("Betty") Starnes, the eighteen-year-old daughter of a coal mine foreman. Soon afterward, his unit shipped out for Guam to join the air offensive against the Japanese home islands. Erwin flew in a B-29 familiarly known as *Snatch Blatch*, a suggestive play on a black witch character from the writings of French author Francois Rabelais. *Snatch Blatch* became more formally known as *The City of Los Angeles* after the military was pressured into cracking down on plane titles viewed as too risqué for prudish home front patriots. Nevertheless, a witch riding a broom, presumably the bawdy Snatch Blatch herself, continued to adorn the nose of the bomber.

The airplane commander and pilot was thirty-year-old Capt. George A. ("Tony") Simeral, a calm and steady veteran originally from Salem, Oregon. Simeral had flown thirty combat missions as a B-24 pilot in the Mediterranean theater, followed by a year as a B-24 instructor, before he volunteered for B-29s. Other crew members were copilot 2nd Lt. Leroy

C. ("Roy") Stables, flight engineer Sgt. Vern W. Schiller, navigator Capt. Pershing Younkin, bombardier 1st Lt. William Loesch, radar operator 2nd Lt. Leo D. Connors, gunner Sgt. Howard Stubstad, gunner Sgt. Herbert Schnipper, gunner Sgt. Vernon G. Widemeyer, and tail gunner Sgt. Kenneth E. Young.

"We were regular guys," said Erwin. "We took pride in how we functioned as a crew."[4] Perhaps inevitably, his fellow crew members took to calling their redheaded radioman "Red," and "Red" he would remain for the rest of his life. He was "a country boy, quiet, unassuming, religiously devout," remarked Simeral, volunteering his personal opinion that Erwin was also the best radioman in the 52nd Bombardment Squadron.[5]

From late February to April 1, the crew participated in unescorted bombing raids against Japan. Their first, on February 25, was a disappointment. The bomb bay doors froze shut, forcing them to abort and dump their ordnance in the ocean on their return to Guam. Following missions were more routine. "I sat in the front compartment on the right side up against the fuselage," remembered Erwin.

> I didn't have a window and was wedged in by equipment and the .50-calber gun turret. It was a lonely post. I couldn't see anything outside. All I had to sit on was a little fabric chair for a fifteen-hour mission. Some other radio operators griped it was the worst job on the plane—absolutely boring! It was twelve hours of boredom mixed with an hour of pure terror. I wore a flight suit on every mission, plus a skull cap, parachute, life preserver and boots. I sat on my parachute for a cushion, but I wore my Mae West life preserver at all times. I couldn't swim.[6]

One of the more memorable missions occurred on March 10 when *Snatch Blatch* was selected to carry wing commander Brig. Gen. Thomas ("Tommy") Power on the first low-level firebomb attack against the Japanese capital. Involving some 330 B-29s, the incendiary attack transformed 16 square miles of Tokyo into cinders and may have killed as many as 120,000 people. Using an extension cord to his interphone, Erwin climbed up to the navigator's astrodome and looked out in awe over the burning city below. It was, as one of the other crew observed, like the ninth and lowest level of Dante's Inferno.[7]

The general's diligence in surveying the dramatic results of the raid made *Snatch Blatch*'s crew more than a little nervous. Thermals from the massive fires below were tossing some of the big bombers around like toys. "Power wasn't content to fly over the target just once," Erwin recalled. "He wanted to go over Tokyo a second time, and a third, to see how it was going."[8] Fuel concerns finally persuaded Power to authorize *Snatch Blatch*'s departure. They returned to Guam without further incident, but that would not be the case a month later, on April 12, 1945, Red Erwin's eleventh combat mission.

"We were flying out of North Field, Guam, and we were designated the lead plane. . . . [W]e were going up to Koriyama, Japan, which was a high octane plant," recalled Erwin, "and we had seventy-five to eighty B-29s in the rear. . . . This particular morning, I guess it was about 9:30 or 10 o'clock, we'd been flying about seven hours because Koriyama was the longest target we had flown from North Field since we'd been over there."[9]

As this was a daylight raid, the procedure was a little different. "On the night raids, we were the pathfinder," explained Erwin. "We would go in and light it up and get out. On the daylight raids we would form up about 50 miles off the coast and go into the formation with the lead crew. Of course, that's when the Japs would fight us all the way in and all the way out."[10]

Arriving at the assembly point over Aogashima, a small volcanic island 223 miles south of Tokyo, *Snatch Blatch* circled, waiting for the remaining B-29s to form up. Erwin's job at this point was to drop flares and then a phosphorus smoke bomb canister through a chute in the floor of the aircraft to mark the assembly location for the arriving bombers. "When they're dropped out of the chute in the radio operator position, they explode and give out a vast amount of smoke for the others to come in on us," explained Erwin.[11]

The phosphorus smoke pot canister was a cylinder about 16 inches long and weighing about 20 pounds. Phosphorus burns at about 1,300 degrees Fahrenheit—it can cut through metal like butter—so the device was equipped with a six-second delayed-action fuse that allowed the canister to fall about 300 feet from the aircraft before igniting. Simeral signaled for Erwin to begin launching the flares. Erwin, in his shirtsleeves for the low-level mission, busied himself dropping the flares. Finally he picked up the phosphorus bomb, set the six-second fuse, positioned it over the 3.5-foot-long chute, and let it go. Almost immediately, he knew something wasn't right. "I knew it was coming back and I tried to put my foot on it and kick it out, but it came on into the plane. . . . I knew that sucker was coming back."[12]

For reasons that were not clear—a defective fuse, an air pocket, or failure of the gate at the bottom of the chute—the device exploded while still in the chute. "It was just a matter of feet or inches," said Erwin. "If it had just gone a little farther, the signal bomb would have cleared the body of the aircraft and fired outside."[13] Instead, the smoking, burning canister rocketed from the chute like a fireball, spewing chunks of 1,300-degree phosphorus. The accompanying blast of white fire hit Erwin in the face, blinding him, burning off his hair, most of his right ear, part of his nose, and large areas of skin. His clothing was on fire. "I was completely aflame," he said.[14]

A thick cloud of phosphorus pentoxide smoke immediately billowed through the aircraft and into the cockpit area, making it impossible for Simeral and copilot Lieutenant Stables to see the instrument panel. The pilots had no idea what had happened. "You could see nothing, absolutely nothing," Simeral said. "Not even your hand before your face."[15]

The burning canister had somehow missed Erwin as it shot back up out of the tube. It smashed into the overhead and dropped back down somewhere at the blinded radioman's feet. Despite the agonizing pain from his injuries, Erwin's first thought was that he mustn't panic. His greatest fear was that the device would burn through the metal floor and into the bomb bay. He asked God to help him. Miraculously, the incredible pain subsided.

"I realized I had to get it out of there, otherwise we were all going to die," he said. "So I looked for it, but I couldn't find it and I kept [searching] with my right hand moving and just said 'Lord, I need your help.' And instantly I found it." Their only hope now was his getting forward to throw the canister out the cockpit window 13 feet away. He could feel the plane descending as he grabbed the superheated device with his bare hands in an agony of searing flesh. "And I began to crawl with it toward the cockpit. I knew we were going down."[16]

Covered with burning phosphorus, Erwin crawled around the gun turret, only to find the way blocked by the navigator's folding table. Hinged to the wall, the table had been left down and locked in place when navigator Younkin went aft to the celestial navigation dome to fix their position. Unable to raise the table with one hand, Erwin tucked the canister between his right arm and his ribcage and fumbled with the latches as the phosphorus burned his flesh to the bone. The seared skin came off his hand onto the table as he lifted it. "You could see the imprint of his whole hand seared on the table," an officer said later.[17] "Kind of difficult, but the good Lord led me through that," Erwin said.[18]

Still on fire, he moved on past the now open table, past flight engineer Vern Schiller at his station, and into the smoke-filled cockpit where Simeral and Stables were struggling to keep the big bomber under control as it lost altitude. A third officer in the cockpit, squadron commander Col. Eugene Strouse, who had come along as an observer, had been catapulted into the nose section of the aircraft as it lurched downward. "Fortunately, we were on autopilot except for the elevators and that saved us," recalled Simeral. "But what I was fearful of was stalling out if I put any back pressure on the elevators."[19]

Stables suddenly saw a burning figure stumble toward him through the smoke, shouting, "Open the window! Open the window!" From the pilot's seat, Simeral shouted, "Get it out the window!"[20]

Stables unlatched his window and slid it back on its tracks. Erwin stumbled blindly toward the rush of cold air. Stables reached to help him, but Erwin managed to shove the phosphorus bomb out the window before collapsing on the deck. Simeral had already opened his own window in an unsuccessful effort to clear some of the smoke. "But after Red threw that bomb out the copilot's window . . . the smoke cleared out, and I could see the instruments and at that point we were at 300 feet," Simeral recalled. "If he hadn't gotten it out of there, well then, why, we probably would have gone on in."[21]

It had taken Erwin about fifteen seconds to negotiate the 13 feet from the radio compartment to Stables's window, but he admitted later that "it seemed like miles when you are burning."[22] Somehow, despite the excruciating pain, he managed to maintain a modicum of control. "I was burning alive," he recalled. "I couldn't see. I asked God to guide me."[23] Lying on the deck, he heard someone ask, "Red, are you all right?" Despite all evidence to the contrary, he replied, "I'm fine."[24]

Vern Schiller used a fire extinguisher to put out what was left of Erwin's burning clothing, but the phosphorus in his flesh continued to smolder. "My flight suit was gone," Erwin remembered. His injuries, horrific as they were, would have been even worse except for his Mae West life jacket. "That's the only thing that saved my chest," he said later. "Otherwise, I was burned all over."[25]

Colonel Strouse took one look at Erwin and ordered Simeral to abort the mission. "Open those bomb bay doors and drop those bombs right now," he directed. "We are going to head for Iwo Jima."[26] Climbing back up to altitude, they jettisoned their bomb load. Simeral radioed the alternate leader to take over the formation and turned *Snatch Blatch* toward Iwo Jima, which had the nearest medical facilities. Erwin was coughing and crying. "He was praying to God and to his mother," recalled gunner Herb Schnipper.[27]

Crew members tried to treat Erwin's injuries but were severely limited as Erwin himself was the crew's first-aid man. Loesch stuck him with a morphine syrette. Erwin was in terrible agony but managed to warn the bombardier, "Don't give me too much of that stuff, you'll kill me."[28] They smeared unguent on him to cut off the oxygen to the burning phosphorus embedded in his flesh. Loesch tried to inject plasma, but Erwin's arms were so badly burned he had trouble finding a vein. "We didn't discover until after, much later, that, after we landed and talked to people, you could do it through any vein . . . ankle, or someplace else," Simeral said.[29] Gunner Schnipper finally managed to get some plasma into Erwin that probably kept him from dying of shock.

Erwin lapsed into silence but never lost consciousness. "I was never unconscious," he said. "I was still alert; I couldn't see them. I could respond to their talking. . . . I was in pain and agony, and I was actually wishing to die. I was so badly burned.... It would have been a blessing if I had been unconscious."[30] Halfway back to Iwo, he spoke up again to ask, "Is everybody else all right?"[31] Crewmates saw that smoke was coming from his mouth.

He was still alive when *Snatch Blatch* touched down on Iwo over two hours later. "Fortunately, Iwo Jima was wide open, and we made a straight-in approach and parked on the runway until the medics got Red out of the aircraft," Simeral said. By then his body had become so rigid they had to ease him out through the engineer's window. Rushed to an underground hospital, he was still exhaling smoke. When medical personnel removed the unguent pads the crew had applied and exposed his flesh to the air, the phosphorus particles began to smolder again. "I remember going to this cave, and this doctor was working on my eyes [and saying], 'We've got to get this phosphorus out of his eyes. Otherwise, he's going to be blind,'" Erwin recalled.[32]

Doctors labored over him for hours, administering whole blood transfusions and antibiotics and picking flecks of white phosphorus from his eyes and body. As each fleck emerged into the open air, it would burst into flame. Erwin hung on through it all. He said later there was an angel by his side reassuring him, "Go, go, go. You can make it."[33]

No one else held out much hope for his survival. The rest of his crew took *Snatch Blatch* back to Guam where, still stunned, they told of Erwin's incredible act. That night officers in the unit prepared a recommendation for the Medal of Honor. At 5 the next morning, they awakened Twentieth Air Force commander Gen. Curtis LeMay at his headquarters on Guam and enlisted his assistance. LeMay immediately forwarded the recommendation to Washington, throwing his full weight behind it to expedite the award before Erwin succumbed. Approval came through in record time. Finding that the nearest Medal of Honor was locked up in a display case in Hawaii, LeMay dispatched a crew to retrieve it. When the emissaries could not locate a key to the case, they broke it open, snatched the medal, and rushed back to Guam.

On Iwo, Erwin continued to cling to life. Three days after his arrival he was airlifted to the Navy hospital on Guam, which had better facilities. There, one week after he was wounded, wrapped in bandages like a mummy with only slits for eyes that still could not see, he was presented the Medal of Honor as his crew looked on. LeMay did the honors, telling him, "Your effort to save the lives of your fellow airmen is the most extraordinary kind of heroism I know."

From behind the bandages, Erwin replied, "Thank you, sir."[34]

In addition to receiving what had to be the most rapidly approved Medal of Honor in history, Erwin would be the only Superfortress crewman to receive the decoration for action aboard a B-29. "They put the medal on my deathbed," he said. "They told me later that I was coming and going. But I knew the good Lord wouldn't let me die."[35]

Day after day, he hung on. "I was losing weight all the time," he said. "In fact, I got down to 87 pounds, skin and bones, because I couldn't open my mouth to eat. I didn't give up. . . . They kept me soaked in saline solution so what little flesh I had wouldn't come off." When General LeMay asked him if there was anything he wanted, Erwin asked for his brother Howard, who was serving with the 2nd Marine Division on nearby Saipan. Movie star Tyrone Power, a Marine Corps transport pilot, flew Howard over to Guam. "He stayed with me for twenty-four hours," said Erwin. "I couldn't see him but I knew he was there and that was a great comfort."[36]

Soon afterward, he was airlifted back to the United States. "They were scraping phosphorous out of my eyes," he said. "I was still smoldering thirty days later when I got to Sacramento."[37] Both his eyes were periodically sewn shut for over a year. His mouth was sewn shut for the skin grafts to replace his lips. Flaps of skin were used to reconstruct the ear that had burned off. His right arm was sewn to his abdomen for several months to grow new flesh on the damaged limb. Doctors wanted to amputate the arm, but Erwin begged them not to. Wife Betty stood by him through it all.

By late 1947, after forty-one surgeries, he was able to see from his left eye and could use one of his arms. The right hand was reconstructed but remained useless. "When I got out in October 1947, they still wanted to do more surgery, but at that time I had had it," he recalled. "I was married. I wanted to go home and go to work."[38] Given a choice, he would have stayed in the Army, he admitted—"I love the military," he said—but given the nature of his injuries, that was not an option.[39] "I knew that the TCI Company would never give me my job back at the plant due to the loss of my arm," he said. "I went to work for the Veterans Administration as a veterans' benefits counselor."[40] He subsequently served for thirty-seven years as a counselor at the veterans' hospital in Birmingham, Alabama. He and Betty raised a son and three daughters.

Their son, Hank Erwin, who went on to become a state senator, recalled his father as "a man of manners," always polite and courteous. He loved sports. Though he could not use his right arm, he directed a local Little League for several years, using his good arm to hit fly balls into the outfield. Despite his limited eyesight, he was also a "news junkie," poring over the newspaper every day. He was dedicated to his job. "He would get up at 4:30 in the morning to make the rounds with the doctors," recalled Hank. "He would visit every patient in every ward."[41]

In 1951, his story was briefly related in the movie *The Wild Blue Yonder*, in which he was portrayed by actor Dave Sharpe. The Air Force honored him in 1997 with creation of the Henry E. Erwin Outstanding Enlisted Aircrew Member of the Year Award. The award is presented annually to an airman, noncommissioned officer, or senior noncommissioned officer in the flight engineering, loadmaster, air surveillance, and related career fields. It is only the second Air Force award named for an enlisted person.

Erwin survived a stroke in his later years. He died at his home on January 16, 2002, and was buried at Elmwood Cemetery in Birmingham. He was eighty years old. "He got many awards, but he never looked for any special recognition," son Hank told a newspaper reporter shortly after Erwin's death. "If he knew you were writing this story, he would probably say something like, 'Why don't you find someone important to write about? I'm just a little guy.'"[42]

Appendix

JAPANESE PLANES

Betty: The Mitsubishi G4M3 Model 34 was a land-based, twin-engine Japanese Navy bomber. It carried a seven-man crew and was armed with four 7.7mm machine guns (two in the nose, two in the waist) and two 20mm cannon, one each in the dorsal and tail turrets. It could carry an aerial torpedo or a 2,000-pound bomb load and had a range of over 2,500 miles and a cruise speed of 195 mph. The most famous Japanese bomber of the war, it was dubbed the "Flying Lighter" by Allied pilots because it would burn like a torch when the unprotected fuel tanks were hit. It saw service throughout the war.

Claude: The Mitsubishi A5M was a single-seat carrier-based fighter, predecessor to the famous Mitsubishi A6M Zero. It was armed with two 7.7mm machine guns above the engine area. The first Japanese Navy monoplane, it first saw combat in China in 1937. Increasingly obsolescent after Pearl Harbor, most ended up in second-line or training functions.

Dinah: The Mitsubishi Ki-46 was a twin-engine Army reconnaissance aircraft. It carried a two-man crew and had a maximum speed of 370 mph, a service ceiling of just over 35,000 feet, and a range of over 1,500 miles. It was armed with a 7.7mm machine gun mounted in the rear cockpit. Popular among crews, the Dinah could fly high and fast, making it difficult for Allied pilots to intercept.

Emily: Called one of the "most outstanding water-based combat aircraft of the war," the Kawanishi H8K was a four-engine Navy flying boat used for patrol duties and long-range bombing attacks. Carrying a crew of ten, it had a nearly 125-foot wingspan, a length of just over 92 feet, and a ferry range of just over 4,400 statute miles. Heavily armed with five 20mm guns and five 7.7mm machine guns, it was sometimes called the "Flying Porcupine." It could carry two torpedoes or 4,400 pounds of bombs.

Frances: The Yokosuka P1Y Ginga ("Milky Way") was a Japanese Navy three-seat, twin-engine bomber. Entering service in 1944, the P1Y was intended to be comparable to the American B-25 Mitchell. It was highly maneuverable and could outrun many Allied fighters at low altitude. It was armed with four 7.7mm machine guns (two in the nose, two in the waist) and two 20mm cannon (one each in the dorsal and tail turrets) and could carry one torpedo or twenty 200-pound bombs. However, only eight of the fourteen fuel tanks were protected, and armor was limited to a single plate behind the pilot's head.

Frank: The Nakajima Ki-84 Hayate ("Storm") was a single-seat Army fighter/bomber considered by some to be the best Japanese fighter of World War II. Armed with two 20mm cannon in the nose and two in the wings, it could carry two externally mounted bombs. It had a maximum speed of 430 mph at 25,000 feet and was a match for any Allied fighter. The Hayate first appeared in service in April 1944, but the bulk of production occurred late in the war.

Hamp: *See* Zeke/Zero.

Helen: The Nakajima Ki-49 Donryu ("Storm Dragon") was a Japanese Army heavy bomber. With an eight-man crew, the Ki-49 was armed with two 7.7mm machine guns (one each to port and starboard), a 20mm cannon in a dorsal turret, and three 12.7mm machine guns (one each in the nose, ventral, and tail positions). It could carry 2,200 pounds of bombs but was underpowered and relatively easy prey for Allied fighters. By late 1944 most had transitioned into noncombat roles.

Irving: The Nakajima J1N1 was intended as a twin-engine, three-seat reconnaissance aircraft. However, after experimentation at Bougainville in 1943 with modifying Irvings as night fighters with upper oblique firing cannons, the J1N1-S Gekko ("Moonlight") night fighter was introduced with both upward and lower oblique firing cannons. The Gekko had a two-man crew, eliminating the previous navigator position.

Jack: The Mitsubishi J2M Raiden was a single-seat, land-based Navy interceptor introduced in early 1944. In a departure from convention, design requirements for the aircraft focused more on speed and climb than on maneuverability, specifying that it be able to climb to 19,685 feet in about five minutes and have a speed of 373 mph at that altitude. First versions featured two 20mm guns and two 7.7mm guns; later versions replaced the 7.7mm machine guns with two additional 20mms. Later models proved formidable against high-flying B-29s.

Jake: The Aichi E13A was a long-range single-engine reconnaissance seaplane. It served many roles, including air/sea rescue. With a three-man crew, the floatplane could handle a 550-pound bomb load and had a range of 1,298 statute miles. Armament consisted of one flexible, rearward-firing 7.7mm machine gun for the observer.

Jill: The B6N Tenzan ("Mountain of the Sky") replaced the Nakajima B5N2 Kate as the standard Navy carrier-based torpedo bomber in the latter part of the war. It had a three-man crew, was armed with three 7.7mm Type 97 machine guns (one rear firing, one in a ventral tunnel, and a third forward-firing gun in the left wing), and could carry a torpedo or up to 1,764 pounds of bombs.

Judy: The Yokosuka D4Y Suisei ("Comet") was a carrier-borne Navy dive bomber introduced to replace the obsolete Aichi D3A2 Val dive bomber. Crewed by a pilot and a backseat gunner, it was one of the fastest dive bombers of the war, superior to the U.S. Helldiver, but lacked armor and self-sealing fuel tanks, a vulnerability not addressed until later in the war. Armed with two 7.7mm machine guns in the nose and a flexible machine gun in the rear position, it typically carried one 1,100-pound bomb.

Kate: The Nakajima B5N2, a single-engine carrier-based torpedo bomber, was among the aircraft that attacked Pearl Harbor on December 7, 1941, where it proved spectacularly successful carrying the lethal Japanese Long Lance torpedo. Kates also participated in the sinking of U.S. carriers *Yorktown*, *Lexington*, *Wasp*, and *Hornet*. With a three-man crew, the Kate was armed with one rear 7.7mm machine gun and could carry one 1,764-pound torpedo or the same weight in bombs. Though it had a good bomb load and range, its slow cruise speed (161 mph), lack of armor or self-sealing fuel tanks, and sole rear gun for defense made it very vulnerable to fighters. It was largely removed from frontline service in 1944.

Lily: Introduced in 1940, the Kawasaki Ki-48-II Type 99 was a Japanese Army twin-engine light bomber. Slow and inadequately armed, it had a four-man crew and was armed with three 7.7mm machine guns, one each in the nose and the dorsal and ventral turrets. Attempts were made to upgrade later versions with more powerful engines, better weaponry, armor, and protected fuel tanks, but production was finally stopped in 1944.

Mavis: The Kawanishi H6K was a Japanese Navy flying boat used for maritime patrol duties. The four-engine craft had a wingspan of just over 131 feet, a length of just over 84 feet, and a range of nearly 3,000 statute miles; it could remain in the air for twenty-six hours. With a nine-man crew, the H6K was armed with 7.7mm machine guns in the nose, spine, and two waist blisters and a 20mm cannon in the tail turret. It could carry two torpedoes or 2,200 pounds of bombs. The transport version could accommodate eighteen passengers.

Nate: The highly maneuverable Nakajima Ki-27 was the Japanese Army's first low-wing monoplane fighter. The single-seat fighter was armed with two fixed forward-firing 7.7mm machine guns. Extensively used in China during the late 1930s, it saw service during the early part of the greater Pacific war before being relegated to homeland defense.

Nell: The Mitsubishi G3M Japanese Navy bomber was developed in the mid-1930s and remained in production until 1943. The twin-engine, long-range, land-based bomber had a seven-man crew. Its most famous action was the sinking of HMS *Prince of Wales* and *Repulse* on December 10, 1941. Armed with four 7.7mm machine guns (two in the waist, one in the dorsal, one in the cockpit), and one 20mm cannon in a dorsal turret, the Nell could carry a bomb load or a torpedo. It had a range of 3,871 statute miles and a cruise speed of 184 mph. By 1943, most were in second-line service.

Nick: The Kawasaki Ki-45 Toryu ("Dragonslayer") was a two-seat, twin-engine heavy fighter flown by the Japanese Army. Early types were armed with two 12.7mm machine guns in the nose, a single 20mm cannon in the belly, and a 7.7mm machine gun in the rear. Another version replaced the 20mm with a 37mm gun in an effort to counter B-17 Flying Fortress bombers.

Oscar: The Nakajima Ki-43 Hayabusa ("Peregrine Falcon") was an Army fighter routinely mistaken for the Zero by Allied pilots. Smaller, lighter, and cheaper to produce than the Zero, the Oscar could outmaneuver virtually any opponent. Armament varied but commonly featured two 12.7mm machine guns. Maximum speed was 336 mph. A favorite among Japanese Army aces, it was the most numerous of all Imperial Army warplanes. However, its light construction left it extremely vulnerable to enemy gunfire.

Pete: The Mitsubishi F1M floatplane was originally developed as an observation plane catapulted from surface vessels but ended up filling a variety of roles during the war, including patrol and rescue plane, defense fighter, convoy escort, and bomber. The last Japanese Navy biplane type, the F1M carried a pilot and observer/gunner and was armed with two fixed forward-firing 7.7mm machine guns and a 7.7mm machine gun for the rear-seat observer.

Rufe: The Nakajima A6M2-N was a single-seat floatplane virtually identical to the Mitsubishi A6M Zero except for the central and side floats. It had a maximum speed of 270 mph. Armed with two 7.7mm Type 97 machine guns in the forward fuselage and two 20mm guns in the wings, it could carry two 132-pound bombs.

Sally: The Mitsubishi Ki-21 was a Japanese Army twin-engine heavy bomber that first saw action in China in the late 1930s. Crewed by seven men, it was armed with five 7.7mm machine guns (one each in the nose, ventral, and tail positions and two in the waist) and a 12.7mm machine gun in a dorsal turret; it could carry a 2,205-pound bomb load. Like most Japanese bombers, it was lightly constructed and initially had no self-sealing fuel tanks, which made it easy prey for U.S. fighters. By 1944 it was essentially obsolete but remained in service due to lack of a suitable replacement.

Tojo: The Nakajima Ki-44 Shokie ("Devil-Queller") went into production in late 1940 for Army service. It was designed as an interceptor fighter with a higher rate of climb and overall speed (maximum 376 mph) than the Ki-43 Oscar. However, it was also much less maneuverable, which made it unpopular with many pilots. Armament consisted of two 12.7mm machine guns in the wings and two in the fuselage. Most Tojos were employed in defense of Japan later in the war.

Tony: The Kawasaki Ki-61 Hien ("Swallow") was the only fighter with a liquid-cooled engine fielded by the Japanese Army during the war. The Ki-61 went into combat around New Guinea in April 1943. Outwardly it somewhat resembled the U.S. P-51 Mustang. Well-armed with two 7.7mm machine guns in the nose and two 20mm guns in the wings, with protective armor and capable of high speed in dives, it was a good match for Allied fighters. Due to its sleek lines, it was initially mistaken by Allied pilots as a German Me 109 or Italian fighter. It had a top speed of 368 mph.

Val: The Aichi D3A single-engine, two-seat carrier bomber was among the aircraft that attacked Pearl Harbor at the beginning of the war. Crewed by a pilot and backseat gunner, it was armed with 7.7mm machine guns in the nose and a flexible 7.7mm in the rear position. It could carry a 551-pound bomb under the fuselage and two 132-pound bombs under the wings. Easily recognizable by its fixed landing gear, it was considered an excellent dive bomber in the early part of the war but eventually became obsolete and was replaced by the Aichi D4Y Suisei Judy.

Zeke/Zero: The fast, highly maneuverable Mitsubishi A6M2 Model 21 carrier-borne Zero was the preeminent fighter during the first year of the war. Though superior to Allied planes of the period, it sacrificed weight in the form of armor and self-sealing fuel tanks to increase speed and agility. The single-seat fighter carried two 7.7mm Type 92 machine guns in the nose and two 20mm cannons in the wings. The official Allied reporting name was Zeke, although the use of the name Zero was common. A clipped-wing variation with minor differences was called a Hamp. The second main version of the Zeke, the A6M3, came out in mid-1942 and had a more powerful engine. The A6M5 version appeared in 1943 with heavier armament and an attempt to provide more protection for the pilot and fuel tanks.

U.S. PLANES

A-20 Douglas Havoc was an Army twin-engine medium bomber/attack aircraft introduced in 1941. With a three-man crew (bombardier, pilot, and rear gunner), it was armed with six fixed forward-firing .50-caliber Browning machine guns in the nose, two .50-caliber machine guns in a dorsal turret, and a flexible .50-caliber machine gun mounted behind the bomb bay. It could carry 4,000 pounds of bombs. The A-20 was used in the Pacific primarily in low-level strikes against enemy airfields and supply dumps and in skip-bombing attacks on Japanese ships.

A-24 Banshee. *See* SBD Dauntless.

B-17 Flying Fortress was introduced in 1939 as a strategic heavy bomber. The four-engine bomber was just over 74 feet long, with a wingspan of just under 104 feet and a range of 2,000 statute miles. It carried a crew of ten (pilot, copilot, navigator, bombardier/nose gunner, flight engineer/top turret gunner, radio operator, two waist gunners, ball turret gunner, and tail gunner). The Fortress was armed with thirteen .50-caliber machine guns in nine positions and could carry 8,000 pounds of bombs. Though developed for high-altitude bombing, in the Pacific it was found more effective at lower altitudes, including in skip-bombing attacks on ships.

B-24 Liberator was a four-engine heavy bomber introduced in 1941. Most crews preferred the B-17 as the B-24 was less robust, had a lower ceiling, was difficult to fly, and performed poorly at low speeds. Its typical ten-man crew consisted of pilot, copilot, navigator, bombardier, radio operator, and gunners for nose turret, top turret, waist, ball turret, and tail. Later versions replaced the glassed "greenhouse" nose with a nose turret to combat head-on attacks and for strafing. It had a range of 1,540 statute miles and was armed with ten .50-caliber machine guns in four turrets and two waist positions. Its bomb load was comparable to the B-17's.

B-25 Mitchell was a twin-engine medium bomber named after Maj. Gen. William "Billy" Mitchell. The Mitchell proved most lethal in low-level attacks on enemy facilities and shipping. Squadrons adapted strafer versions by increasing the number of forward-firing guns. With a length of just under 53 feet and a wingspan of just under 68 feet, the B-25 carried a five-man crew (pilot, navigator/bombardier, turret gunner/engineer, radio operator/waist gunner, and tail gunner). The plane was armed with anywhere from twelve to eighteen .50-caliber machine guns and could carry 3,000 pounds of bombs.

B-26 Marauder was a fast twin-engine Army medium bomber that proved tricky to handle during takeoffs and landings, earning it an early reputation as a "widow maker." Its seven-man crew included pilot, copilot, bombardier/radio operator, navigator, and three gunners. First used in the Pacific theater in early 1942, it was armed with twelve .50-caliber Browning machine guns and could carry 3,000 pounds of bombs.

B-29 Boeing Superfortress was a four-engine, long-range heavy bomber introduced in May 1944 and intended for high-altitude strategic bombing. With a range of 3,250 statute miles, B-29s based in the Mariana Islands were well within striking distance of the Japanese home islands and soon began to lay waste to Japan's cities. A massive 99 feet long with a wingspan just over 141 feet, it had state-of-the-art features, including a pressurized cabin and an analog computer-controlled fire system with four remote machine-gun turrets. The eleven-man crew included pilot, copilot, bombardier, flight engineer, navigator, radio operator, radar observer, right gunner, left gunner, central fire controller, and tail gunner. It could carry 12,000 pounds of bombs 1,600 miles at medium altitude and just less than half that weight at high altitude.

F4F Grumman Wildcat was the frontline U.S. Navy carrier fighter at the beginning of the war, replacing the disappointing Brewster Buffalo. Though generally outperformed by the faster, nimbler Zero, the Wildcat, with its armor, self-sealing fuel tanks, and tougher airframe could survive more damage than the Zero. This toughness, plus adaptive tactics against the A6M Zero, allowed it to hold its own in aerial combat. Armament in the earlier model F4F-3s consisted of four .50-caliber wing-mounted machine guns. That number was increased to six in the later F4F-4.

F4U Vought Corsair was originally designed as a fast and powerful carrier-borne fighter, but difficulties with deck landings prompted the Navy to turn the planes over to the Marine Corps for land-based use when they first debuted. Armed with six .50-caliber wing-mounted machine guns, the big, tough, gull-winged fighter became a legend in the move up the Solomon Islands chain after Guadalcanal was secured in 1943. The problems with carrier landings were subsequently resolved, and the Corsair also saw wide service with the Navy, achieving an 11:1 kill ratio. Many Japanese pilots considered the Corsair the most formidable U.S. fighter of the war.

F6F Grumman Hellcat was a carrier-based fighter introduced in 1943 to replace the Wildcat. Powerful and rugged, armed with six .50-caliber wing-mounted machine guns, the Hellcat was more than a match for the once-feared Mitsubishi Zero. It became the dominant U.S. Navy fighter in the latter half of the war. Hellcats were credited with the destruction of 5,223 enemy aircraft between their combat debut in September 1943 and the end of the war.

P-38 Lightning was an Army twin-engine fighter with distinctive twin booms and a central nacelle containing the cockpit and armament. Its great range made it especially valuable in the Pacific theater with the long distances to targets. It was armed with four Browning .50-caliber machine guns and a 20mm cannon in the nose. While vulnerable at lower altitudes, it was faster than a Zero, and its firepower was devastating. This was the plane Ace of Aces Dick Bong flew while scoring his forty victories and in which second-ranking ace Tommy McGuire scored thirty-eight.

P-39 Airacobra was the principal U.S. fighter in service when the war began. In a departure from convention, the engine was located in the center fuselage behind the pilot. The plane's weaknesses included limited range and the lack of an efficient turbo-supercharger, which limited it to medium and lower altitudes. The P-39 was armed with a 37mm cannon and two .30-caliber machine guns on top of the nose and one .50-caliber machine gun in each wing, later increased to two .50s in the nose and two others in each wing. Though outclassed by Japanese fighters, it performed well in ground-support roles.

P-40 Curtiss Warhawk was the main U.S. Army fighter in the Southwest Pacific and Pacific Ocean theaters during 1941 and 1942; it was also the plane flown by the famed Flying Tigers in China prior to America's entry into the war. First flown in 1938, the single-seat Warhawk was intended as a pursuit aircraft but, like the P-39, suffered from a lack of power at higher altitudes and was at a disadvantage dogfighting with the nimble Zero. It was armed with six .50-caliber machine guns in the wings. Though it remained in service throughout the war, the P-40 was gradually replaced by the superior P-38 Lightning, the P-47 Thunderbolt, and the P-51 Mustang.

P-47 Thunderbolt, nicknamed the "Jug," was one of the heaviest fighters of the war. Fully loaded, it weighed up to eight tons and was armed with eight .50-caliber machine guns. Pilots learned to use the Jug's dive speed to their advantage in aerial combat, rocketing down on the enemy and using the momentum to pull back up to altitude before making another attack. The plane lacked the range of the P-38 Lightning but was effective as a short- to medium-range escort.

P-51 Mustang was a single-seat fighter introduced later in the war and commonly used for long-range bomber escort. Fast and maneuverable, it far surpassed most Japanese fighters. Armament consisted of six .50-caliber Browning machine guns. It had a maximum speed of 440 mph at 30,000 feet, a service ceiling of 41,900 feet, and a maximum range of 950 miles.

PBY-5 Catalina was a twin-engine maritime patrol bomber and search-and-rescue seaplane or "flying boat." Just over 63 feet long, with a wingspan of 104 feet, it carried a ten-man crew (pilot, copilot, bow turret gunner, flight engineer, radio operator, navigator, radar operator, two waist gunners, ventral gunner) and had a range of 2,500 miles and a cruise speed of 125 mph. Armament consisted of three .30-caliber machine guns (two in a nose turret and one in a ventral hatch at the tail) and two .50-caliber machine guns (one each in waist blisters). It could also carry 4,000 pounds of bombs or depth charges.

SB2U Vought Vindicator was a carrier-based dive bomber developed in the 1930s. The first monoplane in this U.S. Navy role, it was already obsolete by the outbreak of World War II. Sometimes referred to derisively as the "wind indicator," the SB2U was crewed by a pilot and a tail gunner.

It could carry a 1,000-pound bomb in the bomb bay and other bombs under the wings up to a maximum load of about 1,500 pounds. Armament included one wing-mounted forward-firing .30-caliber machine gun and a twin .30-caliber tail gun for the rear gunner. The rear part of the fuselage was canvas. Though in the process of being replaced by Dauntless dive bombers in 1942, Vindicators saw action at the Battle of Midway, where they suffered heavy losses.

SBD Dauntless was the U.S. Navy's main carrier-based scout/dive bomber from mid-1940 through mid-1944. Its armament consisted of two .50-caliber forward-firing machine guns in the engine cowling and a .30-caliber flexible-mounted machine gun for the rear gunner. Crewed by a pilot and rear gunner, the Dauntless could carry 2,250 pounds of bombs. An excellent dive bomber (crews translated "SBD" as "Slow but Deadly"), it was the plane that savaged Japanese carriers at Midway. An Army version, which omitted the tailhook for carrier landings, was designated the A-24 Banshee.

TBD Douglas Devastator was a Navy torpedo bomber that entered service in 1937. It carried a three-man crew (pilot, torpedo officer/navigator, and radioman/gunner). Designed to carry a bomb load or single torpedo, it was outdated by the outbreak of war. Slow, poorly armored, and forced to make long, gliding torpedo attacks, it was easy meat for Japanese fighters. During the Battle of Midway, 41 Devastators were launched. Only six made it back to their carriers. The plane was withdrawn from frontline service and replaced by the Avenger.

TBF Grumman Avenger was a Navy torpedo bomber introduced in 1942 that first saw action at Midway. Considered one of the outstanding torpedo bombers of World War II, it had a three-man crew (pilot, radioman, and turret gunner) and was armed with two .50-caliber wing-mounted machine guns, a dorsal-mounted .50-caliber machine gun, and a .30-caliber ventral-mounted machine gun. It could carry up to 2,000 pounds of bombs or one Mark 13 torpedo.

Notes

INTRODUCTION

1. John T. Correll, "The Air Force on the Eve of World War II," *Air Force Magazine,* October 2007.
2. Kent G. Budge, "Casualties," *Pacific War Online Encyclopedia,* http://www.pwencycl .kgbudge.com/C/a/Casualties.htm; Robert Sherrod, *History of Marine Corps Aviation in World War II* (Washington, DC: Combat Forces Press, 1952), 430; "US Navy Personnel in World War II Service and Casualty Statistics," Naval History and Heritage Command, https://www.history.Navy.mil/research/library.
3. *Army Air Forces Statistical Digest World War II* (Washington, DC: Office of Statistical Control, December 1945).

CHAPTER 1

1. John William Finn, interviewed by Carl Raymond Cox, September 21, 2004, John William Finn Collection (AFC/2001/001/21692), Veterans History Project, American Folklife Center, Library of Congress (henceforth Cox interview).
2. Ibid.
3. John William Finn, interviewed by Mike Russert and Wayne Clark, October 6, 2006, New York State Military Museum (henceforth Russert interview).
4. John William Finn, interviewed by Richard Erickson, John William Finn Collection (AFC/2001/001/19400), Veterans History Project, American Folklife Center, Library of Congress (henceforth Erickson interview).
5. Tyler Barker, "The Warrior of Kāneʻohe: Pearl Harbor's First Medal of Honor Recipient," *The Sextant,* Naval History and Heritage Command, December 6, 2016.
6. John William Finn, interviewer unknown, Medal of Honor Foundation. John William Finn Collection (AFC/2001/001/89678), Veterans History Project, American Folklife Center, Library of Congress (henceforth Finn interview).
7. Larry Smith, *Beyond Glory: Medal of Honor Heroes in Their Own Words* (New York: W. W. Norton & Company, 2003), 55.
8. Ibid., 56; Cox interview.
9. Finn interview.
10. Cox interview.
11. Finn interview.

12. "John Finn: Medal of Honor Recipient," *The Hoist* (newspaper of Naval Training Center, undated article).

13. VP-14 underwent three or four numerical designation changes prior to taking up station at Kaneohe before reverting once again to VP-14; to avoid confusion I have chosen to simply refer to the squadron throughout as VP-14.

14. War Diary, Patrol Squadron Fourteen, December 7, 1941–July 1942 (henceforth VP-14 War Diary).

15. Russert interview.

16. Ibid.

17. Erickson interview.

18. Smith, *Beyond Glory*, 61.

19. Russert interview.

20. Erickson interview.

21. Cox interview.

22. Russert interview.

23. Erickson interview.

24. Ibid.

25. Cox interview.

26. Erickson interview.

27. VP-14 War Diary.

28. Russert interview.

29. Smith, *Beyond Glory*, 62.

30. Erickson interview.

31. Ibid.

32. Smith, *Beyond Glory*, 65.

33. Erickson interview.

34. Ibid.

35. Smith, *Beyond Glory*, 62.

36. Erickson interview.

37. Report of Japanese Raid on Pearl Harbor, 7 December 1941, Commander-in-Chief US Pacific Fleet.

38. VP-14 War Diary.

39. J. Michael Enger, Robert J. Cressman, and John F. Di Virgilio, *No One Avoided Danger* (Annapolis: Naval Institute Press, 2015), 127–28.

40. Russert interview.

41. Cox interview.

42. Erickson interview.

43. Ibid.

44. Smith, *Beyond Glory*, 69.

45. Gregg K. Kakesako, "Dec. 7 Hero at Kaneohe Is Honored," *Honolulu Star-Bulletin*, June 30, 1999.

46. Mary Katherine Ham, "Lt. John William Finn: Pearl Harbor's Last Hero, 68 Years Later," *WWII Magazine*, December 7, 2009.

47. Robert A. Cressman, *A Magnificent Fight: Marines in the Battle for Wake Island.* Marines in World War II Commemorative Series (Washington, DC: Marine Corps Historical Center, 1992), 3.

48. William L. Ramsey and Henry Elrod Ramsey, *Elrod's Wake* (unpublished draft manuscript, 2005).

49. Ibid.

50. Ibid.

51. Ibid.

52. Ibid.

53. Ibid.

54. John F. Kinney, *Wake Island Pilot: A World War II Memoir* (Washington, DC: Brassey's, 1995), 33.

55. Bill Sloan, *Given Up for Dead: America's Heroic Stand at Wake Island* (New York: Bantam Books, 2003), 56.

56. Kinney, 48.

57. Ibid., 49.

58. Walter Baylor and Cecil Carnes, *Last Man off Wake Island* (New York: Bobbs-Merrill Company, 1943), 71.

59. Cressman, 66.

60. Saul Braun, *Seven Heroes: Medal of Honor Stories of the War in the Pacific* (New York: G. P. Putnam's Sons, 1965), 11.

61. Gregory J. W. Urwin, *Facing Fearful Odds: The Siege of Wake Island* (Lincoln: University of Nebraska Press, 1997), 247.

62. Ramsey and Ramsey, unpaged.

63. Cressman, 107; Urwin, 300.

64. Urwin, 393.

65. If that is the case, Elrod stands as the first U.S. pilot of the war to sink a warship with small bombs.

66. Baylor and Carnes, 96.

67. Elrod's exact words vary, according to the teller; Baylor and Carnes, 96; Urwin, 333; John Wukovits, *Pacific Alamo: The Battle for Wake Island* (New York: New American Library, 2003), 82 (henceforth *Pacific Alamo*).

68. *Pacific Alamo*, 94.

69. Cressman, 170–71; *Pacific Alamo*, 129.

70. Urwin, 393–94.

71. Ibid., 406.

72. Ibid., 439.

73. Ibid., 489.

74. *Pacific Alamo*, 171.

75. James P. S. Devereaux, *The Story of Wake Island* (New York: J. B. Lippincott, 1947), 182.

76. Ramsey and Ramsey, unpaged.

77. Ibid.

78. Following the fall of Wake, Elizabeth Elrod joined the Marine Corps Women's Reserve, eventually rising to the rank of captain. She later remarried but remained close to Elrod's nephews until her death in 1988.

79. Another was Jimmy Doolittle.

80. Steve Ewing and John B. Lundstrom, *Fateful Rendezvous: The Life of Butch O'Hare* (Annapolis: Naval Institute Press, 1997), 19.

81. Ibid., 89.

82. Ibid., 71–72.

83. Adm. John Smith Thach, USN (Ret.), interview #2, by Cmdr. Etta-Belle Kitchen, USN (Ret.), August 8, 1970, US Naval Institute, Coronado, California.

84. Bruce Gamble, *Fortress Rabaul: The Battle for the Southwest Pacific, January 1942–April 1943* (Minneapolis: Zenith Press, 2013), 74 (henceforth *Fortress Rabaul*).

85. *Fortress Rabaul*, 77; John S. Thach, "The Red Rain of Battle: The Story of Fighter Squadron 3," *Collier's Magazine*, December 5, 1943.

86. Adm. John S. Thach, "Butch O'Hare and the Thach Weave," *Naval History Magazine*, Spring 1992.

87. *Fortress Rabaul*, 80.

88. Ewing and Lundstrom, 128.

89. *Fortress Rabaul*, 87; Thach, "Red Rain of Battle."

90. Ewing and Lundstrom, 130.

91. Ibid., 130.

92. *Fortress Rabaul*, 88.

93. Ewing and Lundstrom, 131.

94. Ibid., 135.

95. Ibid., 137.

96. Ibid., 140.

97. Ibid., 140–41.

98. Ibid., 162.

99. Ibid., 175.

100. Ibid., 174.

101. Ibid., 175.

102. Ibid., 235.

103. Ibid., 267.

104. Alvin Kernan, *Crossing the Line: A Bluejacket's World War II Odyssey* (Annapolis: Naval Institute Press, 1994), 112.

105. Ibid.

106. Ewing and Lundstrom, 276.

107. Ibid., 278; Kernan's memoir differs somewhat in details.

108. Kernan, 113–14.

109. Matt Schudel, "Warren A. Skon, Navy Ace Pilot in WWII, and Wife Hazel Skon, Both 92, Die Days Apart," *Washington Post*, February 25, 2012.

110. Ewing and Lundstrom, 279.

111. Schudel.

112. Ewing and Lundstrom, 282.

113. Ibid., 288.
114. Rita O'Hare married one of Butch's Annapolis classmates in 1945. John Phillips was shot down and killed on February 16, 1944, in the vicinity of Truk Atoll.

CHAPTER 2

1. Carroll V. Glines, *The Doolittle Raid: America's Daring First Strike against Japan* (Atglen, PA: Schiffer Publishing, 1991), 30.
2. Craig Nelson, *The First Heroes: The Extraordinary Story of the Doolittle Raid—America's First World War II Victory* (New York: Penguin Books, 2002), 33.
3. James M. Scott, *Target Tokyo: Jimmy Doolittle and the Raid That Avenged Pearl Harbor* (New York: W. W. Norton & Company, 2015), 88.
4. Gen. James H. "Jimmy" Doolittle, *I Could Never Be So Lucky Again* (New York: Bantam Books, 1992), 46.
5. Doolittle, 44.
6. Nelson, 43.
7. Scott, 44–45.
8. Doolittle, 176–77.
9. Scott, 56.
10. Doolittle, 212; Scott, 57.
11. Scott, 58.
12. Ibid., 62.
13. Ibid., 58.
14. Ibid., 71.
15. Ibid., 72.
16. Nelson, 19.
17. Scott, 96–97.
18. Doolittle, 230; Scott, 97.
19. Doolittle, 230; Scott, 99.
20. Scott, 108.
21. Doolittle, 242.
22. Doolittle, 243; Scott, 129.
23. Scott, 129.
24. Nelson, 61.
25. Doolittle, 246; Scott, 147–48.
26. Nelson, 69.
27. Scott, 149.
28. Doolittle, 250; Scott, 148–49.
29. War Diary, Task Force Sixteen, US Pacific Fleet, April 1–30, 1942; Scott, 163.
30. Scott, 173.
31. Ibid., 176; Doolittle, 254.
32. Nelson, 121.
33. Scott, 179.
34. Nelson, 121–22.
35. Ibid., 126.

36. *Hornet*'s log indicates first plane left ship at 8:15 a.m.

37. Nelson, 135.

38. Doolittle, 7.

39. Scott, 196.

40. Ibid., 197.

41. Doolittle, 8.

42. Scott, 245.

43. Doolittle, 9.

44. Ibid.; Scott, 246.

45. Doolittle, 10.

46. Ibid.

47. Ibid.

48. Ibid., 12.

49. Ibid., 265.

50. Albin Krebs, "James Doolittle, 96, Pioneer Aviator Who Led First Raid on Japan, Dies," *New York Times*, September 28, 1993.

51. Scott, 479.

CHAPTER 3

1. *Lucky Bag, 1935* (Annapolis: US Naval Academy, 1935), 110.

2. Edward F. Murphy, *Heroes of World War II* (Novato, CA: Presidio Press, 1990), 45.

3. Stuart D. Ludlum, *They Turned the War Around at Coral Sea and Midway: Going to War with Yorktown's Air Group Five* (Bennington, VT: Merriam Press, 1991), 42.

4. Ibid., 44.

5. Ibid., 63.

6. Stephen L. Moore, *The Battle for Hell's Island* (New York: New American Library, 2015), 112.

7. John B. Lundstrom, *The First Team: Pacific Air Naval Combat from Pearl Harbor to Midway* (Annapolis: Naval Institute Press, 1984), 259.

8. Ludlum, 131.

9. Ibid., 133; Talbert Josselyn, "Courage . . . beyond Duty," *Atlanta Constitution*, November 15, 1942.

10. Lynn Forshee, *Standby, Mark!*, msmeck.com, https://msmeck.com/standby-mark-by-lynn-forshee/chapter-12.

11. Ludlum, 135.

12. Ibid., 292.

13. Ibid., 135.

14. Moore, 132.

15. Ludlum, 137.

16. Ibid.

17. Stanley Johnston, *Queen of the Flat-Tops* (New York: E. P. Dutton & Co., 1942), 174.

18. "Oakland Boy Missing with Navy Medal of Honor Pilot," *Oakland [California] Tribune*, September 9, 1942.

19. "Not Doing Enough toward Winning War Roosevelt Tells Nation," *Des Moines [Iowa] Register*, September 8, 1942.

20. Edward Illon and Howard Whitman, "Mother Sobs As F.D.R. Lauds Son," *New York Daily News*, September 8, 1942.

21. "Navy Hero's Mother Gets Medal of Honor," *Daily [New York] News*, September 18, 1943. As far as I can determine, Everett Clyde Hill received no decoration for his part in the attack on *Shōkaku*. He left his mother and father, owner of a printing company, and two older brothers, Stanford, twenty-five, a lieutenant in the U.S. Army, and Milton, twenty-seven, a draftsman at an aircraft plant in Seattle.

22. "Combat Bravery Brings Citations for Six Utahns in U.S. Service," *Salt Lake City Telegram*, October 24, 1942.

23. Ibid.

24. "Top Utah Hero Home, Asks, 'Why the Fuss?,'" *Salt Lake City Tribune*, October 4, 1945.

25. http://www.navalaviationmuseum.org/history-up-close/william-hall-hero-coral-sea.

26. "Wounded Flier Tells of Coral Sea Battle," *Salt Lake City Tribune*, July 6, 1942.

27. Ibid.

28. Moore, 146.

29. "Wounded Flyer Tells."

30. Moore, 151.

31. "Wounded Flyer Tells."

32. Ibid.; Moore, 151.

33. Moore, 152.

34. Ibid., 153–54.

35. Ibid., 154.

36. Ibid.

37. "Wounded Flyer Tells"; Moore, 154.

38. Moore, 158.

39. Ibid., 159.

40. "Wounded Flyer Tells."

41. John B. Lundstrom and James C. Sawruk, "Courage and Devotion to Duty: The SBD Anti-torpedo Plane Patrol in the Coral Sea, 8 May 1942," *The Hook: Journal of Carrier Aviation*, Winter 1988.

42. "Wounded Flyer Tells."

43. Moore, 177–78.

44. "Top Utah Hero Home, Asks."

45. Ibid.

46. Ken Hornby, "Capt. Richard E. Fleming USMCR and the Battle of Midway," Battle of Midway Roundtable, June 2016, Hornby6.nwww.midway42.org/Backissues/2016/20160601.aspx.

47. Rolfe Boswell, *Medals for Marines* (New York: Thomas Y. Crowell Company, 1945).

48. Ibid., 40–41.

49. Ibid., 42.

50. Hill Goodspeed, "Always Faithful," *Naval Aviation News*, May/June 2003.

51. Ibid.

52. Capt. Sumner H. Whitten, letter, Naval Aviation Museum, https://www.navalaviationmuseum.org/history-up-close/from-the-cockpit-stories-of-naval-aviation/memories-midway.

53. David Hawley, "Memories of a Hero: The Dakota County Historical Society Honors Richard Fleming, a WWII Pilot Credited with the Sinking of a Japanese Warship," *St. Paul [Minnesota] Pioneer Press*, December 2, 1996.

54. Jim Klobuchar, "Foundation Will Honor Her War-Hero Sweetheart," *Star Tribune* (Minneapolis, MN), August 22, 1995.

55. Hawley.

56. Hornby.

57. Barrett Tillman, *U.S. Marine Corps Fighter Squadrons of World War II* (New York: Osprey Publishing, 2014), 11.

58. War Diary, Marine Scout-Bombing Squadron Two Forty-One, Marine Aircraft Group Twenty-Two, Second Marine Aircraft Wing, FMF, June 1–30, 1942.

59. Walter Lord, *Incredible Victory: The Battle of Midway* (New York: Harper & Row, 1967), 120.

60. Ibid., 121.

61. Ibid.

62. Frank Tremaine, "Midway Hero Killed Making Sure of Direct Hit on Carrier," *Eugene [Oregon] Guard*, June 25, 1942.

63. War Diary, Marine Scout-Bombing Squadron Two Forty-One.

64. Lord, 122.

65. "Salem Youth with the Navy Tells of Exciting Action near Midway Island," *Daily Herald* (Provo, UT), July 8, 1942.

66. *Hiryū*'s respite was brief; she was mortally wounded by a U.S. carrier aircraft later in the day and was deliberately torpedoed by the Japanese the following morning.

67. Goodspeed.

68. "Salem Youth with Navy Tells."

69. Hornby.

70. Samuel Eliot Morison, *History of United States Naval Operations in World War II*, vol. 4: *Coral Sea, Midway and Submarine Actions, May 1942–August 1942* (Boston: Little, Brown and Company, 1958), 110; Hornby.

71. War Diary, Marine Scout-Bombing Squadron Two Forty-One.

72. Tremaine.

73. United States Strategic Bombing Survey, Interrogation No. 83, 1946.

74. Hawley; a photograph of wreckage atop *Mikuma*'s aft turret has been cited as evidence of the crash, but that claim has been largely disproven. There is also no good evidence to support another claim: that flames from the crash were sucked into the *Mikuma*'s air intake, igniting gas fumes in the starboard engine room and incinerating the crewmen there.

75. Whitten.

76. Klobuchar.

77. Peggy Crooks loaned this letter and other items in 1996 for an exhibit mounted by the Dakota County Historical Society in Saint Paul.

78. Gene Eric Salecker, *Fortress against the Sun: The B-17 Flying Fortress in the Pacific* (Conshohocken, PA: Combined Publishing, 2001), 153–55.

79. Roland Bixby, *And Some Gave All The Story of Plymouth N.H.'s Congressional Medal of Honor Winner, Captain Harl Pease, Jr.* (Hooksett, NH: Granite State Copy, 2007), 84.

80. John H. Mitchell, *In Alis Vicimus: On Wings We Conquer: The 19th and 7th Bomb Groups of the United States Air Force in the Southwest Pacific in the First Year of World War Two* (Springfield, MO: G. E. M. Publishers, 1990), 73.

81. Bixby, 212.

82. Ibid.

83. Mitchell, 130.

84. Bruce Gamble, *Fortress Rabaul: The Battle for the Southwest Pacific, January 1942– April 1943* (Minneapolis: Zenith Press, 2013), 216 (henceforth *Fortress Rabaul*); Salecker, 226.

85. Mitchell, 130.

86. Salecker, 227.

87. Ibid.

88. See the account of Edward M. Jacquet at "B-17E 'Why Don't We Do This More Often' Serial Number 41-2429," Pacific Wrecks, https://www.pacificwrecks.com/aircraft/b-17/41-2429.html.

89. Mitchell, 130; *Fortress Rabaul*, 221.

90. Mitchell, 125, 130.

91. Gen. George C. Kenney, *General Kenney Reports: A Personal History of the Pacific War* (New York: Duell, Sloan and Pearce, 1949), 59 (henceforth *General Kenney Reports*).

92. "Determination of Status of an Airplane Missing in Action in the Southwest Pacific Area since 7 August 1942," August 18, 1943; Mitchell, 133.

93. Mitchell, 135.

94. Ibid., 136.

95. Ibid.

96. Ibid., 137.

97. Testimony of Minoru Yoshimura, B5563, 2249, item 5428717, National Archives of Australia; *Fortress Rabaul*, 232.

98. Staff Sgt. Ginger Dempsey, "Keeper of a Legacy," *New Hampshire National Guard Magazine*, Fall 2009.

CHAPTER 4

1. Louise Smith obituary, *Daily Progress* (Charlottesville, VA), April 13, 2007.

2. Richard Tregaskis, *Guadalcanal Diary* (Garden City, NY: Blue Ribbon Books, 1943), 167.

3. Maj. Gen. Marion B. Carl and Barrett Tillman, *Pushing the Envelope: The Career of Fighter Ace and Test Pilot Marion Carl* (Annapolis: Naval Institute Press, 1994), 27.

4. Joseph Foss, interviewed by Jon Seal and Michael Ahn, March 2000, WW2aircraft.net, December 9, 2004, https://ww2aircraft.net/forum/threads/

joe-foss-interview-the-man-the-legend.511 (henceforth Seal and Ahn interview); Joe
Foss, with Donna Wild Foss, *A Proud American: The Autobiography of Joe Foss* (New York:
Pocket Star Books, 1992), 79, 109 (henceforth *Proud American*).

5. Carl and Tillman, 27, 92.

6. Richard Wilcox, "Captain Smith and His Fighting 223," *LIFE Magazine*, December 7, 1942.

7. Rolfe Boswell, *Medals for Marines* (New York: Thomas Y. Crowell Company, 1945), 72.

8. Peter B. Mersky, *Time of the Aces: Marine Pilots in the Solomons, 1942–1944.* Marines
in World War II Commemorative Series (Washington, DC: History and Museums
Division, Headquarters, US Marine Corps, 1993), 2; War Diary, Marine Fighting
Squadron 223, Marine Aircraft Group 23, August 1–31, 1942 (henceforth War Diary
VMF-223).

9. Max Brand, *Fighter Squadron at Guadalcanal* (Annapolis: Naval Institute Press,
1996), 76.

10. War Diary VMF-223.

11. Edward H. Sims, *Greatest Fighter Missions of the Top Navy and Marine Aces of World
War II* (New York: Ballantine Books, 1962), 22.

12. Boswell, 77.

13. Ibid.

14. Ibid.; "Chicago Cheers Oklahoma's Ace, Smith, Companion Heroes," *Daily Oklahoman*, December 6, 1942.

15. Boswell, 77.

16. Sims, 26.

17. Tom Yarbrough, "Jap Bomber Squadron Routed by Yank," *Daily Oklahoman*, October 31, 1942.

18. Boswell, 79.

19. "Five Japs Just About Balance an American's Fighting Power," *Daily Oklahoman*,
October 31, 1942.

20. War Diary VMF-223.

21. Mersky, 11.

22. Japanese records indicate that this plane was not shot down.

23. Thomas G. Miller Jr., *The Cactus Air Force* (New York: Bantam Books, 1981), 108.

24. Wilcox.

25. Report of Action of Marine Aircraft Group 23 for the Period of 31 August to 15
September 1942.

26. "Major John L. Smith Isn't Interested in Exploits of Major John L. Smith," *Valley
Morning Star* (Harlingen, TX), November 4, 1942.

27. Medal of Honor citation, John L. Smith.

28. "Wife Sent Love in Wartime Mail," *Daily Oklahoman*, April 18, 1999.

29. Edward F. Murphy, *Heroes of World War II* (Novato, CA: Presidio Press, 1990),, 59.

30. Carl and Tillman, 92.

31. "Jobless War Hero Dies by Own Hand," *Van Nuys [California] News*, June 16, 1972.

32. Charles T. Jones, "Oklahoma Monument Dedicated to John L. Smith," *Plain Dealer* (Cleveland, OH), December 2, 1998.

33. Boswell, 85–87.

34. Ibid., 88.

35. Brendan Gill, "A Reporter at Large: Where They Wanted to Be," *New Yorker*, March 13, 1943.

36. Tim Frank, "Medal of Honor Series," *Naval Aviation News*, July/August 1998.

37. Robert E. Galer, interviewed by Ronald E. Marcello, August 27, 1998, University of North Texas Oral History Collection, Number 1265 (henceforth Marcello interview).

38. J. Michael Parker, "Nimitz Ace Flier in Pacific War to Be Part of 1942 Symposium," *San Antonio Express-News*, March 26, 1992.

39. Robert E. Galer, interviewed by Bill Alexander, March 14, 1998, Admiral Nimitz Museum and University of North Texas Oral History Collection (henceforth Alexander interview); Marcello interview; Mary Ann Bodine, "Military Business Not Connected with Hero's Visit Here," *Hutchinson [Kansas] News*, April 5, 1943.

40. "Shot Down Three Times, Pilot Gets 13 Jap Planes," *Akron Beacon Journal*, January 17, 1943; Robert E. Galer, interviewed by Dr. Dave Thompson, February 12, 2004, Palm Springs Air Museum, California (henceforth Thompson interview). This was not the first time Galer lost an aircraft. As a first lieutenant with VMF-2 in 1940, he had to ride his Grumman F3F biplane fighter in while approaching the carrier *Saratoga* (CV-3). The Grumman sank and stayed on the bottom off San Diego for forty years. It was discovered by a Navy exploration team and raised, somewhat the worse for wear. Retired Brig. Gen. Galer was at the dock when his old mount found dry land once more.

41. Mersky, 6; Report of Action of Marine Aircraft Group 23.

42. Gill.

43. Seal and Ahn interview.

44. Thompson interview.

45. Mersky, 12.

46. Ibid.

47. Ibid.

48. Kendall Anderson, "A Hero's Welcome," *Dallas Morning News*, March 25, 2000.

49. Gill; Bodine; "Shot Down Three Times"; Walter Baylor and Cecil Carnes, *Last Man off Wake Island* (New York: Bobbs-Merrill Company, 1943), 326.

50. Boswell, 84.

51. Parker.

52. Alexander interview.

53. Thompson interview.

54. Alexander interview; Anderson.

55. "Shot Down Three Times."

56. Alexander interview; Marcello interview; Frank.

57. Alexander interview.

58. Adam Bernstein, "Brig. Gen. Robert E. Galer Dies; Highly Decorated Pilot in 2 Wars," *Washington Post*, July 1, 2005.

59. Robert E. Galer, interviewed by Larry Arnold, October 8, 2002, Robert Edward Galer Collection (AFC/2001/001/12798), Veterans History Project, American Folklife Center, Library of Congress; "Honor Medal Winner Experiences Miracle Escape in Korean War Crash," *Arizona Republic*, August 21, 1952.

60. Bernstein.

61. Alexander interview.

62. Peter C. Lemon, *Beyond the Medal: A Journey from Their Hearts to Yours* (Golden, CO: Fulcrum Publishing, 1997), 55.

63. Brand, 46.

64. Kent Brown, "Lt. Col. Harold William 'Indian Joe' Bauer," World War Two and Aviation History, http://www.acepilots.com/bauer/usmc_bauer1.html; Kent Brown, a nephew of Bauer, has compiled a wealth of information on his uncle, including letters and Bauer's diary; G. D. Provenza, "The Life and Legend of 'Indian Joe' Bauer," *Leatherneck*, November 1992.

65. Brown.

66. Ibid.; 1930 United States Federal Census.

67. Brand, 44.

68. Brown.

69. Boswell, 137; Brand, 38.

70. Brand, 38, 111.

71. Joseph N. Renner, "Interview of Major J. N. Renner, USMC," Bureau of Aeronautics, July 17, 1943 (henceforth Renner interview).

72. Eric Hammel, *Aces against Japan* (Novato, CA: Presidio, 1992), 99 (henceforth *Aces against Japan*).

73. Brand, 44.

74. Ibid., 46.

75. Ibid., 98.

76. Brown.

77. Brand, 98.

78. Brown.

79. Ibid.

80. Brown; Brand, 102.

81. Brown; Brand, 102–4.

82. Renner interview.

83. Brand, 128.

84. Ibid., 104; Provenza.

85. *Proud American*, 149.

86. Carl and Tillman, 19.

87. Brand, 148.

88. Seal and Ahn interview.

89. Ibid.

90. Ibid.; Brown.

91. Seal and Ahn interview.

92. Brown.

93. Ibid.
94. Ibid.
95. James P. Lucier, "At Home and in Combat, Foss Led by Example," *Insight on the News*, January 8, 2001.
96. *Proud American*, 33.
97. Ibid., 45.
98. Ibid., 51.
99. Ibid.
100. Ibid., 87.
101. Ibid., 95–96.
102. Ibid., 113–16.
103. Ibid., 120.
104. Gill.
105. *Proud American*, 95.
106. Ibid., 122.
107. Ibid., 129–30.
108. Ibid., 130–31.
109. Ibid., 131.
110. Ibid., 132.
111. Ibid., 134.
112. Ibid., 137.
113. Ibid., 145.
114. Ibid., 164, 205.
115. Baylor and Carnes, 304.
116. *Proud American*, 157.
117. Ibid., 162.
118. Ibid., 163.
119. Ibid.
120. Ibid., 167–69.
121. Ibid., 169.
122. Capt. Garrett Graham, "Our Number One Ace Comes Home," *Saturday Evening Post*, April 3, 1943.
123. *Proud American*, 383.
124. Ibid., 280.
125. Ibid., 244.

CHAPTER 5

1. Martha Byrd, *Kenneth N. Walker: Airpower's Untempered Crusader* (Maxwell Air Force Base, AL: Air University Press, 1997), xi.
2. Byrd, 36.
3. Ibid., 30, xxvii.
4. Ibid., 30–31.
5. Ibid., 73.

6. Gen. George C. Kenney, *General Kenney Reports: A Personal History of the Pacific War* (New York: Duell, Sloan and Pearce, 1949), 143 (henceforth *General Kenney Reports*).

7. Byrd, 88.

8. Silver Star citation, Headquarters, Allied Air Forces, Southwest Pacific Area, General Orders No. 39, August 20, 1942.

9. Bernhardt Mortenson, "Personal Account of Bomber Command Station Life (A Story about Fifth Bomber Command)," Australia@War, https://www.ozatwar.com/ozatwar/morternson.htm.

10. "General Walker Aims at Flying with His Boys," Associated Press, September 21, 1945.

11. Ibid.

12. Byrd, 97–98.

13. *General Kenney Reports*, 143.

14. Ibid., 167.

15. Ibid.

16. Ibid., 175–76.

17. Ibid.

18. Ibid., 176.

19. Byrd, 113.

20. Lawrence Hickey, *Ken's Men against the Empire: The Illustrated History of the 43rd Bombardment Group, January 1941–October 1943* (Boulder, CO: International Historical Research Associates, 2020), 106.

21. Frederick Wesche III, interviewed by Shaun Illingworth and Kathryn Tracy, Rutgers Oral History Archives of World War II, Rutgers University, May 10, 2001 (henceforth Wesche interview).

22. US Strategic Bombing Survey (Pacific), *The Allied Campaign against Rabaul* (Washington, DC: Naval Analysis Division, Marshalls–Gilberts–New Britain Party, September 1, 1946).

23. Wesche interview.

24. Byrd, 112–13.

25. Ibid., 114.

26. Richard L. Dunn, "The Search for General Walker: New Insights," *Air Power History*, Fall 2014.

27. Byrd, 114.

28. Dunn, "The Search for General Walker."

29. Wesche interview.

30. Byrd, 114.

31. Missing Air Crew Report B-17F, 41-24458, 43rd Bomb Group (H), 64th Bomb (H) Squadron, Rabaul, Jan. 5, 1943.

32. Dunn, "The Search for General Walker."

33. Byrd, 115.

34. *General Kenney Reports*, 176.

35. Hickey, 108–9.

36. Ibid., 177.

37. Walker's mother had died in 1938.

38. Dunn, "The Search for General Walker"; Byrd, 129; Hickey, 109.

39. Byrd, 129.

40. Ibid., 125.

41. Ibid., 121.

42. Medal of Honor citation, War Department, General Orders No. 13, March 11, 1943.

43. *General Kenney Reports*, 216–17.

44. Wesche interview.

45. Peter C. Lemon, *Beyond the Medal: A Journey from Their Hearts to Yours* (Golden, CO: Fulcrum Publishing, 1997), 161.

46. Jefferson J. DeBlanc, interviewer unknown, Jefferson J. DeBlanc Collection (AFC/2001/001/89660), Veterans History Project, American Folklife Center, Library of Congress (henceforth DeBlanc interview).

47. Jefferson J. DeBlanc, *The Guadalcanal Air War: Colonel Jefferson DeBlanc's Story* (Gretna, LA: Pelican Publishing Company, 2008), 35.

48. Ibid.

49. Robert Buckman, "Medal of Honor Winner Recalls South Pacific Saga," *New Orleans Times-Picayune*, January 31, 1993; DeBlanc interview.

50. DeBlanc, 61.

51. Ibid., 62.

52. Ibid., 67.

53. DeBlanc, 83; Eric Hammel, *Aces against Japan* (Novato, CA: Presidio, 1992), 94 (henceforth *Aces against Japan*).

54. DeBlanc, 84–85; *Aces against Japan*, 95.

55. DeBlanc interview.

56. Bruce Schultz, "A Hero Comes Full Circle," *The Advocate* (Baton Rouge, LA), July 8, 2000.

57. *Aces against Japan*, 96.

58. DeBlanc, 85–86; *Aces against Japan*, 96.

59. Buckman.

60. DeBlanc, 86–87; *Aces against Japan*, 97.

61. DeBlanc, 87; *Aces against Japan*, 97.

62. DeBlanc, 89; *Aces against Japan*, 99.

63. Buckman; Schultz, "A Hero Comes Full Circle."

64. DeBlanc interview.

65. DeBlanc, 91–93; *Aces against Japan*, 101–2.

66. Buckman; DeBlanc, 93–94; *Aces against Japan*, 102.

67. Schultz, "A Hero Comes Full Circle"; DeBlanc, 100–101; DeBlanc interview.

68. Schultz, "A Hero Comes Full Circle."

69. Buckman; Schultz, "A Hero Comes Full Circle"; DeBlanc, 102.

70. Buckman.

71. DeBlanc interview.

72. Joe Gyan Jr., "Parade Greets Museum Wing," *The Advocate* (Baton Rouge, LA), November 18, 2002.

73. Clint Hayes, *Zeamer's Eager Beavers: The Incredible True Story*, Zeamer's Eager Beavers, http://zeamerseagerbeavers.com/download-zeamers-eager-beavers-the-story (henceforth *Eager Beavers*).

74. Bob Drury and Tom Clavin, *Lucky 666: The Impossible Mission That Changed the War in the Pacific* (New York: Simon & Schuster, 2016), 16.

75. *Eager Beavers*.

76. Ibid.

77. Drury and Clavin, 178.

78. Ibid., 154.

79. Ibid., 153.

80. Eric M. Bergerud, *Fire in the Sky: The Air War in the South Pacific* (Boulder, CO: Westview Press, 2000), 551.

81. Ibid., 551.

82. Ibid.

83. Drury and Clavin, 194.

84. *Eager Beavers*.

85. Ibid.

86. Jay Zeamer, interviewer unknown, video posted to YouTube by MedalOfHonor Book, September 27, 2011, https://www.youtube.com/watch?v=VGt8gQulPcM (henceforth Zeamer interview).

87. "Old '666,'" video posted to YouTube by bbottlezigzag, March 4, 2009, https://www.youtube.com/watch?v=6Im086TCu3I (henceforth "Old '666'").

88. Drury and Clavin, 210–21; *Eager Beavers*.

89. Drury and Clavin, 225; *Eager Beavers*.

90. Drury and Clavin, 260.

91. Zeamer interview.

92. Ibid.; Drury and Clavin, 251–52.

93. Zeamer interview.

94. "Old '666.'"

95. Drury and Clavin, 264.

96. Charles J. Hanley, "A Team Again: World War II Pilot Recalls the Bombardier Who Didn't Make It," *The Times* (Munster, IN), September. 3, 1995.

97. Drury and Clavin, 266.

98. Ibid.

99. "Old '666.'"

100. Zeamer interview.

101. Ibid. Understandably, considering the confusion and stress, Zeamer and his crew overestimated the number of enemy attackers. The B-17 was actually attacked by eight enemy fighters.

102. Crew statement, July 1943, cited in Drury and Clavin, 284.

103. Zeamer interview.

104. "Old '666'"; Drury and Clavin, 286.

105. Zeamer interview.

106. Hanley.

107. "Jay Zeamer, a Decorated Pilot in World War II, Dies at 88," *Los Angeles Times*, March 26, 2007.

108. Hanley.

109. Hal Boyle, "Correspondent's Notebook," *Rocky Mount [North Carolina] Telegram*, January 6, 1947.

CHAPTER 6

1. Eric Hammel, *Aces against Japan* (Novato, CA: Presidio, 1992), 105 (henceforth *Aces against Japan*).

2. Rolfe Boswell, *Medals for Marines* (New York: Thomas Y. Crowell Company, 1945), 141.

3. Edward H. Sims, *Greatest Fighter Missions of the Top Navy and Marine Aces of World War II* (New York: Ballantine Books, 1962), 52.

4. Boswell, 142.

5. Sims, 55.

6. James E. Swett, interviewer unknown, James E. Swett Collection (AFC/2001/001/89783), Veterans History Project, American Folklife Center, Library of Congress (henceforth Swett interview); *Aces against Japan*, 106; Robert Kirk (director), *Dogfight Guadalcanal*, Digital Ranch, 2006; Sims, 56.

7. Sims, 57; Boswell, 43.

8. Swett interview.

9. "Guadalcanal."

10. *Aces against Japan*, 106–7.

11. "Guadalcanal."

12. *Aces against Japan*, 107.

13. "Guadalcanal."

14. *Aces against Japan*, 108; Swett interview; "Guadalcanal."

15. Swett interview.

16. *Aces against Japan*, 108.

17. Ibid., 109.

18. War Diary, Marine Fighting Squadron Two Twenty-One, Marine Aircraft Group Twenty-One, First Marine Aircraft Wing, April 1–30, 1943.

19. "Swett Family Deluged with Good Wishes," *San Mateo [California] Times*, April 22, 1944.

20. Boswell, 148.

21. Action Report, Marine Fighting Squadron 221, Report of Action between Two Planes of VMF-221 and Fifteen Bombers with Zero Escort over Munda and Kula Gulf on July 11, 1943.

22. Ibid.

23. Ibid.

24. Ibid.

25. Ibid.

26. Swett interview.

27. Eric Hammel, *Aces against Japan II* (Pacifica, CA: Pacifica Press, 1996), 284.

28. Swett interview.

29. Jim Schultz, "Medal of Honor Recipient James Swett of Redding Dies at 88," *Redding [California] Record Searchlight*, January 21, 2009.

30. Richard Goldstein, "James Swett, Who Downed 7 Planes in Attack, Dies at 88," *New York Times*, January 25, 2009.

31. Sims, 71.

32. Boswell, 156.

33. Edward Humes, "Medal of Honor Ken Walsh: Ex-Flier Credits Decoration to Experience, Luck," *Orange County [California] Register*, November 8, 1987.

34. Kenneth N. Jordan Sr., *Men of Honor: Thirty-Eight Highly Decorated Marines of World War II, Korea and Vietnam* (Atglen, PA: Schiffer Military History, 1997), 124.

35. Boswell, 156.

36. Ibid., 157.

37. War Diary, Marine Fighting Squadron One Twenty-Four, August 1943 (henceforth War Diary VMF-124).

38. Ibid.

39. Ibid.

40. Ibid.

41. Ibid.

42. Ibid.

43. Humes.

44. Ralph T. Eubanks, *Once a Marine: Memoirs of a World War II Marine* (Bloomington, IN: AuthorHouse, 2008), 70.

45. Boswell, 158.

46. War Diary VMF-124.

47. Sims, 75–77.

48. Humes.

49. Sims, 80.

50. War Diary VMF-124.

51. Sims, 76-86.

52. Gary A. Warner, "W.W.II Ace Was Man of Few Words in Memorable Meeting with FDR," *San Jose [California] Mercury News*, February 22, 1994.

53. Boswell, 160.

54. "Marine Ace Sets Sights on New Record," *Austin [Texas] American-Statesman*, July 9, 1945.

55. Warner.

56. Humes.

57. Ibid.

58. Gregory Boyington, *Baa Baa Black Sheep* (New York: G. P. Putnam's Sons, 1958), 384.

59. Bruce Gamble, *Black Sheep One: The Life of Gregory "Pappy" Boyington* (Novato, CA: Presidio, 2000), 5 (henceforth *Black Sheep One*).

60. Ibid., 38.

61. Ibid., 124.

62. Boyington, 63; *Black Sheep One*, 177.

63. Colin Heaton, "Black Sheep Leader" (interview with Gregory Boyington), *Aviation History Magazine*, May 2001.

64. *Black Sheep One*, 221.

65. Frank E. Walton, *Once They Were Eagles: The Men of the Black Sheep Squadron* (Lexington: University Press of Kentucky, 1986), 11.

66. Boyington, 150. Biographer Gamble suggests Boyington's inattentiveness was the result of a hangover.

67. Ibid., 151.

68. Ibid., 153.

69. U.S. pilots claimed sixteen victories in the aerial melee. Japanese records indicate the loss of six, possibly seven planes. As was often the case before the widespread implementation of gun camera footage, Boyington was taken at his word. Claims on both sides were typically greatly exaggerated. Gamble offers an interesting insight into this process in *Black Sheep One*.

70. Boyington, 154.

71. Ibid., 165; *Black Sheep One*, 259.

72. *Black Sheep One*, 266–67.

73. Ibid., 258.

74. Walton, 89.

75. Ibid., 127.

76. Ibid., 132.

77. *Black Sheep One*, 279.

78. Boyington, 215.

79. *Black Sheep One*, 292.

80. John Wukovits, "Fred Avey: Flying with the Black Sheep Squadron in World War II," *Aviation History*, May 1997.

81. Walton, 90.

82. Ibid., 95.

83. Boyington, 229.

84. Gamble notes that other pilots confirmed one Zero only and makes a strong case that Boyington's other claims were fabricated.

85. Boyington, 231.

86. Ibid., 233.

87. *Black Sheep One*, 220.

88. John W. Faust, "Boyington according to Scott and Me," Angelfire.com, October 6, 1998, http://www.angelfire.com/ca/dickg/vignettes11.html.

89. Walton, 189.

90. Tom Griffin, "Gregory Boyington—Our 'Black Sheep' Hero," *Our Back Pages: A Look Back at UW History* (University of Washington), December 1998.

91. "Pappy Boyington Hospitalized: Health Shooting Him Down, War Ace Says," *Los Angeles Times*, March 10, 1972; "WWII Flying Ace Pappy Boyington Dead," *Sunday Times-Sentinel* (Fresno, CA), January 12, 1988.

92. "Pappy Boyington, Marine Ace, Outspoken in Print, in Person," *Palm Beach Post* (West Palm Beach, FL), October 5, 1958.

93. Faust.

94. Wukovits, "Fred Avey."

95. Walton, 189.

96. "WWII Flying Ace Pappy Boyington Dead."

97. Walton, 157.

98. Frances Burns, "The Story of Newton's Heroic Ace Bob Hanson of the Marines," *Boston Globe*, February 14–17, 1944.

99. Ibid.

100. Ibid.

101. Bruce Gamble, *The Black Sheep: The Definitive Account of Marine Fighting Squadron 214 in World War II* (Novato, CA: Presidio Press, 2003), 139–40 (henceforth *The Black Sheep*).

102. Ibid., 157; "Missing Newton Flyer Writes Home He's Safe," *Boston Sunday Globe*, November 21, 1943.

103. Staff Sgt. Pen T. Johnson, "Newtonville Flyer Fought Japs with Faulty Engine," *Boston Globe*, October 28, 1943.

104. War Diary, Marine Corps Marine Fighting Squadron 214, August 1–31, 1943.

105. War Diary, VMF-215, November, December 1943, January 1944 (henceforth VMF-215 War Diary).

106. Ibid.

107. Ibid.

108. Saul Braun, *Seven Heroes: Medal of Honor Stories of the War in the Pacific* (New York: G. P. Putnam's Sons, 1965), 104; Boswell, 199.

109. VMF-215 War Diary.

110. Ibid.

111. Ibid.

112. Gamble notes in *Target Rabaul* that Japanese sources indicate only three fighters were missing.

113. VMF-215 War Diary.

114. "Missing Newton Ace Wins Nation's Highest Award," *Boston Globe*, August 1, 1944.

115. Braun, 105.

116. Ibid., 106.

117. VMF-215 War Diary.

118. Ibid.

119. "Missing Newton Ace Wins Nation's Highest Award."

120. VMF-215 War Diary.

121. Bruce Gamble, *Target Rabaul: The Allied Siege of Japan's Most Infamous Stronghold, March 1943–August 1945* (Minneapolis: Zenith Press, 2013), 303 (henceforth *Target Rabaul*).

122. Ibid., 304.

123. Ibid.

124. Ibid., 305.

125. VMF-215 War Diary.

126. Boswell, 197; Braun, 122.

127. "Newton Marine Ace Reported Missing Again," *Boston Globe*, February 6, 1944.

128. Burns, "Story of Newton's Heroic Ace."

129. Ibid.

130. Frances Burns, "Medal of Honor for Lt. Hanson Is Presented Mother," *Boston Globe*, August 20, 1944.

131. Fred Hampson, "How Newton Ace Died: Mishap Ended Career of Man Who Bagged 25 Jap Planes," *Boston Globe*, February 8, 1944.

CHAPTER 7

1. *Lucky Bag, 1929* (Annapolis: US Naval Academy, 1929).

2. Ibid.

3. Van Voorhis personnel file, National Personnel Records Center, St. Louis, MO.

4. Ibid.

5. Wade Cavanaugh, "Bruce Van Voorhis Nevada's WWII Hero," *Las Vegas Sun*, November 12, 1977.

6. Adm. Marc Mitscher, letter to the secretary of the Navy (Board of Decorations and Medals), May 7, 1946, Van Voorhis personnel file.

7. James Claire Nolan, *This Damn Navy: The Diary of a Naval Aviator*, http://thisdamn Navy.com (henceforth Nolan diary).

8. Mitscher letter in Voorhis file.

9. Ibid.

10. Nolan diary, July 6.

11. Mitscher letter in Voorhis file.

12. Nolan diary, July 7.

13. Letter from Lillie V. Pinger to Navy Department, Bureau of Personnel, July 31, 1945, Van Voorhis personnel file.

14. Landing Force Detachment USS *Heyliger* DE 510, "Remains of Allied Personnel Found on Kapingamarangi Atoll," Van Voorhis personnel file.

15. Ibid.

16. Cavanaugh.

17. On her 1920 passport Julia lists the infant as "Raphael," but there is no indication he ever went by anything but Ralph.

18. Ann Kovalenko, "Honor Lehigh World War II Hero," *Morning Call* (Allentown, PA), June 9, 1968.

19. Garrett Middlebrook, *Air Combat at 20 Feet: Selected Missions from a Strafer Pilot's Diary* (Bloomington, IN: AuthorHouse, 2004), 3.

20. Ibid., 76–79.

21. Ibid., 79, 112.

22. Ibid., 182.

23. "Army & Navy Heroes—Pronounced 'Kelly,'" *TIME*, September 6, 1943.

24. Middlebrook, 451.

25. Walter Krell, letter to author Lawrence J. Hickey, 38th Bomb Group Association, January 14, 1989, http://www.sunsetters38bg.com/index.php/articles/stories2/106-a-young-mans-airplane.

26. Middlebrook, 460.

27. Ibid., 467–68.

28. Alma De Coen, "Day's Job Depends on What's to Be Done, Not the Hours That Are Spent at Work," *Journal News* (White Plains, NY), May 7, 1945.

29. Bruce Gamble, *Fortress Rabaul: The Battle for the Southwest Pacific, January 1942–April 1943* (Minneapolis: Zenith Press, 2013), 109 (henceforth *Fortress Rabaul*).

30. Final Mission Report, 38th Bomb Group, August 18, 1943.

31. De Coen.

32. Middlebrook, 474.

33. *Looking Backward: A Lehigh University Scrapbook* (Bethlehem, PA: Lehigh University, 1991).

34. Middlebrook, 485.

35. "Major Cheli Killed in Raid: Famed Flyer Casualty of Wewak Assault," *San Francisco Examiner*, August 26, 1943.

36. "Californians in War News: Hero, Believed Killed, Now Reported Prisoner," *San Francisco Examiner*, February 10, 1944.

37. "Maj. Ralph Cheli Reported Jap Prisoner," *Morning Call* (Allentown, PA), February 10, 1944.

38. "Maj. Ralph Cheli Still Alive," *Morning Call* (Allentown, PA), May 3, 1944.

39. Clyde Beal, "Closure for Family of Purple Heart Recipient," *Herald Dispatch* (Huntington, WV), March 3, 2013.

40. Testimonial of Jose Holguin to Sanford H. Bullock, Special Agent, 115th CIC Detachment, 1948 (henceforth Holguin testimony).

41. Bruce Gamble, *Target Rabaul: The Allied Siege of Japan's Most Infamous Stronghold, March 1943–August 1945* (Minneapolis: Zenith Press, 2013), 112–13 (henceforth *Target Rabaul*).

42. Casualty Branch, Status Review and Determination Section, Review and Determination under Section 5, Public Law 400, 7 March 1942 as Amended, Status of Crew of a B-25 Aircraft Missing in Action in the Southwest Pacific Area since 18 October 1943; *Target Rabaul*, 113.

43. Casualty Branch Status Review; Lee Van Atta, "Lump All Jap Atrocities and You Have Rabaul in Nutshell," *Tipton [Indiana] Daily Tribune*, September 22, 1945.

44. 1st Lt. James McMurria, Perpetuation of Testimony of Former 1st Lieut. James A. McMurria, O-373644. In the matter of the POW Camp operated by the 6th Field Kempai Tai Headquarters in Rabaul, New Britain—Tunnel Hill POW Camp. For the

Chief, War Crimes Branch Civil Affairs Division—War Department. Taken at Columbus, Georgia, July 21, 1948 (henceforth McMurria testimony).

45. *Target Rabaul*, 324.

46. McMurria testimony.

47. Holguin testimony.

48. Ibid.; *Target Rabaul*, 326–27.

49. Kovalenko.

50. "Fire Hits 2 City Firms, Woman's Death Probed," *Morning Call* (Allentown, PA), April 22, 1971.

51. Steve Birdsall, *Flying Buccaneers: The Illustrated Story of Kenney's Fifth Air Force* (Garden City, NY: Doubleday & Company, Inc., 1977), 129.

52. "Article from Home of Heroes," 8th Attack Squadron Association, http://8thattacksqdnassoc.tripod.com/WWIIa.html#ARTICLE.

53. William H. Webster, transcript of interview by unknown interviewer, 3rd Attack Group/3rd Bombardment Group 1919–2019, September 9, 2002, http://3rdstories.yola site.com/william-h-webster.php (henceforth Webster interview).

54. History, 8th Bombardment Squadron (L), 3d Bombardment Group (L) AAF, May 31, 1917–March 31, 1944 (compiled September 1945).

55. "Article from Home of Heroes."

56. Andrew H. Weigel, letter to Dwight Turner, 3rd Bombardment Group—WWII: Stories: Dwight E. Turner, September 3, 1998, http://3rdstories.yolasite.com/resources/Dwight_Turner/Andrew%20Weigel%20Letter%20to%20Dwight%20Turner%20%201999.pdf.

57. Lee Van Atta, "Eye Witness Story of Rabaul Smash," International News Service, October 12, 1943.

58. William H. Webster, letter to Larry Hickey, 3rd Attack Group/3rd Bombardment Group 1919–2019, June 15, 1989, http://3rdstories.yolasite.com/william-h-webster.php (henceforth Webster letter).

59. Ibid.

60. Ibid.

61. Dick Walker, "Raid on Rabaul on 2 November 1943 as Told by Dick Walker, 13th Bomb Squadron, 3rd Bomb Group, Their Part in the Raid on Rabaul on 2 November 1943," Australia@War, https://www.ozatwar.com/usaaf/rabaul2nov43.htm.

62. Webster letter.

63. Joseph A. Pratt, "Memorials and Memories," *Houston Review*, Spring 2005.

64. Webster letter.

65. Ibid.

66. Ibid.

67. Webster interview.

68. Webster letter.

69. Ibid.

70. Ibid.

71. Ibid.

72. Missing Air Crew Report 41-30311 (Rpt. No. 1458), November 2, 1943, 8th Bomb Squadron, 3rd Bomb Group.

73. Webster letter.

74. Ibid. Trout was flying as Keyes's copilot.

75. Ibid.

76. Pratt.

77. Martin J. Radnick, Recollections, http://3rdstories.yolasite.com/dwight-turner.php.

78. Webster interview.

79. Steven D. Smith, "Flight out of Hell: The Harrowing Bombing Mission to Kavieng," Warfare History Network, December 9, 2017.

80. This according to Smith, "Flight out of Hell"; other records claim it was Gross.

81. Chris Pyle, "In the Line of Fire," *Arkansas Democrat-Gazette*, October 22, 2006.

82. "Nathan Gordon, Medal of Honor, WWII," video posted to YouTube by MedalOf HonorBook, September 27, 2011, https://www.youtube.com/watch?v=zR2iWFqTarQ (henceforth Gordon interview).

83. Jack Schnedler, "Nathan Gordon Won the Medal of Honor for His Heroics during World War II," *Arkansas Democrat-Gazette*, August 4, 2002.

84. Pyle.

85. Schnedler.

86. "Nathan G. Gordon," Pacific Wrecks, https://www.pacificwrecks.com/people/vet erans/gordon/index.html.

87. Pyle; Pearson and his gunner, Sgt. Nathaniel D. Gamage of Somerville, Massachusetts, were never found.

88. Smith, "Flight out of Hell."

89. "Nathan G. Gordon."

90. Schnedler.

91. Ibid.

92. "Nathan G. Gordon."

93. Ibid.; Gordon interview.

94. Birdsall, 147.

95. Schnedler.

96. "Nathan G. Gordon."

97. Schnedler.

98. Ibid.

99. "Nathan G. Gordon."

100. Gordon interview.

101. Ibid.

102. Pyle.

103. Schnedler.

Chapter 8

1. Gen. George C. Kenney, *General Kenney Reports: A Personal History of the Pacific War* (New York: Duell, Sloan and Pearce, 1949), 264 (henceforth *General Kenney Reports*).

2. Founded in 1891, the annual parade in honor of the defenders of the Alamo and Texas's independence draws tens of thousands of spectators.

3. *General Kenney Reports*, 264.

4. It was probably a Sally.

5. John C. Stanaway, *Kearby's Thunderbolts: The 348th Fighter Group in World War II* (Atglen, PA: Schiffer Publishing, 1997), 35 (henceforth *Kearby's Thunderbolts*).

6. Ibid., 36–37.

7. Steve Birdsall, *Flying Buccaneers: The Illustrated Story of Kenney's Fifth Air Force* (Garden City, NY: Doubleday & Company, Inc., 1977), 107.

8. Ibid., 108.

9. Ibid.

10. Hamp was a name initially used for the A6M3 Model 32, with a square wingtip, but it was nevertheless still a Zero.

11. *Kearby's Thunderbolts*, 44. The Americans later estimated they encountered about forty enemy fighters, but the actual number was probably about half that.

12. Birdsall, 108.

13. Ibid.; *Kearby's Thunderbolts*, 46.

14. *Kearby's Thunderbolts*, 50; *General Kenney Reports*, 311.

15. *General Kenney Reports*, 311.

16. *Kearby's Thunderbolts*, 48.

17. Ibid., 40.

18. Dean Schedler, "He Just Likes to Hunt—Fiery Ginger's Thunderbolt Ace Pilot Has Ration Trouble Too," *Abilene Reporter News*, December 13, 1943.

19. *Kearby's Thunderbolts*, 8–9.

20. Schedler.

21. *Kearby's Thunderbolts*, 65.

22. Gen. George C. Kenney, *Dick Bong: Ace of Aces* (New York: Popular Library, 1962), 54 (henceforth *Dick Bong: Ace of Aces*); *General Kenney Reports*, 345.

23. *Kearby's Thunderbolts*, 80–81.

24. *Dick Bong: Ace of Aces*, 53; *General Kenney Reports*, 345.

25. *Kearby's Thunderbolts*, 88. On January 15, Joe Foss had tied Rickenbacker's record of twenty-six kills.

26. Missing Air Crew Report 42-22668 on the loss of Neel Kearby.

27. Ibid.

28. Ibid.

29. Ibid.

30. Ibid.

31. "Wife Won't Give Up Hope for Kearby," *San Antonio Light*, March 15, 1944.

32. "General Tells How Air Ace Was Shot Down," *San Antonio Express*, March 23, 1944.

33. Richard L. Dunn, "Double Lucky? The Campaigns of the 77th Hiko Sentai, Part 9," The Warbird's Forum, http://www.warbirdforum.com/lucky9.htm; Richard L. Dunn, "248th Hiko Sentai: A Japanese 'Hard Luck' Fighter Unit, Part 3," j-aircraft.com, http://www.j-aircraft.com/research/rdunn/248th/248th-3.htm.

34. Ibid.

35. Described as an inventive genius, John G. Kearby III was project manager of Project MX-117, a highly classified program designed to develop experimental high-altitude pressure suits. On October 2, 1942, at the Aero Medical Laboratory at Wright Field in Ohio, he ascended to a simulated altitude of 60,200 feet in an altitude chamber, a new record at that time. He and six others died in the crash of a twin-engine training plane while testing equipment in Michigan.

36. "U.S. at War: Missing—Texas," *TIME*, March 27, 1944.

37. Charles A. Martin, *The Last Great Ace: The Life of Major Thomas B. McGuire, Jr.* (Fruit Grove, FL: Fruit Cove Publishing, 1998), 321.

38. Ibid., 9.

39. Ibid., 79, 81.

40. Bill Yenne, *Aces High* (New York: Berkley Caliber Publishing Group, 2010), 116, 135.

41. Ibid., 136–37.

42. Martin, 198.

43. Ibid., 325–26.

44. Ibid., 203–5; Yenne, 150.

45. Martin, 236.

46. Yenne, 247–48.

47. Martin, 309, 312.

48. Ibid., 293.

49. Ibid., 323.

50. Ibid., 279–80.

51. Ibid., 283.

52. Ibid., 286–88.

53. Ibid., 325.

54. Ibid., 318.

55. David Mason, "McGuire Final Report: Investigation into the Final Combat Mission of Major Thomas B. McGuire, Jr." (self-published, January 7, 2009).

56. Ibid.

57. Ibid.

58. Martin, 334.

59. Mason.

60. Martin, 360.

61. "Richard I. Bong, Ace Fighter Pilot, Is Killed," *[Butte] Montana Standard*, August 7, 1945; Yenne, 294.

62. Carl Bong and Mike O'Connor, *Ace of Aces: The Dick Bong Story* (Mesa, AZ: Champlin Fighter Museum, 1985), 2.

63. Ibid., 4.

64. "Richard I. Bong, Ace Fighter Pilot, Is Killed."

65. Bong and O'Connor, 7–8.

66. Ibid., 11, 46.

67. Ibid., 13.

68. *Dick Bong: Ace of Aces*, 13–14.
69. Yenne, 68–69.
70. Bong and O'Connor, 21.
71. Ibid.
72. Ibid., 21–22; Yenne, 93.
73. Bong and O'Connor, 45.
74. Ibid., 49.
75. Yenne, 114.
76. Bong and O'Connor, 48, 50.
77. Ibid., 55, 58; Yenne, 123, 126–27.
78. Bong and O'Connor, 58–59.
79. Garrett Middlebrook, *Air Combat at 20 Feet: Selected Missions from a Strafer Pilot's Diary* (Bloomington, IN: Author House, 2004), 521–22.
80. Martin, 309.
81. Middlebrook, 522.
82. Yenne, 154.
83. Kyle Crichton, "Captain Bong Comes Home—Small Town Hero from Superior, Wisconsin," *Collier's*, February 26, 1944; Bong and O'Connor, 68.
84. Yenne, 174.
85. Bong and O'Connor, 72.
86. Ibid., 70–71; Yenne, 174.
87. Bong and O'Connor, 72; Yenne, 175.
88. *Dick Bong: Ace of Aces*, 56–57.
89. Bong and O'Connor, 73–74; Yenne, 179–80.
90. Bong and O'Connor, 75–76.
91. Yenne, 186.
92. Bong and O'Connor, 89–90.
93. Yenne, 189.
94. Ibid., 190.
95. Bong and O'Connor, 93.
96. Ibid., 97; Yenne, 222.
97. *Dick Bong: Ace of Aces*, 83.
98. Bong and O'Connor, 107; Yenne, 228–29.
99. *Dick Bong: Ace of Aces*, 96.
100. Ibid., 106; Bong and O'Connor, 102.
101. Bong and O'Connor, 103.
102. Ibid., 107.
103. *Dick Bong: Ace of Aces*, 106–7.
104. Bong and O'Connor, 107.
105. *Dick Bong: Ace of Aces*, 114–15.
106. Bong and O'Connor, 112.
107. Ibid.
108. Ibid., 128.

109. "Maj. Richard Bong, America's Top Ace, Killed as Jet-Propelled Plane Explodes in Midair," *Palladium-Item* (Richmond, IN), August 7, 1945.

110. "Richard I. Bong, Ace Fighter Pilot, Is Killed."

111. "Bong Killed in Jet Plane Crash," *Waukesha [Wisconsin] Daily Freeman*, August 7, 1945.

CHAPTER 9

1. Thomas McKelvey Cleaver, *Fabled Fifteen: The Pacific War Saga of Carrier Air Group 15* (Philadelphia: Casemate Publishers, 2014), 76.

2. West Palm Beach Florida, City Directory, 1927.

3. Capt. David McCampbell, US Navy (Ret.), transcript of interview by Paul Stillwell, 2010, US Naval Institute, Annapolis, Maryland (henceforth Stillwell interview).

4. *Lucky Bag, 1933* (Annapolis: US Naval Academy, 1933).

5. Stillwell interview.

6. Ibid., 101–2; Cleaver, 56–57.

7. Cleaver, 15, 63; Stillwell interview.

8. Cleaver, 79.

9. Stillwell interview.

10. Ibid.

11. Cleaver, 89–90; Stephen Sherman, "Cdr. David McCampbell Top Navy Ace of WW2, Shot Down 34 Japanese Planes," February 2000 (updated July 2, 2011), World War Two and Aviation History, http://acepilots.com/usn_mccampbell.html.

12. Cleaver, 92.

13. Ibid., 102.

14. Stillwell interview.

15. Report of Air Operations conducted by Carrier Air Group Fifteen during the period 19 June to 3 July 1944, inclusive.

16. Ibid.

17. Ibid.

18. Ibid.

19. Cleaver, 110.

20. Stillwell interview.

21. Ibid.

22. Cleaver, 127–28.

23. Ibid., 143–44.

24. Cleaver, 17; Stillwell interview.

25. Stillwell interview.

26. Edward H. Sims, *Greatest Fighter Missions of the Top Navy and Marine Aces of World War II* (New York: Ballantine Books, 1962), 164; Cleaver, 19.

27. Stillwell interview.

28. Ibid.

29. Ibid.

30. Ibid.

31. Ibid.

32. Ibid.

33. Ibid.

34. "David McCampbell: Ace of Aces," video posted to YouTube by US Naval Institute, July 21, 2011, https://www.youtube.com/watch?v=Wx-c0BpFbSU.

35. Stillwell interview.

36. Ibid.

37. Carroll V. Glines, *Chennault's Forgotten Warriors: The Saga of the 308th Bomb Group in China* (Atglen, PA: Schiffer Publishing, 1995), 248 (henceforth *Forgotten Warriors*).

38. James R. Woodall, *Texas Aggie Medals of Honor* (College Station: Texas A&M University Press, 2010), 77.

39. *Forgotten Warriors*, 250.

40. Ibid., 249; Woodall, 83.

41. *Forgotten Warriors*, 253.

42. Ibid.

43. Ibid., 254.

44. "14th AF B-24 Sinks Two Warships," *CBI Roundup* 3, no. 7 (October 26, 1944).

45. Clyde A. Farnsworth, "Pilot in Historic Bombing Raid Sacrifices Life to Save Mates, Texan Stands by Pal with Ruined Parachute," *Amarillo Daily News*, November 24, 1944.

46. Ibid.

47. Ibid.

48. Ibid.

49. *Forgotten Warriors*, 258.

50. "14th AF B-24 Sinks Two Warships"

51. Missing Air Crew Report, 308th Bombardment Group, October 29, 1944.

52. "14th AF Hero Makes Gallant Rendezvous with Death," *CBI Roundup* 3, no. 16 (December 28, 1944).

53. Ibid.; Farnsworth; *Forgotten Warriors*; Missing Air Crew Report, 308th Bombardment Group.

54. Farnsworth.

55. Missing Air Crew Report, 308th Bombardment Group.

56. Ibid.

57. Woodall, 88.

58. Katherine Sams Wiley, *The Strafin' Saints: The 71st Tactical Reconnaissance Group: Memories* (privately printed, 1994), 47.

59. Ibid., 86.

60. William Shomo, interviewer unknown, 1981, video posted to YouTube by Ron Terpko, September 21, 2011, https://www.youtube.com/watch?v=A4LUG1Ix4KE (henceforth Shomo interview).

61. Wiley, 72.

62. Ibid., 160.

63. Ibid., 304.

64. "Sees His First Jap Planes in 15 Months in Pacific, Downs Seven," *Evening Times* (Sayre, PA), January 18, 1945.

65. Ibid.

66. Wiley, 305.

67. Shomo interview.

68. Wiley, 305.

69. Ibid.; John C. Stanaway, *Mustang and Thunderbolt Aces of the Pacific and CBI* (London: Osprey Publishing, 1999).

70. Wiley, 305.

71. "Jeannette, Pa., Pilot Shoots Way to Fame," *Altoona [Pennsylvania] Tribune*, January 18, 1945.

72. Wiley, 306.

73. Ibid., 306–7.

74. "William Shomo Wingman—Paul Lipscomb," video posted to YouTube by Ron Terpko, October 10, 2011, https://www.youtube.com/watch?v=YOc51Rh-ivw (henceforth Snooks II interviews).

75. Wiley, 307.

76. "Sees His First Jap Planes in 15 Months in Pacific, Downs Seven,"

77. Wiley, 156.

78. Ibid., 146–47.

79. John E. Jones, "Jeannette Pilot Wants to Return to His P-51: Medal Winner Restless on Ground," *Pittsburgh Post-Gazette*, August 10, 1945.

80. Snooks II interviews.

81. "Ace Who Made Air History in Pacific Will Stay to End," *Tipton [Indiana] Daily Tribune*, June 15, 1945.

82. Snooks II interviews.

83. Andrew Sheehan, "Tale of 3 Heroes," *Pittsburgh Post-Gazette*, July 7, 1983.

84. Snooks II interviews.

85. Shomo interview.

CHAPTER 10

1. Judd A. Katz, "Red Erwin and the Medal of Honor," *Alabama Heritage*, Winter 1996.

2. John T. Correll, "A Brave Man at the Right Time," *Air Force Magazine*, June 2007.

3. Robert F. Dorr, "Medal of Honor Recipient: Henry 'Red' Erwin," *WWII Quarterly*, November 20, 2018.

4. Ibid.

5. John L. Frisbee, "Valor: Triumph and Tragedy," *Air Force Magazine*, August 1988.

6. Jon Erwin and William Doyle, *Beyond Valor* (Nashville, TN: Nelson Books, 2020), 37.

7. Robert F. Dorr, *Mission to Tokyo: The American Airmen Who Took the War to the Heart of Japan* (Minneapolis: Zenith Press, 2012), 151.

8. Dorr, "Medal of Honor Recipient."

9. "The Red Erwin Story Archives.qt," video posted to YouTube by HETV44, July 31, 2012, https://www.youtube.com/watch?v=wtPc9_teMgY (henceforth Erwin interview).

10. Katz.

11. Ibid.

12. Ibid.

13. Ibid.

14. Correll.

15. Ibid.

16. Erwin interview.

17. Correll.

18. Erwin interview.

19. Correll.

20. Dorr, "Medal of Honor Recipient."

21. Correll.

22. Katz.

23. Mark Alpert, "Three Medal of Honor Winners Praised," *Montgomery [Alabama] Advertiser*, March 6, 1986.

24. Correll.

25. Ibid.

26. Katz.

27. Erwin and Doyle, 75.

28. Erwin interview.

29. Correll.

30. Katz.

31. Correll.

32. Ibid.

33. Dorr, "Medal of Honor Recipient."

34. Ibid.

35. Alpert.

36. Correll.

37. Ibid.

38. Katz.

39. Correll.

40. Ibid.

41. Ben Windham, "Southern Lights: One Heroic Moment—But It Didn't End There," *Tuscaloosa News*, January 27, 2002.

42. Ibid.

Bibliography

ORAL HISTORIES AND INTERVIEWS

Adm. Marc Mitscher, letter to the secretary of the Navy (Board of Decorations and Medals), May 7, 1946, Van Voorhis personnel file.

DeBlanc, Jefferson J. Interviewer unknown. Jefferson J. DeBlanc Collection (AFC/2001/001/89660), Veterans History Project, American Folklife Center, Library of Congress.

Finn, John William. Interviewed by Carl Raymond Cox, September 21, 2004. John William Finn Collection (AFC/2001/001/21692), Veterans History Project, American Folklife Center, Library of Congress.

Finn, John William. Interviewed by Mike Russert and Wayne Clark, October 6, 2006. New York State Military Museum.

Finn, John William. Interviewed by Richard Erickson. John William Finn Collection (AFC/2001/001/19400), Veterans History Project, American Folklife Center, Library of Congress.

Finn, John William. Interviewer unknown. Medal of Honor Foundation. John William Finn Collection (AFC/2001/001/89678), Veterans History Project, American Folklife Center, Library of Congress.

Foss, Joseph. Interviewed by Jon Seal and Michael Ahn, March 2000. WW2aircraft.net, December 9, 2004. https://ww2aircraft.net/forum/threads/joe-foss-interview-the-man-the-legend.511.

Galer, Robert E. Interviewed by Bill Alexander, March 14, 1998. Admiral Nimitz Museum and University of North Texas Oral History Collection.

Galer, Robert E. Interviewed by Dr. Dave Thompson, February 12, 2004. Palm Springs Air Museum, California.

Galer, Robert E. Interviewed by Larry Arnold, October 8, 2002. Robert Edward Galer Collection (AFC/2001/001/12798), Veterans History Project, American Folklife Center, Library of Congress.

Galer, Robert E. Interviewed by Ronald E. Marcello, August 27, 1998. University of North Texas Oral History Collection, Number 1265.

Gordon, Nathan. Interviewed by Chuck Norwood. YouTube, June 24, 2016. https://www
.youtube.com/watch?v=mC8rwOJFSsI.

Gordon, Nathan. Interviewer unknown. Medal of Honor Society. Vimeo. https://vimeo
.com/398042775.

Gordon, Nathan. Interviewer unknown. Nathan Green Gordon Collection
(AFC/2001/001/89690), Veterans History Project, American Folklife Center,
Library of Congress.

McCampbell, Capt. David, US Navy (Ret.). Transcript of interview by Paul Stillwell,
2010. US Naval Institute, Annapolis, Maryland.

Renner, Joseph N. "Interview of Major J. N. Renner, USMC," Bureau of Aeronautics,
July 17, 1943.

Shomo, William. Interviewer unknown, 1981. Video posted to YouTube by Ron Terpko,
September 21, 2011. https://www.youtube.com/watch?v=A4LUG1Ix4KE.

Swett, James E. Interviewer unknown. James E. Swett Collection
(AFC/2001/001/89783), Veterans History Project, American Folklife Center,
Library of Congress.

Thach, Adm. John Smith, USN (Ret.). Interview #2 by Cmdr. Etta-Belle Kitchen, USN
(Ret.), August 8, 1970. US Naval Institute, Coronado, California.

Webster, William H. Transcript of interview by David Gregory, February 13, 1999. 3rd
Attack Group/3rd Bombardment Group 1919–2019. http://3rdstories.yolasite
.com/william-h-webster.php.

Webster, William H. Transcript of interview by unknown interviewer. 3rd Attack
Group/3rd Bombardment Group 1919–2019, September 9, 2002. http://3rdstories
.yolasite.com/william-h-webster.php.

Wesche, Frederick, III. Interviewed by Shaun Illingworth and Kathryn Tracy. Rutgers
Oral History Archives of World War II, Rutgers University, May 10, 2001.

Zeamer, Jay. Interviewer unknown. Video posted to YouTube by MedalOfHonorBook,
September 27, 2011. https://www.youtube.com/watch?v=VGt8gQulPcM.

BOOKS, ARTICLES, AND REPORTS

"Ace Who Made Air History in Pacific Will Stay to End." *Tipton [Indiana] Daily Tribune*, June 15, 1945.

Action Report, Marine Fighting Squadron 221. Report of Action between Two Planes
of VMF-221 and Fifteen Bombers with Zero Escort over Munda and Kula Gulf
on July 11, 1943.

Air Operations of Lexington, 7–8 May 1942—Report of. Account of Action, Morning
of May 7th.

Alpert, Mark. "Three Medal of Honor Winners Praised." *Montgomery [Alabama] Advertiser*, March 6, 1986.

Anderson, Carroll R. "McGuire's Last Mission." *Air Force Magazine*, January 1975.

Anderson, Kendall. "A Hero's Welcome." *Dallas Morning News*, March 25, 2000.

*Annual Register of the United States Naval Academy Annapolis, MD. September 27, 1929,
Eighty-Fifth Academic Year, 1929–1930.* Washington, DC: US Government Printing Office, 1929.

Army Air Forces Statistical Digest World War II. Washington, DC: Office of Statistical Control, December 1945.

"Army & Navy Heroes—Pronounced 'Kelly.'" *TIME*, September 6, 1943.

Astor, Gerald. *Semper Fi in the Sky: The Marine Air Battles of World War II.* New York: Ballantine Books, 2005.

Barker, Tyler. "The Warrior of Kāne'ohe: Pearl Harbor's First Medal of Honor Recipient." *The Sextant.* Naval History and Heritage Command, December 6, 2016.

Barnes, Pete. *Richard Bong: World War II Flying Ace.* Madison: Wisconsin Historical Society Press, 2009.

Baylor, Walter, and Cecil Carnes. *Last Man off Wake Island.* New York: Bobbs-Merrill Company, 1943.

Beal, Clyde. "Closure for Family of Purple Heart Recipient." *Herald Dispatch* (Huntington, WV), March 3, 2013.

Bergerud, Eric M. *Fire in the Sky: The Air War in the South Pacific.* Boulder, CO: Westview Press, 2000.

Bernstein, Adam. "Brig. Gen. Robert E. Galer Dies; Highly Decorated Pilot in 2 Wars." *Washington Post,* July 1, 2005.

Birdsall, Steve. *Flying Buccaneers: The Illustrated Story of Kenney's Fifth Air Force.* Garden City, NY: Doubleday & Company, Inc., 1977.

———. *Saga of the Superfortresses: The Dramatic Story of the B-29 and the Twentieth Air Force.* Garden City, NY: Doubleday & Company, Inc., 1980.

Bixby, Roland. *And Some Gave All (The Story of Plymouth N.H.'s Congressional Medal of Honor Winner, Captain Harl Pease, Jr.).* Hooksett, NH: Granite State Copy, 2007.

Bodine, Mary Ann. "Military Business Not Connected with Hero's Visit Here." *Hutchinson [Kansas] News,* April 5, 1943.

Bong, Carl, and Mike O'Connor. *Ace of Aces: The Dick Bong Story.* Mesa, AZ: Champlin Fighter Museum, 1985.

"Bong Killed in Jet Plane Crash." *Waukesha [Wisconsin] Daily Freeman,* August 7, 1945.

Boswell, Rolfe. *Medals for Marines.* New York: Thomas Y. Crowell Company, 1945.

Boyington, Gregory. *Baa Baa Black Sheep.* New York: G. P. Putnam's Sons, 1958.

Boyle, Hal. "Correspondent's Notebook." *Rocky Mount [North Carolina] Telegram,* January 6, 1947.

Brand, Max. *Fighter Squadron at Guadalcanal.* Annapolis: Naval Institute Press, 1996.

Braun, Saul. *Seven Heroes: Medal of Honor Stories of the War in the Pacific.* New York: G. P. Putnam's Sons, 1965.

Buckman, Robert. "Medal of Honor Winner Recalls South Pacific Saga." *New Orleans Times-Picayune,* January 31, 1993.

Burns, Frances. "Medal of Honor for Lt. Hanson Is Presented Mother." *Boston Globe,* August 20, 1944.

———. "The Story of Newton's Heroic Ace Bob Hanson of the Marines." *Boston Globe,* February 14–16, 1944.

Byrd, Martha. *Kenneth N. Walker: Airpower's Untempered Crusader.* Maxwell Air Force Base, AL: Air University Press, 1997.

"Californians in War News: Hero, Believed Killed, Now Reported Prisoner." *San Francisco Examiner*, February 10, 1944.

Carey, Alan C. *We Flew Alone: Men and Missions of the United States Navy's B-24 Liberator Squadrons*. Atglen, PA: Schiffer Military History, 2017.

Carl, Maj. Gen. Marion B., and Barrett Tillman. *Pushing the Envelope: The Career of Fighter Ace and Test Pilot Marion Carl*. Annapolis: Naval Institute Press, 1994.

Casualty Branch, Status Review and Determination Section, Review and Determination under Section 5, Public Law 400, 7 March 1942 as Amended. Status of Crew of a B-25 Aircraft Missing in Action in the Southwest Pacific Area since 18 October 1943.

Cavanaugh, Wade. "Bruce Van Voorhis Nevada's WWII Hero." *Las Vegas Sun*, November 12, 1977.

"Chaplain Gives McGuire Hope for Hero Son." *Herald News* (Passaic, NJ), February 8, 1945.

"Chicago Cheers Oklahoma's Ace, Smith, Companion Heroes." *Daily Oklahoman*, December 6, 1942.

Cleaver, Thomas McKelvey. *Fabled Fifteen: The Pacific War Saga of Carrier Air Group 15*. Philadelphia: Casemate Publishers, 2014.

Cohen, Stan. *Destination Tokyo: A Pictorial History of Doolittle's Tokyo Raid, April 18, 1942*. Missoula, MT: Pictorial Histories Publishing Company, 1983.

Cohn, Art. "Z Is for Zeamer." *Liberty*, January 15, 1944.

"Combat Bravery Brings Citations for Six Utahns in U.S. Service." *Salt Lake City Telegram*, October 24, 1942.

Correll, John T. "The Air Force on the Eve of World War II." *Air Force Magazine*, October 2007.

———. "A Brave Man at the Right Time." *Air Force Magazine*, June 2007.

Cressman, Robert J. *A Magnificent Fight: The Battle for Wake Island*. Annapolis: Naval Institute Press, 1995.

———. *A Magnificent Fight: Marines in the Battle for Wake Island*. Marines in World War II Commemorative Series. Washington, DC: Marine Corps Historical Center, 1992.

Crichton, Kyle. "Captain Bong Comes Home—Small Town Hero from Superior, Wisconsin." *Collier's*, February 26, 1944.

Daso, Dik Alan. *Doolittle: Aerospace Visionary*. Washington, DC: Brassey's, Inc., 2003.

DeBlanc, Jefferson J. *The Guadalcanal Air War: Colonel Jefferson DeBlanc's Story*. Gretna, LA: Pelican Publishing Company, 2008.

De Chant, Jack. "Sweating It Out with Swett." *Leatherneck*, October 1944.

De Coen, Alma. "Day's Job Depends on What's to Be Done, Not the Hours That Are Spent at Work." *Journal News* (White Plains, NY), May 7, 1945.

Dempsey, Staff Sgt. Ginger. "Keeper of a Legacy." *New Hampshire National Guard Magazine*, Fall 2009.

"Determination of Status of an Airplane Missing in Action in the Southwest Pacific Area since 7 August 1942," August 18, 1943. Adjutant General's Department, U.S. Army, August 1945.

Devereaux, James P. S. *The Story of Wake Island*. New York: J. B. Lippincott, 1947.

Doolittle, Gen. James H. "Jimmy." *I Could Never Be So Lucky Again.* New York: Bantam Books, 1992.

Dorr, Robert F. "Medal of Honor Recipient: Henry 'Red' Erwin." *WWII Quarterly,* November 20, 2018.

———. *Mission to Tokyo: The American Airmen Who Took the War to the Heart of Japan.* Minneapolis: Zenith Press, 2012.

Drury, Bob, and Tom Clavin. *Lucky 666: The Impossible Mission That Changed the War in the Pacific.* New York: Simon & Schuster, 2016.

Dunn, Richard L. "The Search for General Walker: New Insights." *Air Power History,* Fall 2014.

Dunnigan, James F., and Albert A. Nofi. *Victory at Sea: World War II in the Pacific.* New York: William Morrow and Company, Inc., 1995.

Enger, J. Michael, Robert J. Cressman, and John F. Di Virgilio. *No One Avoided Danger.* Annapolis: Naval Institute Press, 2015.

Erwin, Jon, and William Doyle. *Beyond Valor.* Nashville, TN: Nelson Books, 2020.

Eubanks, Ralph T. *Once a Marine: Memoirs of a World War II Marine.* Bloomington, IN: AuthorHouse, 2008.

Ewing, Steve, and John B. Lundstrom. *Fateful Rendezvous: The Life of Butch O'Hare.* Annapolis: Naval Institute Press, 1997.

Farnsworth, Clyde A. "Pilot in Historic Bombing Raid Sacrifices Life to Save Mates, Texan Stands by Pal with Ruined Parachute." *Amarillo Daily News,* November 24, 1944.

"Fire Hits 2 City Firms, Woman's Death Probed," *Morning Call* (Allentown, PA), April 22, 1971.

"Five Japs Just About Balance an American's Fighting Power." *Daily Oklahoman,* October 31, 1942.

Ford, Lt. Col. Corey, and Maj. Alastair MacBain. "The Heroes: A Gallery of United Nations Patriots. No. 41 Staff Sergeant Henry E. Erwin." *Collier's,* August 4, 1945.

Foss, Joe, with Donna Wild Foss. *A Proud American: The Autobiography of Joe Foss.* New York: Pocket Star Books, 1992.

"14th AF B-24 Sinks Two Warships." *CBI Roundup* 3, no. 7 (October 26, 1944).

"14th AF Hero Makes Gallant Rendezvous with Death." *CBI Roundup* 3, no. 16 (December 28, 1944).

Frank, Tim. "Medal of Honor Series." *Naval Aviation News,* July/August 1998.

Frisbee, John L. "Valor: Triumph and Tragedy." *Air Force Magazine,* August 1988.

Gamble, Bruce. *The Black Sheep: The Definitive Account of Marine Fighting Squadron 214 in World War II.* Novato, CA: Presidio Press, 2003.

———. *Black Sheep One: The Life of Gregory "Pappy" Boyington.* Novato, CA: Presidio, 2000.

———. *Fortress Rabaul: The Battle for the Southwest Pacific, January 1942–April 1943.* Minneapolis: Zenith Press, 2013.

———. *Target Rabaul: The Allied Siege of Japan's Most Infamous Stronghold, March 1943–August 1945.* Minneapolis: Zenith Press, 2013.

"General Tells How Air Ace Was Shot Down." *San Antonio Express,* March 23, 1944.

"General Walker Aims at Flying with His Boys." Associated Press, September 21, 1945.

Gill, Brendan. "A Reporter at Large: Where They Wanted to Be." *New Yorker*, March 13, 1943.

Glines, Carroll V. *Chennault's Forgotten Warriors: The Saga of the 308th Bomb Group in China*. Atglen, PA: Schiffer Publishing, 1995.

———. *The Doolittle Raid: America's Daring First Strike against Japan*. Atglen, PA: Schiffer Publishing, 1991.

Goldstein, Richard. "James Swett, Who Downed 7 Planes in Attack, Dies at 88." *New York Times*, January 25, 2009.

Goodspeed, Hill. "Always Faithful." *Naval Aviation News*, May/June 2003.

Graham, Capt. Garrett. "Our Number One Ace Comes Home." *Saturday Evening Post*, April 3, 1943.

Griffin, Tom. "Gregory Boyington—Our 'Black Sheep' Hero." *Our Back Pages: A Look Back at UW History* (University of Washington), December 1998.

Gyan, Joe, Jr. "Parade Greets Museum Wing." *The Advocate* (Baton Rouge, LA), November 18, 2002.

Ham, Mary Katherine. "Lt. John William Finn: Pearl Harbor's Last Hero, 68 Years Later." *WWII Magazine*, December 7, 2009.

Hammel, Eric. *Aces against Japan*. Novato, CA: Presidio, 1992.

———. *Aces against Japan II*. Pacifica, CA: Pacifica Press, 1996.

Hampson, Fred. "How Newton Ace Died: Mishap Ended Career of Man Who Bagged 25 Jap Planes." *Boston Globe*, February 8, 1944.

Hanley, Charles J. "A Team Again: World War II Pilot Recalls the Bombardier Who Didn't Make It." *The Times* (Munster, IN), September 3, 1995.

Hawley, David. "Memories of a Hero: The Dakota County Historical Society Honors Richard Fleming, a WWII Pilot Credited with the Sinking of a Japanese Warship." *St. Paul [Minnesota] Pioneer Press*, December 2, 1996.

Heaton, Colin. "Black Sheep Leader." *Aviation History Magazine*, May 2001.

Hickey, Lawrence. *Ken's Men against the Empire: The Illustrated History of the 43rd Bombardment Group, January 1941–October 1943*. Boulder, CO: International Historical Research Associates, 2020.

History, 8th Bombardment Squadron (L), 3d Bombardment Group (L) AAF, May 31, 1917–March 31, 1944 (compiled September 1945).

History of Marine Fighting Squadron Two Twenty-Four, January 6, 1945.

Holguin, Jose. Testimonial of Jose Holguin to Sanford H. Bullock, Special Agent, 115th CIC Detachment, 1948.

"Honor Medal Winner Experiences Miracle Escape in Korean War Crash." *Arizona Republic*, August 21, 1952.

Hoyt, Edwin P. *McCampbell's Heroes: The Story of the U.S. Navy's Most Celebrated Carrier Fighters of the Pacific War*. New York: Van Nostrand Reinhold Company, 1983.

Humes, Edward. "Medal of Honor Ken Walsh: Ex-Flier Credits Decoration to Experience, Luck." *Orange County [California] Register*, November 8, 1987.

"If Ace M'Guire Keeps Shooting Down Japs, His Dad Will Probably Go Out of Business." *The Record* (Hackensack, NJ), December 29, 1944.

Illon, Edward, and Howard Whitman. "Mother Sobs As F.D.R. Lauds Son." *New York Daily News*, September 8, 1942.

"It's 28 Jap Planes for McGuire Now." *Herald News* (Passaic, NJ), November 13, 1944.

"Jay Zeamer, a Decorated Pilot in World War II, Dies at 88." *Los Angeles Times*, March 26, 2007.

"Jeannette, Pa., Pilot Shoots Way to Fame." *Altoona [Pennsylvania] Tribune*, January 18, 1945.

"Jobless War Hero Dies by Own Hand." *Van Nuys [California] News*, June 16, 1972.

"John Finn: Medal of Honor Recipient." *The Hoist*, n.d.

Johnson, Staff Sgt. Pen T. "Newtonville Flyer Fought Japs with Faulty Engine." *Boston Globe*, October 28, 1943.

Johnston, Stanley. *Queen of the Flat-Tops.* New York: E. P. Dutton & Co., 1942.

Jones, Charles T. "Oklahoma Monument Dedicated to John L. Smith." *Plain Dealer* (Cleveland, OH), December 2, 1998.

Jones, John E. "Jeannette Pilot Wants to Return to His P-51: Medal Winner Restless on Ground." *Pittsburgh Post-Gazette*, August 10, 1945.

Jordan, Kenneth N., Sr. *Men of Honor: Thirty-Eight Highly Decorated Marines of World War II, Korea and Vietnam.* Atglen, PA: Schiffer Military History, 1997.

Josselyn, Talbert. "Courage . . . beyond Duty." *Atlanta Constitution*, November 15, 1942.

Kakesako, Gregg K. "Dec. 7 Hero at Kaneohe Is Honored." *Honolulu Star-Bulletin*, June 30, 1999.

Katz, Judd A. "Red Erwin and the Medal of Honor." *Alabama Heritage*, Winter 1996.

Kenney, Gen. George C. *Dick Bong: Ace of Aces.* New York: Popular Library, 1962.

———. *General Kenney Reports: A Personal History of the Pacific War.* New York: Duell, Sloan and Pearce, 1949.

Kernan, Alvin. *Crossing the Line: A Bluejacket's World War II Odyssey.* Annapolis: Naval Institute Press, 1994.

Kinney, John F. *Wake Island Pilot: A World War II Memoir.* Washington, DC: Brassey's, 1995.

Kleinberg, Eliot. "Humble Men, High Honors." *Palm Beach Post* (West Palm Beach, FL), November 11, 1992.

Klobuchar, Jim. "Foundation Will Honor Her War-Hero Sweetheart." *Star Tribune* (Minneapolis, MN), August 22, 1995.

Kovalenko, Ann. "Honor Lehigh World War II Hero." *Morning Call* (Allentown, PA), June 9, 1968.

Krebs, Albin. "James Doolittle, 96, Pioneer Aviator Who Led First Raid on Japan, Dies." *New York Times*, September 28, 1993.

Lemon, Peter C. *Beyond the Medal: A Journey from Their Hearts to Yours.* Golden, CO: Fulcrum Publishing, 1997.

Looking Backward: A Lehigh University Scrapbook. Bethlehem, PA: Lehigh University, 1991.

Lord, Walter. *Incredible Victory: The Battle of Midway.* New York: Harper & Row, 1967.

Lucas, Laddie, ed. *Voices in the Air, 1939–1945.* London: Arrow Books, 2003.

Lucier, James P. "At Home and in Combat, Foss Led by Example." *Insight on the News*, January 8, 2001.

Lucky Bag, 1935. Annapolis: US Naval Academy, 1935.

Ludlum, Stuart D. *They Turned the War Around at Coral Sea and Midway: Going to War with Yorktown's Air Group Five.* Bennington, VT: Merriam Press, 1991.

Lundstrom, John B. *The First Team: Pacific Air Naval Combat from Pearl Harbor to Midway.* Annapolis: Naval Institute Press, 1984.

Lundstrom, John B., and James C. Sawruk. "Courage and Devotion to Duty: The SBD Anti-torpedo Plane Patrol in the Coral Sea, 8 May 1942." *The Hook: Journal of Carrier Aviation*, Winter 1988.

"Maj. Ralph Cheli Reported Jap Prisoner." *Morning Call* (Allentown, PA), February 10, 1944.

"Maj. Ralph Cheli Still Alive." *Morning Call* (Allentown, PA), May 3, 1944.

"Maj. Richard Bong, America's Top Ace, Killed as Jet-Propelled Plane Explodes in Mid-air." *Palladium-Item* (Richmond, IN), August 7, 1945.

"Major Cheli Killed in Raid: Famed Flyer Casualty of Wewak Assault." *San Francisco Examiner*, August 26, 1943.

"Major John L. Smith Isn't Interested in Exploits of Major John L. Smith." *Valley Morning Star* (Harlingen, TX), November 4, 1942.

"Marine Ace Sets Sights on New Record." *Austin [Texas] American-Statesman*, July 9, 1945.

Martin, Charles A. *The Last Great Ace: The Life of Major Thomas B. McGuire, Jr.* Fruit Grove, FL: Fruit Cove Publishing, 1998.

Mason, David. "McGuire Final Report: Investigation into the Final Combat Mission of Major Thomas B. McGuire, Jr." Self-published, January 7, 2009.

McGuire, Dan. "McCampbell, Navy's Leading Ace, Says Team Work Most Important." *Press-Courier* (Oxnard, CA), December 7, 1944.

McMurria, 1st Lt. James. Perpetuation of Testimony of Former 1st Lieut. James A. McMurria, O-373644. In the matter of the POW Camp operated by the 6th Field Kempai Tai Headquarters in Rabaul, New Britain—Tunnel Hill POW Camp. For the Chief, War Crimes Branch Civil Affairs Division—War Department. Taken at Columbus, Georgia, July 21, 1948.

Mersky, Peter B. *Time of the Aces: Marine Pilots in the Solomons, 1942–1944.* Marines in World War II Commemorative Series. Washington, DC: History and Museums Division, Headquarters, US Marine Corps, 1993.

Middlebrook, Garrett. *Air Combat at 20 Feet: Selected Missions from a Strafer Pilot's Diary.* Bloomington, IN: AuthorHouse, 2004.

Miller, John, Jr. *Cartwheel: The Reduction of Rabaul.* United States Army in World War II: The War in the Pacific. Washington, DC: Office of the Chief of Military History, Department of the Army, 1959.

Miller, Thomas G., Jr. *The Cactus Air Force.* New York: Bantam Books, 1981.

Missing Air Crew Report, 308th Bombardment Group, October 29, 1944.

"Missing Newton Ace Wins Nation's Highest Award." *Boston Globe*, August 1, 1944.

"Missing Newton Flyer Writes Home He's Safe." *Boston Sunday Globe*, November 21, 1943.

Mitchell, John H. *In Alis Vicimus: On Wings We Conquer: The 19th and 7th Bomb Groups of the United States Air Force in the Southwest Pacific in the First Year of World War Two.* Springfield, MO: G. E. M. Publishers, 1990.

Moore, Stephen L. *The Battle for Hell's Island.* New York: New American Library, 2015.

Morison, Samuel Eliot. *History of United States Naval Operations in World War II.* Vol. 4: *Coral Sea, Midway and Submarine Actions, May 1942–August 1942.* Boston: Little, Brown and Company, 1958.

Murphy, Edward F. *Heroes of World War II.* Novato, CA: Presidio Press, 1990.

"Navy Aviator Wins Top Medal." *Reno Gazette-Journal*, July 31, 1944.

"Navy Hero's Mother Gets Medal of Honor," *Daily [New York] News*, September 18, 1943.

Nelson, Craig. *The First Heroes: The Extraordinary Story of the Doolittle Raid—America's First World War II Victory.* New York: Penguin Books, 2002.

"Newton Marine Ace Reported Missing Again." *Boston Globe*, February 6, 1944.

"Not Doing Enough toward Winning War Roosevelt Tells Nation." *Des Moines [Iowa] Register*, September 8, 1942.

"Oakland Boy Missing with Navy Medal of Honor Pilot," *Oakland [California] Tribune*, September 9, 1942.

"Pappy Boyington, Marine Ace, Outspoken in Print, in Person." *Palm Beach Post* (West Palm Beach, FL), October 5, 1958.

"Pappy Boyington Hospitalized: Health Shooting Him Down, War Ace Says." *Los Angeles Times*, March 10, 1972.

Parker, J. Michael. "Nimitz Ace Flier in Pacific War to Be Part of 1942 Symposium." *San Antonio Express-News*, March 26, 1992.

Parshall, Jonathan B., and Anthony P. Tully. *Shattered Sword: The Untold Story of the Battle of Midway.* Washington, DC: Potomac Books, 2007.

Pratt, Joseph A. "Memorials and Memories." *Houston Review*, Spring 2005.

Provenza, G. D. "The Life and Legend of 'Indian Joe' Bauer." *Leatherneck*, November 1992.

Pyle, Chris. "In the Line of Fire." *Arkansas Democrat-Gazette*, October 22, 2006.

Ramsey, William L., and Henry Elrod Ramsey. *Elrod's Wake.* Unpublished draft manuscript, 2005.

Report of Action of Marine Aircraft Group 23 for the Period of 31 August to 15 September 1942.

Report of Air Operations conducted by Carrier Air Group Fifteen during the period 19 June to 3 July 1944, inclusive.

Report of Japanese Raid on Pearl Harbor, 7 December 1941, Commander-in-Chief US Pacific Fleet.

"Richard I. Bong, Ace Fighter Pilot, Is Killed." *[Butte] Montana Standard*, August 7, 1945.

Salecker, Gene Eric. *Fortress against the Sun: The B-17 Flying Fortress in the Pacific.* Conshohocken, PA: Combined Publishing, 2001.

"Salem Youth with the Navy Tells of Exciting Action near Midway Island." *Daily Herald* (Provo, UT), July 8, 1942.

Schedler, Dean. "He Just Likes to Hunt—Fiery Ginger's Thunderbolt Ace Pilot Has Ration Trouble Too." *Abilene Reporter News*, December 13, 1943.

Schnedler, Jack. "Nathan Gordon Won the Medal of Honor for His Heroics during World War II." *Arkansas Democrat-Gazette*, August 4, 2002.

Schudel, Matt. "Warren A. Skon, Navy Ace Pilot in WWII, and Wife Hazel Skon, Both 92, Die Days Apart." *Washington Post*, February 25, 2012.

Schultz, Bruce. "A Hero Comes Full Circle." *The Advocate* (Baton Rouge, LA), July 8, 2000.

Schultz, Duane. *The Doolittle Raid.* New York: St. Martin's Press, 1988.

Schultz, Jim. "Medal of Honor Recipient James Swett of Redding Dies at 88." *Redding [California] Record Searchlight*, January 21, 2009.

Scott, James M. *Target Tokyo: Jimmy Doolittle and the Raid That Avenged Pearl Harbor.* New York: W. W. Norton & Company, 2015.

Sears, David. *Pacific Air: How Fearless Flyboys, Peerless Aircraft, and Fast Flattops Conquered the Skies in the War with Japan.* Cambridge, MA: Da Capo Books, 2011.

"Sees His First Jap Planes in 15 Months in Pacific, Downs Seven." *Evening Times* (Sayre, PA), January 18, 1945.

Sheehan, Andrew. "Tale of 3 Heroes." *Pittsburgh Post-Gazette*, July 7, 1983.

Sherrod, Robert. *History of Marine Corps Aviation in World War II.* Washington, DC: Combat Forces Press, 1952.

"Shot Down Three Times, Pilot Gets 13 Jap Planes." *Akron Beacon Journal*, January 17, 1943.

Simmons, Walter. *Joe Foss Flying Marine.* New York: E. P. Dutton & Company, 1943.

Sims, Edward H. *Greatest Fighter Missions of the Top Navy and Marine Aces of World War II.* New York: Ballantine Books, 1962.

Sloan, Bill. *Given Up for Dead: America's Heroic Stand at Wake Island.* New York: Bantam Books, 2003.

Smith, Larry. *Beyond Glory: Medal of Honor Heroes in Their Own Words.* New York: W. W. Norton & Company, 2003.

Smith, Steven D. "Flight out of Hell: The Harrowing Bombing Mission to Kavieng." Warfare History Network, December 9, 2017.

Stanaway, John C. *Kearby's Thunderbolts: The 348th Fighter Group in World War II.* Atglen, PA: Schiffer Publishing, 1997.

———. *Mustang and Thunderbolt Aces of the Pacific and CBI.* London: Osprey Publishing, 1999.

"Swett Family Deluged with Good Wishes." *San Mateo [California] Times*, April 22, 1944.

Thach, Adm. John S. "Butch O'Hare and the Thach Weave." *Naval History Magazine*, Spring 1992.

———. "The Red Rain of Battle: The Story of Fighter Squadron 3." *Collier's Magazine*, December 5, 1943.

38th Bomb Group, Final Mission Report, August 18, 1943.

Tillman, Barrett. *Hellcat Aces of World War 2*. London: Osprey Publishing, 1996.

———. *U.S. Marine Corps Fighter Squadrons of World War II*. New York: Osprey Publishing, 2014.

———. *Wildcat Aces of World War 2*. London: Osprey Publishing, 1995.

"Top Utah Hero Home, Asks, 'Why the Fuss?'" *Salt Lake City Tribune*, October 4, 1945.

Tregaskis, Richard. *Guadalcanal Diary*. Garden City, NY: Blue Ribbon Books, 1943.

Tremaine, Frank. "Midway Hero Killed Making Sure of Direct Hit on Carrier." *Eugene [Oregon] Guard*, June 25, 1942.

Urwin, Gregory J. W. *Facing Fearful Odds: The Siege of Wake Island*. Lincoln: University of Nebraska Press, 1997.

"U.S. at War: Missing—Texas." *TIME*, March 27, 1944.

USS Essex Action Report: Attack on Marcus and Wake Islands, 15–25 May 1944.

United States Strategic Bombing Survey (Pacific). *The Allied Campaign against Rabaul*. Washington, DC: Naval Analysis Division, Marshalls–Gilberts–New Britain Party, September 1, 1946.

United States Strategic Bombing Survey, Interrogation No. 83, 1946.

Van Atta, Lee. "Eye Witness Story of Rabaul Smash." International News Service, October 12, 1943.

———. "Lump All Jap Atrocities and You Have Rabaul in Nutshell." *Tipton [Indiana] Daily Tribune*, September 22, 1945.

VF-15 Aircraft Action Report, June 19, 1944.

Walsh, Lt. Kenneth A. "Narrative by Lieutenant Kenneth A. Walsh, Aviation, Solomon Islands Area. October 25, 1943." Naval Records and Library, CNO, Micro Serial Number 138303, Reel A1828.

Walton, Frank E. *Once They Were Eagles: The Men of the Black Sheep Squadron*. Lexington: University Press of Kentucky, 1986.

War Diary, Marine Air Group 23, August 20, 1942–November 16, 1942.

War Diary, Marine Corps Marine Fighting Squadron 214, August 1–31, 1943.

War Diary, Marine Fighting Squadron 223, Marine Aircraft Group 23, August 1–31, 1942.

War Diary, Marine Fighting Squadron One Twenty-Four, August 1943.

War Diary, Marine Fighting Squadron Two Twenty-One, Marine Aircraft Group Twenty-One, First Marine Aircraft Wing, April 1–30, 1943.

War Diary, Marine Scout-Bombing Squadron Two Forty-One, Marine Aircraft Group Twenty-Two, Second Marine Aircraft Wing, FMF, June 1–30, 1942.

War Diary, Patrol Squadron Fourteen, December 7, 1941–July 1942.

War Diary, Task Force Sixteen, US Pacific Fleet, April 1–30, 1942.

War Diary, VMF-215, November, December 1943, January 1944.

Warner, Gary A. "W.W.II Ace Was Man of Few Words in Memorable Meeting with FDR." *San Jose [California] Mercury News*, February 22, 1994.

"Wife Sent Love in Wartime Mail." *Daily Oklahoman*, April 18, 1999.

"Wife Won't Give Up Hope for Kearby." *San Antonio Light*, March 15, 1944.

Wilcox, Richard. "Captain Smith and His Fighting 223." *LIFE Magazine*, December 7, 1942.

Wiley, Katherine Sams. *The Strafin' Saints: The 71st Tactical Reconnaissance Group: Memories*. Privately printed, 1994.

Windham, Ben. "Southern Lights: One Heroic Moment—But It Didn't End There." *Tuscaloosa News*, January 27, 2002.

Woodall, James R. *Texas Aggie Medals of Honor*. College Station: Texas A&M University Press, 2010.

"Wounded Flier Tells of Coral Sea Battle." *Salt Lake City Tribune*, July 6, 1942.

Wukovits, John. "Fred Avey: Flying with the Black Sheep Squadron in World War II." *Aviation History*, May 1997.

———. *Pacific Alamo: The Battle for Wake Island*. New York: New American Library, 2003.

"WWII Flying Ace Pappy Boyington Dead." *Sunday Times-Sentinel* (Fresno, CA), January 12, 1988.

Yarbrough, Tom. "Jap Bomber Squadron Routed by Yank." *Daily Oklahoman*, October 31, 1942.

Yenne, Bill. *Aces High*. New York: Berkley Caliber Publishing Group, 2010.

Yoshimura, Minoru. Testimony on executions, B5563, 2249, item 5428717, National Archives of Australia.

WEBSITES AND VIDEOS

"B-17F-10-BO 'San Antonio Rose' Serial Number 41-24458." Pacific Wrecks. http://www.pacificwrecks.com/aircraft/b-17/41-24458.html.

Bauer, Harold W. "A War Diary Kept by Harold W. Bauer." World War Two and Aviation History. http://www.acepilots.com/bauer/bauer_diary.html.

Brown, Kent. "Lt. Col. Harold William 'Indian Joe' Bauer." World War Two and Aviation History..http://www.acepilots.com/bauer/usmc_bauer1.html.

Budge, Kent G. "Casualties." *Pacific War Online Encyclopedia*. http://www.pwencycl.kgbudge.com/C/a/Casualties.htm.

"David McCampbell: Ace of Aces.." Video posted to YouTube by US Naval Institute, July 21, 2011. https://www.youtube.com/watch?v=Wx-c0BpFbSU.

Dunn, Richard L. "Double Lucky? The Campaigns of the 77th Hiko Sentai, Part 9." The Warbird's Forum. http://www.warbirdforum.com/lucky9.htm.

———. "248th Hiko Sentai: A Japanese 'Hard Luck' Fighter Unit, Part 3." j-aircraft.com. http://www.j-aircraft.com/research/rdunn/248th/248th-3.htm.

8th Attack Squadron. http://8thattacksqdnassoc.tripod.com.

Faust, John W. "Boyington according to Scott and Me." Angelfire.com, October 6, 1998. http://www.angelfire.com/ca/dickg/vignettes11.html.

Forshee, Lynn. *Standby, Mark!* msmeck.com. https://msmeck.com/standby-mark-by-lynn-forshee/chapter-12.

Hayes, Clint. *Zeamer's Eager Beavers: The Incredible True Story*. Zeamer's Eager Beavers. http://zeamerseagerbeavers.com/download-zeamers-eager-beavers-the-story.

"Henry Erwin, Medal of Honor, WWII." Video posted to YouTube by MedalOfHonorBook, September 27, 2011. https://www.youtube.com/watch?v=tzx8BkSwwWk.

Hornby, Ken. "Capt. Richard E. Fleming USMCR and the Battle of Midway." Battle of Midway Roundtable, June 2016. www.hornby6.nwww.midway42.org/Backissues/2016/20160601.aspx.

Jacquet, Edward M. Account at "B-17E 'Why Don't We Do This More Often,' Serial Number 41-2429." Pacific Wrecks. https://www.pacificwrecks.com/aircraft/b-17/41-2429.html.

"Jay Zeamer: There's Always a Way." Zeamer's Eager Beavers. http://zeamerseagerbea vers.com/biographies/jay-zeamer.

Kenneth N. Walker—US Army Air Force Brigadier General. http://www.kennethn walker.org.

Kirk, Robert, dir. *Dogfight Guadalcanal*. Digital Ranch, 2006.

Krell, Walter. Letter to author Lawrence J. Hickey. 38th Bomb Group Association, January 14, 1989. http://www.sunsetters38bg.com/index.php/articles/stories2/106-a-young-mans-airplane.

Mortenson, Bernhardt. "Personal Account of Bomber Command Station Life (A Story about Fifth Bomber Command)." Australia@War. https://www.ozatwar.com/ozat war/morternson.htm.

"Nathan G. Gordon." Pacific Wrecks. https://www.pacificwrecks.com/people/veterans/gordon/index.html.

"Nathan Gordon, Medal of Honor, WWII." Video posted to YouTube by MedalOfHonorBook, September 27, 2011. https://www.youtube.com/watch?v=zR2iWFqTarQ.

Naval History and Heritage Command. "US Navy Personnel in World War II Service and Casualty Statistics." https://www.history.Navy.mil/research/library.

Nolan, James Claire. *This Damn Navy: The Diary of a Naval Aviator*. http://thisdamn Navy.com.

"Old '666.'" Video posted to YouTube by bbottlezigzag, March 4, 2009. https://www .youtube.com/watch?v=6Im086TCu3I.

Radnick, Martin J. "Recollections." 3rd Attack Group/3rd Bombardment Group 1919–2019. file:///C:/Users/User/AppData/Local/Temp/Martin%20J.%20Radnik-1.pdf

"Richard L. Walker." 3rd Attack Group/3rd Bombardment Group 1919–2019. http://3rdstories.yolasite.com/richard-walker.php.

Sherman, Stephen. "Cdr. David McCampbell Top Navy Ace of WW2, Shot Down 34 Japanese Planes." World War Two and Aviation History, February 2000 (updated July 2, 2011). http://acepilots.com/usn_mccampbell.html.

Walker, Dick. "Raid on Rabaul on 2 November 1943 as Told by Dick Walker, 13th Bomb Squadron, 3rd Bomb Group, Their Part in the Raid on Rabaul on 2 November 1943." Australia@War. https://www.ozatwar.com/usaaf/rabaul2nov43.htm.

Webster, William H. Letter to Larry Hickey. 3rd Attack Group/3rd Bombardment Group 1919–2019, June 15, 1989, http://3rdstories.yolasite.com/william-h-webster .php.

Weigel, Andrew H. Letter to Dwight Turner. 3rd Bombardment Group—WWII: Stories: Dwight E. Turner, September 3, 1998. http://3rdstories.yolasite.com/dwight -turner.php.

Whitten, Capt. Sumner H. Letter. Naval Aviation Museum. https://www.navalaviation museum.org/history-up-close/from-the-cockpit-stories-of-naval-aviation/memo ries-midway.

"William Shomo Wingman—Paul Lipscomb." Video posted to YouTube by Ron Terpko, October 10, 2011. https://www.youtube.com/watch?v=YOc51Rh-ivw, 2006.

About the Author

James H. Hallas is a graduate of the Newhouse School at Syracuse University and was in the newspaper business for nearly forty years as reporter, editor, and publisher. He is the author of *Saipan: The Battle that Doomed Japan in World War II*, which won the 2020 General Wallace M. Greene Jr. Award for Nonfiction; *Uncommon Valor on Iwo Jima: The Stories of the Medal of Honor Recipients in the Marine Corps' Bloodiest Battle of World War II*; *Killing Ground on Okinawa: The Battle for Sugar Loaf Hill*; *Doughboy War: The American Expeditionary Force in World War I*; *Squandered Victory: The Battle of St. Mihiel*; and *The Devil's Anvil: The Assault on Peleliu*. He lives in Portland, Connecticut.